全国优秀畅销书
全国高校出版社优秀畅销书二等奖

An English Reading Course for Modern Science and Technology

现代科技英语阅读教程

（全新修订版）

程同春　程　欣　编著

东南大学出版社
·南京·

内容提要

本教程系具有强烈时代气息和体现现代科技英语特色的大学英语阅读教材。课文题材广泛,信息量大,内容新颖,并融思想性、趣味性、可读性和实用性于一体。每单元语篇语言规范,篇幅适中,由浅入深,循序渐进,有利教学,便于自学。每篇英语课文均配有语言点和汉译文(Language Points and Chinese Translations)以及练习(Exercises),全书最后还配有五套实践练习题(Practice Exercises)和参考答案,目的是引导读者领会课文重点,掌握常用的现代科技英语专业词汇和短语,通过一定的翻译实践提高科技英语的阅读理解与翻译能力。本教程主要使用对象为高等学校和高等职业技术学院理工类专业和英语专业高年级学生,也可供科技工作者、理工类专业人员或具有中级英语水平以上的广大英语爱好者学习或培训使用。

图书在版编目(CIP)数据

现代科技英语阅读教程/程同春,程欣编著. —2版(修订本). —南京:东南大学出版社,2013.2
ISBN 978-7-5641-4121-9

Ⅰ.①现… Ⅱ.①程… ②程… Ⅲ.①科学技术—英语—阅读教学—教材 Ⅳ.①H319.4

中国版本图书馆 CIP 数据核字(2013)第 034400 号

现代科技英语阅读教程

编 著	程同春 程 欣	责任编辑	刘 坚
电 话	(025)83793329/83362442(传真)	电子邮箱	liu-jian@seu.edu.cn
出版发行	东南大学出版社	出版人	江建中
地 址	南京市四牌楼2号	邮 编	210096
销售电话	(025)83793191/83794561/83794174/83794121/83795801/83792174/83795802/57711295(传真)		
网 址	http://www.seupress.com	电子邮箱	press@seupress.com
经 销	全国各地新华书店	印 刷	南京玉河印刷厂
开 本	890mm×1240mm 1/16 印 张 17.5	字 数	592千字
版 次	2013年4月第2版	印 次	2013年4月第1次印刷
书 号	ISBN 978-7-5641-4121-9		
定 价	32.00元		

* 未经许可,本书内文字不得以任何方式转载、演绎,违者必究。
* 本社图书若有印装质量问题,请直接与营销部联系。电话:025-83791830。

第 9 次印刷出版说明

《现代科技英语阅读教程》自首版以来,已连续印刷出版 8 次,先后被评为"全国优秀畅销书"和全国高校出版社"优秀畅销书二等奖",受到广大读者的欢迎程度出乎作者和出版社之预料。先后有 30 多所大学将此书作为"科技英语"课程的教材,有的高校甚至要求此教材全校文科、理科学生人手一册,以便让当代大学生既增进对现代科学技术知识与发展动态的掌握与了解,又提高英语阅读理解与英汉翻译的能力与素养,扩大科技英语的专业词汇量,拓展专业知识,以利文、理科学生综合素质的培养。

针对许多高校和广大读者的要求,并为反映当下的科技动态和科技成果,出版社建议对此书进行修订。这次修订的原则是:对原有内容作少量修订,在保留原书特色和长处的基础上,按科技分类作了较大调整,特别是增加了反映最近几年来世界科技发展与研究的新成果、新见解等新内容,如:网络生活、网络技术、机器人、生物燃料、纳米技术、绿色革命、转基因作物等方面的最新发展与研究,以便与时俱进,紧跟上当代科学技术的迅猛发展。

全书根据科技内容的不同,细分为 12 个单元,共 40 篇课文。每篇课文配有汉语译文、注释和多项练习题等。每单元开始的第 1 页上,均安排了 3 段简要英文,对本单元内容进行总述、概念定义、要点解释或者列出重点和主题句。有些单元之间内容不同,但也有着内在关联,属于交叉性学科。教师在课堂教学中,可以有重点地选择各单元中有代表性的课文进行讲授,剩余部分可供学生自学或作为课外阅读材料。具体如何组织教学,本书"前言"中所作的建议可供详阅与参考。

本书由程同春教授和程欣副教授任主编,祝长青、钱煜翔、蒋静、袁柯枫、石蕾、蒋文琪、周静、张玲、蒋南珍、王玉芳和蒋夕葆等老师也参加了编写、翻译、修订和校阅等工作。

本书修订中吸收了最新的科技发展和研究成果,参考了有关文章和资料,在此向有关作者表示诚挚的谢意,也向东南大学出版社责任编辑刘坚博士谨致衷心的感谢。

编者
2013 年春于南京理工大学

前 言

回顾过去一百多年的历史,世界科学技术迅猛发展,人类在极短的时间内超越了蒸汽机时代,现在已进入了航天时代和信息时代。从收音机、电视、雷达、汽车、飞机到火箭、激光、电子计算机、航天飞机和人造地球卫星,各种科技发明、创造如雨后春笋般涌现,在工农业生产建设、社会经济发展、文化教育、生命科学、太空研究等各个方面大大促进了世界文明和现代化进程,使世界变得更加丰富多彩,也从根本上改变了人类的生活方式。

科技英语作为英语语言下属的一门专业学科,是专门用途英语(English for Specific Purposes,简称 ESP)的一种,是将要从事或正在从事科技工作和理工类专业人员所教授或应用的专门用途英语。科技英语作为科技交流的工具和科技信息的载体,以英语语言形式反映世界科学技术研究和发展的成果、方法和动态,其重要性已经并将随着现代科技的突飞猛进而日趋增强。

为了使高等教育面向 21 世纪,适应现代化社会对理工类专业人才的需求,我们特编写了这本教材。本教材主要编选了国内外近年来有关科技发展的最新资料,选题广泛,内容翔实,从个人计算机、因特网、网络电话到电子商务、网上生活方式;从电子鼻、传播技术、信息技术到信息高速公路、国际空间站;从基因工程、克隆技术、虚拟现实技术到红外摄影机、太空旅游;从生物节奏、环境保护、治理污染到绿色革命、开发新能源,几乎包括了理工类专业的各个领域和各种高新技术。这些文章材料新颖,语言规范,体裁多样,信息量大,实用性强,具有鲜明的时代气息。

本教材的编写原则是:结合语言学习的特点,体现基础英语、专业英语和专业知识的三结合,力求成为一门系统性、指导性、趣味性和可读性较强的课程,有利教学,便于自学。全书中,每单元的课文段落按顺序编号,课文后配有注释和汉译文,以帮助读者理解。每单元课文后的练习题和全书最后部分的五套实践练习题引导读者领会全文重点,掌握一些必要与常用的现代科技英语词汇,并结合进行适量的多项选择、阅读理解和英汉翻译实践,从而提高科技英语的阅读与翻译能力。本书可作为高等学校和高等职业技术学院英语专业和理工类专业高年级学生教学用书,也可供科技工作者和理工类专业人员阅读、学习之用。

本书可供教学 1 学年(两个学期),每周 2 至 4 课时。也可由教师根据课时安排情况和学生所学专业的不同,选用相近、相关专业内容的课文,进行有重点的教学。就如何进行教学,建议如下:

一、预习

这是教学的首要环节。学生应在上课前认真进行预习,借助工具书以及每单元课文后的 Language Points and Chinese Translations,充分理解课文内容,学习专业知识及其英语表达方法。

二、课堂教学

这是教学的主要环节,对学生来说,它起着学习科技英语主渠道的作用。课堂教学原则上应用英语讲授,也可适当运用汉语,进行英汉两种语言的比较。课堂教学中可以开展如下教学活动:

1. 让学生朗读课文,将课文翻译成汉语,根据课文内容提问等方式检查学生的预习情况与理解能力。

2. 教师介绍必要的背景知识，讲解一些语言点、重点和难点，以及一些常用的现代科技英语词汇、短语、句型等，同时对一些较难较复杂的句子结构进行必要的语法分析。总之，要调动一切教学手段帮助学生充分理解和掌握课文。

3. 在学生掌握课文内容的前提下，有时可组织课堂讨论或分成小组进行活动，就课文内容结合实际各抒己见，相互交流，以提高学生综合理解能力。

4. 课文后的练习题可作为课堂练习，也可作为课外作业，以帮助学生巩固、提高所学的知识。

5. 在教学过程中，教师也可以根据教学内容和学生英语水平的实际情况，进行一些必要的科技英语阅读与翻译技巧的讲解，以提高学生的科技英语实际应用能力，为所学的专业服务。

三、复习

学生应在教师的指导下进行课后复习。复习时，学生要对课文内容有正确的理解；能将课文译成较通顺的中文；能较熟练地说出和应用科技英语的一些常用词汇；掌握与课文内容相关的专业知识；能正确地做课后的各种练习。

程欣同志参与了本书的编写，并为整理文稿做了大量工作。本书编写中吸收了最新的科技研究成果，参考和引用了有关论著、文章，文中不能一一注明，在此向有关作者表示感谢。书中不妥之处，敬请同行专家、广大读者不吝指正。

编者

于南京理工大学

Contents

Unit 1　Web Life Today ··· 1
（第 1 单元　今天的网络生活）

　Lesson 1　Diversifying Your Web Life in One Place ································· 2
　Lesson 2　WWW—Woven Deep into Our Lives ······································· 7
　Lesson 3　The Web Lifestyle ·· 13
　Lesson 4　Prospects of the Web ··· 18

Unit 2　WWW and Web Technology ··· 22
（第 2 单元　万维网和网络技术）

　Lesson 5　World Wide Web ·· 23
　Lesson 6　How the Internet Works ··· 28
　Lesson 7　Waves from Space ··· 34
　Lesson 8　Marketing on the Internet ··· 38

Unit 3　Information Technology ··· 43
（第 3 单元　信息技术）

　Lesson 9　Information Technology ··· 44
　Lesson 10　Speeding on the Data Highway ·· 47
　Lesson 11　Catching the Third Wave ·· 50
　Lesson 12　China's Reform and Information Technology Industry ········ 54

Unit 4　Computer Science and Technology ·· 59
（第 4 单元　计算机科学和技术）

　Lesson 13　End of the PC Era ·· 60
　Lesson 14　Bill Gates' Speech to Tsinghua University ·························· 64
　Lesson 15　The Next Revolution in Computers ····································· 70
　Lesson 16　Virtual Reality Technology ··· 77

Unit 5　Green Revolution
（第 5 单元　绿色革命） ········ 84

    Lesson 17　Green Revolution——Clean Cars and Energy ········ 85
    Lesson 18　Alternative Energy Sources——Solar and Wind Power ········ 91
    Lesson 19　The Trouble with Biofuels ········ 95
    Lesson 20　The Next Green Revolution：GMOs ········ 100

Unit 6　Biotechnology and Cloning
（第 6 单元　生物工程和克隆） ········ 105

    Lesson 21　The Biotech Century ········ 106
    Lesson 22　What Are Biorhythms? ········ 111
    Lesson 23　The Age of Cloning ········ 115
    Lesson 24　Scientific Researches on Body's Rhythms ········ 122

Unit 7　Robots
（第 7 单元　机器人） ········ 126

    Lesson 25　Robot Wars：The Rise of Artificial Intelligence ········ 127
    Lesson 26　Robot Scientist "Adam" Solves Genetic Problems ········ 133
    Lesson 27　Robots of the Future ········ 138

Unit 8　Application of Electronic Technology
（第 8 单元　电子技术应用） ········ 144

    Lesson 28　A Brave New Olfactory World——Applications for Electronic Noses ········ 145
    Lesson 29　Digital Storage Oscilloscopes ········ 150
    Lesson 30　E-mail Phones ········ 156

Unit 9　Environmental Protection and Pollution Treatment
（第 9 单元　环境保护和污染处理） ········ 162

    Lesson 31　Environmental Protection and Pollution Treatment ········ 163
    Lesson 32　A Clean World or a Polluted World? ········ 168
    Lesson 33　Good Effects of El Nino ········ 173

Unit 10　Space Station and Space Technology
（第 10 单元　太空站和空间技术） ········ 177

    Lesson 34　The International Space Station ········ 178
    Lesson 35　A New Concept for Spacecraft Tiles ········ 183
    Lesson 36　Space Travel in the Future ········ 187

Unit 11　Nanotechnology　192
（第 11 单元　纳米技术）
　　Lesson 37　Nanotechnology　193
　　Lesson 38　A New Treatment for Cancer——Nanoparticles　199

Unit 12　Scientific Theory and Scientific Research　204
（第 12 单元　科学理论和科学研究）
　　Lesson 39　What Is a Scientific Theory?　205
　　Lesson 40　New Findings from the Latest Scientific Research　210

Practice Exercises　216
　　Practice Exercise 1　216
　　Practice Exercise 2　225
　　Practice Exercise 3　235
　　Practice Exercise 4　245
　　Practice Exercise 5　255

Key to Practice Exercises　265

Unit 1 Web Life Today

第1单元 今天的网络生活

—— Web technology has generated immense new wealth and transformed the ways we work, learn, and amuse ourselves.

—— Microsoft had a first-rate browser, which it included free with its Windows operating system. This one-two punch destroyed Netscape, and led to antitrust lawsuits against Microsoft in the United States and Europe. But Web access became a global way of life.

—— Still, Windows Live Web services and Essentials provide solid tools that can help you organize your email, messaging, photos, storage, scheduling and social networking in one place with one password.

Lesson 1

Diversifying Your Web Life in One Place

[1] If you use the Internet regularly, your activities are likely spread out all over the Web. You might be sharing photos on Flickr, emailing via Hotmail, posting status updates on Facebook, following tweets on Twitter, sending instant messages on Google Chat and keeping a calendar on Apple's MobileMe. You hop from one site to the next, juggling different user names and passwords.

[2] In Nov., 2008, Microsoft unveiled Windows Live, its Web-based attempt to consolidate many of these activities. Windows Live can be found at home.live.com and includes programs that cover a lot of ground: Hotmail(email), SkyDrive(online storage), Spaces(blogging), Calendar and Events(online invitations). Four new Windows Live categories—Profile, People, Photos and Groups—create a Facebook/MySpace-like feel by following activities of networked users and sharing that data with others.

[3] If you're using a Windows PC, you can additionally download a suite of seven free desktop applications called Windows Live Essentials from download.live.com that enhance and coordinate with the Windows Live services. These include Messenger, Photo Gallery, Mail, Writer, Movie Maker Beta, Family Safety and Toolbar. I downloaded the Essentials and enjoyed using many of them, especially Mail, Messenger and Toolbal. But I focused my testing this week on the Windows Live Web services, which, as advertised, let me control various elements of my digital life in one place with one password. SkyDrive is a simple and approachable online-storage repository that will be truly useful for a lot of folks who want a central place to keep files. The Windows Live Profile offers handsome personalized pages with bright colors and designs; compared side-by-side with a Facebook page, it made Facebook look dull and sparse. I also used Windows Live Photos to upload digital photos onto my Profile and then shared them with friends and family in three quick steps.

[4] Microsoft smartly realized that most people already visit a variety of sites for online pursuits and will want to add those activities to their Windows Live Profile. Users can currently link to 12 other sources, including Twitter, Flickr, Photobucket, WordPress, Pandora and Yelp—but not Facebook or MySpace. Microsoft says that it's working to build relationships with Facebook and MySpace and hopes to have related news next year.

[5] But though various Web activities can be added to a Live Profile, this connection isn't as productive as it could be. Take Twitter, for example. I added my Twitter account to my Live Profile, but on Live Profile I could see only tweets from myself and from people in my Windows Live network. To see tweets from the 50 people I follow on Twitter, I had to go to Twitter.com.

[6] I had a similar experience with Pandora. I added my Pandora account to my Live Profile, and when I book-marked Keith Urban as a favorite artist, this tidbit appeared on my Live Profile page. But when I listened to Christmas tunes for a few hours, nothing on my Profile page reflected this.

[7] After linking my Live Profile to my Flickr account, I posted photos on Flickr.com, and seconds later, these pics appeared on my Live Profile. But other activities from Flickr weren't reflected on my Live Profile, such as when my contacts posted photos or when those in a Flickr group of which I'm a member posted photos. To see this, I had to visit Flickr.com.

[8] Microsoft says that in the case of Web activities, the outside companies choose what to show and what not to show. But I can't use Windows Live as a home base for my other online activities unless it displays useful data that save me trips to other Web sites. Link many social-networking services, Windows Live gives special privileges to those who are in the network. To belong to a Windows Live network, one must first have a Windows Live ID, which anyone can get by signing up for Hotmail, Windows Live Messenger or Xbox Live.

[9] Windows Live also allows interaction with people outside the network. For instance, I can share any of the photos that I upload to my profile with friends and family who don't have Windows Live IDs by simply emailing a link to them. These people don't need a Windows Live ID to look at the photos. When I used Windows Live to share photos with my sister, who had received hundreds of digital shots from me on every photo-sharing Web site I've tested, she wasn't impressed. She correctly pointed out that other sharing sites, like Shutterfly, allow full-screen slideshow views; Windows Live limits slide shows to the size of the browser window. Windows Live Web service works best on Microsoft's own Internet Explorer browser, version 6 and up, and a special quick-photo-upload tool works only with Internet Explorer. This uploading tool doesn't work with Apple's Safari browser or the Mozilla Firefox browser; instead, you must slowly add each photo to your page, selecting them one at a time.

[10] If you're using a Windows PC, the Windows Live Essentials are definitely worth installing. Photo Gallery enables simple photo publishing directly from your computer's collection of My Pictures, and specific faces can be labeled and tagged in each shot. Windows Live Mail, which replaced Outlook Express last year, is a smoothly designed program that I rely on every day for use with three different eamil accounts. Windows Live Messenger links into the Live Web services specifically by retrieving the status updates for each person in your network and displaying those in a ticket-like panel at the bottom of Messenger. The Windows Live Toobal works only in Internet Explorer but shows an at-a-glance view of your network's updates, along with photos, eamil and calendar—all in the top panel of the browser.

[11] Windows Live Essentials are still in beta, or testing, mode, and Windows Live Web services will add more partnerships next month. I'll be anxious to see if these new partnerships operate more productively with the Live Profile. Aggregating content from across the Web isn't worthwhile unless that content is fully and usefully accessible in its new home.

[12] Still, Windows Live Web services and Essentials provide solid tools that can help you organize your email, messaging, photos, storage, scheduling and social networking in one place with one password. That, by itself, is a relief.

Language Points and Chinese Translations

第1课　单一界面,多彩网络生活

[1] 你如果经常使用因特网,则你的上网活动很可能遍及整个网络。你可能会在 Flickr 上共享照片,通过 Hotmail 收发电子邮件,在 Facebook 上更新个人资料,在 Twitter 上搜索短消息,在 Google Chat 上与别人聊天,在苹果公司的 MobileMe 上安排日程。你从一个网站跳到另一个网站,变换着使用不同的用户名和密码。

[2] 2008年11月,微软公司推出了视窗在线服务,试图以网络为基础整合多种网上活动。视窗在线可以在 home.live.com 网站找到,其程序包括很多基础功能:Hotmail(电子邮件)、SkyDrive(在线存储)、Spaces(博客)以及 Calendar and Events(在线邀请)。四项新的视窗在线功能——个人档案、人际交往、照片和群——创建了与

Facebook 或者 MySpace 相类似的功能,即可以跟踪网络用户的各种活动,并与别人分享数据。

　　[3] online-storage repository 硬盘,在线存储硬盘,意指 hard drive

　　你如果正在使用个人电脑视窗操作系统,就能从 download.live.com 另外下载一套名叫"视窗在线必需品"的软件。该软件免费提供七种电脑应用程序,用来增强和协调视窗在线服务。这些应用程序包括即时消息、相册、邮件、写手、电影制作测试板、家庭安全和工具栏。我下载了这套软件,乐于使用其中的许多应用程序,特别是邮件、即时消息和工具栏。但是我本周的测试重点是视窗在线网络服务,正像广告宣传的那样,它能让我在同一个界面用同一个密码控制我各种各样的电子数码生活。SkyDrive 是一个使用简便的在线存储硬盘,对许多人希望拥有一个存储中心保存各种文档确实很有用。视窗在线档案提供的页面精美,富有个性,色彩鲜艳,设计生动;如果与 Facebook 页面互相对比,则 Facebook 的页面就显得单调松散。我也使用过视窗在线相册把数码照片上传到我的"在线档案"里,然后用三个快捷的步骤就能与朋友和家人共享这些照片。

　　[4] 微软公司敏锐地意识到,大多数人为了在线搜索而访问各种网站,同时也希望把那些上网活动添加到视窗在线档案。目前,用户们可以链接使用 12 个网络资源,包括 Twitter、Flickr、Photobucket、WordPress、Pandora 和 Yelp——但是 Facebook 和 MySpace 除外。微软公司声称正在运作与 Facebook 和 MySpace 两家机构建立业务关系,并希望在明年有所进展。

　　[5] 然而,虽然可以把各种各样上网活动添加到在线档案,但是这种链接并不是十分完美。就以 Twitter 为例,我把 Twitter 网站的账号添加到我的在线档案,却只能看到我自己和视窗在线好友发送的短消息。要看到在 Twitter 上所搜索到的 50 个人的信息,我还必须登录 Twitter.com。

　　[6] 我使用 Pandora 也有过相似的经历。我把自己的 Pandora 账号加入在线档案,当我把最喜爱的艺术家凯斯·厄尔本加入收藏夹后,在线档案页面上就出现了相关的珍闻。但是我听了几个小时的圣诞曲调后,我的在线档案页面上有关此项的信息就一无所有了。

　　[7] 我把自己的 Flickr 账号输入在线档案后,在 Flickr.com 上传送了几张照片,数秒钟后,这些照片就出现在了我的在线档案上。但是,Flickr 上其他一些活动并不能在我的在线档案上显示出来,例如我所联系的人或 Flickr 群上的那些成员发送的照片。真要想看到的话,我必须登录 Flickr.com。

　　[8] 微软公司声称,对于一些相关的网络活动,其他一些网站可以选择显示什么,不显示什么。然而,我现在还不能把视窗在线用作我参与其他在线活动的基础平台,除非视窗在线能显示有用的数据以使我不必再去登录其他网站。像许多网络社交服务一样,视窗在线使同一网络的用户拥有一些特权。要想加入视窗在线网络者首先要有一个视窗在线的用户名,该用户名只要在 Hotmail、Windows Live Messenger 或者 Xbox Live 签名登记,任何人都可获取。

　　[9] 视窗在线也能使我与本网络外的人进行互动交流。例如,我能够与朋友和家人共享我上传到"个人档案"的任何照片,尽管他们没有视窗在线的用户名,我只要把相关链接以电子邮件发送给他们即可,即他们不必有视窗在线用户名照样能看到这些照片。我测试过一些照片共享网站。当我使用视窗在线与我的妹妹共享照片时,她收到了我发出的数以百计的数码照片,但她印象不深。她指出其他一些照片共享网站,像 Shutterfly 可以允许全屏的幻灯片播放,而视窗在线只限于在浏览器边框内显示。视窗在线网络服务在微软公司的 IE6 及以上版本的浏览器中运作效果最好,其独特的照片快速上传功能仅适用于 IE 操作系统。这种上传功能不适用于苹果公司的 Safari 或 Mozilla Firefox 浏览器;你必须一次一张地慢慢地将每张照片添加到页面。

　　[10] 你如果是个人电脑视窗用户,那么视窗在线必需品就肯定值得安装。相册能让你把电脑里"我的图片"文件夹中的照片直接发布到网上去,同时能把每张照片中的特定面容进行标记加注。视窗在线邮箱已经替代了去年的 Outlook Express,是一个设计绝妙的程序软件,我每天用它收发三个不同邮箱账号里的电子邮件。Windows Live Messenger 链接进视窗在线网络服务,可以把你网络上每个人的即时更新信息显示在 Messenger 底部的标签状面板上。视窗在线工具栏只能在 IE 操作系统中运作但却可以一目了然地显示出你的网络更新信息,以及照片、电子邮件和日程表——它们都位于浏览器上部的控制面板上。

　　[11] 视窗在线必需品现在仍处于尚不完善或测试模式,而视窗在线网络服务将在下个月增加更多的合作伙伴。我渴望看到这些新的合作关系能在"在线档案"运作得更有效能。要把网络上各种纵横交叉的内容整合到一起并不合算,除非确保这些内容能够完整、实用地进入新的主页。

　　[12] 而且,视窗在线网络服务和视窗在线必需品所提供的软件功能强大,能够帮助你在同一个界面用同一个密码构建网络生活:进行电子邮件收发、即时聊天、照片共享、在线存储、日程安排和网上社交活动。仅此就足以慰藉。

Exercises

I. Answer the following questions:

1. Why are your activities likely spread out all over the Web if you often use the Internet?

2. What did Microsoft unveil in Nov., 2008? And Why?

3. What programs does Windows Live include?

4. What applications do Windows Live Essentials include?

5. Why is SkyDrive very useful?

6. What does Windows Live Profile offer? How about Windows Live Photos?

7. How Many sources can users at present link to via Windows Live Profile? Please list some of them.

8. How does Windows Live allow us to interact with people outside the network?

9. Why are Windows Live Essentials worth installing?

10. Why is Windows Live Toolbar very useful when working in Internet Explorer?

11. What are the functions of Windows Live Web services and Essentials?

II. Translate the following words and phrases:

A. From Chinese into English.
1. 用户名和密码
2. 个人电脑视窗
3. 增强和协调视窗在线服务
4. 在线存储硬盘
5. 在线搜索
6. 珍闻,珍品
7. 网络社交服务
8. 与某人共享照片
9. 全屏幻灯片播放
10. 照片快速上传

B. From English into Chinese.
1. to spread out all over the Web
2. to send instant messages on Google Chat
3. to consolidate a lot of activities

4. to share data with others _____
5. digital life in one place _____
6. to build relationships with… _____
7. to have a similar experience with… _____
8. special privileges _____
9. to email a link to sb. _____
10. to show an at-a-glance view of sth. _____

III. Translate the following passage into Chinese:

Today the center of gravity in technology has shifted from PCs to the Internet, altering the old rules of competition that were so lucratively mastered by Microsoft.

For millions of users, mobile devices like cellphones are beginning to edge out PCs as the tool of choice for many computing tasks. And Google, the front-runner in the current wave of Internet computing, has wrested the mantle of high-tech leadership from Microsoft.

Although Mr. Gates will spend one day a week at the company, it will be up to his successors, led by Steven A. Ballmer, the chief executive, to master the challenges of the Internet or watch Microsoft's wealth and stature in the industry steadily erode. "Bill's legacy is Windows and Office, and that will be a rich franchise for years to come, but it's not the future," said David B. Yoffie, a professor at the Harvard Business School.

Still, the Gates legacy is impressive. In addition to the software itself, Mr. Gates and his company have fundamentally shaped how people think about competition in many industries where technology plays a central role. Today, there are more than one billion copies of the Windows operating system on PCs around the world.

Industry experts and economists say that Windows is not necessarily the best or most admired software for running the basic operations of a personal computer—Apple's Macintosh can claim the most devout fan club. But Mr. Gates grasped and deployed two related concepts on a scale no one ever had in the past: the power of network effects and the value of establishing a technology platform.

Put simply, the network effect describes a phenomenon in which the value of a product goes up as more people use it. E-mail messaging and telephones are classic examples. A technology platform is a set of tools or services that others can use to build their own products or services. The more people who use the tools, the more popular the platform can become.

Mr. Gates took advantage of both notions and combined them to build Microsoft's dominance in PCs, spreading its influence with computer makers and software developers. Today, there are many thousands of software applications that run on the Windows platform, not just word processing and spreadsheets but also the specialized programs in doctors' offices, factory floors and retail stores—a very broad network on a nearly ubiquitous technology platform.

"Gates saw software as a separate market from hardware before anyone else, but his great insight was recognizing the power of the network effects surrounding the software," said Michael A. Cusumano, a professor at the Massachusetts Institute of Technology's Sloan School of Management.

Well-known Sayings

△ *Take time before time takes you.*
△ *He who hunts for flowers will find flowers; and he who loves weeds will find weeds.*
△ *The greatness of art is not to find what is common but what is unique.*

Lesson 2

WWW—Woven Deep into Our Lives

[1] It was a technical paper with the simple title "Information Management: A Proposal", written by a researcher at a European physics laboratory and filled with esoteric terms like hypertext and browser.

[2] It was also the birth certificate of the World Wide Web, a technology that's generated immense new wealth and transformed the ways we work, learn, and amuse ourselves.

[3] Twenty years ago this month, Tim Berners-Lee, then a researcher at Conseil Européen pour la Recherche Nucléaire, or CERN, in Switzerland, handed in his proposal for a new kind of computer network. That paper and the technology it envisioned would spawn such giant enterprises as Google, Facebook, MySpace, Yahoo, Amazon, and eBay. At the same time, the Web "has replaced countless other services and resources," said Ted Schadler, an Internet analyst at Forrester Research in Cambridge. Newspaper circulation dwindled as readers turned to the Web instead; travel agents shut down as tourists book their trips online. And millions of us started to watch our favorite shows on computer instead of TV sets.

[4] Berners-Lee, now based at the Massachusetts Institute of Technology, oversees W3C, the global organization that maintains the Web's technical standards. Instead of patenting his 1989 brainstorm, Berners-Lee insisted the idea must be given away at no charge, or few people would use it. "It took 18 months for my colleague Robert Cailliau and me to persuade the CERN directors not to charge royalties for use of the Web," said Berners-Lee in a speech last year. "Had we failed, the Web would not be here today."

[5] The World Wide Web giveaway spawned an entrepreneurial frenzy as companies sought new ways to profit from Berners-Lee's generosity. But nobody could make money on the Web until people began to use it.

[6] Berners-Lee built his first primitive browser in late 1990. It was entirely text-based, with none of the pretty pictures you find on the Web today, and you had to type commands to move from page to page. But it caught the attention of two University of Illinois students, Marc Andreessen and Eric Bina, who created a new browser that could show photos and could be controlled by clicking a mouse. Mosaic was the first browser to be widely used.

[7] When computer entrepreneur Jim Clark saw Mosaic, "it dawned on me, this was going to be massive," he said. So in 1994, Clark and Andreessen formed Netscape Communications Corp. "There were a lot of people who thought I was absolutely nuts," said Clark. "The Internet is free. How was I going to make any money out of this business?"

[8] Clark found he could sell Netscape browsers to businesses even as he gave them away to the general public. He built Netscape with the ability to encrypt financial transactions and helped create the market for online retailers like eBay and Amazon.

[9] In 1995, Clark sold stock in Netscape to the public. It was one of the most successful stock offerings ever, raising $2 billion almost overnight.

[10] It was also the last straw for software giant Microsoft, which declared war on upstart Netscape.

Benjamin Slivka, a codeveloper of Microsoft's rival Internet Explorer browser, remembers a desperate effort to catch up. "I and the rest of the team worked pretty insane hours," Slivka said—as much as 100 hours a week for 17 months.

[11] By 1996, Microsoft had a first-rate browser, which it included free with its Windows operating system. This one-two punch destroyed Netscape, and led to antitrust lawsuits against Microsoft in the United States and Europe. But Web access became a global way of life.

[12] People used Web publishing tools to celebrate their hobbies and passions online, using personal websites or quickly updated personal newsletters known as blogs. In 2001, a website called Wikipedia began an encyclopedia composed entirely by volunteers, and today, Wikipedia boasts 10 million articles written in 260 languages by 75,000 unpaid contributors.

[13] Of all the uses to which the Web was put, "the incredible willingness of people, to share the information they have" was a huge surprise to Vint Cerf, chief Internet evangelist at Google Inc. and coinventor of the Internet's core data protocols. "I hadn't anticipated that there would be such a huge response."

[14] Cerf also noted the social power of the Web, which lets people seek out others who share their tastes. "With the World Wide Web and search engines," said Cerf, "you had ways of finding people who had common interests, without knowing who they are." That insight has spawned sites like Facebook and MySpace where it's easy to interact online with likeminded people.

[15] The Web keeps changing the world, with help from wireless data networks and cheap handheld Internet devices. Netscape cofounder Jim Clark is an investor in Clearwire Corp., which is building a network to deliver high-speed data to handheld devices. Google's Cerf said the idea is to expand Web services into poorer countries where people can afford a phone but not a full-fledged computer.

[16] Other innovators are making the Web smarter, with software to help Web computers "understand" data. Mathematician Stephen Wolfram recently disclosed plans for a new website, Wolfram Alpha, that will answer questions typed in ordinary English. Ask Google "what was the Beatles' biggest hit?" and you get 2.3 million Web pages written by Beatles fans. If Alpha works as advertised, it will simply respond, "Hey Jude."

[17] Tim Berners-Lee, notorious for being press-shy, turned down requests for an interview. But today, he will be at CERN, celebrating his own biggest hit.

Language Points and Chinese Translations

第 2 课　万维网——深深融入我们的生活

[1] WWW 是 World Wide Web 的缩写,万维网,环球网。具体来说,WWW 是一个基于超文本方式的信息检索服务工具,可以提供丰富的文本和图形、音频、视频等多媒体信息,并将这些内容集合在一起,也提供导航功能,使用户可以方便地在各个页面之间进行浏览。由于 WWW 内容丰富,浏览方便快捷,目前已成为互联网最重要的服务。

《信息管理:一份建议书》是一篇题目简单的科技论文,作者是欧洲物理实验室的一位研究人员,该论文中充满了诸如超文本和浏览器这类深奥难懂的术语。

[2] 该论文也是万维网的出生证明书。这一技术,已创造了巨大的新型财富,并且深刻影响工作、学习和娱乐,改变了我们的生活方式。

[3] 20年前的这个月,当时在瑞士的欧洲粒子物理研究所(CERN)担任研究员的蒂姆·伯纳斯·李提交了一份创建一种新型计算机网络的建议书。该建议书与其中所设想的技术将会催生出像Google、Facebook、MySpace、Yahoo、Amozon和eBay这样的许多巨头企业。同时,万维网"已经替代了其他无数的服务和资源",剑桥大学福瑞斯研究所的因特网分析师特德·谢德勒说。随着读者转向互联网,报纸发行量逐步缩减;随着旅游者在线预订行程,旅行社纷纷关闭。我们之中的数百万人开始通过电脑而不是电视机观看自己所喜爱的节目。

[4] W3C万维网联盟,又称W3C理事会,是World Wide Web Consortium的缩写。W3C于1994年10月在麻省理工学院计算机科学实验室成立,建立者是万维网的发明者蒂姆·伯纳斯·李。万维网联盟是国际著名的标准化组织,自成立以来,已发布近百项相关万维网的标准,对万维网的发展作出了杰出的贡献/to patent 取得(发明物或方法)之专利权/brainstorm 绝妙的主意,突然想到的好方法,灵感/to give away 分发,分送,让别人获取/royalty 专利使用费,特许使用费,专利权税,版税

现在任职于麻省理工学院的伯纳斯·李监管着万维网联盟。这是一个全球性组织机构,专门维护万维网的技术标准。伯纳斯·李并没有为其1989年的奇思妙想申请专利权,而是坚持认为其创意必须让所有人免费分享,否则几乎就不会有人去使用它。"我和同事罗伯特·卡里奥用了18个月说服CERN的管理者不要征收万维网的专利使用费,"伯纳斯·李在去年的一次演讲中说。"如果我们失败了,今天这里就不会有万维网了。"

[5] giveaway n. 赠品,免费样品

当许多公司探求新的途径从伯纳斯·李的慷慨中获取利益时,万维网的免费大餐激发了一场创业热潮。然而只有当人们开始使用网络,才能从中赚钱。

[6] 1990年末,伯纳斯·李研制出了他的第一个原始浏览器。它完全基于文本,没有你今天可在网上找到的漂亮图片,并且你必须输入指令才能从一个页面转到另一个页面。但是这引起了伊利诺斯大学的两位学生马克·安德里森和埃里克·比纳的关注,他们研发出一种新型的浏览器,能够显示图片,并能够通过点击鼠标进行操作。Moaic成为第一个被广泛使用的浏览器。

[7] 计算机企业家吉姆·克拉克见到Moaic浏览器时说:"我开始感悟到它将有巨大的发展前景。"因此,在1994年,克拉克和安德里森组建了网景通讯公司。克拉克说,"当时有很多人认为我一定是发疯了。因特网是免费的,我怎么能从中赚到钱呢?"

[8] 克拉克发现即使让公众免费使用网景公司的浏览器,但仍然可以将其出售给一些企业。他研制了能够为金融交易编制密码的网景浏览器,并且帮助诸如eBay和Amazon这样的在线零售商开拓市场。

[9] 1995年,克拉克向公众出售了网景公司的股票。这是空前的最成功的股票之一,几乎在一夜之间就融资了20亿美元。

[10] the last straw(一系列重压,打击中)终于使人不能忍受的最后一击,终于使人不支而倒下的因素/upstart 崛起者,暴发户

这也是令软件巨头微软公司无法忍受的打击,微软公司继而对崛起者网景公司宣战。微软公司与之竞争的Internet Explorer浏览器的合作研发人本杰明·斯利夫卡回忆起他们为了迎头赶上而孤注一掷的努力时说:"我和团队的其他成员疯狂地长时间工作。"——一连17个月每星期工作长达100小时。

[11] 到1996年,微软公司已经有了第一流的浏览器,并将其包含在免费提供的视窗操作系统中。这合二而一的重拳组合击垮了网景公司,从而引发了美国和欧洲对微软公司的反垄断诉讼。但是使用万维网已成为了一种全球性的生活方式。

[12] 通过使用个人网站或快速更新被称作博客的个人资讯等万维网发布工具,人们可以在网上谈论自己的爱好,抒发自己的激情。2001年,一家称为"维基百科"的网站开始创建了一部完全由志愿者编写的百科全书。至今,"维基百科"宣称已经拥有75 000位免费撰稿人使用260种语言编写的1 000万篇文章。

[13] 在万维网的所有应用中,"人们分享其信息的意愿令人难以置信。"这使文特·瑟夫感到非常意外,他是Google公司主要的因特网使用宣传者和因特网核心数据协议合作发明人。他说:"我没有预料到会有如此巨大的反响。"

[14] 瑟夫也注意到了万维网的社交威力,它可以让人们寻找到与其趣味相投的人。他说:"使用万维网和搜索引擎,你就会有方法找到有共同兴趣爱好的人而不必知道他们是谁。"这一洞察已经催生出诸如Facebook和MySpace这样的网站,在这些网站上可以非常容易地与志趣相投者在线互动。

[15] 借助无线数据网络和便宜的因特网便携装置,万维网正在不断地改变着世界。网景公司的合作创始人吉姆·克拉克是 Clearwire 公司的投资人,该公司正在创建一个向便携装置高速传输数据的网络系统。Google 公司的瑟夫说,这一设想目的在于把万维网的服务扩展到一些贫穷国家。在这些国家,人们能够买得起电话,但是买不起装置齐全的电脑。

[16] 其他的创新者正在使用软件来帮助万维网计算机"理解"数据,从而使网络变得更加精明。数学家斯蒂芬·沃尔弗拉姆最近公布了创建新网站 Wolfram Alpha 的计划,该网站将会回答以普通英语输入的问题。询问 Google"甲壳虫最热门的歌曲是什么?"你会得到甲壳虫乐队粉丝们所撰写的 230 万网页。如果 Alpha 网站能像所宣称的那样运作,它将简单地回答:"Hey Jude."

[17] press-shy 不愿或讨厌面对媒体,-shy 表示"怕……的","讨厌……的"。

蒂姆·伯纳斯·李不愿面对媒体是众所周知的。他曾拒绝了许多采访请求。但是今天,他将在 CERN 庆祝自己的巨大成功。

Exercises

I. Answer the following questions:

1. What is the title of the technical paper according to the text?

2. Who handed in the proposal for a new kind of computer network?

3. Why has the Web replaced countless other services and resources?

4. What is W3C?

5. What did Berners-Lee do instead of patenting his 1989 brainstorm?

6. What did Berners-Lee do in late 1990?

7. How about Berners-Lee's first primitive browser?

8. Why did Microsoft declare war on Netscape?

9. What did people do by using Web publishing tools?

10. Say something about the website Wikipedia.

11. What is the social power of the Web?

12. Why does the Web keep changing the world?

II. Translate the following words and phrases:

A. From Chinese into English.
1. 科技论文 _____
2. 欧洲物理实验室 _____
3. 超文本 _____
4. 万维网技术标准 _____
5. 专利使用费 _____
6. 点击鼠标 _____
7. 为金融交易编制密码 _____
8. 第一流的浏览器 _____
9. 反垄断诉讼 _____
10. 因特网核心数据协议 _____
11. 搜索引擎 _____
12. 在线互动 _____
13. 因特网便携装置 _____
14. 高速传输数据 _____

B. From English into Chinese.
1. to be filled with esoteric terms _____
2. a new kind of computer network _____
3. an Internet analyst _____
4. to turn to _____
5. to book one's trips online _____
6. brainstorm _____
7. an entrepreneurial frenzy _____
8. the first primitive browser _____
9. to type commands to move from page to page _____
10. online retailers _____
11. a global way of life _____
12. quickly updated personal newsletters _____
13. to share the information _____
14. wireless data networks _____
15. a full-fledged computer _____
16. to turn down requests for an interview _____

III. Translate the following passage into Chinese:

In a Harvard Business School case study, Mr. Gates spoke of Microsoft's strategy in terms of network effects and technology standards that, combined, enabled the company to command markets. "We look for businesses where we can garner large market shares, not just 30 or 35 percent," he said.

In the past, Microsoft has beaten back challenges and vanquished rivals, even when it came late to markets, as it did in the first wave of Internet technology. Mr. Gates's shrewd 1995 decision to embrace Internet browsing technology and attack the early leader, Netscape Communications, started a pitched antitrust battle with the government. "But he extended Microsoft's hegemony for a decade," said Mitchell Kapor, a longtime rival.

However, Microsoft is lagging badly in current round of Internet competition and, analysts say, is facing more formidable challengers this time—notably Google. Microsoft's share of Internet search in the United States is less than 10 percent, while Google holds more than 60 percent and Yahoo has about 20 percent. And search is only part of the new platform on the Web, which includes social networks like Facebook and MySpace and Internet-based alternatives to traditional desktop software, including e-mail messaging, word processors and spread-sheets.

Traditional desktop software—and the technology standards Microsoft controls there—matter far less when more software is accessed with a Web browser and delivered over the Internet from vast data centers run by Google and others. The new approach is known as "cloud computing," and the business model behind it is typically to sell online advertising and software services.

Well-known Sayings

△ *The brighter you are, the more you have to learn.*
△ *Courage and resolution are the spirit and soul of virtue.*
△ *It has been my philosophy of life that difficulties vanish when faced boldly.*

Lesson 3

The Web Lifestyle

[1] If you asked people today why they used the telephone to communicate with their friends or why they turned to the television for entertainment, they would look at you as if you were crazy. We don't think about a telephone or a television or a car as being oddities. These things have become such an integral part of life that they are no longer noticed, let alone remarked upon.

[2] In the same way, within a decade no one will notice the Web. It will just be there, an integral part of life. It will be a reflex to turn to the Web for shopping, education, entertainment and communication, just as it is natural today to pick up the telephone to talk to someone.

[3] There is incredible interest in the Web. Yet it is still in its infancy. The technology and the speed of response are about to leap forward. This will move more and more people to the Web as part of their everyday lives. Eventually, everyone's business card will have an electronic mail address. Every lawyer, every doctor and every business—from large to small—will be connected.

[4] In United States' elections, people now turn to the Internet to see real-time results. The Pathfinder mission to Mars and the problems with the Mir space station drew millions of people to the Web for more up-to-date detail than were available elsewhere.

[5] A change like this is often generational. Where older people have to learn something new outside their everyday experiences, kids, who grow up with a new technology simply treat it as given. College campuses in particular are providing the ingredients to generate the critical mass for a Webready culture.

[6] Today in the United States, there are over 22m adults using the Web, about half of whom access the Internet at least once a day. Meanwhile, the variety of activities on the Web is broadening at an amazing rate. There is almost no topic for which you cannot find fairly interesting material on the Web. Many of these sites are getting excellent traffic flow. Want to buy a dog? Or sell a share? Or order a car? Use the Internet. Where are we going to get the time to live with the Web? In some instances, people will actually save time because the Web will make doing things more efficient than in the past. Being able to get information about a major purchase, for example. Or finding out how much your used car is worth. Or what is your cheapest way of getting to Florida. That is very easy to find on the Web, even today. In other instances, people will trade the time they now spend reading the paper, or watching television, for information or entertainment they will find on the computer screen. Americans, particularly young ones, will spend less time in front of a television screen, more on the Web.

[7] One great benefit of the Web is that it allows us to move information online that now resides in paper form. Several states in America are using the Web in a profound way. You can apply for various permits or submit applications for business licenses. Some states are putting up listings of jobs—not just state government jobs, but all the jobs available in the state. I believe, over time, that all the information that governments print, and all those paper forms they now have, will be moved on to the Internet. Electronic commerce notches up month-by-month too. It is difficult to measure, because a lot of electronic commerce involves existing buyers and sellers who are simply moving paperbased transactions to the Web. That is not new business. Microsoft, for example, purchases millions of dollars of PCs online instead of by

paper. However, that is not a fundamental change; it has just improved the efficiency of an existing process. The biggest impact has occurred where electronic commerce matches buyers and sellers who would not previously have found each other. When you go to a book site and find an obscure book that you never would have found in a physical bookstore, that is a new type of commerce.

[8] Today, about half of all PCs are still not connected to the Web. Getting communications costs down and making all the software simpler will bring in those people. And that, in turn, will move us closer to the critical mass that will make the Web lifestyle everyone's lifestyle. One element that people underestimate is the degree to which the hardware and software will improve. Just take one aspect: screen technology. I do my e-mail on a 20-inch liquid crystal display (LCD) monitor. It is not available at a reasonable price yet, but in two years it will be. In ten years, a 40-inch LCD with much higher resolution will be commonplace.

[9] The boundary between a television set and a PC will be blurred because even the set-top box that you connect up to your cable or satellite will have a processor more powerful than what we have today in the most expensive PC. This will, in effect, make your television a computer.

[10] Interaction with the Web also will improve, making it much easier for people to be involved. Today the keywords we use to search the Web often return to too many articles to sort through, many of them out of context. If you want to learn about the fastest computer chip available, you might end up getting responses instead about potato chips being delivered in fast trucks. In the future, we shall be either speaking or typing sentences into the computer. If you ask about the speed of chips, the result will be about computers, not potatoes. Speech recognition also means that you will be able to call in on a phone and ask if you have any new messages, or check on a flight, or check on the weather.

[11] To predict that it will take over ten years for these changes to happen is probably pessimistic. We usually overestimate what we can do in two years and underestimate what we can do in ten. The Web will be as much a way of life as the car by 2008. Probably before.

Language Points and Chinese Translations

第3课 网络生活方式

[1] to communicate with sb. 与某人联系,交际/crazy 疯狂的,发疯的/oddity 奇妙,奇异,奇特的人或物/integral 不可缺少的/to let alone 更不用说,莫说,不在话下

今天你如果问别人为什么使用电话与朋友联系或为什么打开电视机进行娱乐,他们会惊异地看着你,以为你发疯了。我们已不再认为电话、电视机或小轿车是什么奇特的东西了,这些东西已成为生活中不可分割的一部分而被我们熟视无睹,更不用说对之评头论足了。

[2] reflex 反射,反映,本文中意指由于条件反射而逐渐形成了一种习惯。to turn to 借助于,依靠/to pick up 拿起

同样道理,在十年之内人们将不再注意互联网络。它的存在只是生活的一部分。人们将习惯成自然地依靠互联网进行购物、教育、娱乐和交际,就像今天人们很自然地拿起电话与某人交谈。

[3] incredible 可惊的,不可思议的,难于置信的/to be in its infancy 处于初级阶段,处于初期,infancy 幼小,婴儿期

虽然互联网络现在还处于初级阶段,但人们对之有着惊人的兴趣。网络技术将迅速发展并导致人们快速的反应。这将使越来越多的人把互联网络作为他们生活的一部分。最终,每个人在名片上将都印有电子邮件地址。

每位律师,每位医生,每个企业——从大企业到小企业——都将互相联系在一起。

[4] Pathfinder "探路者号",指美国发向火星的科学探测器/Mir 指俄罗斯的"和平号"空间站

今天在美国的选举中,人们依靠互联网观看选举的实况,数以百万计的人依靠互联网了解有关"探路者号"飞向火星的使命以及"和平号"空间站问题的最新详细情况,而且这些信息要比以前从别处所获得的信息新得多。

[5] generational 时代性,时代特征的/ingredient 成分,组成部分

像这样的变化具有时代性。老一辈的人必须学习他们日常生活以外的新事物,而和新技术一起成长的年轻人对之习以为常。特别是大学校园正在为网上文化提供关键性的要素。

[6] 今天在美国,有 2 200 多万成年人在使用互联网,大约有一半的人每天至少一次进入因特网。同时,网上的活动种类正以令人惊奇的速度在扩展。在互联网上你将会发现几乎没有什么题目不含有相当有趣的材料。许多网址都有极其良好的路径。你想买条狗?还是销售股票?还是订购一辆小轿车?请使用因特网。我们将在何处获得时间进行网络生活?在某些情况下人们实际上已在节省时间,因为依靠互联网办事将比过去更加有效。例如:要购买大商品,我们就能通过互联网获得有关的信息。或者你想了解使用过的汽车价值多少,或者什么才是最便宜的方式到达佛罗里达州。在今天,这些都可以很容易地在互联网上找到答案。在另一些情况下,人们将会把读报看电视的时间用于在网上寻找信息或进行娱乐。美国人,特别是年轻人,看电视的时间将越来越少,而用更多的时间上网。

[7] 互联网的一大优点就是使我们可以把书面信息搬到网上。美国的一些州正在以一种具有深远意义的方式使用互联网。你可以申请各种许可证或者为营业执照提交申请书。一些州建立起了招工栏目——不仅有州政府机构的工作,而且还有州内可提供的所有工作。我相信,过一段时间,政府所印发的信息和书面资料都将被搬上因特网。电子商务也将逐月扩展。这一切都很难估量,因为大量的电子商务都涉及买卖双方,他们只是简单地把纸上贸易搬到网上进行。这并不是什么新的行业。例如,微软公司购买了数以百万美元计的个人电脑网线以代替纸张。然而,这还不是根本的变化,这只是使现行的程序提高了效率,其最大的作用是使以前互不了解的买卖双方可以相互沟通。当你进入一个图书网址并找到了你在书店里永远都不会找到的一本毫无名气的书,这才是一种新型的商业。

[8] 今天,大约有一半的个人电脑还未与互联网连接。降低通讯费用,开发更简单的软件就可以使这些人也加入互联网。而反过来,这将促使我们开发出更关键性的要素,从而使网络生活方式成为每个人的生活方式。人们过低估计的一项要素就是硬件和软件的改进程度。就拿屏幕技术来说,我是在 20 英寸的液晶显示器上写电子邮件。这在目前还不能提供合理的价格,但再过 2 年就可以了。再过 10 年,40 英寸高清晰度的液晶显示器将极为普通。

[9] boundary 分界线/to blur 弄模糊,涂污/processor 处理器

电视机与个人电脑将不会有很明显的区别,因为和有线网或卫星相连的机顶盒都将有一个处理器,其功能将比我们现在最昂贵的个人电脑还要强得多。实际上,这将使电视机变成了电脑。

[10] interaction 相互作用,相互影响,本文中意指互联网的信息功能/keywords 主题词,主要词,指令/to sort 分类,拣选/computer chip 电脑芯片

互联网的功能将进一步改善,使人们更加容易进入。今天我们在互联网上用以搜寻的主题词经常涉及太多的东西而不能分拣,而且它们没有上下文。如果你想了解最快速的电脑芯片,结果你得到的答复竟是用快速卡车运送的土豆片。将来,我们将把所说或打出的句子输进电脑。如果你询问电脑芯片的速度,结果将是有关电脑方面的内容,而不再是土豆了。话语识别系统也表示你将能打电话查询你是否有新的信息,或查询航班或天气情况。

[11] to predict 预言,预示/pessimistic 悲观的/to overestimate 估计过高,高估/to underestimate 估计过低,低估

认为以上这些变化将过十多年才能发生,这很可能是悲观的预言。我们常常过高估计在 2 年内所能做的事而过低估计在 10 年内所能做的事。到 2008 年,也很可能在 2008 年之前,互联网将像小轿车一样成为人们的一种生活方式。

Exercises

I. Answer the following questions:

1. Why will the Web be an integral part of our life within a decade?

2. How do the American people watch the real-time results of elections and the Pathfinder mission to Mars?

3. Why does the author say that the change is often generational?

4. How many people are using the Web now in the U. S. A. ?

5. Do you think that we shall save time when using the Web? Why?

6. What is one great benefit of the Web?

7. What is a new type of commerce?

8. According to the author, what measures can be taken to bring in more people to use the Internet?

9. Why will the boundary between a TV set and a PC be blurred?

10. According to the author's prediction, when will the Web become a way of our life and work?

II. Translate the following words and phrases:

A. From Chinese into English.
1. 与某人联系 ____
2. 电子邮件地址 ____
3. 最新的详情 ____
4. 电子商务 ____
5. 纸上贸易 ____
6. 液晶显示器 ____
7. 处理器 ____
8. 主题词,关键词 ____
9. 电脑芯片 ____
10. 网上生活方式 ____

B. From English into Chinese.
1. an integral part of life ____
2. to let alone ____
3. real-time results ____
4. to grow up with a new technology ____
5. Webready culture ____

6. a major purchase _____
7. a fundamental change _____
8. to improve the efficiency of the existing process _____
9. speech recognition _____
10. to turn to the Web for shopping, education, entertainment and communication
_____

Ⅲ. Translate the following passage into Chinese:

E-Commerce has changed the way businesses sell, package and ship consumer goods, and as a result, it has put pressure on information technology staffs to help online retailers fulfill customer orders.

IT people are key players in e-commerce fulfillment because they handle the vital inventory-control and warehouse-management software that allows e-commerce operations to sell and distribute items one or two at a time. In traditional retail, IT's role is less critical because most companies ship consumer goods in bulk to retail stores.

Much of the change in approach involves split-case distribution—a logistics term that means cases of goods are split open on the receiving dock and the individual items from the cases are stored on shelves or in bins in the warehouse.

In e-commerce, there is a different value proposition. Your distribution center becomes your store.

[online retailers 在线零售商/inventory-control 库存控制/split-case distribution 开箱批发/logistics 后勤的,后勤供应的/receiving dock 接收货台/bin 货箱]

Well-known Sayings

△ Beauty, unaccompanied by virtue, is as a flower without perfume.

△ Our greatest glory consists not in never falling, but in rising every time we fall.

△ Your philosophy should encompass this truism: if you choose to find the positive in virtually every situation, you will be blessed, and if you choose to find the awful, you will be cursed.

Lesson 4

Prospects of the Web

[1] A decade after the World Wide Web first became popular, it's hard to imagine life without it. Now imagine this: Ten years hence, the Web as we know it will have largely vanished.

[2] It isn't going away, but the Web—and the Internet behind it—will go underground, undercover, and maybe even under our skin (via chip implant). It will melt into our surroundings. We won't speak of accessing the Web any more than we speak of accessing the highway system or the electric power grid. "Computers and the Web will disappear into our lives," says Paul Saffo, director of the California-based Institute for the Future.

[3] Ten years ago, Netscape's initial stock sale launched the dot-com boom, and the Web was thrust into our PCs. A decade from now, we'll rarely use a traditional computer to chat, shop, or entertain ourselves on the Internet. Its connections are already moving beyond PCs, a trend that will accelerate as the Internet goes wireless.

[4] What will become of websites, with their distinct personalities and dot-com extensions? They, too, will slip behind facades. Yahoo! will deliver its stock quotes directly into a television, iPod earbuds, or both. Google will learn our tastes and deliver tailored information and entertainment as they become available, or as they fit into our schedules. We'll still have computers and will surf for what's new and different. But so-called push services "will deliver what you care about all of the time, or don't want to ignore," says Jun Yang, a computer science professor at Duke University. Some will be highly personal: The news from MSN might be that a sensor chip in your toddler's skin has been detected slipping past the front door.

[5] Big issues loom, not least of which is figuring out how companies get paid for all this. It's one thing to have a banner ad atop MapQuest directions—it's another to endure an annoying 10-second ad before the directions are read aloud. Even tougher to foresee is the future of Web features that have transformed mass media into personal media: blogging, picture sharing, podcasting. "We used to press our nose to the glass and watch," says Saffo. "It will no longer be a one-way trip."

Language Points and Chinese Translations

第4课 网络前景

[1] World Wide Web 环球信息网,中文名为万维网或环球网,通常缩写为 WWW,也可简称为 Web。万维网与因特网(Internet)有着本质的区别。因特网指的是一个硬件的网络,全球所有的电脑通过网络链接后就成了因特网。而万维网更倾向于一种浏览网页的功能,是一个基于超文本方式的信息检索服务工具。

万维网广受欢迎,风靡10年之后,很难想象没有它,我们的生活会是怎么样。现在就想象一下这样的场景:我们所熟知的万维网将会大部分消失不见。

[2] 万维网并不会离我们远去,但是它——以及支持它的因特网——将会隐藏不露,甚至可能(通过芯片移

植)进入我们的皮下。它将和我们的生存环境有机地融为一体。将来我们谈起上网就像现在谈论进入高速公路系统或电网系统那样平常。加利福尼亚州的未来研究所所长保罗·萨佛说:"电脑和万维网将会悄然融入我们的生活。"

[3] Netscape 网景公司,是美国的一家计算机服务公司,以其生产的同名网页浏览器(Netscape Navigator)而闻名。

10 年前,网景公司首次发行股票引发了 .com 时代的迅速发展,紧接着万维网进入了我们的个人电脑。从现在开始 10 年后,我们将很少使用传统意义上的电脑在因特网上聊天、购物或享受娱乐。网络链接已经超越了个人电脑领域,这一趋势还将随着因特网的无线化而不断增强。

[4] extension 扩张,延长,本文中与 dot-com 连用,译为"扩展名"/iPod 是苹果电脑公司推出的一种大容量 MP3 播放器,同时也可作为高速移动硬盘使用,是一种数字音频视频播放器。所有的 iPod 都配有 earbud(耳塞式耳机),使用一种特殊的白色线,以搭配 iPod 的设计/push service 推送服务。"推"技术(push technology)能够向客户机传送数据而无需其发出请求,如发送电子邮件。传统的万维网是基于拉技术(pull technology),客户端浏览器必须事先向网页发出请求,所需信息才能被传送过来/MSN 是 Microsoft Service Network 的缩写,微软网络服务,是微软公司推出的即时消息软件,可以与亲人、朋友、工作伙伴进行文字聊天、语音对话、视频会话。

具有鲜明个性、以.com 为扩展名的网站将会变成什么样子呢? 它们也将悄悄地隐入幕后。Yahoo! 将直接把它的股票报价分别或同时传输进电视和 iPod 耳塞式耳机。Google 会了解我们的兴趣爱好,并在可行或适合时段向我们发送精心选择的资讯和娱乐节目。我们仍将会使用电脑上网搜索新的不同信息。杜克大学计算机科学教授杨军说,所谓的"推送"服务"将每时每刻为你提供所关注的或不想错过的信息"。有些信息将是非常个人化的:从 MSN 上所显示的消息可能是,植入你蹒跚学步的孩子皮肤下的传感器芯片已经探测出孩子正在悄悄地溜出大门。

[5] MapQuest 是美国一家专门为用户提供网上地图查询服务的网络公司/blogging 博客,以网络作为载体,便捷地发布自己的心得,及时与他人进行交流,是集丰富多彩的个性化展示于一体的综合性平台/podcasting 播客,是数字、网络广播技术发展的一种产物,其全称是 Personal Optional Digital Casting(个性化的可自由选择的数字化广播)。具体来说,这是一种让用户自由地在互联网上发布文件,并允许用户采用订阅 feed 的方式来自动下载文件的技术和理念,是一种全新的广播形式。Podcasting 源于苹果公司的 iPod,兼具 broadcasting(广播)和 Webcasting(网络广播)之意。

一些重大的问题也随之而来,特别是诸如:网络公司为用户提供了这些服务,而收取报酬该如何计算。在 MapQuest 查询系统的方位指示栏上插入一条通栏广告是一回事——在方位指示信息出来之前让用户忍受一条恼人的 10 秒钟广告则是另一回事。现在,网络的特色是把大众传播媒介转变成了一些个性化的媒介:博客、图片共享、播客等,网络的未来特色会是如何,这就更难预测了。萨佛说:"我们过去总是把鼻子紧凑到屏幕前去观看,而将来就不再是单向旅行了。"

Exercises

I. Answer the following questions:

1. What will happen to the Web in ten years according to the author?

2. Why does Paul Saffo say that computers and Web will disappear into our lives?

3. What happened ten years ago?

4. What will happen to websites with the distinct personalities and dot-com extensions? How about Yahoo! and Google?

5. What are the big issues according to the author?

6. What are the Web features at present? How about the future of the Web? Please use your imaginations.

II. Translate the following words and phrases:

A. From Chinese into English.
1. 万维网
2. 芯片移植
3. 电网系统
4. 网上聊天
5. 鲜明的个性
6. 扩展名
7. "推"服务
8. 博客

B. From English into Chinese.
1. to melt into our surroundings
2. to access the highway system
3. to shop on the net
4. to go wireless
5. a sensor chip
6. mass media
7. picture sharing
8. podcasting
9. one-way trip

III. Translate the following passage into Chinese:

Gates explained how Media-room, the Internet-based television platform that Microsoft created for telecommunications companies to sell, will work with TNT and Showtime to let users select their own camera angles when viewing sports. For example, a Nascar fan could maintain a constant view from his favorite driver's car, or plug into a certain ringside shot in a boxing match. For now, though, Mediaroom is mainly used for TV services in other countries.

Microsoft will have another chance to show its video talents this summer, when it runs NBC's online Olympics portal, which is designed to let people zero in on specific events that interest them.

"Building great connected TV experiences is not just a hobby for Microsoft," Bach said.

Gates and Bach talked up improvements in ways for people to interact with software by voice, touch and gesture. In addition to the speech-recognizing functions in Sync-enabled cars, Microsoft plans to soon upgrade the voice-activated information searches available through its subsidiary Tellme. It also will augment the system underlying Surface, Microsoft's computer in a table that responds to users' touches and gestures.

Surface is debuting as a virtual concierge in hotels, but Gates hopes it will soon be used in retail stores. For example, Gates showed how an outdoors-shop customer could use a Surface table to customize a snowboard and transfer an image of his creation to a mobile device simply by putting it on the table.

It was that kind of demonstration that inspired thousands of techies to begin lining up for the speech more than four hours before it started.

[TNT 特纳电视网络,是 Turner Network Television 的缩写/Showtime 娱乐时间电视网络,是 Showtime Network Inc 的缩写/NBC（美国）国家广播公司,是 National Broadcasting Company 的缩写/to zero in on 集中关注,把……对准目标,对……集中注意力/to talk up 赞扬,为引起兴趣而讨论/Tellme（美国）语音搜索专业网络公司/Surface 微软公司研发的触控屏幕电脑,用手指即可进行浏览图片、挑选乐曲等多项操作/to customize 定制,定做,按规格改制]

Well-known Sayings

△ Imagination is more important than knowledge.

△ The way to get started is to quit talking and begin doing.

△ Perfection is achieved, not when there is nothing more to add, but when there is nothing left to take away.

Unit 2 WWW and Web Technology

第 2 单元 万维网和网络技术

—— The World Wide Web is a system of interlinked hypertext documents accessed via the Internet. With a web browser, one can view web pages that may contain text, images, videos, and other multimedia, and navigate between them via hyperlinks.

—— The Internet and the World Wide Web are not one and the same. The Internet is a global system of interconnected computer networks. In contrast, the Web is one of the services that runs on the Internet. It is a collection of text documents and other resources, linked by hyperlinks and URLs, usually accessed by web browsers from web servers. In short, the Web can be thought of as an application "running" on the Internet.

—— The WWW is a powerful hyper-textual medium for integrating all of the resources of the Internet. You can read through a page of text, and on the spur of the moment, link to related information anywhere in the world. ... There are thousands of computers throughout the world on the Web, and literally millions of interconnected WWW pages, and all are easily accessible from your desktop computer.

Lesson 5

World Wide Web

[1] "World Wide Web for Everyone" is an eight week long distance learning workshop conducted entirely by e-mail. It introduces the beginner to the World Wide Web(WWW), (the Internet's distributed hypermedia intered mound deep formation system) and enhances the skills of the somewhat more experienced user as well.

[2] The WWW is a powerful hyper-textual medium for integrating all of the resources of the Internet. You can read through a page of text, and on the spur of the moment, link to related information anywhere in the world. For example, after reading a short piece on twentieth century abstract art, you can link to and view a collection of color prints of paintings by Picasso, Klee, and Mondrian. High school history students reading about Sir Winston Churchill can link to a page where, at the click of a mouse button, recordings of his actual speeches can be played. A business woman in Paris, France can check out the "home page" of her counterpart in Montreal, Canada, complete with her picture and professional vita. There are thousands of computers throughout the world on the Web, and literally millions of interconnected WWW pages, and all are easily accessible from your desktop computer.

[3] The first graphical WWW browsers became available in 1993. Since the introduction of the hugely successful Netscape Navigator in 1994, WWW browsers have provided access to most of the main Internet functions, including the WWW, FTP, gopher, telnet, USENET news, e-mail, and real-time audio and video. The WWW, or simply, "the Web" has become the Internet's "killer application" that integrates a variety of media, including text, images, sound, video and small computer programs called applets. For example, a chemistry student can view a three-dimensional picture of a molecule, and view it from any direction or simply make it appear to slowly rotate in space on the screen. New programming languages, such as Java and JavaScript, have been developed for creating a myriad of imaginative applets on the Web.

[4] Online commerce has become a reality through the magic of HTML forms and CGI (Common Gateway Interface) scripts. For example, you can view an on-line catalog of CD-ROM games with Netscape, fill a virtual shopping card with CDs you have selected, pay for your order electronically, and have your games delivered by express mail the following day.

[5] Having a WWW home page providing one's personal information has become the 1990's version of the business card, resume, voice mail, and on occasion, electronic recreation area, all rolled into one. In fact, the WWW provides an opportunity to participate and collaborate with others at many levels. It can be a great way to network with colleagues and associates or even to reach potential customers concerning products or services.

[6] "World Wide Web for Everyone" will focus on how to gain maximum advantage from this simple use, yet very sophisticated, Internet tool. During the Workshop, you will learn:

[7] How to gain access to the WWW, including information on setting up a direct TCP/IP connection to the Internet (SLIP/CSLIP/PPP).

[8] How to link to specific Web resources using Uniform Resource Locators (URLs). This includes how to construct URLs for various kinds of resources, such as WWW, gopher, FTP, telnet, etc.

[9] How to distinguish between various kinds of WWW browsers, including Netscape Navigator, Microsoft Internet Explorer, NCSA Mosaic, Arena, Lynx, etc. and the strengths and weaknesses of each.

[10] How to navigate Webspace and use various searching tools such as Alta Vista, Inforseek, Inktomi, Wandex, CMU Lycos, WebCrawler, and others.

[11] How to make WWW bookmarks and organize your bookmarks with Hypertext Markup Language (HTML).

[12] How to effectively and efficiently design your own home page with HTML, and how to install it on a server.

[13] The principles of good home page design, in order to project a favorable image for you and/or your employer or business.

[14] The advantages and disadvantages of HTML editors, such as Hot Dog, Page Mill, Hot Metal, and HTML Assistant, and related utilities.

[15] How to understand the multimedia formats used on the Web, including those for images, audio and video.

Language Points and Chinese Translations

第5课　环球网

[1] workshop 讲习班,研讨会,工场/to conduct 进行,实施/hypermdia 超媒体,hyper 词的前缀,表示"超""过于"之意/to enhance 提高,增加,增强/somewhat 有点、稍微

"人人环球网络"是一个为期八个星期的、全部由电子邮件运作的远距离讲习班。它向初学者介绍环球网知识(WWW)(因特网分布式超媒体信息系统),同时也可提高稍有经验的用户使用环球网的技能。

[2] to integrate 使结合,使并入,使一体化/on the spur of the moment 马上,立即,不假思索地/mouse 鼠标/home page 主页/counterpart 地位相同的人,对手,对方/vita 个人简历

万维网是一种功能强大的超文本媒体,使所有的因特网资源一体化。你可以阅读网页,并可以链接到世界任何地方的相关信息。例如:你阅读了有关20世纪抽象艺术的一个简短网页后,就可以链接并观赏到毕加索、克利和蒙德里安所画的一大批彩色油画。中学生学习历史读到有关温斯顿·丘吉尔爵士的材料时,敲击鼠标键,链接相关网页,即可播出他演讲时的实况录音。法国巴黎的一位女商人可以检索到加拿大蒙特利尔的同行的"主页",该主页材料完全,并有照片和个人职业简历。万维网上全世界各地成千上万的计算机都连接在一起,实际上就是数以百万计的相互连接的环球网页。你可以通过你的计算机非常容易地进入所有的网页。

[3] browser (计算机)浏览器/Netscape Navigator 是 Netscape 电信公司制造的浏览器的名称/FTP 文件传输协议,是 File Transfer Protocol 的简略形式/gopher 原意指北美产的一种地鼠,本文中为计算机用语,地鼠服务器/telnet 远程登录/USENET news 新闻论坛/audio 音频的/video 视频的/to rotate 旋转,转动/a myriad of 无数的

最早的万维网图像浏览器于1993年开始使用。自1994年引进了 Netscape 公司的获得巨大成功的 Navigator 浏览器以来,环球网络浏览器提供了可使用因特网大部分主要功能的通道,包括环球网络、文件传输协议、地鼠服务器、远程登录、新闻论坛、电子邮件和实时音频、视频节目。环球网络,或者简称为 Web,已经成为因特网上的"应用杀手",它集各种媒体为一体,包括文本、图像、声音、视频和被称作 applets 的计算机小型程序。例如,化学专业的学生可以观察到分子的三维图像,可以从各个方向进行观察或者使该图像在屏幕上呈现出在空中慢慢旋转。Java 和 JavaScript 等新程序设计语言亦已开发,以在万维网上开发无数富于想象力的 applets 程序。

[4] HTML 超文本标记语言,是 Hypertext Markup Language 的缩写形式/CD-ROM(指信息量极大的)压缩

光盘只读存储器,是 Compact Disk Read Only Memory 的缩写形式

通过神奇的超文本标记语言(HTML)和通用网关接口程序(CGI),网上交易已成为现实。例如,你可以使用 Netscape 浏览器收看网上光盘只读存储器(CD-ROM)的游戏目录单,插入你所挑选的光盘虚拟购物卡,以电子货币进行付款预订,第二天你即可收到快递发来的游戏光盘。

[5] 利用环球网主页提供个人信息已成为 20 世纪 90 年代提供信息的一种形式,它集名片、简历、声音邮件甚至有时候电子娱乐区于一体。实际上,环球网提供了与别人进行多层次参与和合作的机会。它是与同事或伙伴进行网络联系的最佳途径,甚至可以和潜在的客户进行有关产品或服务的直接联系。

[6] sophisticated 复杂的

"人人环球网络"讲习班将主要教授如何通过简易的方式学会使用很复杂的因特网工具从而获得最有利的效果。在该讲习班期间,你将学习到:

[7] access to 接近,进路,进出/TCP/IP 传送控制协议、网间互联协议,是 Transmission Control Protocol、Internet Protocol 的缩写形式

如何进入环球网,包括与因特网建立直接的传送控制协议(网间互联协议)的相关信息(SLIP/CSLIP/PPP)。

[8] Uniform Resource Locators 统一资源定位器

如何利用统一资源定位器(URLs)连接到特定的网络资源上,包括如何为环球网、地鼠服务器、文件传输协议、远程登录等各种资源建立统一资源定位器。

[9] to distinguish 区别,分别,辨别

如何辨别各种各样的环球网浏览器以及它们的优缺点,包括 Netscape 公司的"Navigator",微软公司的"Internet Explorer",国家超级计算中心的"Mosaic","Arena"和"Lynx"等浏览器。

[10] to navigate 航行

如何游历环球网和使用各种检索工具,如:Alta Vista,Inforseek,Inktomi,Wandex,CMU Lycos,WebCrawler 等。

[11] WWW booktmarks 环球网书签,计算机用语,指用某种标记制作成索引,以便用户在网上查寻资料

如何制作环球网书签和使用超文本标记语言编制你的书签。

[12] to install 安装/server 服务器

如何有效地使用超文本标记语言设计你的主页,如何接入服务器。

[13] to project 设计,计划,投射/image 形象,肖像,影像

学习如何设计好的主页,以便为你、你的雇主及你的业务设计出令人愉悦的形象。

[14] related 相关的,有关的/utility 设施,公用事业,有用物

了解超文本标记语言编辑器如 Hot Dog,Page Mill,Hot Metal 和 HTML 辅助器等的优缺点及其相关的用具。

[15] format 格式,版式,构造,形式

如何理解环球网上所使用的多媒体格式,包括图像、音频和视频等功能。

Exercises

I. **Answer the following questions:**

1. Why is the WWW a powerful hyper-textual medium for integrating all of the resources of the Internet? Give one or two examples.

2. When did the first graphical WWW browsers come into use?

3. What Internet functions do WWW browsers provide access to?

4. Why has the WWW become the Internet's "killer application"?

5. Why has online commerce become a reality?

6. Why does the WWW provide an opportunity to participate and collaborate with others at many levels?

7. According to the text, what shall we learn during the workshop?

8. According to the text, how many kinds of WWW browsers do we have now and what are their names?

9. What searching tools can we use when navigating Webspace?

10. Why must we study the principles of good home page design?

II. Translate the following words and phrases:

A. From Chinese into English.
1. 远距离教育
2. 环球网浏览器
3. 主页
4. 光盘
5. 远程登录
6. 鼠标
7. 三维图像
8. 程序设计语言
9. 网上贸易
10. 声音邮件
11. 虚拟购物卡
12. 统一资源定位器
13. 检索工具
14. 超文本标记语言
15. 服务器
16. 多媒体格式

B. From English into Chinese.
1. distributed hypermedia intered mound deep formation system
2. hyper-textual medium
3. FTP
4. gopher
5. real-time audio and video
6. to pay for orders electronically
7. to reach potential customers
8. WWW bookmarks
9. a myriad of imaginative applets on the Web

10. the advantages and disadvantages of HTML editors _____

III. Translate the following passage into Chinese:

In Feb. 1999, representatives of corporations and Internet user groups as well as a handful of governments met in Geneva to discuss the need to improve the system for assigning names to World Wide Web sites, so as to satisfy the growing demand around the world for easily remembered names for Internet sites, such as "www. ibm. com" or "www. microsoft. com".

Under the system currently administered for the world by the Virginia-based Network Solutions, Inc. or NSI, there are seven categories of extensions.

The current list includes. com (pronounced dot-com) for commercial firms, . org for non-profit organizations, . net for networks, . edu for educational institutions, . gov for government operations, . mil for the military, and two-letter country codes, such as . us for the United States or . uk for the United Kingdom.

To that would be added seven more extensions: . firm for businesses, . store for companies selling products, . web for sites emphasizing the World Wide Web, . arts for cultural sites, . info for information services, . nom for individuals and . rec for recreational activities.

Well-known Sayings

△ *He that can have patience can have what he will.*

△ *Confidence in yourself is the first step on the road to success.*

△ *When we seek to discover the best in others, we somehow bring out the best in ourselves.*

Lesson 6

How the Internet Works

[1] To see how big carriers could control the online world, you must understand its structure.

How does E-mail travel on the Internet to reach someone far away?

[2] When Jennifer, who lives in Pasadena, Calif., wants to send an E-mail message from her home computer to her mother in Washington, D. C., she uses a local Internet service provider(ISP) such as EarthLink Network Inc. (ELNK). EarthLink gives Jennifer access to the Internet, much in the way that an on-ramp puts a driver on the national highway system.

[3] After Jennifer's computer makes a local telephone call to EarthLink's local bank of modems, Jennifer types in her E-mail message and hits "send". Based on Mom's E-mail address, EarthLink will recognize that Mom is a customer of an ISP in Washington called Erols Internet Inc. (RCNC). EarthLink will then send the E-mail to an Internet "backbone provider", such as GTE Corp. (GTE), to route it along its way.

What is a backbone provider and why is it important on the Internet?

[4] Backbone providers are the Internet players that typically own and lease longhaul fiber-optic cables spanning a large region. They also own the communications gear that directs traffic over the Internet. There are only a handful of major backbone providers, including MCI, WorldCom, Sprint Corp. (FON), GTE, and PSINet Inc. (PSIX).

[5] Backbone providers connect to each other to exchange data between their customers. They also pick up and deliver traffic for a fee from the 7 000 or so smaller ISPs, who give residential and small-business users access to the Internet. Backbone carriers are like the highway system over which most of the freight of the Internet travels to reach its destination.

How did the current backbone providers come to be?

[6] When the Internet was still a government-run system, there was only a single Internet backbone: the NSFNET, operated by the National Science Foundation, which connected the regional government-funded Internet networks that were run by various research universities. When the government privatized the NSFNET in 1995, companies such as MCI, UUNET Technologies (now owned by WorldCom), BBN (now owned by GTE), and PSINet stepped into the breach by setting up commercial Internet backbone services. Now, instead of one NSFNET backbone, there are many of them that link together to provide the global connectivity, that is the Internet.

How do Internet companies connect to each other?

[7] When the NSFNET was privatized, the government set up three locations in the U. S. where various Internet backbone companies could place their communications gear side by side and connect to each other. These so-called "public peering points" are in Chicago, Palo Alto, Calif., and Pennsauken, N. J. Later, the government sanctioned two industry-run public peering points called Metropolitan Access Exchange East and West—MAE-East, in Vienna, Va., and MAE-West in San Jose, Calif.

[8] The problem was, as the Internet grew, the public points became overburdened and traffic slowed at these bottlenecks. So backbone providers started making arrangements with each other, called "private peering". These are direct, bilateral connections between two carriers in which no fees are charged.

Do the largest backbone providers charge each other?

[9] Backbone providers aren't charging peers now, but there is a lot of discussion about whether they should. Most industry experts say the Internet needs to develop some payment scheme. After all, it is now a commercial, profit-making business, not a government freebie.

[10] But the industry has not figured out how to calculate who owes what to whom. Without an industry standard or government regulation, smaller companies fear that larger ones will set these charges in an arbitrary and discriminatory fashion. There could be a lot of "cockamamie measurements", says Leonard Kleinrock, an Internet founder and computer science professor at the University of California at Los Angeles.

What is the solution to safeguarding competition on the Internet?

[11] Since the Internet was privatized, it has grown by leaps and bounds into a remarkably successful communications medium without government regulation—and most want it to stay that way.

[12] But the Internet has matured to a point that more uniform rules are needed to safeguard competition. As a first step, experts argue that backbone providers should have to disclose the criteria for becoming a peer. This would allow companies to see whether they are being discriminated against.

[13] An industry group called the Global Internet Project—whose members include such major backbone providers as MCI, GTE, and AT&T—is developing a longer-term solution. The group advocates a fair and public system under which all backbone providers would pay each other for carrying Net traffic.

[14] "We need a market mechanism to ensure peering for all," says Daniel Schulman, president of AT&T WorldNet Service, a project member. Many issues need to be worked out, including who would do the policing. Still, with a clear payment system, those who can afford to pay the price can become peers. Peering would be determined by the market rather than by a private company with its own competitive interests.

Language Points and Chinese Translations

第6课 因特网的运作

[1] carrier 递送人,转运工具,运载工具,媒介物,本文中意指电信公司/to control 控制
要了解大型的电信公司是如何控制网上世界的,就必须知道其结构。

[2] E-mail 电子邮件/internet 因特网/provider 供应者,提供者,准备者/access 通路,通道,指 way to a place/ramp 斜坡,坡道,滑行道
电子邮件是如何通过因特网到达远方的收信人?
Jennifer 居住在加利福尼亚州的帕萨迪纳,当她打算从家里的电脑上给住在哥伦比亚特区华盛顿市的母亲发送电子邮件时,她使用当地的如 EarthLink 网络公司(ELNK)这样的因特网服务提供商(ISP)所提供的服务。

EarthLink 公司为 Jennifer 提供入网通路,这很像一条上坡道让驾驶员进入国家公路网。

[3] bank of modems 调制解调器库/to recognize 认识,认出,知道/backbone provider 主干网提供商/to route 经由某特定路线将……送达

当 Jennifer 的计算机与当地的 EarthLink 公司的调制解调器库接通电话后,Jennifer 就输入电子邮件的内容,并击"发送"键。EarthLink 公司根据 Jennifer 母亲的电子邮件地址,识别出其母亲是华盛顿市名叫 Erols 因特网公司(RCNC)的因特网服务提供商的一个用户。Earth-Link 公司然后将电子邮件发送给像 GTE 公司(GTE)这样的因特网"主干网提供商",将该电子邮件按其路径送达收信人。

[4] typically 典型地,代表性地,象征性地/to lease 出租,租借/long-haul 远程,长距离,haul 指拖曳或输送的距离/fibre-optic cables 光纤电缆,optic 光学的,视觉的,眼睛的/to span 跨越,横跨/communications gear 通讯控制装置,gear 原意指传动装置,齿轮,用具

什么是主干网提供商?为什么它在因特网上很重要?

主干网提供商是因特网的运营者,典型的因特网提供商拥有并出租地域覆盖面很广的远程光纤电缆。他们还拥有通讯控制装置管理因特网上的信息传递。现今有几家较大的主干网提供商,包括 MCI,WorldCom,Sprint Corp(FON),GTE 和 PSINet Inc.(PSIX)。

[5] data 数据,事实资料,是 datum 的复数形式/to pick up 拾起,拣起,获得/to deliver 递送,交付/freight 运输的货物,本文中意指在因特网上传递的信息/destination 目的地

主干网提供商互相连接在一起,在其用户之间交换数据。他们还有偿地为 7 000 家左右小型的因特网服务提供商提供获取并递送信息的服务。这些小型的因特网服务提供商向居民和规模小的商业用户提供因特网接入服务。主干网通讯公司就像公路网,通过该网将因特网上的大部分信息传递至目的地。

[6] NSFNET 国家科学基金会网络,是 National Science Fouhdation Net 的缩略形式/to privatize 私有化/step into the breach 前往帮助,上前帮助,相当于 to come forward to help/to set up 建立,设立

现行的主干网提供商是如何形成的?

当因特网还是一个由政府管理的系统时,只有一个主干网:NSFNET,由国家科学基金会操作。该主干网把地区性的由政府资助,由各个从事研究的大学所管理的因特网络连接起来。在 1995 年政府将 NSFNET 私有化时,MCI、UUNET Technologies(现在为 WorldCom 公司所拥有)、BBN(现在为 GTE 公司所拥有)和 PSINet 等公司都前往帮助,建立商业性的因特网主干网服务机构。现在,已不再是 NSFNET 一家,而是有许多家主干网提供商了,他们互相连接在一起,提供全球性的联通服务,这就是因特网。

[7] public peering points 公共对等连接点,即把各个因特网主干网对等地连接起来/peering 对等,匹敌,同等/to sanction 批准,认可

因特网公司是如何相互连接的?

在 NSFNET 公司私有化时,美国政府在国内指定了三个地点让各个因特网主干网公司把他们的通讯控制装置排放在一起并相互连接。这些所谓的"公共对等连接点"位于芝加哥,加州的帕罗阿尔托和新泽西州的宾索肯。之后,政府又批准了两个行业经营的公共对等连接点,称作东区城域通道交换点(MAE-East)和西区城域通道交换点(MAE-West)——分别位于弗吉尼亚州的维也纳和加州的圣何塞。

[8] bilateral 双向的,双边的/to charge 收(费),要(价)

随着因特网的发展而产生的问题是这些公共对等连接点变得负担过重,信息传送在这些瓶颈处变慢。因此主干网提供商开始进行相互之间的连接安排,称作"私有对等连接"。这是两个电信公司之间直接、双向的连接,并不收取任何费用。

[9] scheme 计划,规划,方案/freebie 免费品,免费的东西

最大的主干网提供商是否互相收费?

目前主干网提供商并不互相收费,但是对是否应该收费这一问题已进行过许多讨论。大多数行业专家说因特网需要制订某种收费计划。现在它毕竟是一个商业性、盈利性的行业,并不是政府提供的免费品。

[10] to figure out 想出，理解，计算出，断定/to calculate 计算，核算，预测/arbitrary 专断的，武断的，任意的，专横的/discriminatory 差别对待的，歧视性的/cockamamie 令人难以置信的/measurement 测算，计算

但是该行业尚未想出计费标准和收费对象。由于没有行业标准或政府法规，小公司害怕大公司将会以专断和带有歧视性的方式规定这些费用。因特网的创建人、加利福尼亚大学洛杉矶分校的计算机科学教授 Leonard Kleinrock 说，可能会有很多"令人难以置信的测算办法"。

[11] to safeguard 保护，防卫/by leaps and bounds 飞跃地，极迅速地

因特网上保护公平竞争的解决办法是什么？

因特网自从私有化以来，在没有政府管理的状况下，迅速地发展成为一个非常成功的通讯媒介——而且大多数人希望它继续这样发展下去。

[12] to mature 成熟/uniform 相同的，一致的，一贯的/to disclose 公布，揭开，揭发/criteria 标准，准则，尺度（其单数形式为 criterion）/peer 原意为同等的人或同等地位的公民，在网络术语中指对等接入装置或接入网络的单位/to discriminate against 歧视

但是因特网已经发展得相当成熟，需要有更多统一的规则来保护公平竞争。一些专家们主张，作为第一步，主干网提供商必须公布入网标准，这样可以使入网公司看清他们是否遭受不公正对待。

[13] to advocate 提倡，拥护，鼓吹

被称作全球因特网项目的行业集团——其成员包括 MCI，GTE 和 AT&T 这些主要的主干网提供商——正在制订一个长期的解决办法。该集团提倡建立一个公平、公开的体系。在该体系下，所有的主干网提供商都要为网络通信业务互相支付费用。

[14] mechanism 机制，机构/to work out 作出，设计出，制订出/to police 管辖，控制

项目成员之一 AT&T 世界网络服务公司的总裁 Daniel Schulman 说，"我们需要一种市场机制保证所有公司都可以开展入网服务的业务"。很多问题需要解决，其中包括由谁来统管的问题。另外，还要有明确的支付体制，只有那些付得起钱的公司才能开展入网服务。而且开展入网服务应该由市场来决定，而不是由为了自己竞争利益的私营公司来决定。

Exercises

I. Answer the following questions:

1. How does E-mail travel on the Internet to reach someone you want to contact?

2. What is a backbone provider?

3. What can a backbone provider do?

4. What does NSFNET stand for?

5. By whom was NSFNET operated?

6. When was NSFNET privatized?

7. What companies helped to set up commercial Internet backbone services?

8. What are "public peering points"? And where are they?

9. Why does the Internet need to develop some payment scheme?

10. How has the Internet developed since it was privatized?

11. According to some experts, what should be done as a first step?

12. What does the Global Internet Project advocate?

13. Why does Daniel Schulman say that they need a market mechanism?

II. Translate the following words and phrases:

A. From Chinese into English.

1. 因特网服务提供商
2. 调制解调器库
3. 主干网提供商
4. 远程光纤电缆
5. 交换数据
6. 公共对等连接点
7. 双向连接
8. 通讯媒介
9. 市场机制
10. 接入网标准

B. From English into Chinese.

1. to control the online world
2. access to the Internet
3. to route it along its way
4. to span a large region
5. communications gear
6. government-funded Internet networks
7. to privatize
8. to step into the breach
9. overburdened and traffic slowed
10. a commercial, profit-making business
11. by leaps and bounds
12. to safeguard competition
13. to discriminate against
14. an industry standard and government regulation

III. Translate the following passage into Chinese:

The Internet, unlike other media such as TV or radio, is inherently a "two-way" medium. The ease with which a computer user can communicate to the rest of the world has created a sense of "global community" that's found almost nowhere else. People around the world post web sites, exchange e-mail, and participate in online chats.

Going online means not just surfing the Web and reading e-mail. It means getting involved in the whole Net community.

The earliest Internet-based communication was e-mail. Then came electronic bulletin boards. Both of these systems are still used today. And the Web is very true to them.

While most people are assigned e-mail addresses through their ISPs, free accounts are available to anyone who has access to a web-ready computer. Services such as Yahoo! Mail allow users to access their e-mail from work, home, or anywhere they can launch a web browser.

Once you've got e-mail, you'll find plenty of uses for it on the Web.

[true(to) adj. 忠诚的,忠实的,这里指互联网忠实地服务于电子邮件和电子公告板两个通讯系统。/ISPs 因特网服务提供商,是 Internet Service Providers 的缩写形式。]

Well-known Sayings

△ Living without an aim is like sailing without a compass.

△ An optimist sees an opportunity in every calamity; a pessimist sees a calamity in every opportunity.

△ Don't aim for success if you want it; just do what you love and believe in and it will come naturally.

Lesson 7

Waves from Space

[1] The Internet on the television screen? Data access at super-high speed? That sounds alien to a lot of people. After all, only a fraction of Asians outside Japan, Singapore and Hong Kong has experienced the Internet on a personal computer. In many places, the advanced infrastructure to support networks, including the Internet, is simply not available.

[2] But American computer-processor maker Intel is not satisfied with the pace at which the personal-computer market is growing in Asia. So it has taken the next step in anticipation of the success of broadband services. Together with the Pacific Century Group of Hong Kong, it has formed Pacific Convergence, a company that aims to boost the use of broadband services—audio and visual data transmitted digitally.

[3] Satellite data-delivery systems will be a major part of the company's operations, say Pacific Convergence executives. Already, the company has made plans to develop its own satellites to cover Asia.

[4] Pacific Century, which owns 60% of Pacific Convergence, has the kind of track record that suggests it can make satellite data delivery in Asia work. The company was responsible for launching StarTV in Asia in 1991, racking up more than 50 million subscribers in three years. "Our satellite network will be the backbone for delivery of digital services," says Joseph Spitzer, senior vice-president, public relations, at Pacific Century. "Eventually our network will have a footprint larger than Star's."

[5] Consumers can access broadband services in three ways: through telephone lines; cable-TV lines; or directly from the satellite via an antenna. Satellite data distribution's major advantage is its ability to cover a vast area. Delivering broadband services through cable or telephone wires is cost-effective in Asian cities where population density is high. But there are large numbers of people spread thinly in countries such as China or Indonesia that could be more effectively reached by satellite.

[6] Peter Jackson, chief executive of Asiasat, one of the region's leading service suppliers, says bringing multimedia quickly to China, for example, will not be as difficult as might be expected. "China is already a very sophisticated user of satellites," says Jackson. He says government offices and businesses now use them to run telecommunications and network applications.

[7] To begin with, the broadband service could have a possible turbo Internet application—one that would allow users to access the Internet at high speeds.

[8] Jackson says the major constraint to interactive satellite services is the return line: Internet users must send instructions back to the Internet to demand new information, for instance. This line has to run overland via regular telephone lines. However, since Internet consumers usually only send small amounts of data to the Internet, they do not necessarily require a high-quality landline.

[9] Hardware for fast satellite Internet services direct to a PC already exists. Hughes Network Systems of the United States now offers its DirecPC product for Japan and North America. With a land connection to a local Internet Service Provider, download speeds of 400 kilobits per second are available via satellite, compared with 56 kbps from the fastest available regular modem.

[10] The high initial cost of installation and the subscription fee makes such satellite turbo Internet systems better suited to organizations such as companies or schools rather than individuals. Industry analysts say a satellite data set-up costs about $500 to install and between $20 and $50 per month to support.

[11] Spitzer says that while direct-to-home Internet is a possible application for the new company, it

will focus mainly on delivering data to commercial service providers such as cable operators or Internet Service Providers.

[12] For Intel, the initial number of computers sold may be less of a issue than seeding the market by exposing people to PCs in everyday life. The joint venture with Pacific Century is part of Intel's global strategy to encourage computer applications that use the full power of its latest processors.

[13] Pacific Convergence's eventual market, however, is the end user. Spitzer foresees a time when the technology will allow data access alongside interactive television services. "We want to sell to the family group," he says.

Language Points and Chinese Translations

第 7 课　来自太空的无线电波

[1] alien 异样的,陌生的/fraction 小部分,一些/infrastructure 基础设施/available 有用的,可取得的

电视屏幕上的因特网？超高速数据存入？这对很多人来说听起来非常奇异。除了日本、新加坡和香港以外,毕竟只有极少数亚洲人使用个人电脑进入因特网。在很多地方,甚至连支持互联网络(包括因特网)的先进基础设施都没有。

[2] pace 步速,步调,速度/anticipation 预期,预料/broadband service 宽带服务,宽带业务/to boost 提高,推广,支援,发展/audio 音频的,听觉的/visual 视力的,视觉的

但是美国的计算机处理器制造商英特尔公司对于亚洲地区个人电脑市场的发展速度并不满意,所以该公司已采取了下一个步骤以期在宽带业务上获得成功。该公司也已经和香港太平洋世纪集团一起组建了太平洋协作公司,目标是推广使用宽带业务——声像数据的数字化传送。

[3] 太平洋协作公司的管理层说卫星数据传送系统是该公司的主要运营业务。该公司已经制订了计划发展自己的卫星以覆盖亚洲地区。

[4] to rack up 累计,累积/backbone 骨干,支柱/foot print 足迹,脚印,本文中指网络覆盖面

太平洋世纪集团占有太平洋协作公司60％的股份,其跟踪记录表明它能够在亚洲地区进行卫星数据传送。在1991年,该公司负责在亚洲发送卫星电视,在三年期间用户数累计达五千多万。太平洋世纪集团公共关系部的资深副总裁 Joseph Spitzer 说:"我们的卫星网络将是数字化传送服务的支柱。我们的网络覆盖面最终将超过星空卫视。"

[5] via 经,由,通过/antenna 天线

用户可以通过三种方式进入宽带服务:电话线,电缆电视线或直接用天线接收卫星信号。卫星数据传播的主要优点是它能覆盖广大的区域。在人口稠密的亚洲城市通过电缆或电话线进行宽带传送业务是很经济的,但是在中国或印度尼西亚这些人口大量散居的国家,使用卫星传送则更加有效。

[6] multimedia 多媒体/sophisticated 不简单的,深于世故的

亚洲卫星公司是亚洲地区主要的服务提供商之一,该公司总经理 Peter Jackson 说,在中国快速普及多媒体将不会像预料的那么难。Jackson 说,"中国现在已经能很熟练地使用卫星了"。他说政府机构和企业部门正在用卫星进行电信和网络应用服务。

[7] constraint 强制,抑制,拘束/interactive 相互影响、作用或制约的

首先,宽带服务可能适用于超级因特网——即可以让用户高速进入因特网。

[8] Jackson 说交互式卫星服务的主要障碍是回程线路。例如:因特网用户必须向因特网回送指令以便要求获取新的信息。这条线路要通过通常的电话线在陆地上运行。然而因特网客户一般只向因特网输入极少量的数据,所以他们并不一定要求高质量的陆上线路。

[9] download 卸载,下载

现在已经出现了可以直接向个人电脑提供快速卫星因特网服务的硬件。美国的 Hughes 网络系统现在已向日本和北美地区提供 DirecPC 产品。与当地的因特网服务提供商进行陆上连接后,就可以通过卫星使下载速度

提高到每秒 400 千毕特,而现在最快的普通调制调解器的速度是每秒 56 千毕特。

[10] initial 首次的,初次的/installation 安装/Subscription 预约,订购

由于这种卫星超级因特网系统的初装费和订购费很昂贵,因此更适合公司或学校等机构使用,而不适合于个人。行业分析家们说安装一个卫星数据系统的费用大约要 500 美元,每月的维护费用在 20~50 美元之间。

[11] to focus on (使)集中,聚集

Spitzer 说,虽然新公司可以提供直通家庭用户的因特网服务,但是它主要是向有线电视或因特网服务提供商这样的商业服务系统传送数据。

[12] 对于英特尔公司来说,起初阶段电脑的销售数字并不重要,主要是使人们在日常生活中接触个人电脑而培育市场。和太平洋世纪集团举办合资企业是英特尔公司全球战略的一个部分,其目的是鼓励使用具有该公司最新处理器全套功能的电脑。

[13] to foresee 预见,预知

但是,太平洋协作公司的最终市场是终端用户。Spitzer 已预见到这种技术将使数据存取和交互式电视服务结合在一起。他说,"我们希望销售给家庭用户"。

Exercises

I. Answer the following questions:

1. Why is Intel not satisfied with the PC market development in Asia?
2. What step has the Intel taken?
3. What company does the Intel set up with the Pacific Century Group of Hong Kong? And what is the purpose of the new company?
4. What will be the main part of the new company's operations?
5. What achievements did the Pacific Century make after launching StarTV in Asia in 1991?
6. In how many ways can consumers access broadband services? What are they?
7. Why does Peter Jackson say that it will not be as difficult as expected to bring multimedia quickly to China?
8. What are the download speeds via satellite?
9. What does the new company focus on?
10. What is the Intel's global strategy?

II. Translate the following words and phrases:

A. From Chinese into English.

1. 因特网
2. 超高速

3. 天线 _____
4. 电脑处理器 _____
5. 宽带业务 _____
6. 声像数据数字化传送 _____
7. 卫星数据传送系统 _____
8. 卫星网络 _____
9. 多媒体 _____
10. 交互式电视业务 _____
11. 卸载,下载 _____
12. 调制解调器 _____

B. From English into Chinese.
1. to be alien to _____
2. a fraction of _____
3. advanced infrastructure _____
4. in anticipation of _____
5. to be responsible for _____
6. to rack up _____
7. a sophisticated user of satellites _____
8. to begin with _____
9. hardware _____
10. direct-to-home Internet _____
11. joint venture _____
12. to focus on delivering data to commercial service providers _____

Ⅲ. Translate the following passage into Chinese:

Intel began an exploration of China's wireless Internet market by launching its third wireless competence centre and the fastest Pentium Ⅲ processor during the Intel Developer Forum(IDF) which was held in Beijing on April 24~25.

"Wireless access to the Internet will become a major trend throughout the world in the coming years," said Ron Smith, vice-president of Intel and general manager of the wireless communications and computing group, during the centre's inaugural ceremony.

Intel established its first wireless competence centre in Stockholm, Sweden, in November 1999 and a second in Tsukuba, Japan, in February.

With the establishment of the new centre in China, Intel will help pioneer the development of technologies and solutions for next-generation cellular phones. The centre will also provide a venue for Chinese companies to develop technologies enabling new content and services for broadband Internet connections via cellular phones, according to Smith.

Well-known Sayings

△ *Experience is a good teacher.*
△ *Action without study is fatal. Study without action is futile.*
△ *A little competition is a good thing and severe competition is a blessing. Thank God for competition.*

Lesson 8

Marketing on the Internet

[1] Ira Carlin, worldwide media director of the world's largest advertising agency, McCann Erickson, is quite candid about using fear to sell his message about the communication revolution.

[2] One prediction shows that 55 percent of advertising by volume will be carried on the Internet by 2005. Consumers will have control and choice of communication; they will also have control over what advertisements they watch, and how. But that will only apply to the "information enabled", says Carlin. "There'll be an upstairs-downstairs schism ... The widening gap between the information enabled and information disabled is going to be a greater social problem than any seeming social problem we've ever had in the past, including racial and economic problems."

[3] Look at what is already happening, Carlin says. Living in Manhattan, he can choose the way he receives his daily news. He can open his front door and pick up his own personal copy of the *New York Times*. He can tune to the radio station of the *New York Times*, WQXR, and listen to the same news. "Or I can simply click into newyorktimes. com on the Internet and get the print electronically; or hear the audio files or see the video that the *New York Times* stringers have supplied, through my computer. It's the same news, but I choose the media modality."

[4] The revolution goes further. Carlin's computer can currently stream videos to him at 22 frames per second, with the picture big enough to occupy one-quarter to one third of the monitor screen. "Six months from now, I guarantee that I will be able to receive a full-screen video at 30 frames per second. That means I'll be watching television, but I'll be getting it through a telephone connection." McCann Detroit, says Carlin, put out the world's first video ad, in early 1997, on Pointcast. Pointcast. com is a free news and information service, "fully supported by advertising". It was set up in early 1996 and has 2. 1 million subscribers in the US. Pointcast. com uses a special software program to work out what ads a person might be interested in, by monitoring their selection of news and information on the Net. "I do a lot of technology and marketing work," says Carlin. "Because of that, the computer program thinks I'm rich. It sends me stockbroker ads and technology ads." The person in the office next door, who has chosen celebrity news, gets ads for movies and television programmes and entertainment.

[5] By June 1997, nearly 400 channels of cable television were available in the US. In the near future, thanks to revolutionary developments in computer technology, computer users will be able to access those channels via their computer screens. "How can anyone fill 400 channels of television?" asks Carlin. He answers himself promptly: "Customised programming, that's how." Giant multinational food company Nestle is already setting up a cable channel showing cooking programmes based on its products. "All you need is a convivial host and high-quality guests and recipes," Carlin points out.

[6] Businesses will need to cross-market in the future, Carlin says. So Nestle might still run its popular television ad about a couple who fall in love over a cup of Nescafe coffee, "but they would also produce a CD of all the love songs the couple would listen to, and a novelisation of their relationship." Teenage product ads might have an associated video game. And successful businesses in the future, Carlin says, will draw customers into their own loyal "family" by talking to them directly and providing services

via the Internet.

[7] The Internet is proving a powerful ally for small firms as well as the industry giants. "There's a Midwest company in the States that only employs 16 people in the entire company, but they make quality lathes," says Carlin. "They have tripled their orders by setting up a Web site, and all that incremental revenue is coming from outside the United States."

[8] The Amazon bookstore—amazon.com—was started in a garage in Colorado "by a guy with electronic links to the major book distributors". He thought of a way to provide added service to any customers looking for a book from his Internet book-store. Today, his agent assesses what books people are interested in from their enquiries via the Internet. Amazon then sends them book news automatically: for example, "This author is currently in the chat area" or "We have these new books." "That guy in Colorado is making a lot of money!" says Carlin.

[9] The "roughly right" approach to targeting an audience is not good enough in today's electronic age, Carlin says. "But, quite frankly, with the right message and the right modality and the right timing, we can end up selling the consumer anything, anywhere, anytime." Now are you scared?

Language Points and Chinese Translations

第8课　网上营销

[1] candid *adj.* 坦白地，率直的/message 消息，信息/communication revolution 信息革命

Ira Carlin 是世界上最大的广告公司麦肯·埃里克森的全球媒体总监，当他在谈及利用商家的恐惧心理销售他的有关通讯革命的信息时，显得非常坦诚。

[2] prediction *n.* 预测，预言/upstairs-downstairs schism 两极分化，schism 分裂，分化，分立/the information enabled 擅长使用信息技术的人/racial 种族的

一项预测显示，到2005年全世界55％的广告将在因特网上进行播放，消费者将能控制和选择通讯；他们还能操纵决定看什么样的广告及怎样收看。但是这只适用于那些"擅长使用信息技术的人"，Carlin 说，"两极分化现象将会出现，擅长使用信息技术的人与不擅长使用信息技术的人之间日益拉大的差距将会成为一个更严重的社会问题，其严重性远远超过了我们过去所遇到的任何表面上的社会问题，包括种族和经济问题。"

[3] click into 点击进入/com 作为后缀用在因特网上的域名中，是 commercial 的缩写形式/audio files 音频文件/modality *n.* 形式，方式

Carlin 说，看看正在发生的吧！他住在曼哈顿，能够自己选择每日接收新闻的方法，他可以打开前门，拾起自己订阅的《纽约时报》，也可以将收音机调到《纽约时报》的广播电台 WQXR，收听同样的新闻。"或者我只要点击进入因特网上的《纽约时报》网址（newyorktimes.com），调出电子刊物；或者通过我的电脑收听或收看由《纽约时报》特约记者提供的音频文件或视频图像节目。接收同样的新闻，但我可随意选择各种媒体方式。"

[4] to stream 连续提供/frame 帧/monitor *n.* 监听器，监测器；*v.* 监听，监测，监视/Subscriber 订购者/celebrity 名望，名人，著名

（通讯）革命在进一步深入，Carlin 的电脑目前能以每秒22帧的速度为他连续提供视频图像，其图像大到可占电脑显示器屏幕的1/4到1/3。"从现在起6个月后，我保证能以每秒30帧的速度接收全屏视频图像。这就意味着我是在看电视，但我将是通过电话连接而接收到的。"Carlin 说，麦肯·底特律公司早在1997年初就在点播公司网站（Pointcast.com）播出了世界上第一个视频广告。点播公司网站是一个"完全靠广告来支持"的免费的新闻与信息服务网站，它于1996年初开通，现在美国已有210万个网上用户。通过监测人们对网上新闻与信息的选择，点播公司使用一种特殊的软件程序来获悉人们对什么样的广告感兴趣。"我做大量的技术和市场营销工作"，

Carlin 说,"正因为如此,电脑程序认为我富裕,它就发给我证券经纪人广告和技术广告。"隔壁办公室的一个人,经常选看名人新闻,因而总是收到电影、电视和娱乐节目的广告。

[5] customised 这一过去分词,相当于形容词,表示按规格、特殊需要定制或定做的/multinational 多国的/convivial 欢乐的,饮酒作乐等的

到 1997 年 6 月,近 400 个有线电视频道在美国开通。在不久的将来,由于计算机技术的革命性发展,电脑用户将能通过计算机屏幕进入到这些频道。Carlin 问"有谁能知道怎样来排满 400 个电视频道的节目?"他随即自问自答:"安排不同特殊需要的节目,这就是办法。"大型跨国食品企业雀巢公司已在设立一个有线频道,播放以其产品为根据的烹饪节目。"你所需的只是一个爱饮宴作乐的主持人、高品位的来宾和高档次的菜谱",Carlin 这样说道。

[6] cross market 交叉营销/novelisation 改编的小说/teenage 青少年的

Carlin 说,在将来,企业需要使用交叉营销术。因此,雀巢公司仍会秉承其一贯的颇受欢迎的电视广告,即描述一对男女在喝雀巢咖啡时坠入爱河,"但他们同时还将推出一张 CD 唱片,灌有那对情侣想听的所有爱情歌曲,和一本根据他们的密切关系所改编而成的小说。"青少年产品广告也许会有与产品相关联的电子游戏。Carlin 讲道,未来成功的企业将会把顾客吸引到他们自己的忠实的"家族"中来,其方法就是通过因特网,与顾客直接交流并提供各种服务。

[7] ally n. 联盟,同盟/industry giants 工业巨头/lathe n. 车床,旋床/to triple (使)成为三倍/incremental (利润)增加的

除了工业巨头外,因特网同时也是小型企业强大的同盟。Carlin 说,"在美国有个中西部公司,全公司仅仅雇佣 16 个人,但他们却生产出了高质量的车床。他们通过设立一个互联网网址,使订单增加到 3 倍,而这所有增加的收入均来源于美国以外的地区。"

[8] garage 车库/distributor 分销商,分配者/to assess 评估,评定/chat area 指网上的闲聊区或聊天室

亚马逊书店(amazon.com)创建于科罗拉多州的一个车库里,"当时是由一个年轻人将计算机连接到许多主要的图书分销商而形成的。"他想出一个方法能为所有在他的网上书店查书的顾客提供额外的服务。现今,他的代理商根据用户的网上查询来评估他们对哪些书籍感兴趣。然后,亚马逊书店会自动发给他们书讯。例如,"该书作者现正在聊天室"或者"我店现有这些新书"。Carlin 说,"科罗拉多州的那个年轻人正在大笔大笔地赚钱!"

[9] to target 把……作为目标/to scare 害怕,恐吓

Carlin 说,那种"大概正确"的确定观众(或用户)目标的方法在今天的电子时代已不适用了,"但是,坦率地说,有了正确的信息,正确的方式,并利用正确的时机,我们最终就能在任何地方、任何时间,出售给消费者任何商品。"现在你还害怕吗?

Exercises

I. **Answer the following questions:**

1. How much advertising by volume will be carried on the Internet by 2005 according to one prediction?

2. What does "the information enabled" mean?

3. According to Carlin, what will become a great social problem?

4. In what ways does Carlin receive his daily news?

5. Who put out the world's first video ad? And when?
   _____
6. In what way does Pointcast.com work out what ads a person might be interested in?
   _____
7. Why does Carlin often receive stockbroker ads and technology ads?
   _____
8. What will happen to computer users owing to revolutionary developments in computer technology?
   _____
9. Will businesses need to cross market in the future? Give an example.
   _____
10. Why does the author say that the Internet is providing a powerful ally for small businesses? Give an example.
    _____
11. Say something about the Amazon bookstore.
    _____
12. According to Carlin, how can we sell the customer anything, anywhere, anytime?
    _____

II. Translate the following words and phrases:

A. From Chinese into English.
1. 通讯革命 _____
2. 全球媒体 _____
3. 音频文件 _____
4. 监视器屏幕 _____
5. 视频广告 _____
6. 影视节目 _____
7. 有线电视频道 _____
8. 交叉营销 _____
9. 互联网网址 _____
10. 网上查询 _____
11. （网上）聊天室 _____
12. 电子时代 _____

B. From English into Chinese.
1. the information enabled _____
2. upstairs-downstairs schism _____
3. to click into _____
4. to get the print electronically _____
5. the media modality _____
6. a full-screen video _____
7. stockbroker _____
8. celebrity _____
9. host _____
10. incremental revenue _____
11. to assess _____
12. an approach to targeting an audience _____

III. Translate the following passage into Chinese:

The information highway will extend the electronic marketplace and make it the ultimate go-between, the universal middleman. Often the only humans involved in a transaction will be the actual buyer and seller. All the goods for sale in the world will be available for you to examine, compare and, often, customize. You'll be able to tell your computer to find the best price offered by any acceptable source or ask it to "haggle" with the computers of various sellers. Information about vendors and their products and services will be available to any computer connected to the highway… This will carry us into a new world of low friction, low-overhead economy, in which market information will be plentiful and transaction cost low. It will be a shopper's heaven.

[the electronic marketplace 电子购物市场/customize 按规格定做,定制/haggle 讨价还价/vendors 卖主/low friction, low-overhead economy 摩擦少,管理费用低的经济]

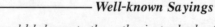

— *Well-known Sayings* —

△ *The world belongs to the enthusiast who keeps cool.*

△ *If A equals Success, then the formula is A equals X plus Y plus Z, with X being Work, Y Play, and Z Keeping Your Mouth Shut.*

△ *In order to build, you have to know, you have to master science. But in order to know, you have to study, to study steadfastly, patiently.*

Unit 3　Information Technology

第 3 单元　信息技术

——Information technology is the study, design, development, implementation, management or support of the computer-based information systems. Information technology actually deals with the usage of all the electronic computers and all the computer software in order to produce, store, transform or convert, process, transmit, protect and retrieve the retained information.

——Infotech is the "marrying-up" of products from several key industries: computers, telephones, television, satellites. It means using micro-electronics, telecommunication networks, and fibre optics to help produce, store, obtain and send information by way of words, numbers, pictures and sound more quickly and efficiently than ever before.

——Information technology is the science—the underlying science—of institutional restructuring. It is the science you use to restructure institutions. It is the basis and tools by which you build systems that allow institutions to be efficient and globally competitive.

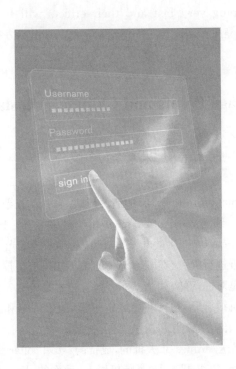

Lesson 9

Information Technology

[1] What exactly is infotech? 85% of people polled recently had not a clue what it is meant, although 53% of those polled said they thought it sounded pretty important. They were right. It is. So what is it? Well, put simply, it is the "marrying-up" of products from several key industries: computers, telephones, television, satellites. It means using micro-electronics, telecommunication networks, and fibre optics to help produce, store, obtain and send information by way of words, numbers, pictures and sound more quickly and efficiently than ever before.

[2] The impact infotech is having and is going to have on our lives and work is tremendous. It is already linking the skills of the space industry with those of cable television so programmes can be beamed directly into our homes from all over the world. Armies of "steel collar" workers, the robots, will soon be working in factories doing the boring, complex and unpleasant jobs which are at present still done by man. In some areas such as the car industry this has already started. Television will also be used to enable customers to shop from the comfort of their homes by simply ordering via the TV screen, payment being made by direct debit of their credit cards. Home banking and the automatic booking of tickets will also be done through the television screen. Cable television which in many countries now gives a choice of dozens of channels will soon be used to protect our homes by operating burglar and fire alarms linked to police and fire stations. Computers will run our homes, controlling the heating, air conditioning and cooking systems while robots will cope with the housework. The friendly postman will be a thing of the past as the postal service and letters disappear with the electronic mail received via viewdata screens.

[3] All these things are coming very fast and their effects will be as far-reaching as those of the industrial revolution. Infotech is part of the technological revolution and that is with us now.

Language Points and Chinese Translations

第9课 信息技术

[1] infotech 信息技术，是 information technology 的简写形式/to poll 投票，民意测验，舆论调查，在本句中为过去分词，修饰前面的 people/clue 线索，had not a clue 相当于 did not know/marrying-up 嫁接，结合/key industries 主要工业，基本工业/micro-electronics 微电子学/fibre optics 纤维光学

信息技术究竟是什么？根据最近进行的民意测验，85%的人不知道信息技术是什么，虽然53%的被调查者说他们认为这听起来十分重要。他们是对的，确实如此。那么信息技术是什么？简单地说来，它是计算机、电话、电视、卫星等若干主要工业产品的"有机结合"。它指使用微电子学、通讯网络和纤维光学，以文字、数字、图像和声音的方式，比以前更快速有效地制作、储存、获取和发送信息。

[2] to beam（无线电等）传送，播送/armies of 大批的，成批的/steel collar 是作者模仿 white collar（白领）而创造的一个新词汇，"steel collar" workers "钢领"工人，意指机器人，后面的 the robots 是其同位语/via, *prep.* 通过，经过，相当于 by the way of/…payment being made by direct debit of their credit cards 是独立结构，在本句中作状

语用/home banking 家庭银行业务/the automatic booking of tickets 自动订票/dozens of channels 几十个电视频道/to run 管理,经营/to cope with 处理,应付/the postal service 邮政服务/electronic mail 电子邮件,现在一般简写为 E-mail/viewdata screen 指提供可视资料与数据的屏幕,即计算机屏幕

  信息技术正在和将要对我们的生活和工作产生极其巨大的影响。它正在把太空工业技术和有线电视技术结合起来以便把电视节目直接传送到世界各地、千家万户。大批的"钢领"工人,即机器人,不久将在工厂里做那些枯燥乏味而又复杂的工作,而这些工作目前仍然由人在操作。但在汽车工业等一些领域,已经开始这样做了。电视也可以用来帮助顾客在舒适的家中购物,他们只要通过电视屏幕订货,并用信用卡直接借记付款。也可以通过电视屏幕办理家庭银行业务以及自动订票。现在在很多国家有线电视可以提供几十个电视频道供人们选择,这种有线电视不久将可与警察局、消防站的防盗、防火警报装置连接,实现对家的安保。计算机将管理家庭,控制取暖、空调和烹饪系统,而机器人则将处理所有家务劳动。通过计算机屏幕接收电子邮件,邮政服务和信函将消失,友好可亲的邮递员也将成为历史。

  [3] 所有这一切事物都将迅速来临,其作用将像工业革命一样影响深远。信息技术是技术革命的一部分,现在它已和我们息息相关。

Exercises

Ⅰ. Answer the following questions:

1. What is infotech?

2. What does infotech mean?

3. What are the impact and the function of infotech?

4. How can we use cable television to protect our homes?

5. How can we use computers to run our homes?

6. Why will the postmen be a thing of the past?

Ⅱ. Translate the following words and phrases:

A. From Chinese into English.
1. 信息技术
2. 主要工业
3. 微电子产品
4. 通讯网络
5. 纤维光学
6. 有线电视
7. 机器人
8. 技术革命

B. From English into Chinese.
1. to produce, store, obtain and send information _____
2. by way of words, numbers, pictures and sound _____
3. to link... with... _____
4. the skills of the space industry _____
5. the boring, complex and unpleasant jobs _____
6. to order via the TV screen _____
7. credit cards _____
8. dozens of channels _____
9. to cope with the housework _____
10. to control the heating, air conditioning and cooking systems _____

III. Translate the following passage into Chinese:

Information Technology (IT) has arisen as a separate technology by the convergence of data processing techniques and telecommunications, the former providing the capability for processing and storing information, the latter the vehicle for communicating it. The main contributing branches are computing, microelectronics and telecommunications but others include optoelectronics, office equipment technology, systems theory and artificial intelligence theory and practice.

The rapid advances in telecommunications and computer technology are causing the information and telecommunications industries to converge. Everything is going digital—telephones, televisions, radios. Soon it will be difficult or impossible to distinguish between a cable television company and a telephone company. Both will be providing high-speed, two-way, digital video services as well as ordinary phone service.

Well-known Sayings

△ *Progress begins with the belief that what is necessary is possible.*
△ *Human progress is furthered, not by conformity, but by aberration.*
△ *The people who get on in this world are the people who get up and look for circumstances they want, and if they cannot find them, make them.*

Lesson 10

Speeding on the Data Highway

[1] The US's largest telecommunications company has overtaken its rivals in the battle to keep ahead on the information superhighway by sending data down a sub-sea fibre optic cable four times faster than is usual on today's commercial cables. The increased transmission speed was made possible by amplifying the signals optically rather than electronically.

[2] Last month AT&T sent the information as pulses of light at a rate of 10 billion bits per second over a 2 000-kilometre stretch of cable under the Caribbean Sea. Although even higher rates have been attained in research the test proves that commercial cables can also be made to work at higher speeds.

[3] Today's fastest commercial fibre optic cables carry 2.5 billion bits per second, but as services such as video phone calls develop, their capacity will have to be increased.

[4] AT&T ran the tests on a cable stretching from Florida to the American Virgin Islands. When fully operational in December, the cable will connect the US, Mexico, Italy, Portugal and Spain. But it will not work at the higher speed immediately because customers do not yet need it.

[5] To transmit information through a fibre optic cable, the signal is converted into pulses of light. As the signal travels down the cable it gradually becomes fainter, so it must be boosted every 40 miles or so. In the past this was achieved by electronic repeaters, which convert the light pulses into electronic signals, boost them, and then convert them back into light before sending them on. But electronic repeaters must be preset to process a certain amount of information. So increasing the capacity of the cable would mean replacing every repeater along its length.

[6] This problem can be avoided by using optical repeaters. These are stretches of cable that contain the light-emitting element erbium and a "pump" laser. The laser keeps the erbium section of fibre at an energy state on the brink of emitting light. This means that when the light pulse hits the erbium section, it boosts the erbium's energy just enough to push it over the edge and emit light, sending the refreshed signal onto the next repeater.

[7] Using a method called wavelength division multiplexing, AT&T's engineers sent four colours of light simultaneously down the cable. The signals were then sorted out according to wavelength and converted back into information.

Language Points and Chinese Translations

第10课 在信息高速公路上疾驰

[1] rival 竞争者,对手/sub-sea 海底,海底的,sub 为词的前缀,表示下、低、次等含义。/to amplify 放大,扩大,延伸/signal 信号

美国最大的电信公司通过海底光纤电缆发送信息,其速度比今天的商业电缆快四倍,从而大大超过了其竞争对手,保持了在信息高速公路上的领先地位。该公司通过光学而不是电子学的方法放大信号因而提高了传送

速度。

　　[2] pulses of light 光脉冲波，pulse 脉，脉搏，脉冲波/bit(binary digit) 毕特，二进位制信息单位/stretch 伸长，伸展，延亘，连绵

　　上个月 AT&T 公司通过加勒比海海底长达 2 000 公里的光纤电缆，以速度为每秒 100 亿个毕特的光脉冲波输送了信息。虽然在研究中可以达到更高的速度，但是这次测试表明商业电缆也能以更高的速度运行。

　　[3] video phone 可视电话，电视电话，video 电视的/capacity 容量，容积

　　今天最快速的商业光纤电缆传送速度为每秒 25 亿个毕特，但是随着可视电话的发展，其容量也将必须增加。

　　[4] operational 操作上的，运作上的，业务上的

　　AT&T 公司在佛罗里达州至美属维尔京群岛的海底光纤电缆上作过多次试验。在 12 月全线运行时，这条电缆将把美国、墨西哥、意大利、葡萄牙和西班牙互相连通。但是该电缆不会立即以更高的速度运行，因为用户们还没有这样的需求。

　　[5] to convert…into… 把……转变成……/to boost 抬高，升高/electronic repeater 电子中继器

　　为了通过光纤电缆传送信息，就必须把信号转换成光脉冲。由于信号在沿着电缆传输时会逐渐减弱，因此每隔 40 英里左右，就必须把信号放大一次。这在过去是靠电子中继器来实现的。电子中继器把光脉冲转变成电子信号，加以放大，然后再转变成光继续进行传送。但是电子中继器必须预设才能处理一定数量的信息，因此增加电缆的容量就意味着要替换整个电缆上的每个中继器。

　　[6] erbium 铒/on the brink of 濒于，濒临，在……的边缘/to refresh 提神，振作，更新，本文中 refreshed 作形容词用，修饰 signal，表示"增强的，提高的，扩大的"之意

　　可以使用光学中继器来避免这个问题。光学中继器是含有发光元素铒和"泵"激光的长段的光缆。激光使光纤电缆的含铒部分处于濒临发光的能量状态。这意指：当光脉冲打击含铒部分时，使铒的能量增加到足以推动它超越边缘能态而发光，这样把增强了的信号传送给下一个中继器。

　　[7] wave-length 波长/simultaneously 同时，相当于 at the same time/to sort out 拣选，分类

　　AT&T 公司的工程师们使用波长分隔多路传送的方法，把四种颜色的光同时输入电缆，然后信号就按不同的波长被分拣并转换成信息。

Exercises

I. Answer the following questions:

1. In which respect has the US's largest telecommunications company overtaken its rivals?

2. How fast does a sub-sea fibre optic cable transmit signals?

3. What is the rate of pulses of light?

4. What does the test made by AT&T prove?

5. How is information transmitted through a fibre optic cable?

6. What is an optical repeater?

7. What method do AT&T's engineers adopt to transmit information through a fibre optic cable?

II. Translate the following words and phrases:

A. From Chinese into English.
1. 信息高速公路 _____
2. 电信公司 _____
3. 海底光纤电缆 _____
4. 光脉冲 _____
5. 电视电话 _____
6. 电子中继器 _____
7. 光学中继器 _____
8. 波长 _____

B. From English into Chinese.
1. commercial cables _____
2. to amplify the signals optically _____
3. at a rate of _____
4. at a high speed _____
5. every 40 miles or so _____
6. a certain amount of information _____
7. to convert...into... _____
8. at an energy state _____
9. on the brink of _____
10. to sort out signals _____

III. Translate the following passage into Chinese:

An undersea fibre optic cable stretching from China to the United States in a loop system more than 25 000 kilometres underwater will soon expand China's links with the world.

This new fibre optic technology system will transmit voice, data and images at up to a total of 80 gigabits per second. The capacity of 80 gigabits per second is a massive speed advance on previous technology, and allows the transmission of more than one million calls simultaneously.

The $1.5 billion China-US Cable Network, as it is called, provides a digital connection between China and the US, and overcomes the small fibre optic capacity which has been available, and which, among other things, affects the ability to expand Internet capacity (currently all links are via satellite). China Telecom has been trying for some time to set up a direct link with the US. The cable will be used for all communications such as telephone line services including Internet connections and e-mail links.

Well-known Sayings

△ *The most incomprehensible thing about the world is that it is comprehensible.*

△ *The trouble with our times is that the future is not what it used to be.*

△ *The natural progress of the works of men is from rudeness to convenience, from convenience to elegance and from elegance to nicety.*

Lesson 11

Catching the Third Wave

[1] Tomorrow's economy is developing from an information revolution that futurist Alvin Toffler termed the Third Wave. Just as the Second Wave, the Industrial Revolution, transformed the lives of the eighteenth-century agrarians, the Third Wave is re-making the world and the future.

[2] "In the past ten years or so, much of the established world order has crumbled," write management consultants Jermy Hope and Tony Hope in their new book, *Competing in the Third Wave*. "We are currently in the dislocation phase between the second and third-wave economies."

[3] Suddenly, companies born and raised in the second-wave economy are struggling to overcome profound shock, trying to learn new skills, and searching for third-wave opportunities all at once. Managers face a host of new business realities, including.

[4] • A rapidly accelerating high-tech sector driving a third-wave economy of constant change;
• The rise of world markets and the global nature of money and information;
• The fall of government monopolies and the breakup of conglomerates;
• A dramatic reduction of inventory levels as technology allows companies to manufacture products on demand;
• The emergence of knowledge as the key economic resource;
• Changing patterns of employment that include an explosion of outsourcing and new alliances.

[5] The authors suggest a number of ways that managers can learn to ride the third wave successfully.

[6] Finding and keeping loyal and profitable customers is essential. The route to long-term success is to find loyal customers who represent a close strategic fit with the company and are also likely to be profitable. Rather than trying to meet the needs of a larger group of people, third-wave managers work to attract and keep the right customers. Loyalty-based strategies yield spectacular results for some companies.

[7] MBNA, a credit card company, targets specific affinity groups whose members have above-average earnings: sports clubs, universities, and associations. The company produces Visas and Mastercards for 4 300 such groups, usually with personal logos. MBNA's strategy is hitting the bull's-eye: The average balance held by its cardholders is three times the national average.

[8] Technology is creating unprecedented opportunities to build a loyal consumer base by customizing products. Levi-Strauss offers its Personal Pair outlets for women who want a perfectly fitting pair of jeans. A computer picks out exactly the right size and sends the woman's specifications to the factory. For an added $10 fee, her made-to-measure jeans arrive a few days later.

[9] Third-wave organizations realize the power that resides in the minds of their best people, embedded in systems, databases, and competencies. Successful managers learn how to acquire, define, and use knowledge to build long-term capabilities.

[10] Chaparral Steel is a working prototype of a knowledge-based organization. The company has set world records for producing low-cost, high-quality steel. The company invests heavily in education,

training, arid formal apprenticeship programs.

[11] "Expertise must be in the hands of the people who make the product," says CEO Gordon Forward. Along with strong incentive and education systems, Chaparral maintains an openness to outside ideas and a tolerance for failure that help to keep innovative thinking alive.

Language Points and Chinese Translations

第11课 迎接第三次浪潮

[1] to transform 改变,转变,改革/agrarian 主张平均地权的人

明天的经济正从信息革命中发展起来。未来学家 Alvin Toffler 把信息革命称作第三次浪潮。正像第二次浪潮——工业革命改变了18世纪主张平均地权的人的生活方式一样,第三次浪潮在又一次改变着世界与未来。

[2] to crumble 崩溃,瓦解,灭亡/dislocation 断层,错位

经济管理顾问 Jenny Hope 和 Tony Hope 在他们的新书《在第三次浪潮中竞争》中这样写道:"在过去的十年左右时间里,已经建立起来的世界秩序大多已经土崩瓦解","目前我们正处在第二次浪潮向第三次浪潮的经济转型时期。"

[3] shock 冲击,震荡/a host of 许多,一大堆

突然间,许多在第二次浪潮经济中诞生和成长起来的公司都在努力奋斗,克服转型时期的巨大冲击,学习新的技术,寻求第三次浪潮所带来的机遇。管理者们正面临着商界许多新的现实,其中包括:

[4]monopoly 垄断,独占/breakup 解体,解散,分裂/conglomerate 联合大企业/explosion 爆炸,剧变,激增/to outsource 外部采办,外购

- 加速发展的高科技推动不断变化的第三次浪潮的经济;
- 世界市场的兴起和资金信息的全球化;
- 政府失去垄断和联合大企业的解体;
- 公司依靠技术按需制造产品从而大大降低了库存;
- 知识作为主要的经济资源;
- 就业方式的变化,包括外包和企业重组的激增。

[5] 作者提出了一些方法,管理者们可以学习以便能够成功地迎接第三次浪潮。

[6] route 路径,路线/strategic 战略的/spectacular 引人注意的,惊人的

发现并留住那些忠实可靠的有利可图的顾客很重要。长期成功的途径就是寻找那些忠实的顾客,他们代表着完全适合公司发展的战略需求,而且对于公司来说他们很可能有利可图。第三次浪潮中的管理者们不是试图去满足大批人群的需求,而是吸引并留住适合的顾客。对于一些公司来说,以忠实顾客为基础的战略会产生惊人的效果。

[7] to target 把……作为目标/affinity 亲和性,吸引力/Visa 威世信用卡/Mastercard 万事达信用卡/logo 标识,作为标志的语句,标识语/bull's eye 靶的中心,打中靶心的一击,to hit the bull's eye 正中要害

信用卡公司 MBNA 把运动俱乐部,大学和协会等一些社团作为目标,这些团体成员的收入超过平均水平。该公司为4 300个这样的团体制作威世信用卡和万事达信用卡,通常带有个人的标识。MBNA 公司的战略抓住了关键,该公司信用卡持有人的平均结余是全国平均水平的三倍。

[8] unprecedented 无前例的,空前的/to customize 定制,定做,按规格改制/outlet 销路,商店/made-to-measure 根据测量而制作的

技术正在以为顾客定制产品的方式,为建立一支忠实可靠的消费者队伍而创造前所未有的机遇。Levi-Strauss 商店为想要购买完全合身的牛仔裤的妇女提供了专门行销的商品。计算机准确地量出女顾客身材的尺

寸,并将其规格发送至工厂。只要另外多付十美元的费用,按测量身材定做的牛仔裤几天后就可到手了。

[9] to reside in 存在于,归于,属于/embedded in 留在……中,嵌入,埋置/competence 能力,胜任/to acquire 获取,取得/define 定义,规定,限定/capability 能力,才能

第三次浪潮下的企业界都认识到竞争力在其精英的大脑中,植根于各种系统、数据库和能力之中。成功的经营管理人员知道如何获取、确定和使用知识以便培养长期发展的能力。

[10] working prototype 足有成效的典型、范例或样板/apprenticeship program 学徒训练计划

Chaparral 钢铁公司是一家典型的知识型企业。该公司以生产低成本、高质量的钢铁创造了世界纪录,并且在教育、培训和正式的学徒训练计划方面投入巨大。

[11] expertise 专门知识或技能,专长/CEO 首席执行官,是 chief executive officer 的缩略语/incentive 激励,刺激/tolerance 宽容,容忍/innovative 革新的,创新的,富有革新精神的

公司首席执行官 Gordon Forward 说,"专业技术必须掌握在制造产品的人手里。"该公司除了有强有力的激励机制和教育体系外,还保持对外开放的思想和容忍失败,这些都有助于保持富于革新精神的思想与活力。

Exercises

I. Answer the following questions:

1. What does the Third Wave refer to?

2. What was the result of the Second Wave?

3. Which phase are we currently in according to the authors of *Competing in the Third Wave*?

4. What are the third-wave opportunities?

5. How can we ride the third wave successfully?

6. "Loyalty-based strategies yield spectacular results for some companies." Please say something about such companies according to the text.

7. Why does the author say that the power resides in the minds of the best people?

8. What does the Chaparral Steel do to keep innovative thinking alive?

II. Translate the following words and phrases:

A. From Chinese into English.
1. 专门技能或知识 _____
2. 信息革命 _____
3. 工业革命 _____
4. 转型时期 _____
5. 高科技 _____
6. 资金、信息的全球化 _____

7. 经济资源 _____
8. 以知识为本 _____
9. 投资于教育和培训 _____
10. 激励机制 _____

B. From English into Chinese.
1. the established world order _____
2. companies born and raised in the second-wave economy _____
3. a host of new business realities _____
4. to manufacture products on demand _____
5. changing patterns of employment _____
6. loyal and profitable customers _____
7. to meet the needs of _____
8. three times the national average _____
9. to create unprecedented opportunities _____
10. to customize products _____
11. to build long-term capabilities _____
12. a working prototype _____
13. in the hands of _____
14. to maintain an openness to outside ideas _____

Ⅲ. Translate the following passage into Chinese:

In 1906, the public radio broadcasting first appeared in Massachusetts. In 1936, the first public television company was set up in London. TV development speeds up after the invention of the cathode ray tube "kinescope" by Vladimir Zworykin, head of RCA's TV research. This tube displaces John Logie Baird's mechanical system. Worldwide television broadcasts are now possible through satellite technology.

In 1960, laser technology was developed by Charles H. Townes and Arthur Schawlow of Columbia University, and Dr Theodore H. Maiman working at the Hughes Research Labs. Laser technology is now vital in telecommunications, medicine, the defence industry, mass production, ozone measurements, and supermarkets (bar-code reading). Travelling through fibre optic cables, lasers carry phone, fax, computer, TV and radio communications and are used in medical operations, business, industry, commerce, construction and in the home.

Well-known Sayings

△ *Memory is the mother of knowledge.*
△ *The wish is the father of the thought.*
△ *Life is measured by thought and action, not by time.*

Lesson 12

China's Reform and Information Technology Industry

[1] China is embarking on an extraordinary new stage of its economic and industrial development. The restructuring of the state-owned enterprises is as big a transformation as any country has ever seen, let alone implemented.

[2] The process of transformation of the state-owned enterprises is well under way. Today it is working at the first stage of enterprise restructuring, which is to align industries, align assets, merge companies, and to create an industry infrastructure that is organizationally capable of becoming a globally successful enterprise or globally successful industry.

[3] However, there's another phase to economic reform of state-owned enterprises that goes beyond structure, that goes beyond merging, that goes beyond aligning. It's about the processes by which the enterprises are managed.

[4] Building the systems of cost control, of accounting, of inventory management, of supply chain management, of cash management, of customer relationships, and of benchmarking. These are all systems that aren't created through structural change. They're created through process and cultural change.

[5] And underpinning all of those systems—what drives the creation of those systems—is information technology. Information technology is the science—the underlying science—of institutional restructuring. It is the science you use to restructure institutions. It is the basis and the tools by which you build systems that allow institutions to be efficient and globally competitive.

[6] China's information technology industry needs to evolve today along with the state-owned enterprises to support the transformation of China's enterprises.

[7] Today China's information technology industry is principally a hardware-based industry. But it is absolutely critical that China builds a software and services industry along with its hard-ware industry if the transformation of the state-owned enterprises is going to take place.

[8] Because what we need in China is applications. We already have the computers, but what China needs now are the applications that run on the computers that will allow the state-owned enterprises to achieve this transformation.

[9] I'm not talking about simple, unsophisticated software like spreadsheets, word processing, or games. I'm talking about large, complex software that allows these companies to do all the things I talked about before: transaction processing, data management, billing, cash management, managing platforms, e-business opportunities.

[10] China needs to build the industry that will adapt applications for abroad and build new applications out of the intellectual capital of the Chinese people.

[11] And then a services industry has to emerge that will help China's institutions apply these technologies to their state-owned enterprises.

[12] And finally there is, in my opinion, a very big opportunity for China to lead in the transformation of small and medium sized companies, including smaller state-owned enterprises. Because

what will happen in the future is that software applications that allow companies to become efficient and globally competitive will be embedded in a network.

[13] Small and medium sized companies will not have to build those applications. They will not have to pay for those applications. If China's telecom industry develops in the way we expect it will, and if focus is given to these Chinese applications, small and medium sized businesses will be able to, in effect, rent the applications, dial up on their telephone, and have a billing application, an accounting application, or an e-business application, to use without having to build it, pay up front, or maintain it.

[14] But again, this requires a focus in China on the next stage of development of the information technology industry, which is to move beyond just making PCs and hardware to making intellectual capital, to making the real heart of an information technology system which is the application, not the hardware.

[15] So it's interesting to see how China's extraordinarily important priority of restructuring the state-owned enterprises aligns very clearly and carefully with the next stage of development of the information technology industry in China. It aligns very clearly with the next phase of the information technology, which is e-business.

[16] And through the evolution of Chinese-based applications, building on the e-business concept, there's a lot of opportunity and, I think, a lot of optimism about the success of the state-owned enterprise reformation program.

Language Points and Chinese Translations

第12课　中国的改革与信息技术产业

▲ 本文为国际商用机器制造公司(IBM)董事长兼首席执行总裁 Gerstner 先生在北京所作的演讲词摘选。在该文中他以一个外国人的立场评述了中国的改革和信息技术产业。

[1] to embark on 从事，着手，开始搞/to restructure 重组，改组，调整/state-owned 国有的，国营的/transformation 改革，改造，转变/to let alone 更不用说/to implement 贯彻，完成，实施

中国已经进入了经济和工业发展的一个崭新阶段。国有企业重组的大规模改革是任何国家都未曾经历过的，更不用说实施这一改革了。

[2] to be under way 前进着，进行中/to align 调整，匹配，使密切合作/assets 资产，财产/to merge 使合并，使结合/infrastructure 基础，基础结构/to be capable of 有……的能力

国有企业改革的进程正在顺利进行中。现在改革正处于企业重组的第一阶段，即产业调整、资产调整、公司合并，创建行业基础，以便在组织结构上能够成为全球性的成功企业或行业。

[3] phase 方面，侧面，阶段/to go beyond（表示范围、限度）超出，超过

但是，国企经济改革的另一方面超越了结构改革、合并和调整，它涉及企业经营管理的方式方法。

[4] inventory 库存，存货/benchmarking 水准基点，基准/cultural 文化的

建立成本控制、财务、库存管理、供应链管理、现金管理、客户关系管理、标杆分析等体系，所有这些体系的创建并不是通过企业结构变化，而是通过企业经营管理和企业文化的转变而实现的。

[5] to underpin 支持，巩固，加强……的基础/underlying 根本的，基础的/institutional 公共机构的，制度的，其名词为 institution

所有这些体系的基础——促进创建这些体系的——是信息技术。信息技术是科学——是机构改革的基础科

学。它是你用以重组机构的科学,是你建立体系的基础和工具,从而提高机构的效率和全球竞争力。

　　[6] to evolve 发展,进展/transformation 转轨,转化,改革,变化

　　中国的信息技术产业需要与国有企业同步发展以便支持中国企业的转轨。

　　[7] critical 紧要的,关键性的,重要的

　　今天,中国的信息技术产业主要是以硬件为基础。但是,中国如果要进行国企转轨,就必须建立与硬件产业同步发展的软件和信息服务产业。这是极其关键的。

　　[8] 其原因是,在中国我们所需要的是软件的应用。中国已经有了计算机,但现在所需要的是在计算机上运行,使国有企业达到转轨目的的软件应用。

　　[9] managing platform 管理平台

　　我这里所谈论的并不是像空白表格程序、文字处理或游戏等简单软件,而是大型、复杂的软件,它们能使这些公司完成我前面所谈及的各种业务:交易处理,数据管理,开账收费,现金管理,管理平台,电子商务机会等。

　　[10] to adapt for 使适合,使适应/capital 资本

　　中国需要建立的产业是使软件应用适合国外需求,同时运用中国人自己的智力资本研制出新型的应用软件。

　　[11] to emerge 出现,形成/to apply to 把……应用于

　　然后还必须有信息服务产业。信息服务产业将有助于中国的机构把这些技术应用于国有企业。

　　[12] to be embedded in 嵌入,印入,埋置

　　最后,我认为中国有极大的机会在包括小型国企在内的中小型公司的改革中走在前列。因为在未来,能提高公司效率和全球竞争力的软件将应用于网络。

　　[13] telecom=telecommunication 电信/in effect 实际上/up front 预先,在前面

　　中小型公司不必自行研制这些应用软件,也不必为此付费。如果中国电信业能以我们所期望的方式发展,如果重点放在中文应用软件的开发上,那么实际上,中小型企业就能够租用应用软件,拨电话上网,就能获取收费、财务或电子商务的应用软件,也就是说使用这些软件而无需投入先期研制和后期维护费用。

　　[14] 因而,中国在下一阶段发展信息技术产业的重点不只是制造个人电脑和硬件,而是积累智力资本,确立信息技术体系的核心,即应用软件,而不是硬件。

　　[15] priority 优先权,优先,重点

　　所以,观察一下中国重中之重的国企重组是怎样与中国下一阶段信息技术产业清晰而又精心地联系在一起,这是十分有趣的。很显然,这与信息技术的新阶段,即电子商务,也是密切联系在一起的。

　　[16] concept 观念,概念,思想

　　而且,依托于电子商务理念的中文版应用软件的发展,为国有企业改革的成功提供了许多机遇和乐观的前景。

Exercises

Ⅰ. **Answer the following questions:**

1. What stage is China embarking on according to the text?

2. What is the first stage of enterprise restructuring?

3. What is another phase to the reform of state-owned enterprises?

4. What is the function of information technology?
   _____

5. Why is it very critical that China builds a software and services industry along with its hardware industry?
   _____

6. According to China's actual condition, what kind of software should be developed?
   _____

7. Why do we have to develop a services industry?
   _____

8. What is the focus in China on the next stage of development of the information technology industry?
   _____

II. Translate the following words and phrases:

A. From Chinese into English.
1. 国有企业重组 _____
2. 国企改革进程 _____
3. 调整产业 _____
4. 资产调整 _____
5. 成本控制 _____
6. 库存管理 _____
7. 企业文化 _____
8. 信息技术产业 _____
9. 空白表格程序 _____
10. 电子商务 _____
11. 数据管理 _____
12. 管理平台 _____
13. 智力资本 _____
14. 应用软件 _____

B. From English into Chinese.
1. to embark on _____
2. a globally successful enterprise _____
3. cash management _____
4. supply chain management _____
5. institutional restructuring _____
6. a hardware-based industry _____
7. small and medium-sized enterprises _____
8. China's telecom industry _____
9. to be under way _____
10. in effect _____
11. to build on the e-business concept _____
12. priority _____
13. opportunity _____
14. evolution _____

III. Translate the following passage into Chinese:

What we need is a nationwide network of "information superhighways", linking scientists, business people, educators and students by fiber-optic cable to process and deal with information that is available but unused.

Such a network is the single most cost-effective step America could take to become more competitive in the world economy. It is also the single most important step the United States could take to improve its proficiency in science, technology and research.

Of course, today, scientists, engineers and a few million computer hobbyists know the power of computer networking, and they take the convenience of networking for granted. But imagine that the network could transmit not just text but video and voice. Already there's electronic mail, electronic banking, electronic shopping, electronic tax returns and electronic newspapers, but these applications are limited severely by the speed and size of our networks.

[cost-effective 节省成本的/hobbyist 业余爱好者/networking 联网/tax-returns 纳税报表]

Well-known Sayings

△ *Brevity is the soul of Wit.*

△ *No sweet without sweat.*

△ *Ask not what your country can do for you but ask what you can do for your country.*

Unit 4 Computer Science and Technology

第4单元 计算机科学和技术

—— Computer Science is the study of principles, applications of technologies of computing and computers. Computer science is a discipline that involves the understanding and design of computers and computational processes. In its most general form, it is concerned with the understanding of information transfer and transformation. Particular interest is placed on making processes efficient and endowing them with some form of intelligence. The discipline ranges from theoretical studies of algorithms to practical problems of implementation in terms of computational hardware and software.

—— An explosion of intelligent, networked, single-purpose devices will replace the all-purpose, one-size-fits-all PC. ... Now Windows has spilled over the PC barrier into servers, network computers, handheld devices, Web TV sets, cash registers, automobile dashboards, handheld wireless data entry terminals and other platforms.

—— We see PCs connected to the Internet making the world a smaller place, and that's positive in so many ways: to build understanding between people, to share research in key science areas, including medicine, to allow world commerce to work very well.

Lesson 13

End of the PC Era

[1] You hear a lot these days about the coming demise of the personal computer. But the reality is more complicated and more interesting. Researchers, analysts and other pundits predict that an explosion of intelligent, networked, single-purpose devices will replace the all-purpose, one-size-fits-all PC. The PC is too complicated. It's too hard to use. It's too big. Users are fed up. Meanwhile, prices are falling so rapidly that it will soon be impossible to make money on them. Many predict a cellphone model for PCs: You get the box free but pay for the Internet connection.

[2] So, businesses(and consumers) will dump the PC and embrace easier-to-use network computers, intelligent wallets, networked refrigerators, "ubiquitous computing" offices, smart phones, wired homes and wearable computers, according to this line of thinking.

[3] There's truth in all this. Companies are feverishly pumping out cool new devices that existed previously only in science fiction. They'll be cheap, useful and ubiquitous. But like most paradigm shifts, this one brings erroneous predictions of the demise of what came before. Radio was supposed to kill books. TV was supposed to kill radio. And so on.

[4] Here's what's really happening. Despite the starry-eyed predictions of a world without PCs, the PC, for good or ill, will be around for the foreseeable future. However, it will cede its place at the center of the industry.

[5] Its replacement? Windows.

[6] When Windows first came out, Microsoft hoped the new DOS shell would one day ship on most PCs. That milestone was passed years ago. Now Windows has spilled over the PC barrier into servers, network computers, handheld devices, Web TV sets, cash registers, automobile dashboards, handheld wireless data entry terminals and other platforms.

[7] The next versions of Windows NT and Windows CE are designed to penetrate markets previously too high or too low for Windows. Windows 2000 will run on PCs, workstations and servers all the way up to massive data warehouses. Windows CE will run on everything else, from watches to cell phones to dedicated game machines.

[8] Bottom line: The PC is just one of many Windows platforms.

[9] It'll still be one of the most important platforms, of course, since business users aren't about to replace their PCs with single-purpose devices. You'll still need a powerful processor for speech recognition and number-crunching, fast graphics for that large, flat-screen monitor, and a standard development platform for a wide variety of applications. The PC will remain the central tool for advanced business users and thousands of vertical markets.

[10] Home users may gravitate toward intelligent, Web-aware Windows TV sets, dedicated game machines(running CE and other platforms), and smart, single-purpose devices. It's even feasible that Microsoft may come up with a "PC Lite" platform for consumers based on Windows CE.

[11] Given its already dominant position in the industry, it's hard to think of new places Windows might yet go, but it will. Indeed, while the PC shrinks in importance over the coming years, Windows will

become increasingly important and central to everything we do.

Language Points and Chinese Translations

第13课　个人计算机时代的结束

〔1〕demise 死亡/pundit（某一学科的）权威,权威性的评论者/to predict 预言,预示,预告/to be fed up（对……）感到厌倦/cell-phone 蜂窝式移动电话

最近你听到很多关于个人电脑时代即将结束的说法,但是实际情况更加复杂、有趣。研究人员、分析人员和其他专业权威预言说,智能、网络化的单一用途装置将替代多用途、多功能合一的个人电脑。个人电脑过于复杂,体积又大,难以使用,用户感到厌倦。同时,个人电脑价格下跌很快,很难从中获利。许多人预言,个人电脑将成为蜂窝式移动电话模式:你可以免费获得但是要支付因特网费用。

〔2〕to dump 抛弃/to embrace 接受,抓住,抱住,着手/ubiquitous 无处不在的,普遍存在的/wearable 可穿戴的,可佩戴的

所以,根据这一思路,企业（和消费者）将会抛弃个人电脑,转而接受容易使用的网络计算机、智能钱包、网络冰箱、无处不在的"智能"办公室、智能电话、连接互联网的家用计算机和佩带式计算机。

〔3〕feverishly 狂热,极度兴奋/to pump 用力抽出,打出（水等）,本文中指尽力开发出、推出某事物/cool（美语俚语）极妙的,适意的,好的,相当于 pleasant,fine/paradigm 范例,示例/shift 手段,办法,权宜之计/erroneous 错误的,不正确的

这一切都有成为现实的可能。许多公司都在高度热情地推出以前只存在于科幻小说中的极其美妙的新装置。它们便宜实用,到处都有。但是正像大多数情况一样,这使人们对以前发生的事物总会作出消亡的错误预言,如误认为收音机的出现会使书籍消失,电视的出现会淘汰掉收音机,等等。

〔4〕starry-eyed 对事物持过分乐观看法的,幻想的/foreseeable 可预见的/to cede 让与,放弃

实际发生的情况是这样的,尽管人们对个人电脑将被世界淘汰抱有过分乐观的预测,但是个人电脑,不管是好是坏,都将仍然在可预见到的将来广泛存在。不过它将退出在产业界的中心地位。

〔5〕其替代物是什么？视窗。

〔6〕DOS disk operation system 微软公司研制的磁盘操作系统/to spill 溢出/dashboard（汽车的各种控制器等的）仪表板

当视窗首次出现时,微软公司原指望该新式的磁盘操作系统将会有一天能运行于大多数个人电脑上。但这作为一个里程碑,已是多年前的事了。现在,视窗操作系统已经超越个人电脑的范围,使用于服务器、网络计算机、便携式设备、网络电视机、现金出纳机、汽车仪表板、手持无线数据输入终端和其他一些平台。

〔7〕to penetrate 穿过,渗透入,深入于/massive 大规模的,巨大的,大量的/to dedicate 奉献,把（时间、精力等）用于

现在已经设计出了下一代视窗 NT 和视窗 CE,以便进入以前视窗不能进入的高端或低端市场。视窗 2000 将能运行于个人电脑、工作站和服务器,直至大规模的数据存储库。视窗 CE 将能运用于其他一切东西,如从手表、蜂窝式移动电话到专门的游戏机等。

〔8〕bottom line 最后一行,本文中指最后的结果,结论

最终结果是:个人电脑仅作为许多视窗平台中的一种操作系统。

〔9〕to be about to do sth 即将……/recognition 识别,认出,认识/number-crunching 本文中指处理器进行运算时发出嘎吱嘎吱的声音/vertical 垂直的,竖式的

当然,由于企业用户还不会立即使用专一用途装置替代个人电脑,所以个人电脑目前仍是最重要的操作平台之一。你仍然需要功能强大的处理器进行语言识别和计算运算,需要快速的图像处理器用于大屏幕监视器,需要标准的开发平台用以支持各种应用软件。个人电脑将仍然是先进的企业用户和成千上万个直销市场的主要

工具。

[10] to gravitate toward 倾向于,受……的吸引/feasible 可行的/to come up with 提供,提出

家庭用户可能倾向于智能化的、网络能识别的视窗电视机,专门的游戏机(运行 CE 或其他操作平台)和专一用途的智能设备。微软公司甚至可以为视窗 CE 的消费用户提供一种"轻便式个人电脑"的操作平台。

[11] given 假设的/dominant 占优势的,支配的,统治的/to shrink 缩小,减少

假定视窗在产业界已经占有优势地位,很难想象会发展到何种新的阶段,但是它肯定会向前发展。实际上,随着未来几年个人电脑重要性的不断减弱,视窗将对我们所从事的一切发挥越来越重要的中心作用。

Exercises

I. Answer the following questions:

1. Why will intelligent, networked, single-purpose devices take the place of PCs?

2. What kind of computers will businesses and customers use if they dump PCs?

3. According to the text, do you think PCs will disappear in the near future?

4. What has Windows run on now according to the author?

5. What is the function of Windows 2000?

6. Why will the PC still be one of the most important platforms?

7. What will home users gravitate toward?

8. Do you think Windows will play an important role in our life and work?

II. Translate the following words and phrases:

A. From Chinese into English.
1. 个人电脑 _____
2. 智能、网络化的装置 _____
3. 多用途、多功能合一的计算机 _____
4. 蜂窝式移动电话 _____
5. 网络计算机 _____
6. 智能电话 _____
7. 视窗 _____
8. 服务器 _____
9. 大型数据存储库 _____
10. 操作平台 _____

B. From English into Chinese.
1. pundit _____
2. single-purpose devices _____
3. wearable computers _____
4. starry-eyed predictions _____
5. DOS shell _____
6. Web TV sets _____
7. handheld wireless data entry terminals _____
8. speech recognition _____
9. large, flat-screen monitor _____
10. Web-aware Windows TV sets _____
11. to come up with _____
12. dominant position _____

III. Translate the following passage into Chinese:

The wallet PC will be about the same size as a wallet. It will display messages and schedules and also let you read or send electronic mail and faxes, monitor weather and stock reports and play both simple and sophisticated games. At a meeting, you might take notes, check your appointments, browse information if you're bored, or choose from among thousands of easy-to-call up photos of your kids. You won't need a key or magnetic card key to get through doors, either. Your wallet PC will identify you to the computer controlling the lock. Instead of holding paper currency, the new wallet will store unforgettable digital financial information. Tomorrow, the wallet PC will make it easy for anyone to spend and accept digital funds. If your son needs money, you might digitally slip five bucks from your wallet PC to his.

Well-known Sayings

△ *There is no royal road to learning.*
△ *Smiling wins more friends than frowning.*
△ *Wisdom is knowing when to speak your mind and when to mind your speech.*

Lesson 14

Bill Gates' Speech to Tsinghua University

[1] It's great to be here and have a chance to share some of my excitement with you.

[2] I got involved with computers at 18, and the computer was a very limited teletype that had to be connected through a phone line up to a mainframe-like computer but my friends and I became fascinated with understanding what the computer can do, what was the future, and how would it be used. When we found out about chip technology, and the miracle of being able to improve the power of the chip exponentially, we realized that computers had a very bright future. We spent a lot of our time writing software because we loved writing software, because we thought that the software being written by a lot of big hardware companies wasn't as good as what we could do.

[3] I was 19 when I realized that if I wanted to be the first to do a software company for these new cheap computers, I needed to get my friends together and start right away, so Microsoft became the first company doing software for these new machines. Our vision was a computer on every desk and in every home. In the last 20 years, that vision is certainly becoming a reality. If we had to change it today, we would simply add that now we also want to have a computer in every pocket, every car—many other places that we had not thought about when we first started doing development. I believe software is the key element that really unlocks the power of all this technology, and the idea of making it easy to find information, easy to create information, easy to communicate with other people. Software is at the center of that, and so software will be the fastest growing industry in the world and one that will create lots and lots of great jobs. Certainly here in China the opportunity for hundreds of thousands of great jobs should be very exciting because there is a global shortage in terms of computer skills.

[4] The personal computer revolution got started in 1975, that's when I left college and started Microsoft. These last 22 years have really been amazing, every prediction we've made about improvements have all come true. As we look ahead, that pace of innovation is not slowing down, in fact if anything it's speeding up. Very high speed processors like 300 MHz Pentiums, or new 64-bit processors that we're already developing Windows NT for; incredible storage capacity, which will let us store, not just data, but also digital video as well; great screen technology to create a tablet-like device that would be good enough for reading and writing; advanced graphics and now the ability to connect computers together at very high speed.

[5] The Internet is the way that all these machines can be connected together. And those standards, and the improvement of those standards, is very very important. Some people like to think about how the computer industry compares to other industries. I've shown before what the cost of the typical car was in 1980 in US, and that rose up to be about from 8 000 to 19 000 today, and likewise cereal has increased in price. How does that compare to PCs? If the same model was followed for PCs, you can buy a car for 27 cents and cereal for less than one cent, so there's no other area of the economy that has this rapid improvement, and people just aren't used to it. You almost have to tell people, "What would you do if Internet computing power was free," because that's what we'll be able to deliver with all these improvements.

[6] Microsoft's vision of computing is global computing. We see PCs connected to the Internet making the world a smaller place, and that's positive in so many ways: to build understanding between people, to share research in key science areas, including medicine, to allow world commerce to work very well. And the Internet is driving this already. Microsoft has set up operations around the world, and we are very pleased with the success we're having here in China. We are doing significant software development on products here, and that will continue to increase, and key for us is having very very high quality software people, and we've been lucky to hire a great number of people from this university. Really I'd say that the core of the teams we've put together have come from here, and I've listed some of those employees here, and we certainly hope that in the future this list will increase dramatically, and the quality of our work continues to rise.

[7] Microsoft believes in doing a lot of research because the software of today is not adequate for tomorrow. It's come a long way, such as the graphics interface, the application, and the way we deal with linguistics; it's much better than it was a year ago. Building the Internet into the software has come a long way. Some of the more ambitious things, like teaching the computer to speak or listen or see, still require a lot of software work that's not yet done, and so we've been investing in research, and building the number of research locations which will be increasing in the years ahead. One advance is teaching the computer to pick up sentences and understand them, and not just think of them as a series of characters.

[8] Here we have an example where the word processor is looking at an English sentence, and suggesting that the grammar is not correct, and showing exactly how the grammar might be fixed. That kind of thing has proven to be extremely popular, and it's just a step on the road to getting computers to actually understand what's going on, in the same way that humans do. That pursuit of artificial intelligence is the most exciting thing in computer science. Although the progress in that has been fairly slow, I'm confident that that will be accelerating quite a bit.

[9] Another interesting area that I think people aren't expecting is computer vision. The actual digital cameras that allow you to have an image and scan that image are going down in cost, and software to recognize users, see what they're looking at, what kind of gestures they're making; that kind of software is coming along quite well. In fact I brought a short little film of a demonstration that someone from our vision group did, so let's take a quick look at some of the progress that's been made.

[Demo video]

[10] That just gives you a glimpse of one area that is expected to make the personal computer really disappear into the environment and connect up in a rich way. Tomorrow's PC will be quite different from what we have today, tomorrow's Internet will be much better than what we have today, but it will all evolve out of this technology that we have right now.

[11] It's clear that the reason we refer to this as the information age is that the capabilities available in the information age will let people reach out and get what they need, whether it's business learning, or for entertainment. Microsoft feels in a very lucky position to be helping to drive these things, and key for us is working with other software companies so that they can build other applications on top of the system. Every industry needs a lot of software work there, and so I talk about the software industry creating so many great jobs in the years ahead. I think you picked a great field to be in, and we look forward to working with you.

Thank you.

Language Points and Chinese Translations

第14课　比尔·盖茨在清华大学的演讲

　　[1] to share sth. with sb. 与某人分享……　本句中 it 是形式主语,后面的动词不定式短语 to be here and…是真正的主语

　　(我)非常高兴有机会来到这里,与你们一起分享我的激动与快乐。

　　[2] to get involved with 原意指卷入,陷入,本文中指开始接触,专注于/mainframe (尤指除外部辅助装置的)计算机/teletype 电传打字机,电传打字电报机/to be(become) fascinated with 对……着迷了,被强烈地吸引住了/chip technology 芯片技术/miracle 奇迹,非凡的事例/exponentially *adv.* 指数的,幂的,本文中意指非常快,迅速地

　　我在18岁时开始接触电脑。那时,电脑是种非常有限的电传打字机,要通过电话线连接到主机上。但是我和我的朋友们都深深地着迷了,都想了解这电脑能做些什么,前景如何,以及怎样使用电脑,当我们发现了芯片技术,以及能奇迹般地以不可思议的速度迅速提高芯片的功能时,我们意识到电脑会有非常光明的前景。我们花费大量时间编写软件,因为我们很喜爱编写软件,也因为我们认为许多大型的硬件公司所编写的软件没有我们编写的那么好。

　　[3] vision 想象力,眼光,视觉,远见/the key element 主要因素,关键因素/shortage 短缺,缺少/in terms of 从……观点出发,以……的措词

　　我19岁时意识到:如果我想第一个为这些新型、便宜的计算机成立软件公司,就必须把我的朋友们组织在一起,并立刻动手。就这样,微软公司成为为这些新型的计算机制作软件的首家公司。我们当时所想象的是在每个办公桌上、每个家庭都有一台电脑。在过去的20年中,这种想象确实变成了事实。如果今天我们要对此作改动的话,我仅简单地补充一点,即现在我们也想让每个人的口袋里,每辆小汽车里——以及我们在当初开始时没有考虑到的许多其他地方也都有一台电脑。我认为软件是关键因素,它能真正地释放出电脑技术的所有潜能,同样重要的是便捷地查找信息、创造信息、与别人交际的创意。软件是电脑技术的核心,所以它将是世界上发展最迅速的产业,也将创造出大量的工作机会。由于目前全球计算机技能的缺乏,在中国能有成千上万个这样的工作机会,这无疑将是非常令人兴奋的。

　　[4] amazing 令人惊异的/prediction 预言,预示/processor 处理器/digital video 数字视频/screen technology 屏幕技术

　　个人电脑革命始于1975年,当时我刚离开大学,创建微软公司。过去的22年确实令人惊异,我们关于电脑技术不断改进的每个预言都变成了现实。展望未来,革新的步伐不是放慢了,而是加速了:像300兆赫兹的奔腾处理器,或者新64毕特处理器等高速处理器,我们已经正在为其研制视窗 NT(Windows NT)操作系统;不可思议的存储容量,我们不但可以存储数据,而且也可以存储数字视频;显示技术创造出了非常适合于读、写的平板式装置;还有先进的图像技术和电脑高速联网能力。

　　[5] to compare to… 与……比较,对照,相比/cereal 谷类,谷类植物/PCs 个人电脑,是 personal computers 的简略形式/to be used to 习惯于

　　因特网使所有的电脑都连接在一起,其标准及标准的完善提高极其重要。一些人喜欢考虑如何把计算机工业与其他工业相比较。以前我曾讲过在美国1980年购买一辆汽车的费用,而在今天价格已上涨到8 000至19 000美元左右。同样粮食价格也已上涨。那么怎样和个人电脑的价格比较呢?如果采取与个人电脑的价格相同的计算模式,则现在你用27美分就可以购买一辆汽车,用不到1美分就可以购买粮食。因此其他经济领域根本没有像计算机行业这么迅速的发展,只是人们还不习惯于这种发展。你几乎不得不告诉人们:"如果因特网的计算功能是免费的,你会怎么做?"因为随着电脑的不断进步,我们将能够提供这种免费服务。

　　[6] global 全球的/commerce 商业,贸易

　　微软公司的发展眼光是全球计算机化。我们看到联结于因特网的个人电脑正在使世界变小,这在许多方面都给我们带来了积极的影响:增进了人们之间的相互了解,分享包括医学在内的主要科学领域的科研成果,使世

界贸易顺利进行。因特网正在朝这些方面发展。微软公司已在全世界建立运营机构,我们也对在中国所取得的成功感到高兴。我们在中国的软件产品发展迅速,并将继续发展。对于我们来说关键是要有高素质的软件设计人员,我们感到幸运的是已在这所大学里聘请了很多人才。确实,我想说组成我们这支队伍的核心来自于这里,我已经列出了其中一些雇员的名单,我们也当然希望这个名单将来会不断增加,我们的产品质量将不断提高。

[7] adequate 足够的/to come a long way 取得进展,明显好转/graphics interface 图形界面/linguistics 语言学/to pick up 识别,认识

微软公司相信要做很多研究工作,因为今天的软件不足以适应明天的需求。我们已经取得了一些进展,如图形界面、应用程序、处理语言的方法等。软件的进展比一年前大得多。开发互联网软件也已取得了进展。还有一些雄心勃勃的计划需要进行大量的软件研究和开发,像教电脑能说,能听或能看。所以我们一直在投资于软件研究,并建立了一些研究基地,其数量在未来几年里也将不断增加。有一个进展是教电脑能识别和理解句子,而不仅仅把它们当作一连串的符号。

[8] word processor 文字处理器/pursuit 追求,追踪,事务

这里有个例子:文字处理器阅读了一个英语句子,提示了语法错误,并准确地显示出应如何修改。这一事例已证实非常受人们欢迎。使计算机像人一样真正理解所正在进行的事情,还只是发展道路上所迈出的一步。对人工智能的探索研究是计算机科学中最令人兴奋的事。虽然在这方面的进展还很慢,但我深信它将会快速地发展起来。

[9] digital 数字的,计数的/to scan 扫描,扫掠,浏览/to recognize 识别,辨别,认识,认出

我认为人们未预料到的另一个有趣领域是计算机视觉。现在既能照相又能扫描图像的数码照相机价格正在下降,软件能辨认用户,看到用户正在看的事物和用户所作的各种姿势,这种软件发展势头很好。事实上,我带来了一个电影短片,这是我们视觉小组成员所做的一个演示,现在让我们很快地看一下我们已经取得的一些进步吧。

[演示录像]

[10] a glimpse of 看见,瞥见/to be different from 与……不同/to evolve 发展,进化,演化

刚才你们只是粗浅地了解了这一领域,它将使个人电脑实际上融入环境并以丰富多样的方式互相联结起来。明天的个人电脑将与今天的截然不同,明天的因特网将比今天的好得多,但它们都将从我们现有的技术中发展起来。

[11] to refer to… as 把……叫做,称为

很清楚,我们把今天称作信息时代,其理由是:在信息时代,人们有能力获得所需要的任何信息,不管是商务、学习还是娱乐活动。微软公司感到很幸运能处于这样的地位帮助促进这些事物的发展。对于我们来说,关键是与其他软件公司共同努力以便他们能在该系统之上开发其他一些应用。每个行业都需要大量的软件工作,因此我谈到了在今后的几年中软件工业将创造许多工作机会。我认为你们已选择了一个伟大的领域,我们期待着与你们一起工作。

谢谢大家。

Exercises

I. **Answer the following questions:**

1. According to the text, what was the computer at the time when Bill Gates was a young man?

2. What was he eager to know about the computer?

3. Why did he think that computers had a very bright future?
   _____

4. When did he set up Microsoft and what was his vision?
   _____

5. Why is software the key element?
   _____

6. What progress has been made in the computer technology?
   _____

7. What is Microsoft's vision of computing?
   _____

8. What benefits has the Internet brought to people?
   _____

9. What kind of research work has Microsoft done and what are Microsoft's ambitious programs?
   _____

10. According to the text, say something about the word processor and computer vision.
    _____

11. Why do we refer to our age today as the information age?
    _____

II. Translate the following words and phrases:

A. From Chinese into English.
1. 芯片技术 _____
2. 软件 _____
3. 硬件 _____
4. 高速处理器 _____
5. 数字视频 _____
6. 屏幕技术 _____
7. 数据 _____
8. 全球计算机化 _____
9. 计算机视觉 _____
10. 图形界面 _____

B. From English into Chinese.
1. to be fascinated with _____
2. teletype _____
3. to communicate with other people _____
4. at the centre of _____
5. in terms of _____
6. to speed up _____
7. 64-bit processor _____
8. incredible storage capacity _____
9. to share research in key science areas _____
10. to come a long way _____
11. to deal with _____
12. a series of _____
13. to scan an image _____

14. demonstration _____

Ⅲ. Translate the following passage into Chinese:

I view WebTV as in its early stages. As the hardware improves, as the speed of connections improves, the concept of something simpler than the PC, but still interactive, is shared by Sony and Microsoft. We're brainstorming together on that.

I think parallel to the personal computer revolution there's an explosion of digital cellular. Today's digital cellular technology can only handle the transmission of voice and simple text data. From around 2001 the next-generation mobile communications service, called IMT-2000, will become available. This will be able to handle transmission of moving pictures.

Today's technology is vertical. I think we need collaboration between Microsoft and Sony, so as to reform the passive viewing habits by computer-based technology. Of course, before a total solution is possible, we need a lot of companies' collaboration, not only Sony and Microsoft, but also operators of cable and satellite TV.

[brainstorm v. 集中每人的智慧解决(难题)/digital cellular 本句中指"数字式蜂窝电话"将爆炸式发展/cable and satellite TV 有线电视和卫星电视]

Well-known Sayings

△ *Diligence is the mother of good luck.*

△ *Progress is a nice word. But change is its motivator.*

△ *The progress of studies comes from hard work and is retarded by frivolities.*

Lesson 15

The Next Revolution in Computers

[1] When I wrote *Automation* over 40 years ago, I wanted to tell people that something so significant was brewing that it would change everything, and that technologies such as computers and automation would transform the way we do business. As we look back, that impact is easy to recognize, but at the time, it was very difficult.

The Road to Automation

[2] It is hard for those who weren't around then to realize, but people had no idea that computers were going to change the world. Instead, they argued arcane things like, "What happens when a truck of scrap metal goes down the street and erases the magnetic records?" There was a lot of missionary work needed in those early years. But, gradually, a few things began to happen, and suddenly there was a rush of developments such as the use of computers by commercial banks, airlines, transportation, and the telephone companies.

[3] Written in the early 1950s, *Automation* focused on the technology that made things happen. But there was more to it than just technology. During the first big rush, people thought they would buy computers and that would solve everything. But people soon discovered they had to figure out how to accomplish their goals in new ways.

[4] We have learned much in the last 40 years that we can apply to thinking about the twenty-first century. Here are a few of my thoughts:

• It is hard to change old patterns of perception. People see things from a particular frame of reference that they are used to. But much of what they must deal with, especially in information technology, represents radical change, and it is hard for people to step outside and look at it afresh.

• Just because something is technologically possible doesn't mean it will necessarily happen. Many forecasts assume that if something can happen technologically, it will happen when it can be done economically. It won't.

• Preconditions are often needed. For example, there is considerable resistance on the part of some doctors to use computers. Once we have a generation of physicians coming out of medical school who have been brought up using computers, however, there will be a completely different approach to medical services.

• Things usually take much longer to happen than you expect them to. Once you have worked out what is possible and figured out what you can do, you think that everyone else will start to do it. However, it often takes much longer for the obvious to happen.

• You cannot anticipate what people will do with a new technology. Until you provide it at the market price, the only certainty is that people will not use a new technology the way you would expect. Therefore, demonstrations, pilot projects, and competition are important.

Always Expecting Change

[5] As the developments of the last 40 years continue to unfold, some patterns are emerging. In my early work, I theorised that computers would, first, change how we do our jobs. Indeed, this pretty much

dominated computer and automation applications in the 1950s and 1960s. Second, I believed computers would change the kind of work we do—as began to happen during the 1970s and 1980s. Third, I believed the technologies would change the world in which we work. This is the beginning of the next great development in computers and automation, which has already begun in the 1990s.

[6] Technology is becoming embedded in all sorts of products and services. It has become a part of our lives. And for the first time, we are seriously altering the way we deliver public services by the use of technology. Public services are typically the most important things we have—education, safety, medical treatment and services, and transportation.

[7] The delivery of public services has tended to be an area where we decorate an obsolete process with technology. We must determine how we can deliver these services in a different way.

Automating Health Care

[8] Health care is an extraordinarily obsolete system. A professor of emergency medicine at a major university sent me a really heartrending letter. He said that physicians have to start from the very beginning with every patient. There is no history, no time to prepare—they know nothing about the patient.

[9] We have inferior medical service because the computer technology that could change it is not being used. The difficulties of just accessing patient records—apart from analysing them properly—are unnecessary and hinder us from providing quality service.

[10] We have the opportunity to do some wholesale rethinking of how we provide health care and turn it into not only medical service, but preventive maintenance that involves the patient in decision making. We can begin through pilot and demonstration projects in hospitals, by doctors, and especially by private sector participation. Physicians can show patients the consequences of their actions and what the alternatives are. Technologies such as multimedia and interactive computers can allow patients, in the privacy of their own homes, to ask questions about these alternatives.

[11] Other countries are moving much more aggressively than the United States in medical information. The computerization and redesign of Sweden's health delivery system has reduced that nation's spending on health care from 12% of GNP to a little over 7%. More than one-third of the population of the Netherlands have their medical records computerised. While some hospitals in the United States keep computerised patient records, these records only cover the time the patient is in the hospital and do not include their entire medical history.

Anticipating the "Infostructure"

[12] Information technologies offer many opportunities for improving the delivery of public services. Infostructure obliterates geographical limitations: we can now communicate with an individual anywhere on the globe. By linking doctors' offices to the information in medical and patient databases, people would be referred to the right specialists, who could see and treat patients much faster. No more sitting for hours in waiting room after waiting room. Immediate access, leading to individualized delivery of service, is the key benefit of the computer revolution.

[13] Transportation is another public service in which information technologies offer vast improvements. While start-up arrangements, pricing schemes, and overall timetables have yet to be resolved, intelligent vehicle/highway systems will allow drivers to pass through a toll gate without even stopping: their accounts are debited automatically.

[14] This transportation infostructure will also tell you where the nearest hotel is and if there is a room available. If your car breaks down, it will direct you to the nearest repair shop that stocks the parts

you need. And if you have an accident or medical emergency, it can tell you where the nearest hospital is, how to get there, and other necessary information. Europe and Japan are already developing such systems. In Japan alone, there are over 250 000 vehicles equipped with position-location devices and electronic maps.

[15] The problems we now face are fundamentally conceptual, rather than technical. Questions about pricing structures and related regulations must still be answered. It is these conceptual problems that prevent society from accruing any benefits from the infostructure that the technologies are making possible, such as improved cost performance, more easily shared resources, and more highly utilised ones.

[16] Society must make public services and the physical infrastructure more effective through an increased interaction between the public and private sectors, so that we can create a demand for the kinds of software and hardware for each specific area—intelligent highways, health care, etc.—that will build the infostructure.

[17] Once this is done, major growth industries—such as real-time data collection, database storage of historical and current information, communications networking, and service-providing software for the users and support staff of the infostructure—will blossom in the years ahead.

Language Points and Chinese Translations

第15课　计算机的下一次革命

[1] automation 自动化/brewing 到来,来临/transform 改变

四十多年前,当我写《自动化》一书时,我是想告诉人们:某种意义深远的事物将要来临,它将改变一切;像计算机和自动化等的技术将会改变我们做生意的方式,现今虽然很容易意识到这种影响,但当我们回首过去,这在当时是难以想到的。

[2] arcane 神秘的/magnetic 磁的/scrap 废料

通向自动化的道路

计算机将改变整个世界,这对当时那些不从事该专业的人来说是很难意识到的,而普通人对此更是一无所知。相反,他们只是在争论一些神秘的事,如"当一卡车金属废料驶过街区,消掉了磁带录音会怎么样?"在早期年代,要进行许多宣传工作。但是,慢慢地开始发生一些新事物,并且突然出现了许多发明成果,如在商业银行、航空公司、交通界和电话公司开始使用计算机。

[3] focus on 集中,着重/accomplish 完成,成功地做完/figure out 算出,想出,理解

《自动化》一书写于50年代早期,它重点论述了使自动化实现的技术,但除了技术外,还有其他更多的因素。在第一次大浪潮中,人们以为买了计算机就可解决一切问题,但很快他们就发现,还必须解决如何用新方法来完成目标的问题。

[4] perception 感觉,领悟力,理解力/radical 根本的,基本的/afresh 重新,再/resistance 抵抗(力),反对,阻止/anticipate 预测,预期/demonstration 演示

在过去40年中,我们已学到许多东西,在考虑21世纪的时候可以加以应用。下面是我的几点思考:

• 旧的理解方式很难改变。人们往往以他们习惯的特有的思维框架来看问题,但是他们必须解决的问题中,尤其是在信息技术方面,都展现出根本的变革,而人们又很难跳出框架去重新看待一切。

• 那些技术上可行的东西并不意味着必定会发生。许多预言都假定,如果某种东西在技术上可行,只要在经济上也合算的话,它就会发生。事实并非如此。

• 先决条件常常是必需的。例如,有些医生对使用计算机有很大的抵触情绪,但一旦我们有一代医学院毕业的医生,他们由计算机陪着成长,那么在医疗服务中就会采用一种完全不同的方法与手段。

• 事情的发生往往比你所预料的时间更长。一旦你解决了什么是可能的,并能想象出你能够做些什么,你就会认为其他人也将开始这样做。然而,明显要发生的事常常需更多的时间才会发生。

• 你不能预期到人们将利用新技术做些什么事。唯一确认无疑的是人们将不会像你期望的那样来使用新技术,直到你能按市场价格提供这一新技术。所以,演示、小规模的试验性项目和竞争都是十分重要的。

永远期待着变化

[5] to unfold 展开,呈现/to emerge 出现,显出,暴露/to dominate 支配,控制

由于最近40年的发展还在继续,一些模式也正在出现。在我的早期著作中,我曾作出这样的推论:第一,计算机将会改变我们的工作方式。确实,在50年代和60年代,这是计算机和自动化的主要应用方式。第二,我认为计算机将会改变我们所做的工作种类——这在70年代和80年代期间已经开始发生。第三,我确信技术将会改变我们所工作的世界,这是下一次计算机和自动化巨大发展的开始,这种发展在90年代就已经开始了。

[6] alter 变更,改变/typically 代表性地,典型地

技术正在被利用于各种产品和服务之中。它已经成为我们生活中的一部分。我们第一次通过应用技术来认真地改变我们提供公共服务的方法。公共服务在我们所从事的各种事务中具有最重要的代表性——教育、安全、医疗服务和运输。

[7] decorate 装饰/obsolete 过时的,作废的

公共服务的提供方式已日趋成为我们利用技术来修改陈旧作业方法的领域。我们必须明确如何用不同的方式来提供这些服务。

保健自动化

[8] extraordinary 特别的,非常的,非凡的/emergency 紧急事件,紧急情况/heartrending 使人悲痛的,令人伤心的

保健系统现在已非常落后。一所重点大学的急救医学教授曾给我来过一封令人难过的信。他说,医生们对每一个病人都不得不从头开始——没有病历,没有准备的时间——他们对病人毫无了解。

[9] access 接近,取得/apart from 除……之外/hinder 阻碍,妨碍

获取病人病历、准确地分析病历都非常困难,而这本应可以克服,它阻碍了医疗服务水平的提高。

[10] wholesale adj. adv. 大规模的(地),批发的(地)/preventive 阻止性的,预防的/pilot 以小规模作试验的,实验的/alternative 可选择的,选择性的/interactive 相互作用的,相互影响的/privacy 独处而不受干扰

我们有机会来全面地重新思考一番,我们究竟如何提供保健服务,不仅把它应用于医疗服务,而且贯彻到需要病人作出决定的预防性保健工作中去。刚开始时,我们可以在医院里让医生,特别是私人医生参与,进行一些小规模试验和演示项目。医生可以向病人演示他们行为的后果以及改正方式。像多媒体、交互式计算机技术可以允许病人在其家中不受干扰的情况下,就改正方式进行咨询。

[11] aggressively 有闯劲的,不怕阻力的/computerization 计算机化/GNP 国民生产总值,是 gross national product 的缩写形式

在医疗信息方面,其他国家要比美国行动得更积极。瑞典对保健系统的计算机化和重新设计已使政府在医疗上的花费从占国民生产总值的12%降到7%略多。荷兰1/3以上人口的病历已计算机化。然而在美国的一些医院里虽然也实行将病人的病历存入计算机,但仅仅是病人在住院期间的情况记录,并不包括他们的全部病史。

憧憬"信息基础设施"

[12] infostructure＝information-based infrastructure 信息基础设施/to obliterate 擦掉,除去/individualized 有个性化的,有特性的

信息技术为改善公用事业服务提供了许多机会。信息基础设施可消除地理局限性:我们现在可以与世界上任何地方的某个人进行交流,通过把医生办公室和医疗及病人数据库的信息连接起来,人们就可找到适合自己的专家进行咨询,并且能更快地得到诊治,而不必再在一个又一个候诊室里等上数小时。快捷地获取信息,从而得到具有针对性的特色服务是计算机革命的主要优点。

[13] vast 巨大的/pricing scheme 定价系统/intelligent 有智力的,聪明的/to debit 将(钱)记入(某人账户的)借方

交通是信息技术催生进步的另一项公共服务。虽然始发安排、定价系统和总的时刻表都尚待解决,但智能型

车辆/智能型公路系统将允许驾驶员顺利通过收费站而无须停车,其费用将自动记入他们的账户内。

[14] break down (汽车)出毛病,坏掉了/position-location device 定位装置

这种交通信息基础设施还会告知你最近的旅馆在哪里,是否还有空房间。如果你的汽车出了故障,它将指引你到最近的修车行,那儿备有你所需的零部件。又如你出了交通意外或要急诊,它会告诉你最近医院的方位,如何到达那里及其他必要的信息。欧洲和日本已经在着手开发这种系统。仅在日本,就有 25 万多辆汽车配置了定位装置和电子地图。

[15] conceptual 观念上的/to accrue 自然增长或产生/utilised 有用的,可利用的

现在,我们面临的问题基本上是观念上的,而非技术上的。有关价格结构及相关的规章制度等方面的问题仍待解决。正是这些观念上的问题,阻碍了社会从技术上可行的信息基础设施上获利,例如提高成本效能,更容易共享的资源以及更能充分利用的资源。

[16] physical 物质的,有形的,确确实实的

社会必须通过增强公共与私人部门之间的相互影响来促进公用服务事业与物质的信息基础设施效率的提高,这样,我们就能在每个具体领域产生各种软件与硬件的需求——智能公路、保健等——这些都将构建信息基础设施。

[17] real-time data collection 快速数据收集/blossom 开花,繁盛,兴旺,发展

一旦做到这点,一些高速发展的重要产业——如快速数据收集、历史及当代信息的数据库储存、通讯网络系统、用户和信息基础设施维护人员所使用的服务软件等——都会在未来几年里得到快速的发展。

Exercises

I. Answer the following questions:

1. What did the author want to tell people when he wrote the book *Automation* in the early 1950s?

2. What did the book *Automation* focus on?

3. Why does the author say that it is hard to change old patterns of perception?

4. The author thinks that we have learned a lot in the past 40 years which we can apply to thinking about the 21st century. What are his thoughts?

5. What did the author theorize about in his early work?

6. Are the technologies of computers and automation becoming embedded in all sorts of products and services?

7. According to the text, what technologies can allow patients, in the privacy of their own homes, to ask questions about the alternatives?

8. Say something about the computerization of health care system in Sweden and Netherlands.

9. What does GNP stand for?

10. What offers many opportunities for improving the delivery of public services?

11. Why does infostructure obliterate geographical limitations?

12. What are the advantages of the transportation infostructure?

13. Are the problems we are now facing fundamentally conceptual or technical? Why?

14. What will blossom in the near future?

II. Translate the following words and phrases:

A. From Chinese into English.
1. 智能公路
2. 信息基础设施
3. 定位装置
4. 电子地图
5. 多媒体技术
6. 交互式计算机技术
7. 保健自动化
8. 定价系统
9. 数据库储存
10. 通讯网络联系
11. 服务供应软件
12. 快速数据收集

B. From English into Chinese.
1. to transform the way we do business
2. to look back
3. a rush of new developments
4. to figure out
5. to accomplish goals in new ways
6. patterns of perception
7. to represent radical changes
8. preconditions
9. a completely different approach to medical services
10. demonstrations and pilot projects
11. to dominate computer and automation applications
12. to provide quality service
13. easily shared resources and highly utilised ones
14. an increased interaction

III. Translate the following passage into Chinese:

In 1900, they never imagined the computer and its miniaturization. Thanks to more and more capacity for memory processing through smaller and smaller silicon chips, the mainframe computer which needed a large room became a desktop computer and workstation, which eventually even had greater capacity.

The personal computer, revolutionized by the introduction of IBM's Personal Computer(PC) in 1981, spread to 245 million PC users by century's end. The PC was not only word processor, business organizer, research and educational tool, home study centre and games player, but allowed global communication through the Internet.

The Internet was prefigured by the communications system ARPANET, initially a US Defense Department network expanded by universities. The Internet is a linked computer communications network used for information, e-mail, business and education. US-based International Data Communications predicts the Internet economy will reach $US 1 trillion by 2002.

Well-known Sayings

△ *Wisdom is to the mind what health is to the body.*

△ *Keep on trying. No matter how hard it seems, it will get easier.*

△ *Just as there is no short cut in other subjects, so there is none in English.*

Lesson 16

Virtual Reality Technology

[1] It's Saturday afternoon and you would love to play a few rounds of golf, but fret that you might not get enough tee time at the closest public links. Instead, you decide to go down to the athletic club a few blocks away. There, you enter a private room, press a button, and look at the large screen on the wall in front of you. The screen flickers, blinks, and presto! —you are suddenly on one of the world's great golf courses, perhaps St. Andrews in Scotland, or Pebble Beach in Monterey, California, U. S. A, or Quinta do Lago in Portugal.

[2] You tee off on the plastic turf whacking your ball against the screen. A blurred facsimile of the ball slices or hooks down the fairway. Computers, infrared beams, and photo-optical detectors track the ball's spin, velocity, and direction. You are totally immersed in the three-dimensional computer generated world.

[3] "Virtual reality is created by using display and control technology to surround its users with an artificial environment that mimics real life," explains Dr. Hasan Alkhatib, professor of computer engineering at Santa Clara University in California, U. S. A. "Through the use of visual and sound effects, things that don't exist can be made to appear to exist. Virtual reality allows users to manipulate objects on the screen so they can become full participants in the three-dimensional setting that envelops them."

[4] Dr. Mark Fishman, professor of computer science at Eckerd College in St. Petersburg, Florida, U. S. A, and a leading authority on artificial intelligence and artificial reality, says virtual reality's effect can be powerful. "Put people in a virtual room and have them walk on a tread mill. They will not want to walk into the abyss they see in front of them, even though they know perfectly well their body is in the real world. They fall right into the illusion, and the illusion is getting better and better."

[5] While this technology's most advanced applications at the moment are in entertainment such as virtual reality golf and the virtual reality arcade game rooms sprouting up all over the world, researchers say its potential is enormous. They see it impacting everything, from education to medicine and science to business and government. "The common perception of virtual reality is that it's some kind of sophisticated computer game in an arcade," explains Dr. Jack Goldfeather, professor of mathematics and computer science at Carleton College in Minnesota, U. S. A, and a designer of hardware and software for three dimensional computer animation. "I don't really know if the public realizes how many uses it's being applied to."

[6] Professor Fishman says that virtual reality has the potential to accelerate scientific advancement. "It could be an intellectual tool that can study some of the diseases and problems threatening mankind's well being, such as AIDS and global warming."

[7] Already, virtual reality systems have many practical applications. Most notably, the technology is being used to make simulations of cars or buildings during the design phase, to provide instruction in technical subjects like engineering, and to introduce new surgical techniques. "Virtual reality offers another window, but one that a scientist can climb through to interact directly with scientific abstractions," says Howard Rheingold, author of *Virtual Reality*. "Virtual reality has the potential to

become a microscope of the mind."

[8] The idea of using computers to render artificial but useful environments began as early as the 1960s, but the computer power needed to generate 3-D graphics was so costly that only government agencies such as the U. S. National Aeronautics and Space Administration (NASA) or the Defense Department, along with a few university labs, could afford it. The field began to grow in the mid 1980s when one-time computer hacker Jaron Lanier coined the term "virtual reality" and founded VPI Research Inc. in Redwood City, California, the first high-tech company dedicated to the virtual reality field.

[9] Since then companies worldwide have come to recognize the technology's commercial potential and have entered the market. In the U. S. for example, the aerospace giant Boeing has organized a company-wide steering committee to explore virtual reality's potential applications, while Caterpillar, based in Peoria, Illinois, has started testing virtual reality models of its earth movers to improve performance and driver visibility.

[10] Current virtual reality research shows numerous potential applications of the interactive technology.

[11] **EDUCATION**: Educators say virtual reality can offer alternatives to the way students learn. Some educators, in fact, are already using virtual reality systems in the classroom. At Rensselaer Polytechnic Institute, architectural students move around in an animated image of the Parthenon, examining that noble structure's roof and columns. At the University of Washington's Interface Technology Laboratory, scientist William Brichen is developing a virtual universe in which objects are controlled by algebra and not physical laws. Working in an artificial universe, students will be able to move city blocks around in various configurations provided they don't violate algebraic laws.

[12] **DESIGN**: Researchers from several universities and corporations around the world are working hard to develop a wide range of virtual reality applications in this area, with designs on everything from automobiles to household appliances. In Detroit, Michigan, powerful computers and graphics stations are letting designers create new car models in 3-D. Boeing uses a virtual reality tunnel to test airplane models. The company says the computer-created model should significantly reduce the time and money spent crafting new models.

[13] Architects are expected to be the biggest users of virtual reality design applications. One experimental system now allows an architect to move through the design of a virtual hospital in a virtual wheelchair to test access to doors, hallways, light switches, and other design elements. The California-based software company Autodesk has developed a computer program that allows architects to take clients on a "walk" through a house or building before construction starts.

[14] "Some of the computer models are so good that you actually feel you're inside the building, not just looking at a monitor," says William Jenks.

[15] **INVESTING**: Computer 3-D graphics are being used to give investors more data than they can possibly absorb from a spreadsheet. Money managers for TIAACREF, the $106 billion college and university teachers pension fund, use a system called Capri to track stocks and bonds. Capri can be designed for any portfolio.

[16] "Some of my colleagues have been working for years on creating a 3-D image of the stock market," Professor Fishman reveals. "It will happen. That's why virtual reality has enormous potential for the financial market."

[17] **MEDICINE**: Virtual reality is giving scientists the ability to work surrounded by images of molecules and other objects that once required an electronic microscope study. Researchers predict that

surgeons in training will be able to practice on electronic cadavers while experienced surgeons will benefit from new techniques developed from virtual reality applications. "The medical impact is limitless," says Professor Goldfeather. "Can you imagine traveling through the blood vessels to study whatever organ you wish? The organs will be modeled inside a computer, but it will seem as if you are actually inside the body."

[18] The technology is hindered right now by the fact that today's computers are simply not fast enough, a quite remarkable revelation given that computer speed is doubling every 18 months to two years. Computer scientists say a massive amount of processing is required to create the various components of an image. Researchers expect a major breakthrough within the next five to ten years. "Computing speed will increase to such levels that we will be able to create more sophisticated images," predicts Professor Fishman. And as the computing power increases, the steep prices of virtual reality systems are expected to drop.

Language Points and Chinese Translations

第 16 课　虚拟现实技术

[1] round（表示比赛等的）回合，场，轮/to fret 着急，烦恼，担忧/tee 球座/links 高尔夫球场/block 街区/flicker 闪烁，摇晃/blinks 闪烁，若隐若现/presto 急速地，相当于 quickly

周六下午，你很想打几场高尔夫，但是又担忧到最近的公共高尔夫球场去没有足够的打球时间，所以你转而决定去几个街区外的体育俱乐部。在那里，你进入一个私人用房间，按一下电钮，然后看着你前面墙上的大屏幕。屏幕急速地闪烁着，突然间，你已置身于一个世界级的大型高尔夫球场，这也许是苏格兰的 St. Andrews 球场，或者是美国加利福尼亚州蒙特里的 Pebble 海滨球场，或者是葡萄牙的 Quinta do Lago 球场。

[2] to tee off 开球/turf 草地/to whack 使劲打/to blur 弄模糊/facsimile 摹写，复制/fairway（高尔夫球场上的）平坦球道/infrared 红外线的/velocity 速度，速率/to be immersed in 投入，沉浸于/dimensional 维数的，线度的，指（长、宽、高）三度的

你在塑料草地上开球，对着屏幕使劲地击球。模拟的高尔夫球忽隐忽现，忽左忽右地飞落在平坦的球道上。计算机、红外线光柱和光学照相检测器追踪测量球的旋转、速度和方向。你完全沉浸在计算机所产生的三维世界里。

[3] virtual 虚的，虚拟的/artificial 人工的，人造的/to mimic 模仿，模拟，酷似/to manipulate 熟练地操作，使用，处理，操纵，摆布/participant 参与者，参加者/to envelop 围绕，包围

美国加利福尼亚州圣克莱拉大学计算机工程教授 Hasan Alkhatib 博士解释说，"虚拟现实是靠使用显示和控制技术创造出来的，使使用者置身于模仿现实生活的人造环境中。""通过运用视觉和音响效果，能够使实际不存在的物体看来好像确实存在着。虚拟现实可以让使用者操作屏幕上的物体，使他们在环绕他们的三维场景中成为完全的参与者。"

[4] tread mill（古时罚囚犯踩踏的）踏车，比喻指单调的工作/abyss 深渊/illusion 错觉，幻觉，幻想

Mark Fishman 博士是美国佛罗里达州圣彼得堡埃克德学院的计算机科学教授，也是人工智能和人造现实的一位权威。他说虚拟现实的效果很强烈，"让人们置身于一个虚拟的房间里，叫他们踩踏车。虽然他们十分清楚地知道自己的身体是在现实世界里，但是他们也不愿意走入他们面前所能看到的万丈深渊。他们沉浸在幻觉之中，而这种幻觉正变得越来越真实。"

[5] entertainment 娱乐，乐趣，欢乐/arcade 骑楼，连环拱廊（指有拱形顶盖的两侧有商店的街道）/to sprout 发芽，很快地生长，发展/perception 感觉，知觉，感性认识/to apply to sth. 适用，应用/animation 动画片，动画片制作

尽管在目前这种技术最先进的应用是在娱乐方面,如虚拟现实的高尔夫球,和在世界各地正在迅速发展的带有拱顶的虚拟现实的游戏机房,但是研究人员们说该技术的潜力是十分巨大的。他们已看到了它对一切事物的强烈影响,从教育到医药,还是从科学到商业和政府。Jack Goldfeather 博士是美国明尼苏达州卡尔顿学院的数学和计算机科学的教授,也是一位三维计算机动画片硬件和软件设计师。他解释说,"人们对虚拟现实的共同感觉是,认为它是拱顶游戏机房里某种复杂的计算机游戏。我并不十分了解公众是否知道它正在被广泛应用。"

[6] to accelerate 加速,加快,促进/well being 健康,幸福,福利

Fishman 教授说虚拟现实具有加快科技进步的潜力。"它可以成为一种智能工具用以研究某些威胁人类健康的疾病和问题,如艾滋病和全球气候变暖等。"

[7] notably 值得注意地,显著地,著名地/simulation 模仿,模拟/to interact 互相作用,互相影响/abstraction 抽象(化),抽象作用,抽象观念

虚拟现实体系现在已经有了许多实际的应用。最值得注意的是,该技术正在应用于设计阶段以对汽车和建筑物进行模拟,从而为工程等技术问题提供指导,或介绍新的外科技术。《虚拟现实》的著作者 Howard Rheingold 说,"虚拟现实提供了另一个窗口,科学家可以通过该窗口与抽象科学进行直接接触。虚拟现实具有潜力成为人类思维的显微镜。"

[8] to render 提供,实施/graphics 图解法,制图法/one-time 从前的,昔时的/hacker 计算机迷,编制程序专家/to coin 杜撰,创造(新词,新语等)

利用计算机提供有用的人工环境这一想法始于 60 年代,但是当时产生三维图像所需要的计算机价格太贵,只有像美国宇航局(NASA)和国防部这样的一些政府机构和少数几个大学的实验室才能承担。该领域在 80 年代中期开始发展,当时,原本就是计算机迷的 Jaron Lanier 创造了"虚拟现实"这个新词语,并在加利福尼亚州的雷德伍德城创建了 VPI 研究公司,该公司是从事虚拟现实领域研究的第一家高科技公司。

[9] aerospace 航空和宇宙航行空间/steering committee (团体组织中的)筹划指导委员会/earthmover 大型挖(或推)土机/visibility 可见度,能见度,视程

自从那时起,世界各地的公司开始意识到该技术的商业潜力,并纷纷投入该市场。例如,在美国,航空巨人波音公司就已经组织了全公司范围的筹划指导委员会探究虚拟现实技术的潜在应用。基地设在伊利诺伊州皮奥利亚的凯特匹拉公司已经开始测试推土机的虚拟现实模型,以便提高机器的效能和驾驶员的可视性。

[10] interactive technology 相互作用技术

目前的虚拟现实研究表明,相互作用技术具有许多潜在的应用。

[11] alternative 两者选一,抉择,可供选择的办法/polytechnic adj. 多种工艺的,多种科技的,n. 综合性工艺学校,工业大学/animated 栩栩如生的,活跃的/algebra 代数/configuration 构造,结构,外形/provided 如果,假若,相当于 if 或 on condition that/to violate 违反,违背

教育:教育工作者说虚拟现实可以向学生提供选择性的学习方式。事实上,一些教育工作者已经在教室里运用虚拟现实系统。在伦塞勒工艺学院,建筑专业的学生们围着栩栩如生的巴台农神庙图像绕行,细心研究这一壮观建筑的屋顶和柱子。在华盛顿大学的相互作用技术实验里,科学家 William Brichen 正在研制一个由代数而不是由物理定律所控制的虚拟宇宙。学生们在人造宇宙里工作时,如果不违反代数法则就能够按各种构造移动城市里的街区。

[12] household appliance 家庭用具,器具/tunnel 隧道,坑道/to craft 精巧地制作

设计:来自世界各地的一些大学和公司的研究人员们正在努力工作,以开发虚拟现实在该领域的广泛用途,其设计范围涉及汽车到家庭用具等一切东西。在密歇根州底特律市,功率强大的计算机和图形工作站正在帮设计人员们创造出三维的新汽车模型。波音公司利用一个虚拟现实隧道测试飞机模型。该公司说这种用计算机创造的模型将明显地节约制作新模型所花费的时间与金钱。

[13] 人们认为建筑师们将是虚拟现实设计的最大应用者。现在一种试验性系统可以让建筑师坐在虚拟的轮椅上在虚拟设计的医院里移动,检测门厅、过道、电灯开关以及其他一些的设计部位。总部设在加利福尼亚州的 Autodesk 软件公司已开发出了一种计算机程序,它可以让建筑师们带领着客户在开始建造前就在房屋或大楼里"行走"。

[14] William Jenks 说,"计算机所设计的一些模型很真实,使你觉得确实是在建筑物里,而不仅仅是看着监

测器。"

[15] spreadsheet（计算机用语）空白表格程序/TIAACREF（美国）教师保险与年金协会和大学退休股票基金会，是 Teachers Insurance and Annuity Association-College Retirement Equities Fund 的缩写形式/pension 养老金，退休金/stock 股票，公债券/bond 债券，公债/portfolio 有价证券

投资：正在使用计算机三维图像给投资者提供比从表格程序中可能获得的更多数据。拥有1 060亿美元的教师保险和年金协会以及大学退休股票基金会(TIAA-CREF)的财务管理人员使用了一种叫做"Capri"的系统来跟踪股票和债券行情。"Capri"能为任何有价证券进行设计筹划。

[16] stock market 证券市场，股票市场/to reveal 透露，泄露

Fishman 教授透露说，"几年来我的一些同事一直在为创建证券公司的三维形象而工作着。它将会建成。这就是虚拟现实在金融市场上具有巨大潜力的原因。"

[17] to predict 预言，预示/surgeon 外科医生/cadaver（用于解剖的）尸体

医药：虚拟现实使科学家们能在分子和其他物体形象的环境中工作，而在过去则要用电子显微镜来研究。研究人员们预言，接受训练的外科医生将能在电子尸体上进行实习，而富有经验的外科医生也将从应用虚拟现实所开发的新技术中受益。Goldfeather 教授说，"虚拟现实在医学上的影响是无限的。你能想象在血管里穿行以研究你想研究的任何器官吗？各种器官将在计算机里被做成模型，但看起来就好像你真的置身于人体内。"

[18] to hinder 阻止，阻碍/revelation 揭示，展示，展现/massive 大规模的，大量的，巨大的/breakthrough 突破/steep 难以接受的，不合理的，过分的

目前该项技术的发展受到的现实阻力，现在的计算机速度还不够快，一个值得注意的发现表明计算机速度每18个月至两年就要增加一倍。计算机科学家们说，形成一个图像的各组成部分需要计算机进行大量的处理。研究人员们期待在下一个 5～10 年的时间里将有重大的突破。Fishman 教授预言，"计算机速度将会增加到让我们将能创造出更加复杂精致的图像来"。随着计算机功能的不断提高，虚拟现实系统昂贵的价格有望下降。

Exercises

Ⅰ. **Answer the following questions**:

1. What is the virtual reality technology?

2. Why can virtual reality users become full participants in the three-dimensional setting?

3. What are the most advanced applications of the technology at the moment?

4. Do you think that the technology's potential is enormous? Why?

5. Why does Professor Fishman say that the technology has the potential to accelerate scientific advancement?

6. Can you tell some of the virtual reality system's practical applications?

7. Who coined the term "virtual reality"?

8. Why can the technology offer alternatives to the way students learn? Please give an example.

9. Please give an example to show the technology's application in the field of architectural design.

10. Please tell the technology's applications in medicine.

11. What is the hindrance of the technology's development?

12. According to researchers, when will there be a major breakthrough in the technology?

II. Translate the following words and phrases:

A. From Chinese into English.
1. 虚拟现实技术
2. 光学照相检测器
3. 计算机产生的三维世界
4. 控制技术
5. 视觉和音响效果
6. 电子显微镜
7. 人造现实
8. 三维图像
9. 相互作用技术
10. 智能工具
11. 计算机程序
12. 监测器

B. From English into Chinese.
1. infrared beams
2. to be totally immersed in
3. an artificial environment that mimics real life
4. hardware and software
5. three-dimensional computer animation
6. scientific advancement
7. to make simulations of building
8. commercial potential
9. to reduce the time and money spent crafting new models
10. enormous potential for the financial market
11. a major breakthrough
12. the steep prices of virtual reality systems
13. scientific abstractions
14. a high-tech company
15. a wide range of virtual reality applications
16. a massive amount of processing

III. Translate the following passage into Chinese:

Hong Kong supermarket chain Wellcome created the city's first major cybergrocery on the Internet and has signed a deal to provide shopping on Hong-kong Telecom IMS's recently launched interactive television service, iTV. "For us this is another means of serving the community," says Wellcome's marketing manager.

On the Web site(www.wellcomehk.com) customers can browse through nearly 3 000 products organized into categories, check delivery details and view special offers, some of which may be available exclusively through the Internet.

Once customers select their items they can opt to read more about them or pop them into their virtual shopping baskets before proceeding to the checkout. Electronic shopping lists can be recorded to reduce time on subsequent visits. Payment clearance is done electronically and goods are delivered from a central warehouse, eliminating the need for retail space and reducing checkout labour costs.

〔cybergrocery 网上食品杂货店/IMS 信息管理系统,是 information management system 的缩写形式/interactive 交互式的/browse v. 随意观看/opt to 选择/pop 放进/virtual shopping baskets 虚拟的购物篮、购物篮/payment clearance 支付清算〕

Well-known Sayings

△ *Truth is the most valuable thing we gave, let us economize it.*

△ *The primary purpose of education is not to teach you to earn your bread, but to make every mouthful sweeter.*

△ *Youth is not a time of life, it is a state of mind; it is not rosy cheeks, red lips and supple knees, it is a matter of the will, a quality of the imagination, it is a vigor of the emotions; it is the freshness of the deep springs of life.*

Unit 5 Green Revolution

第 5 单元 绿色革命

—— *The use of solar and wind power is now increasing rapidly, raising hope that such alternative energy technologies can significantly reduce greenhouse gas emissions and generate new jobs.*

—— *Advances in electronics, biotechnology, and the use of synthetic materials could soon lead to cleaner and more efficient ways to generate energy.*

—— *Genetic engineering and plant manipulation will reduce the harmful impacts of agriculture on the environment. Crops will be engineered to be more resistant to pests and to use their nutrients more efficiently, reducing the need for pesticides and fertilizers, which are major causes of water pollution.*

Lesson 17

Green Revolution
——Clean Cars and Energy

[1] By 2010, you may be driving a pollution-free, recyclable car, eating genetically engineered food grown without pesticides, avoiding rush-hour traffic jams by working and shopping at your home computer, and lighting your home with wind power.

[2] In the 20th century, technology sometimes seemed intent on destroying the environment, bringing us smog-belching cars, toxic waste and polluted waters. But as a new millennium approaches, technology has the potential to help clean up the mess.

[3] We are on the verge of a "green revolution" in the way automobiles are fueled and energy is generated. And, best of all, the revolution may be relatively painless, sparing affluent consumers the need to sacrifice comfortable lifestyles.

[4] The innovation creating the most excitement is the development of "fuel cell" technology, which uses hydrogen and oxygen to set off a chemical reaction that produces electricity.

[5] The fuel cell, originally developed for the U.S. space program and currently in use in the space shuttle, has the potential to replace the internal combustion engine and create motor vehicles that spew harmless water vapor from their tailpipes.

[6] Motorists would refuel at service stations, pumping liquid methanol that would be converted to hydrogen inside their vehicles. Fuel cells also could act as mini power plants producing clean electricity and hot water inside homes and offices.

[7] Today, fuel cell technology is too costly to compete with traditional energy sources, but futurists are heartened by the fact that major automobile companies—including Ford Motor Co.—and oil companies—including Atlantic Richfield Co.—are pumping millions into fuel cell development.

[8] "I think people are realizing that the fastest way to have a positive impact on the environment is not to get rid of automobiles but to make them so that they are much more environmentally benign," said Glen Hiemstra, a futurist who has served as a consultant to corporations ranging from Boeing Co. to Hewlett-Packard Co.

[9] Meanwhile, another clean source of power for homes and offices has the potential to help blow away the pollution from traditional gas or coal-fired power plants. Wind power has become the world's fastest-growing energy source, swelling at a rate of 20% to 30% a year for the past three years to become a $2 billion industry.

[10] Clusters of up to 100 wind turbines rising more than 130 feet high generate electricity from futuristic-looking "wind farms" stretching from Palm Springs, Calif., to Jutland, Denmark. The turbines typically have just two or three rotating blades, giving them the look of Spartan windmills. As the blades turn, they extract energy from the wind by slowing it down. A generator attached to the shaft of the turbine creates electricity.

[11] Although wind power still supplies less than 1% of the world's electricity, its double-digit growth rates and declining costs give it the potential to become a major source of electricity.

[12] Improved technology and government incentive programs have helped to lower the costs of wind power in the United States from about 40 cents per kilowatt-hour to about 5 cents today.

[13] In the new millennium, wind power's share of the worldwide energy market could surpass that of hydropower, which now supplies 20% of the demand for electricity. In European nations such as Germany and Spain, wind power already is becoming a major source of energy. In Denmark, it accounts for 8% of the market.

[14] In the United States, which has lagged in wind power development, Energy Secretary Bill Richardson announced an initiative this summer to ensure that wind power supplies at least 5 % of the nation's electricity by 2020.

[15] "Wind power is still considered a laughing matter by many energy industry executives," an energy expert comments. "But soon, such people may look almost as silly as those who once called the airplane an absurd idea."

[16] In the midst of this revolution in power, continuing advances in computer technology may help us save some human energy as well. Increasingly, U. S. workers will be able to do at least a portion of their work on faster, more efficient home computers, avoiding the need to join rush-hour traffic jams on the way to and from the office.

[17] Corporate attitudes that have slowed the expansion of telecommuting have changed dramatically in the past three years as bosses realize they don't need to be able to gather their employees in the same place to supervise them effectively.

[18] At the same time, early efforts at "e-commerce" will balloon in the next decade, making it routine for American consumers to shop online. That will help the environment by cutting down on the number of car trips we make to run errands.

[19] Here are some of the other environmentally friendly developments that US scientists expect within the next decade.

[20] Genetic engineering and plant manipulation will reduce the harmful impacts of agriculture on the environment. Crops will be engineered to be more resistant to pests and to use their nutrients more efficiently, reducing the need for pesticides and fertilizers, which are major causes of water pollution.

[21] Cars will become lighter, increasing fuel efficiency. Cars that still run on gasoline will get 80 miles to a gallon. This doesn't mean cars will get any smaller. Rather, they will be lighter because they will be built with less steel and more aluminum, magnesium, titanium and composites.

[22] Cars, computers, plastics and paper will become more biodegradable or recyclable. Cars will be built with modular parts that can be removed and reused.

[23] Smart membranes, or filters, will improve water treatment at sewage plants and municipal water supplies, improving the quality of our drinking water.

Language Points and Chinese Translations

第17课 绿色革命
——清洁汽车与清洁能源

[1] recyclable 再循环的,可回收利用的/rush-hour(公共车辆等的)高峰时间,拥挤时刻/traffic jams 交通阻塞,交通拥挤

到2010年时,你可能会驾驶着无污染、可回收利用的小汽车,吃着基因技术培育的无杀虫剂的食物,在自己家中的电脑上工作、购物而不再遭受上班高峰时的那种交通阻塞,并且使用风力来发电照明。

[2] to be intent on (doing) sth. 热切的,专心的/smog-belching 排出烟雾的/toxic: poisonous 有毒的/millennium: period of 1 000 years 一千年

在20世纪,有时候技术似乎"热衷于"破坏我们的环境,给我们带来排放烟雾的汽车、有毒的废物和污染过的水。但是当新千年来临之际,技术已经有潜力帮助我们收拾这残局。

[3] on the verge of 接近于,濒于/affluent: wealthy 富裕的

在给汽车供给燃料和产生能源方面,我们正面临一场"绿色革命"。而且最重要的是,这场革命相对来说没有痛苦,富裕的消费者们没有必要因此牺牲他们舒适的生活方式。

[4] to set off 引发、引爆

最令人激动的革新是开发"燃料电池"技术,该技术利用氢和氧产生化学反应从而产生电能。

[5] the internal combustion engine 内燃发动机/to spew 喷

燃料电池,原来是研制用于美国的太空计划,目前正使用于航天飞机,它有潜力替代内燃发动机,制造出尾管排出无害水蒸气的汽车。

[6] methanol 甲醇

汽车司机在服务站补充燃料时,加入液体甲醇,在汽车内转化成氢气。燃料电池也可以用作微型发电厂,给住家和办公室供应清洁的电源和热水。

[7] 今天,与传统的能源相比,燃料电池技术成本太高,但是未来主义者感到鼓舞,因为一些主要的汽车公司——包括福特汽车公司——和石油公司——包括大西洋福田公司——正投资数百万美元研制燃料电池。

[8] to have a positive impact on… 对……产生积极、正面的作用/to get rid of 清除,摆脱/benign 有利的,有益的

未来主义者Glen Hiemstra是波音公司和Hewlett-Packard公司的顾问,他说:"我认为人们正在认识到对环境产生积极作用的最快捷的方法不是丢弃汽车而是使它们更加环保。"

[9] to swell 增长,增大,膨胀/at a rate of 以……的比率

同时家庭和办公室另一种清洁的能源会有助于清除掉传统燃气或烧煤发电厂所产生的污染。风力发电已成为世界上迅速发展的能源,在过去三年中以每年20%至30%的速度增长,成为价值20亿美元的行业。

[10] turbines 叶轮机,汽轮机,涡轮机/windmill 风车/to extract 吸取,提取/shaft 轴

从加州的棕榈泉到丹麦的日德兰,有很多展示未来风貌的"风力农场",近百个130多英呎高的风力叶轮机在源源发电。这种典型的叶轮机装有两三片旋转的叶片,看起来像是斯巴达式的风车。叶片旋转时,通过对风的阻力产生能量,附加在叶轮机轴上的发电机产生电流。

[11] double-digit 两位数字的

虽然现在风力发电还只占世界供电量不到1%,但是其两位数的增长率和成本的日益降低,将有潜力成为一种主要的电源。

［12］incentive 鼓励的，刺激的

技术的不断改进和政府的鼓励计划已经有助于降低美国风力发电的成本,已从每千瓦时40美分降至大约现在的5美分。

［13］hydropower 水力发电/to account for（指数量等）占

在新千年,风力发电在世界能源市场中所占的份额将超过水力发电,现在水力发电占用电需求量的20%。在德国和西班牙等欧洲国家,风力发电正在成为主要的能源。在丹麦,风力发电占能源市场的8%。

［14］to lag 滞后,落后/initiative 提案

美国在开发风力发电方面已经落后,今年夏季美国能源部长Bill Richardson宣布了一项提案以便确保到2020年风力发电至少占全国总电量的5%。

［15］executive n. 行政官,执行者,管理者/absurd 荒谬的,愚蠢的

一位能源专家评论说,"很多能源工业的管理人员现在仍然认为风力发电是一种可笑的事。但是不会很久,这些人将会像那些曾把飞机称为荒谬想法者一样愚蠢。"

［16］在能源革命的进程中,计算机技术的不断发展也将有助于我们节省人类能源。美国工人们将至少能在更快捷、更有效的家庭电脑上做一部分工作,不必赶着去上下班而加入交通拥挤的行列。

［17］telecommuting 远距离工作,指人们在家中电脑上上班工作,而不必赶往办公室工作。

原来一致的观点是人们应集中在一起工作,这影响了远距离工作的开展。而这种态度在最近三年中发生了很大的变化,因为老板们认识到他们不必要让雇员们集中在同一地点工作也能有效地进行管理。

［18］to balloon 激增,膨胀/e-commerce 电子商务/routine 日常工作,常规,惯例/to run errands 出差办事,跑腿/to shop online 网上购物

同时早期努力开发的电子商务在今后的十年中将会大发展,使美国的消费者在网上购物成为常事。这将使我们减少办事用车的次数而有助于环境保护。

［19］下面是美国科学家期望在今后的十年中在环境保护方面的一些发展：

［20］manipulation 控制,操作,处理/to engineer 设计,操纵,策划

遗传工程技术和植物控制技术将减少农业对环境的有害作用。用遗传工程技术培育的庄稼对害虫有更强的抵抗力,能更有效地利用养分,减少对杀虫剂和化肥的需求量,而杀虫剂和化肥正是引起水污染的主要原因。

［21］小汽车将制造得更轻,以增加燃料效率,仍然使用汽油的小汽车每加仑汽油将可跑80英里,这并不是指汽车将变得更小,而是变得更轻,因为汽车制造将越来越少使用钢铁,而更多使用铝、镁、钛和各种复合材料。

［22］biodegradable 生物可降解性,是一生物化学用语/modular 制成有标准组件的,制成标准尺寸的小汽车

计算机、塑料和纸张将变得更具有生物可降解性,可以回收利用。汽车的各种标准组件都可以拆装,重新利用。

［23］sewage 污水,污物/municipal 市的,市政的

精巧的膜滤器将提高污水处理厂的水处理能力,改善城市供水状况,从而提高我们饮水的质量。

Exercises

Ⅰ. **Answer the following questions：**

1. According to the author, what kind of car shall we drive and what kind of food shall we eat by 2010?

2. Why did technology sometimes seem intent on destroying our environment in the 20th century?

3. What is the "fuel cell" technology?
   _____

4. For what was the fuel cell originally developed? What is its use at present? And what potential does it have?
   _____

5. What are people realizing about the environment?
   _____

6. What has become the world's fastest-growing energy source? Why?
   _____

7. How does a wind turbine work?
   _____

8. Why will the continuing advances in computer technology help us save some human energy?
   _____

9. What have changed greatly in the past three years?
   _____

10. Why will early efforts at "e-commerce" balloon in the next decade?
    _____

11. What will happen to environmental developments within the next decade according to U. S. scientists?
    _____

12. What does the "green revolution" mean?
    _____

II. Translate the following words and phrases:

A. From Chinese into English.
1. 基因技术培育的食物 _____
2. 绿色革命 _____
3. 燃料电池技术 _____
4. 化学反应 _____
5. 甲醇 _____
6. 水力发电 _____
7. 能源市场 _____
8. 网上购物 _____
9. 生物可降解性 _____
10. 每千瓦时 _____

B. From English into Chinese.
1. a pollution-free, recyclable car _____
2. rush-hour traffic jams _____
3. a new millennium _____
4. on the verge of _____
5. to set off _____
6. to have a positive impact on _____
7. to get rid of _____
8. double-digit growth rate _____

9. the potential to become a source of electricity _____
10. incentive programs _____
11. a major source of energy _____
12. in the midst of _____
13. to run errands _____
14. to improve the quality of drinking water _____

III. Translate the following passage into Chinese:

Some environmentalists point to the Twingo, the small car developed by France's Renault company, to show what could be achieved by the world's car industry if it moved away from a trend towards bigger and more powerful cars and radically cut the fuel consumption of its products. Public opinion polls in many countries show motorists wanting access to this kind of environmentally-aware car.

A prototype environmental car, the SmILE (smaller, intelligent, lighten, efficient) has been put together by the environmental group Green-peace. The group hopes the concept will catch on. It depends heavily on supercharging or forcing fuel mixture into the cylinders at higher than normal pressure. Some experts say this is a good way to extract high performance and high fuel efficiency from small engines.

What remains to be seen is whether the enthusiasm of environmental designers catches on with the dollar-driven international car industry, and whether motorists back up with their chequebooks, their desire for "greener" cars.

[access to 接近,进入,本句中指"想购买"之意/prototype 原型,样品/catch on 受到欢迎,喜爱,流行/back up 支持/"greener" cars 指"环保型"汽车]

Well-known Sayings
△ *Kindness is more important than wisdom, and the recognition of this is the beginning of wisdom.*
△ *Character is made up of those principles and values that give your life direction, meaning and depth.*
△ *We can only experience true success and happiness by making character the bedrock of our lives.*

Lesson 18

Alternative Energy Sources
——Solar and Wind Power

[1] The use of solar and wind power is now increasing rapidly, raising hope that such alternative energy technologies can significantly reduce greenhouse gas emissions and generate new jobs.

[2] The global wind power industry, for example, has become a $2-billion-a-year business, expanding at a rate of 25 % per year. India, China, and a dozen European nations have installed thousands of wind turbines that generate electricity at a cost comparable to new coal-fired power plants. In the 1990s, Germany has created 10 000 new jobs in its wind industry. Wind power now provides less than 1% of the world's total electricity, but that figure could climb to 20 % or more within 50 years, according to Worldwatch Institute researchers.

[3] Solar power is the second-fastest-growing energy source today. The cost of buying a kilowatt worth of solar photovoltaic cells dropped from $70 000 in the 1970s to $4 000 in 1997, and in 10 years it could go as low as $1 000. Approximately 400 000 homes—many in remote areas not connected by power lines—already use solar power. Worldwatch studies suggest that covering the rooftops of existing buildings with solar cells could meet more than half of the electricity needs each year.

[4] "During the past few years a host of promising new technologies have moved quietly but decisively from experimental curiosity to commercial reality," write Worldwatch Institute energy analysts Christopher Flavin and Seth Dunn in their report *Rising Sun, Gathering Winds: Policies to Stabilize the Climate and Strengthen Economies*. Advances in electronics, biotechnology, and the use of synthetic materials could soon lead to cleaner and more-efficient ways to generate energy.

[5] A new generation of lightweight hybrid electric vehicles could exceed 100 miles per gallon by utilizing a combination of fuel cells, small piston engines, turbine generators, and highly efficient electric motors. Similar technologies using micro-turbines and fuel cells could generate electricity and heat for commercial buildings and private homes while producing just 10% to 20% of the emissions from today's power plants. Micro-power plants located in buildings are extremely efficient; 90% of the fuel they use can be turned into electricity, usable space heat, and heat for warming water.

[6] Government incentives in Japan have led to plans by housing companies to build 70 000 homes with silicon roofing tiles capable of generating enough electricity to meet most of the residents' needs. Similar programs are under way in the United States and Europe.

[7] India has become the fourth-leading user of wind power by offering tempting investment tax credits and a guaranteed purchase price for wind-generated electricity. A government agency focusing on renewable energy provides loans and grants to further stimulate development.

[8] Since 1989 the Dutch government has reached 28 separate long-term agreements with 1 000 companies that represent 90% of the country's industrial energy use. The government negotiates efficiency targets with each industry group, from giant paper and chemical companies to small businesses such as laundries. The agreements call for an average 20% efficiency improvement by 2000. Two-thirds of the agreements have resulted in an average 9% efficiency gain from 1989 levels.

[9] "The countries that have achieved the most progress are the ones that have done many small

things right—forging an integrated package of mutually supportive policies that bring market forces to bear to solve the climate problem," write Flavin and Dunn.

Language Points and Chinese Translations

第18课　替代能源
——太阳能和风能

［1］greenhouse 温室，暖房/emission 发射，散发，排放/to generate 产生，发生，导致

现在太阳能和风能的利用正在得到迅速的发展，人们希望这些替代能源技术能够有效地减少温室气体的排放，并创造新的工作机会。

［2］to install 安装，设置，安置/comparable 可比较的，比得上的

例如，全球风能工业已成为每年20亿美元的行业，而且以每年25%的增长速度在发展。印度、中国和十多个欧洲国家已经安装了数以千计的风力涡轮机，其发电的成本与新建的燃煤电厂差不多。在90年代，德国已在风能工业方面创造了1万个新的工作机会。根据世界观察学会研究员的研究，风力发电现在占世界总发电量不到1%，但是在今后的50年内该数字会上升到20%其至更多些。

［3］photovoltaic 光伏的，photovoltaic cell 阻挡层光电池，光生伏打电池

今天，太阳能是第二位发展最快的能源。购买可以发电1千瓦的太阳能电池所花的费用已从70年代的7万美元降至1997年的4千美元，十年后将会低至1千美元。大约有4万家庭已经在使用太阳能，其中很多家庭居住在边远地区而无法连接上电网。世界观察学会的研究表明：在现有建筑物的顶部都安装上太阳能电池将能满足每年一半以上的电力需求。

［4］a host of 一大群，许多/curiosity 奇特性，好奇/to stabilize 稳定，安定

世界观察学会能源分析专家Christopher Flavin 和 Seth Dunn 在他们的报告《升起的太阳，聚集的风：稳定气候，增强经济的政策》中这样写道："在过去几年期间，许多有发展前途的新技术已经悄悄地但又明确无疑地从试验性的新奇事物变成了商业现实。"电子、生物技术的发展以及合成材料的使用不久将促使人们以更清洁、更有效的方法产生能量。

［5］hybrid 混合的/combination 联合(体)，结合(体)，组合/piston 活塞

由于燃料电池、小型活塞发动机、涡轮发电机和高效电动马达的组合应用，新一代的轻型混合燃料电动车辆每加仑油能行驶1百多英里。利用微型涡轮机和燃料电池的类似技术可以为商业大楼和私人住宅供电、供热，而所排出的气体仅占现在发电厂所排放气体的10%至20%。安装于建筑物内的微型发电厂效率特别高，其使用的燃料有90%可以转变成电能、适用的空间热量和给水加温的热量。

［6］incentive 刺激，鼓励/silicon 硅/under way 进行中，前进中

在日本，政府的鼓励政策已经使许多房地产公司计划建造7万户屋顶盖有硅瓦的房屋，这种硅瓦能产生足够的电量满足大多数居民的需要。在美国和欧洲，类似的计划也正在实施之中。

［7］tempting 引诱人的，吸引人的，使人发生兴趣的/credit 信用贷款/to focus on 集中/renewable 可更新的，可换新的

印度已成为利用风能的第四大国，政府向人们提供具有吸引力的投资税信用贷款，并确保风能所产生的电力的购买价格。一个专门负责再生能源的政府机构提供贷款与担保，以便进一步促进发展。

［8］target 目标，指标/laundry 洗衣，洗衣店/to call for 号召/to result in 致使，导致

自从1989年以来，荷兰政府已经与能源使用量占全国90%的一千家公司达成了28项单独的长期协议。政府部门和每一个工业集团，无论是大型的造纸和化学公司，还是像洗衣店那样的小型工商企业，都进行了能源使用效率和目标的谈判。这些协议号召到2000年要平均提高20%的效率，而且已经有三分之二的协议使效率在1989年的水平上平均提高了9%。

[9] to forge 锻造,打制,本文中转义为制订/integrated 连接成整体的,结合成一体的/package 一揽子,详细的计划,相当于 detailed plan

Flavin 和 Dunn 写道:"那些已经取得很大进步的国家都是在许多细小的事情上做得正确——制订了完整的相互支持的一揽子政策,从而使市场的力量来解决气候问题。"

Exercises

I. **Answer the following questions:**

1. What is now increasing rapidly?

2. How is the global wind power industry developing?

3. What countries have now installed a large number of wind turbines?

4. How many jobs did Germany create in its wind industry in the 1990's?

5. How about the development of wind power according to Worldwatch Institute researchers?

6. Which power is the second-fastest-growing energy source now? What about its cost?

7. How many homes are now using solar power?

8. What advances will lead to cleaner and more-efficient ways to generate energy?

9. Say something about the new generation of lightweight hybrid electric vehicles.

10. How does the Japanese government encourage housing companies to develop solar energy?

11. Which country is the fourth largest user of wind power? And what measures does it take to develop wind power?

12. How has the Dutch government done to increase the efficiency of energy use?

13. Why have some successful countries made much progress?

II. **Translate the following words and phrases:**

A. From Chinese into English.
1. 风能工业 _____
2. 替代能源技术 _____
3. 风力涡轮机 _____
4. 太阳能光伏电池 _____

5. 燃料电池 _____
6. 燃煤发电厂 _____
7. 新能源 _____
8. 合成材料 _____
9. 涡轮发电机 _____
10. 效率目标 _____

B. From English into Chinese.

1. to generate new jobs _____
2. a $2-billion-a-year business _____
3. at a rate of _____
4. in remote areas _____
5. to meet the needs of sb. _____
6. cleaner and more-efficient ways _____
7. micro-power plants _____
8. to be under way _____
9. to stimulate development _____
10. an integrated package of mutually supportive policies _____
11. to focus on renewable energy _____
12. long-term agreements _____

III. Translate the following passage into Chinese:

We cannot completely eliminate floods and fires and other natural disasters, but we know they will get worse if we do not do something about global warming. There are many people who simply don't believe that anything can be done about it because they don't believe that you can grow an economy unless you use energy in the same way America and Europe have used it for the last 50 years—more and more energy, more and more pollution to get more and more growth. That's what they believe. But I disagree. Without any loss of economic opportunity we can conserve energy much more than we do; we can use clean energy sources, such as solar and wind power, much more than we do; with the development in electronics and biotechnology, we can use synthetic materials to generate new energy; and we can adopt new technologies to make the energy we have go further much more than we do.

Well-known Sayings

△ *Necessity is the mother of taking chances.*
△ *There can be no progress if people have no faith in tomorrow.*
△ *Only those who have the patience to do simple things perfectly will acquire the skill to do difficult things easily.*

Lesson 19

The Trouble with Biofuels

[1] Maybe it was simply too good to be true. For proponents, biofuels—petroleum substitutes made from plant matter like corn or sugar cane—seemed to promise everything. Using biofuels rather than oil would reduce the greenhouse gases that accelerate global warming, because plants absorb carbon dioxide when they grow, balancing out the carbon released when burned in cars or trucks. Using homegrown biofuels would help the U. S. reduce its utter dependence on foreign oil, and provide needed income for rural farmers around the world. And unlike cars powered purely by electric batteries or hydrogen fuel cells—two alternate technologies that have yet to pan out—biofuels could be used right now.

[2] But according to a pair of studies published in the journal *Science* recently, biofuels may not fulfill that promise—and in fact, may be worse for the climate than the fossil fuels they're meant to supplement. According to researchers at Princeton University and the Nature Conservancy, almost all the biofuels used today cause more greenhouse gas emissions than conventional fuels, if the full environmental cost of producing them is factored in. As virgin land is converted for growing biofuels, carbon dioxide is released into the atmosphere; at the same time, biofuel crops themselves are much less effective at absorbing carbon than the natural forests or grasslands they may be replacing. "When land is converted from natural ecosystems it releases carbon," says Joseph Fargione, a lead author of one of the papers and a scientist at the Nature Conservancy. "Any climate change policy that doesn't take this fact into account doesn't work."

[3] Many environmentalists have been making the case against biofuels for some time, arguing that biofuel production takes valuable agricultural land away from food, driving up the price of staple crops like corn. But the *Science* papers make a more sweeping argument. In their paper, Fargione's team calculated the "carbon debt" created by raising biofuel crops—the amount of carbon released in the process of converting natural landscapes into cropland. They found that corn ethanol produced in the U. S. had a carbon debt of 93 years, meaning it would take nearly a century for ethanol, which does produce fewer greenhouse gases when burned than fossil fuels, to make up for the carbon released in that initial landscape conversion. Palm tree biodiesel in Indonesia and Malaysia—one of the most controversial biofuels currently in use, because of its connection to tropical deforestation in those countries—has a carbon debt of 86 years. Soybean biodiesel in the Amazonian rainforest has a debt of 320 years. "People don't realize there is three times as much carbon in plants and soil than there is in the air," says Fargione. "Cut down forests, burn them, churn the soil, and you release all the carbon that's been stored."

[4] Worse, as demand for biofuels go up—the European Union alone targets 5.75% of all its transport fuel to come from biofuel by the end of this year—the price of crops rises. That in turn encourages farmers to clean virgin land and plant more crops, releasing even more carbon in a vicious cycle. For instance, as the U. S. uses more biodiesel, much of which is made from soybeans or palm oil, farmers in Brazil or Indonesia will clear more land to raise soybeans to replace those used for fuel. "When we ask the world's farmers to feed 6 billion people and ask them to produce fuel, that requires them to use additional land", says Fargione. "That land has to come from somewhere."

[5] Industry groups like the Renewable Fuels Association criticized the studies for being too simplistic, and failing to put biofuels in context. And it's true that the switch to biofuels can have benefits that go beyond climate change. Biofuels tend to produce less local pollution than fossil fuels, one reason why Brazil—which gets 30% of its automobile fuel from sugar-cane ethanol—has managed to reduce once stifling air pollution. In the U.S., switching to domestically produced biofuels helps cut dependence on foreign oil, and boosts income for farmers. But in all of these cases, the benefits now seem to pale next to the climate change deficits. Fargione points out that if the U.S. managed to use 15 billion gallons of ethanol by 2015—as is mandated in last year's energy bill—it would still only offset 7% of projected energy demand. That won't put Venezuela or Iran out of business.

[6] This is all depressing news, especially if you're a corn farmer. Biofuels are one of the few alternative fuels that are actually available right now, but the evidence suggests we be better off not relying on them. But even Fargione doesn't argue that we should ditch biofuels altogether. Biofuels using waste matter—like wood chips, or the leftover sections of corn stalks—or from perennial plants like switchgrass, effectively amount to free fuel, because they don't require clearing additional land. "There's no carbon debt," notes Fargione. Unfortunately, the technology for yielding fuel from those sources—like cellulosic biofuels—is still in its infancy, though it is improving fast. In the end, the right kind of biofuel won't be a silver bullet, but just one more tool in the growing arsenal against climate change.

Language Points and Chinese Translations

第19课　生物燃料的弊端

[1] biofuels 生物燃料,泛指生物质组成或萃取的固体、液体或气体燃料,可以替代由石油制取汽油或柴油,是可再生能源开发利用的重要方向。但是生物能源在生产过程与运输过程中消耗掉的水资源、电能、石油等也是巨量的,有专家、学者认为生物能源的开发与利用是人类拆东墙补西墙的愚蠢行为/to pan out (结果)成功

　　生物燃料很好,但很可能并不真是如此。对于支持者来说,生物燃料——利用玉米或甘蔗等植物原料制成的石油替代品——似乎有望解决一切问题。利用生物燃料而不用石油,可以减少使全球气候加速变暖的温室气体,因为植物在生长过程中吸收二氧化碳,从而抵消了汽车或卡车燃油时所排放出来的碳。利用本土生产的生物燃料有助于美国减少对外国石油的完全依赖,同时也为全世界农民提供所必需的收入。并不像完全由蓄电池或氢燃料电池提供动力的汽车那样——这两种替代技术目前尚未发展完善——生物燃料现在就可以利用来为汽车提供动力。

　　[2] 但是根据《科学》杂志上最近发表的两项研究,生物燃料可能不会实现支持者的希望——事实上,可能比其所替代的矿物燃料更加促使气候恶化。根据普林斯顿大学和自然资源保护委员会的研究人员称,如果把生产生物燃料的全部环境成本都作为考虑因素,则今天所使用的所有生物燃料几乎都会比传统燃料引起更多的温室气体排放。由于把未开垦的土地转而用来种植生物燃料作物,二氧化碳就释放到大气中;同时,生物燃料作物本身吸收二氧化碳的效果要比其可能替代的自然森林或草原差得多。约瑟夫·法尔焦内是其中一篇论文的主要作者,也是自然资源保护委员会的一名科学家。他说:"土壤在自然生态体系中被改变时就会释放出碳。任何有关气候变化的政策,如果不考虑这一事实,就不会起作用。"

　　[3] 一段时间以来,许多环境保护论者一直在反对使用生物燃料,他们争辩说,生产生物燃料会占用生产粮食的宝贵的农用土地,从而促使像玉米这样的主要农作物的价格上涨。但是《科学》杂志上的论文提出了更加全面的论据。法尔焦内的团队在他们的论文中计算出了种植生物燃料作物所造成的"碳债"——在把自然土壤转变为庄稼地的过程中所释放出来的碳的总量。他们发现美国生产的玉米乙醇的"碳债"为93年,这意味着与燃烧矿

物燃料相比,乙醇燃烧时所产生的温室气体确实更少,但是补偿最初阶段的土壤转化所释放出的碳要用大约100年的时间。印度尼西亚和马来西亚的棕榈树生物燃料——是目前使用中的最有争议的生物燃料之一,因为它与那些国家砍伐热带森林有关——"碳债"为86年。在亚马逊河流域的雨林中生产的大豆生物柴油的"碳债"是320年。法尔焦内说:"人们并没有认识到植物和土壤中的碳含量是空气中的3倍之多。砍伐树木,烧荒毁林,改变土壤,就把储存的碳全部释放出来了。"

[4] 更为糟糕的是,随着对生物燃料需求的不断增长——仅仅欧盟就制定了这样的目标:今年年底前,生物燃料在所有交通运输业燃料中的比例为5.75%——农作物的价格高涨。这就反过来鼓励农民开垦更多的处女地种植更多的此类作物,释放出更多的碳进而恶性循环。例如,美国在使用更多的生物燃料,其中很多是由大豆或棕榈油制成的,而巴西或印度尼西亚的农民则将开发更多的土地种植大豆,用以替代那些制作燃料的大豆。法尔焦内说:"当我们要求全世界的农民养活60亿人口时,还要求他们生产燃料,那就是要求他们利用额外的土地。那额外的土地只能是来自某个地方。"

[5] to manage to do sth. 设法做到,设法得以,终于/to offset 抵消,补偿

可再生燃料协会等一些工业团体批评这些研究太简单化,没有把生物燃料放在整个大环境中考虑。转而使用生物燃料确实好处很多,并不局限于对气候变化有利。生物燃料造成的局部污染往往比矿物燃料少,正是由于这个原因,巴西——其30%的汽车燃料来自于甘蔗乙醇——已经设法做到了减少曾经令人窒息的空气污染。在美国,转而使用国内生产的生物燃料有助于削减对外国石油的依赖,并且增加了农民的收入。但是在所有这些事例中,这些好处与对气候变化所导致的坏处相比现在看起来微不足道。法尔焦内指出,如果美国在2015年前能设法做到利用150亿加仑的乙醇——这是去年能源法案的强制性要求——这也仅相当于预计能源需求的7%。那也不会使委内瑞拉或伊朗停止石油生意。

[6] to amount to 相当于,等于,就是/in infancy 在初期阶段,在发展初期

这一切都是令人沮丧的消息,特别是对于种植玉米的农民来说。生物燃料是现在就可利用的、少数可供选择的燃料之一,但是有证据显示,我们最好不要依赖它们。然而即使法尔焦内也并不主张我们应该抛弃使用生物燃料。利用废弃物——像木屑、玉米梗——或者像柳枝稷一类的多年生植物而制成的生物燃料,实际上相当于免费的燃料,因为不需要开发额外的土地。法尔焦内指出:"这不存在碳债。"令人遗憾的是,从那些资源中生产燃料的技术——像生产植物纤维素生物燃料——虽然发展迅速,但现在仍处于初期阶段。最终,理想的生物燃料将并不是银弹,而只是在不断增加的对付气候变化武器库中又多了一种工具。

Exercises

I. Answer the following questions:

1. What are the biofuels?

2. Why would using biofuels reduce the greenhouse gases that acclerate global warming?

3. What are the benefits of using biofuels?

4. Why may biofuels be worse for the climate than the fossil fuels?

5. Why are many environmentalists against using biofuels?

6. What is the "carbon debt"?

7. The corn ethanol produced in the U. S. has a carbon debt of 93 years. What does it mean?

8. Why is the palm tree biodiesel produced in Indonesia and Malaysia one of the most controversial biofuels now in use?

9. What is the worse situation in using biofuels?

10. Why does the author say that the benefits seem to pale next to the climate change deficits?

II. Translate the following words and phrases:

A. From Chinese into English.
1. 生物燃料
2. 石油替代品
3. 温室气体排放
4. 加速全球气候变暖
5. 把……释放到大气中
6. 自然生态系统
7. 再生燃料
8. 能源需求

B. From English into Chinese.
1. to absorb carbon dioxide
2. to balance out
3. ulter dependence on
4. fossil fuels
5. staple crops
6. to convert natural landscape into cropland
7. to make up for
8. tropical deforestation
9. in turn
10. to clear virgin land
11. a vicious cycle
12. to manage to do sth.
13. the energy bill
14. to amount to
15. to be in the infancy

III. Translate the following passage into Chinese:

Most politically controversial is the diversion of crops to biofuel production. The White House has been the most aggressive in its promotion of biocrops, but others, such as the European Union, have also set ambitious targets for the new technology. US production of ethanol from corn has gone from 1. 6 billion gallons in 2000 to 5 billion in 2006. President George Bush has set an interim target of 35 billion gallons for 2017 on the way to the administration's ultimate goal of 60 billion by 2030. Brazil and Indonesia are accused by their critics of sacrificing food and biodiversity to bio-ethanol and bio-diesel. Should we grow our biofuel crops in verifiable East Anglia or more efficient South America?

Second, third and fourth-generation biofuels have a much greener impact, but, despite sharply diverging claims, there is little doubt that current biofuel policy is affecting food prices to some extent. Climate change is another unknowable quantity that could transform everything for the worse. Teeming Bangladesh will perhaps be the most notable loser, an impact exacerbated by rising sea levels. A few nations—Argentina, Bolivia, South Africa—will benefit from higher food prices because of the way their economies are structured.

Genetically modified crops are another politically loaded option to boost agricultural productivity massively; population control another way of meeting the challenge. Demographics, biotechnology and the climate will all profoundly affect the number of people in the world with enough food in their bellies and the cost of our weekly shop.

— Well-known Sayings —

△ *Your attitude, not your aptitude, will determine your altitude.*
△ *Great emergencies and crises show us how much greater our vital resources are than we have supposed.*
△ *Courage is rightly esteemed as the first of human qualities because it is the quality which guarantees all others.*

Lesson 20

The Next Green Revolution: GMOs

[1] For a decade Europe has rebuffed efforts by biotechnology firms such as America's Monsanto to promote genetically modified crops. Despite scientific assurances that genetically modified organisms (GMOs) are safe for human consumption, and a ruling by the World Trade Organisation against national import bans in the European Union, many Europeans have yet to touch or taste them. But that may soon change, according to Iain Ferguson, boss of Tate & Lyle, a British food giant. "We sit at a moment of history, when GM technology…is a fact of life," he said.

[2] Mr. Ferguson, who is also the head of Britain's Food and Drink Federation, argues that because many large agricultural exporters have adopted GMOs, it is becoming expensive to avoid them. CopaCogeca, a farmers' lobby, warned that the rising cost of feed could wipe out Europe's livestock industry unless bans on GMOs are lifted. Meanwhile, European agriculture ministers failed to agree on whether to allow imports of GM maize and potatoes; the decision will now be made by the European Commission, which is likely to say yes.

[3] If it does, it will be a victory for Monsanto. But the firm is already enjoying an even sweeter form of revenge: huge commercial success. It has had three straight years of revenue and profit growth, and on February 12th it raised its profit forecast for the fiscal year for the second time in two months. Monsanto made a profit of $993m in the year to August, on revenues of $8.6 billion. The global commodity-price boom helps, but Brett Begemann, a senior executive at Monsanto, insists that it is the firm's advances in GMO technology that are fetching premium prices and will help it to double profits by 2012.

[4] The firm's fortunes have been boosted by the success of GMOs outside Europe. A new report from the International Service for the Acquisition of Agri-biotech Applications (ISAAA), a non-profit outfit that tracks industry trends, charts the dramatic growth in the 12 years that GMOs have been commercially available. The area under cultivation increased by 12% last year, to 114m hectares globally. America topped the list, but there is rapid growth in Argentina, Brazil, India and China. Thomas West of Pioneer Hi-Bred, a division of DuPont, says Europe should get on board, as "the train is leaving the station".

[5] According to Cropnosis, an industry consultancy, the market for agricultural biotechnology grew from about $3 billion in 2001 to over $6 billion in 2006, and is expected to reach $8.4 billion next year. Hans Kast, chief executive of Germany's BASF Plant Science, thinks the figure could reach $50 billion by 2025, as a second generation of GMO technology, now in the pipeline, reaches the market.

[6] Proponents of GMOs are optimistic because a confluence of social, commercial and technological forces is boosting the case for the technology. As India and China grow richer, the world is likely to need much more food, just as arable land, water and energy become scarcer and more expensive. If they fulfil their promise, GMOs offer a way out of this bind, providing higher yields even as they require less water, energy and fertiliser.

[7] Early incarnations of the technology, such as Monsanto's Roundup Ready maize and soyabeans, were genetically engineered to be resistant to herbicides and pesticides, making it easier for farmers to control pests without damaging crops. The second generation will have further traits, such as drought resistance, "stacked" on top. Michael Mack, chief executive of Switzerland's Syngenta, reckons that

farmers will pay extra for these new features.

[8] Indeed, farmers can expect everfaster cycles of product upgrades, thinks David Fischhoff, a senior executive at Monsanto. He likens the industry's situation to the early days of the personal computer, now that the underlying technology is in place. Monsanto predicts that the yield from maize grown in America, which has doubled since 1970, can double again by 2030.

[9] Mr. Mack draws a similar analogy. "Like in the software industry," he says, "intellectual-property rights give our technology value." Farmers paying big licence fees to use the new technology would no doubt agree. But just as with software, GMOs suffer from piracy. In a few countries, the hostile stance toward intellectual-property rights has been blessed by the government itself.

[10] The dirty little secret of the software industry, however, was that companies quietly tolerated some piracy on the basis that once customers went legal, they would probably stick with the products they were already using. The same may be happening with GMOs. Ask Syngenta's boss if he is worried about piracy, and he answers "yes and no". As countries grow richer or embrace WTO rules, he says, their farmers will start paying.

[11] The most important reason to think that GMOs have a brighter future, however, comes not from any of the benefits they offer farmers, large though those will be. The big difference with the next generation of technology, argues Mr. West of Pioneer Hi-Bred, is that it will also provide benefits to consumers. As an example, he points to his firm's high-oleic soyabean oil, which it expects to have on the market next year, Through genetic manipulation, he claims, his firm's researchers have been able to improve soya oil so that it tastes better, is healthier and produces no trans-fats during cooking.

[12] Could such an innovation even persuade sceptical Europeans? The lack of consumer benefits with first-generation GMOs made it easy for activists to whip up opposition. But if future products offer things consumers want, such as healthier food, and address problems that European regulators are worried about, such as obesity and climate change, then GMOs may yet have their day in Europe.

Language Points and Chinese Translations

第20课　下一次绿色革命:转基因作物

[1] genetically modified organisms (GMOs) 转基因生物,指遗传基因被改造修饰过的生物体。本文中主要指转基因作物。genetically modified 转基因,简称 GM,是指运用科学手段从某种生物体中提取所需要的基因,将其转入另一种生物中,使其基因进行重组,再从结果中进行数代的人工选育,从而获得特定的具有变异遗传性状的物质。转基因作物,是利用基因工程将原有作物的基因加入其他生物的遗传物质,并将不良基因移除,从而培育品质更好的作物。转基因作物通常可增加作物的产量,改善品质,提高抗旱、抗寒及其他特性。这是人类9 000年作物栽培史上的一场空前科技革命。

10年来欧洲断然拒绝了生物技术公司(例如美国的孟山都公司)努力促销转基因作物。尽管转基因作物在科学上已证明(GMOs)对人类消费是安全的,并且世界贸易组织就反对欧盟禁止进口这种作物作出了裁决,但是许多欧洲人仍然尚未接触或品尝过它们。然而据英国食品巨头泰勒和莱尔公司的老板伊恩·弗格森称,那种状况可能很快就要改变。他说:"我们现在正处在一个历史性的时刻,即转基因技术……正是一种生活现实。"

[2] lobby 院外活动集团(也称"第三院",指美国垄断组织为了收买或胁迫议员使立法为其服务所派的专人和设立的专门机构,因活动在议会走廊、休息室而得名。)/to wipe out 消灭、肃清,摧毁

弗格森先生也是英国食品和饲料联合会的负责人。他论证说,因为很多大的农业出口商已经采用了转基因作物,现在要回避它们,就得付出昂贵的代价。一个农民的院外活动集团 CopaCogeca 警告说,饲料成本的增长很

可能完全摧毁畜牧业,除非欧盟撤销其对转基因作物的禁令。同时,欧盟的农业部长们就是否允许进口转基因玉米和土豆并没有达成一致的意见;现在欧洲委员会将对此作出决定,很可能会表示同意。

[3] 如果欧洲委员会作出了同意的决定,这对美国孟山都公司来说,将是一次胜利。但是该公司正享受更加喜人的报复性增长:巨大的商业成功。该公司已经整整连续3年在收入和利润上获得增长。2月12日,它在两个月里第2次提高了本财政年度的利润预期。到本财政年度的8月,孟山都公司从86亿美元的收入中已获取了9.93亿美元的利润。全球商品价格激增也对此起到了促进作用,但是孟山都公司的资深经理布雷特·贝格曼坚持认为正是由于公司在转基因技术方面的先进成果才售得了高价,并将促使公司到2012年时利润翻番。

[4] to top the list 名列前茅,领衔/to chart 用图表表示或说明

欧洲以外转基因作物的成功促使孟山都公司财富激增。来自一家跟踪产业动向的非营利机构"探测农业生物技术应用国际服务部"(ISAAA)的一份新报告,以图表的形式显示了12年中转基因作物在商业上引人注目的增长情况。去年转基因作物种植面积增长了12%,全球已达到了1.14亿公顷。美国名列前茅,但阿根廷、巴西、印度和中国也都迅速增长。杜邦公司的一个分部"先驱者 Hi-Bred"的托马斯·韦斯特说,欧洲应该上车了,因为"火车即将离站出发。"

[5] in the pipeline 在运输中,递送中,在进行中,在生产中

据产业咨询公司 Cropnosis 称,农业生物技术的销售额已从2001年大约30亿美元增长到2006年60多亿美元,预计明年可达84亿美元。德国的 BASF 作物科技公司的总经理汉斯·卡斯特认为,到2025年这个数字会达到500亿美元,因为现今正在开发中的第二代转基因技术到时候会进入市场。

[6] 转基因作物的支持者是乐观的,因为社会、商业和技术上三大力量的聚集正在促进这项技术的发展。当印度和中国逐渐富裕起来,世界很可能需要更加多得多的粮食,而同时可耕地、水和能源正变得更为稀缺和更加昂贵。如果真能达到预期的那样,则转基因作物就会提供一种方法摆脱此种困境,因为转基因作物产量更高,而需要的水、能源和肥料却较少。

[7] 这种技术的早期特征,正如孟山都公司"综合制备"的玉米和大豆那样,是经过基因工程研制出来的作物,既能抗除莠剂,又能抗杀虫剂,从而使农民更容易控制害虫而又不会损害庄稼。第二代作物将具有更多的特性,如抗旱、顶端"结实丰满"。瑞士的辛金塔公司总经理迈克尔·麦克推断说农民们将为作物的这些新特性支付额外的费用。

[8] to liken... to... 把……比做,把……比拟

孟山都公司的资深经理戴维·费什科夫认为,农民确实可以期望产品更新升级的周期不断加快。他把转基因作物产业的状况比拟为早期的个人电脑,因为基础性的转基因技术已经成熟。孟山都公司预言美国种植的玉米产量自1970年以来已经翻番,到了2030年可能还会再增长一倍。

[9] 麦克先生作出了一个相似的比拟。他说:"像软件产业一样,知识产权使我们的技术具有价值。"农民们毫无疑问是同意为了使用新技术而支付大笔的特许费用的。然而正像使用软件那样,转基因作物也会遭受到非法侵权。在有些国家,对知识产权的敌视观点一直受到其本国政府的保护。

[10] 然而,软件产业卑劣的小秘密是公司暗地里容忍一些侵权行为,其根据是一旦顾客懂得法律,他们很可能仍会坚持使用已经用惯的产品。在转基因技术上也会发生与之相同的情况。问及辛金塔公司的老板是否会对非法侵权感到忧虑,他回答说"既是又不"。他说一些国家逐渐富裕起来或者接受世界贸易组织的规则时,这些国家的农民就会开始付款。

[11] high-oleic 高油的,高油酸的/genetic manipulation 基因控制,基因操作/trans-fats 反式脂肪

然而,认为转基因作物会有一个更加光辉前景的最重要原因并不是它们给予农民的任何利益,虽然那些利益将会很大。"先驱者 Hi-Bred"分部的韦斯特先生论证说,使用下一代技术的最大差异在于它也将会给消费者提供利益。作为一个例子,他指出他公司的高油酸的大豆油可望在明年投入市场。他声称,通过基因控制,他公司的研究人员已经能够改良大豆油,使其味道更好,更有益于健康,并且在烹调时不会产生反式脂肪。

[12] 这种创新能够说服惯于怀疑的欧洲人吗?没有顾及消费者利益的第一代转基因作物容易使激进主义者提出反对意见。但是,如果将来的产品会给消费者提供想要的东西,如更有益于健康的食品,并且处理好欧洲管理者们所担忧的问题,如肥胖症和气候变化,那么转基因作物仍会在欧洲有它们走运的时期(即成功的时期)。

Exercises

I. **Answer the following questions:**

1. What has happened to biotechnology firms during ten years according to the text?

2. Why is the European Commission likely to agree on the import of GM maize and potatoes?

3. Why does the author say "it will be a victory for Monsanto"?

4. What does a new report from ISAAA chart?

5. Please say something about the market for agricultural biotechnology from 2001 to 2025.

6. Why are proponents of GMOs optimistic?

7. What were the early incarnations of the transgene technology?

8. What kind of analogy does Mr. Mack draw?

9. Why did some software companies quietly tolerate some piracy?

10. Why do GMOs have a brighter future?

11. Why does the author say that GMOs may yet have their day in Europe?

II. **Translate the following words and phrases:**

A. From Chinese into English.
1. 生物技术
2. 转基因作物
3. 世界贸易组织
4. 畜牧业
5. 财政年度
6. 利润翻番
7. 非营利机构
8. 技术力量
9. 可耕地
10. 除莠剂和杀虫剂
11. 产品升级更新的周期
12. 作出一个相似的比拟
13. 知识产权
14. 特许费
15. 非法侵权

16. 高油酸的大豆油 _____
17. 基因控制 _____
18. 反式脂肪 _____

B. From English into Chinese.
1. scientific assurances _____
2. GM technology _____
3. to wipe out _____
4. to agree on _____
5. huge commercial success _____
6. to fetch premium prices _____
7. to top the list _____
8. proponents of GMOs _____
9. to be resistant to sth. _____
10. to pay extra for the new features _____
11. to be in the place _____
12. the software industry _____
13. to have a brighter future _____
14. to whip up opposition _____
15. to have one's day _____

Ⅲ. Translate the following passage into Chinese:

Darwin had the framework of his theory of natural selection as his "prime hobby". His research included animal husbandry and extensive experiments with plants, finding evidence that species were not fixed and investigating many detailed ideas to refine and substantiate his theory.

In the book *On the Origin of Species*, Darwin's allusion to human evolution was the understatement that "light will be thrown on the origin of man and his history". His theory is simply stated in the introduction:

As many more individuals of each species are born than can possibly survive; and as, consequently, there is a frequently recurring struggle for existence, it follows that any being, if it vary however slightly in any manner profitable to itself, under the complex and sometimes varying conditions of life, will have a better chance of surviving, and thus be naturally selected. From the strong principle of inheritance, any selected variety will tend to propagate its new and modified form.

He put a strong case for common descent, but avoided the then controversial term "evolution", and at the end of the book concluded that:

Whilst this planet has gone cycling on according to the fixed law of gravity, from so simple a beginning endless forms most beautiful and most wonderful have been, and are being, evolved.

On the Origin of Species was translated into many languages, becoming a staple scientific text attracting thoughtful attention from all walks of life. Having published *On the Origin of Species* as an abstract of his theory, he pressed on with experiments, research and writing of his "big book", covering humankind's descent from earlier animals including evolution of society and of human mental abilities, as well as diversifying into innovative plant studies and explaining decorative beauty in wildlife.

Well-known Sayings

△ All human wisdom are summed up in two words—wait and hope.
△ Always aim for achievement and forget about success.
△ Who controls the past controls the future; who controls the present controls the past.

Unit 6　Biotechnology and Cloning

第 6 单元　生物工程和克隆

—— Biotechnology is the use of living systems and organisms to develop or make useful products, or any technological application that uses biological systems, living organisms or derivatives thereof, to make or modify products or processes for specific use. In other words, biotechology can be defined as the mere application of technical advances in life science to develop commercial products.

—— Biotechnology has applications in four major industrial areas, including health care (medical), crop production and agriculture, non food (industrial) uses of crops and other products (e.g. biofuels), and environmental uses.

—— Cloning involves the removal of the nucleus from one cell and its placement in an unfertilized egg cell whose nucleus has either been deactivated or removed. Cloning in biotechnology refers to processes used to create copies of DNA fragments (molecular cloning), cells (cell cloning), or organisms.

Lesson 21

The Biotech Century

[1] Ring farewell to the century of physics, the one in which we split the atom and turned silicon into computing power. It's time to ring in the century of biotechnology. Just as the discovery of the electron in 1897 was a seminal event for the 20th century, the seeds for the 21st century were spawned in 1953, when James Watson blurted out to Francis Crick how four nucleic acids could pair to form the self-copying code of a DNA molecule. Now we're just a few years away from one of the most important breakthroughs of all time: deciphering the human genome, the 100 000 genes encoded by 3 billion chemical pairs in our DNA.

[2] Before this century, medicine consisted mainly of amputation saws, morphine and crude remedies that were about as effective as bloodletting. The flu epidemic of 1918 killed as many people(more than 20 million) in just a few months as perished in four years of World War I. Since then, antibiotics and vaccines have allowed us to vanquish entire classes of diseases. As a result, life expectancy in the U. S. jumped from about 47 years at the beginning of the century to 76 now.

[3] But 20th century medicine did little to increase the natural life-span of healthy humans. The next medical revolution will change that, because genetic engineering has the potential to conquer cancer, grow new blood vessels in the heart, block the growth of blood vessels in tumors, create new organs from stem cells and perhaps even reset the primeval genetic coding that causes cells to age.

[4] Our children may be able(I hope, I fear) to choose their kids' traits: to select their gender and eye color; perhaps to tinker with their IQs, personalities and athletic abilities. They could clone themselves, or one of their kids, or a celebrity they admire, or maybe even us after we've died.

[5] In the 5 million years since we hominoids separated from apes, our DNA has evolved less than 2%. But in the next century we'll be able to alter our DNA radically, encoding our visions and vanities while concocting new life-forms. When Dr. Frankenstein made his monster, he wrestled with the moral issue of whether he should allow it to reproduce: "Had I the right, for my own benefit, to inflict the curse upon everlasting generations?" Will such questions require us to develop new moral philosophies?

[6] Probably not. Instead, we'll reach again for a time-tested moral notion, one sometimes called the Golden Rule and which Immanuel Kant, the millennium's most meticulous moralist, gussied up into a categorical imperative: do unto others as you would have them do unto you; treat each person as an individual rather than as a means to some end.

[7] Under this moral precept we should recoil at human cloning, because it inevitably entails using humans as means to other humans' ends—valuing them as copies of others we loved or as collections of body parts, not as individuals in their own right. We should also draw a line, however fuzzy, that would permit using genetic engineering to cure diseased and disabilities but not to change the personal attributes that make someone an individual (IQ, physical appearance, gender and sexuality).

[8] The biotech age will also give us more reason to guard our personal privacy. Aldous Huxley, in *Brave New World*, got it wrong: rather than centralizing power in the hands of the state, DNA technology has empowered individuals and families. But the state will have an important role, making sure that no one, including insurance companies, can look at our genetic data without our permission or use it

to discriminate against us.

[9] Then we can get ready for the breakthrough that could come at the end of the next century and is comparable to mapping our genes: plotting the 10 billion or more neurons of our brain. With that information we might someday be able to create artificial intelligences that think and experience consciousness in ways that are indistinguishable from a human brain. Eventually we might be able to replicate our own minds in a machine, so that we could live on without the "wetware" of biological brain and body. The 20th century's revolution in infotechnology will thereby merge with the 21st century's revolution in biotechnology.

Language Points and Chinese Translations

第21课 生物技术的世纪

[1] to ring farewell to 告别,辞别/to turn silicon into computing power 把硅变成计算的动力/to ring in 迎接/seminal adj. 根源的,种子的/to spawn 产卵/to blurt out 脱口而出,顺口说出/James Watson 和 Francis Crick 分别是美国和英国的生物医学专家,两人在 1962 年共同获得诺贝尔生物学奖。/nucleic acids 核酸/DNA molecule 脱氧核糖核酸分子,DNA 是 deoxyriborlucleic acid 的缩写形式。/to decipher 翻译(密码),解译,辨认/human genome 人类基因组/gene 基因

在物理世纪,我们分裂了原子,把硅变成计算的动力。现在向物理世纪告别吧,该是迎来生物技术的世纪了。正像 1897 年发现电子是为 20 世纪发展奠定基础的重大事件一样,1953 年生物医学家 James Watson 向 Francis Crick 脱口说出了四个核酸如何能够配对组成一个脱氧核糖核酸分子的自我复制编码,这为 21 世纪的发展打下了基础(直译:播散了种子)。只要再过几年我们就能实现划时代的最重大突破:解译人类基因组,即在人类的脱氧核糖核酸(DNA)中由 30 亿个化学配对进行编码的 10 万个基因。

[2] to consist of… 由……组成/amputation (外科)截肢,截断,切除/morphine 吗啡/crude adj. 原始的,天然的,粗鲁的/remedy 治疗法,补救法/bloodletting n. 放血,抽血/flu epidemic 流行性感冒/to perish 死亡,毁灭,本句中 perished 是过去分词,前面省去了 those people,即指在第一次世界大战四年中所死亡的人/antibiotic 抗菌素,抗生素/vaccine 牛痘苗,疫苗,菌苗/to vanquish 制服,克服/life expectancy 指人的预期寿命

在本世纪前,医疗技术主要是由截肢锯、吗啡和像放血疗法一样的原始治疗法组成的。1918 年的流行性感冒仅在几个月内杀死的人(2 000 多万)就和第一次世界大战 4 年中死亡的人一样多。从那时起,各种抗生素和疫苗使我们能够战胜各类疾病。其结果是,美国人的预期寿命从本世纪初的大约 47 岁剧增到现在的 76 岁。

[3] life-span 寿命,也可说成 the span of life/genetic engineering 遗传工程/blood vessels 血管/tumor 肿瘤/stem cells 干细胞/primeval genetic coding 原始遗传编码/…that causes cells to age 引起细胞老化,这是一定语从句,修饰前面的 coding,to age 使变老,老化

但是 20 世纪的医学在增加健康人类的自然寿命方面所作出的贡献甚少。下一次医学革命将改变这种状况,因为遗传工程有潜力征服癌症,在心脏里生长新的血管,阻止肿瘤中血管的生长,从干细胞里造出新的器官,甚至重新设置使细胞老化的原始遗传编码。

[4] traits 特性,性格,品质/to tinker with 修补,拼凑,调整/IQs 智商,是 Intelligence Quotient 的缩写形式/to clone 克隆,无性繁殖

我们的孩子也许能够(我希望,同时也担忧)挑选他们自己子女的特性:选择他们的性别和眼睛的颜色,也许调整他们的智商、个性和体育竞技能力。他们能够克隆自己或自己的一个孩子,或他们所钦佩的一位名人,或在我们去世后甚至克隆我们自己。

[5] hominoids 原始人类/ape 猿,类人猿/to evolve 进化/to encode 译成密码/to concoct 调和,调制,编造/to

wrestle with 与……作苦斗,斗争/to inflict 使受痛苦,折磨/everlasting 永久的,持久的/moral 道德上的

在我们人类和猿分离以来的 500 万年中,我们的 DNA 的只进化不到 2%。但在下个世纪里,我们将能对我们的 DNA 作彻底的改变,在创造新的生命形式时,把我们的远见卓识译成密码。当 Frankenstein 博士制造自己的怪物时,他就为是否应该让它生殖繁衍这个道德问题而苦恼不堪:"我是否有权利为了自身的利益而让生生不息的子孙后代遭殃?"这样的问题是否需要我们发展新的道德哲理?

[6] millennium 一千年/categorical imperative 无条件的,绝对的命令

也许不需要。相反,我们将再次谈及经时间考验过的一个道德观念问题,有时被人们称之为黄金法则,一千年来最谨慎的道德学家 Immanud Kant 将之称誉为绝对的命令:己之所欲,施之于人;把每个人当做一个个体来对待,而不是作为达到某种目的的工具。

[7] precept 戒律,教训,格言/to recoil 退缩,撤回/attribute 属性,品质,特征

在这种道德戒律下,我们应该回避克隆人类,因为这会不可避免地使某些人被利用而成为另一些人达到某种目的的手段——被利用者只被视为我们所喜爱的人的复制品,或者人体各部位的集合体,而不是有自身权利的个体。我们也应该划一条界线,不管这条界线是如何模糊不清,即允许采用遗传工程医治疾病和残疾,但是不允许改变那种使人个性化的个人属性(智商,身体的外貌,性别和特征)。

[8] personal privacy 个人隐私/to get it wrong 将之搞错了,犯了一个错误,这是在动词 get 后带有形容词的复合宾语。/to empower sb. 授权给某人,相当于 to give power to sb. /to discriminate against 以不同的方式对待,歧视

生物技术时代也使我们有更多的理由保护个人隐私。在《挑战新世界》一书中,作者 Aldous Huxley 犯了一个错误:DNA 技术把权力授予了个人和家庭,而不是把权力集中在国家的手里。但是国家将会发挥重要作用,确保包括保险公司在内的任何人,未经我们的允许都不能看我们的遗传因子数据或用它来歧视我们。

[9] breakthrough 突破/to be comparable to 可与相比的,可与比拟的/to map 绘制/neuron 神经原,神经细胞/artificial intelligences 人工智能/to be indistinguishable from 与……相同,难以区分/to replicate 复制,重复,相当于 to make an exact copy/wetware 湿件,这是作者仿照计算机 software 和 hardware 而创造的一个新词,意指人脑和人的身体/to merge with 合并,结合在一起

然后我们就可以为下个世纪末将要来临的突破做好准备,这种突破可与描绘我们的基因图相比较:绘制出我们大脑中 100 亿或更多的神经原。有了这样的信息,我们将来总有一天会创造出人工智能,这种人工智能能用与人类大脑相同的方式进行思考和有意识地感受事物。最终我们也许有可能在机器里复制我们的意识,从而在没有生物大脑和身体"湿件"的状况下照样能生存。20 世纪的信息技术革命将因此和 21 世纪的生物技术革命融为一体。

Exercises

I. Answer the following questions:

1. According to the author, what was a seminal event for the 20th century?

2. What will be one of the most important breakthroughs of all time?

3. Why did life expectancy in the U. S. jump from about 47 years at the beginning of the 20th century to 76 now?

4. What will genetic engineering do to the human health?

5. Has our DNA evolved slowly or fast in the 5 million years?

6. What will happen to our DNA in the 21st century?

7. According to Immanuel Kant, what was the categorical imperative?

8. Why must we recoil at human cloning?

9. What will genetic engineering be used to do?

10. According to the author, what will be the breakthrough at the end of the 21st century?

11. What shall we be able to create in the near future?

12. What will happen to the revolution both in infotechnology and biotechnology in the 21st century?

II. Translate the following words and phrases:

A. From Chinese into English.
1. 生物技术
2. 核酸
3. 脱氧核糖核酸
4. 疫苗
5. 抗生素
6. 放血,放血疗法
7. 遗传工程
8. 人工智能
9. 克隆
10. 智商

B. From English into Chinese.
1. to turn silicon into computing power
2. self-copying code
3. to decipher the human genome
4. as a result
5. to develop new moral philosophies
6. Do unto others as you would have them do unto you.
7. to guard one's personal privacy
8. moral notion
9. to be indistinguishable from
10. infotechnology
11. to discriminate against
12. to merge with
13. attribute
14. to encode

III. Translate the following passage into Chinese:

Now a new kind of biotech, genomics, is mesmerizing Wall Street. Since 1993, when Incyte Pharmaceuticals of Palo Alto made the niche's first *IPO*, eight genomics leaders have racked up average annual share price gains of more than 75%. The leaping stocks look like those in biotech's first wave, yet genomics companies are a different breed.

The drug companies' rush to invest underscores the promise of genomics. While early biotech focused on scanty dozens of genes, Incyte and others now use computers to cull therapeutic gems from genes by the thousand. The international Human Genome Project is expected to decode all 100 000 genes by 2003.

[genomics 基因分析学/mesmerizing 使……迷醉/Incyte Pharmaceuticals 药物公司名/make the niche's 填补……空白/IPO 国际专利标书,是 International Patent Offer 的缩写形式/therapeutic gems 在治疗方面的特效因子]

Well-known Sayings

△ *Vital to every operation is cooperation.*
△ *No question is ever settled until it is settled right.*
△ *Discontent is the first step in progress of a man or a nation.*

Lesson 22

What Are Biorhythms?

[1] At the beginning of last century, medical scientists made a surprising discovery: that we are built not just of flesh and blood but also of time. They were able to demonstrate that we all have an internal "body clock" which regulates the rise and fall of our body energies, making us different from one day to the next. These forces became known as biorhythms; they create the "highs" and "lows" in our everyday life.

[2] The idea of an internal "body clock" should not be too surprising, since the lives of most living things are dominated by the 24-hour night-and-day cycle. The most obvious feature of this cycle is the way we feel tired and fall asleep at night and become awake and alert during the day. If the 24-hour rhythm is interrupted, most people experience unpleasant side effects. For example, international aeroplane travellers often experience "jet lag" when travelling across time zones. People who are not used to shift work can find that lack of sleep affects their work performance.

[3] As well as the daily rhythm of sleeping and waking, we also have other rhythms which last longer than one day and which influence wide areas of our lives. Most of us would agree that we feel good on some days and not so good on others. Sometimes we are all fingers and thumbs but on other days we have excellent coordination. There are times when we appear to be accident-prone, or when our temper seems to be on a short fuse. Isn't it also strange how ideas seem to flow on some days but at other times are apparently nonexistent? Musicians, painters and writers often talk about "dry spells".

[4] Scientists have identified the following three biorhythmic cycles: physical, emotional and intellectual. Each cycle lasts approximately 28 days and each is divided into a high energy period and a low energy period of equal length. During the high energy period of a physical biorhythm we are more resistant to illness, better coordinated and more energetic; during the low energy period we are less resistant to illness, less well coordinated and tire more easily. The low period puts energy into our "batteries" for the next high period.

[5] The "critical" or weakest time is the time of changeover from the high energy period to the low energy period or vice versa. This "critical" time usually lasts a day. On the critical day of a physical biorhythm, there is a greater chance of accident and illness.

[6] Human experience is always individual and we each have our own biorhythmic experiences. Some people experience such enormous physical turbulence on their "physically critical" days that they have to go to bed. Accidents appear to happen so frequently during turbulent biorhythms that some car insurance companies in Japan have issued biorhythm forecasts to policy-holders in order to cut down the number of costly incidents.

Language Points and Chinese Translations

第22课 什么是生物节奏？

[1] to demonstrate 证明,论证,表明/body clock 生物钟/to regulate 调节,调整,控制/biorhythms 生物节奏

在上个世纪初,医学科学家们得出了一个惊人的发现:我们的身体不仅由血、肉构成,而且还包含时间。他们能够证明我们体内都有"生物钟",调节体能的增减,使我们每天的状况各不相同。这种体能力量被称作生物节奏,使我们每天的生活有"高潮"和"低潮"。

[2] to dominate 支配,控制/side effect 副作用/jet lag 时差反应/time zone 时区/shift work 倒班,轮班或调班工作

体内"生物钟"的观点并不令人感到非常惊奇,因为大多数生物的生命都是按日夜24小时的周期运行。这一周期最明显的特征是:在夜晚我们感到疲劳而睡觉;在白天我们清醒而警觉。如果24小时的节奏受到了干扰,大多数人就都会有种种不愉快的感觉。例如:国际航班的旅客在飞越时区时就常有时差感。不适应于倒班工作的人发现缺乏睡眠会影响工作效率。

[3] coordination 协调,配合,协作/prone 易犯的,偏向的/to be on a short fuse 易发怒,脾气急躁的/nonexistent 不存在的/spell (持续的)时间,服务时间/dry spells 意指艺术家们缺乏创作灵感或热情的"枯竭期"

和睡眠及清醒的日常生活节奏一样,我们也有其他一些生物节奏,其持续时间超过一天,并对我们的生活有广泛的影响。大多数人都持有相同的看法,即在一些日子里我们感觉良好,而在另一些日子里感觉不大好。我们有时候笨手笨脚,有时候却极为协调灵巧。也有的时候我们似乎极易发生事故或动辄发脾气。也有的时候我们思路敏捷流畅,而有时候脑海里空白一片,这些难道不很奇怪吗?难怪音乐家、画家和作家常常谈论起"枯竭期"。

[4] to identify 鉴定,辨认,验明/resistant 抵抗的,抗……的

科学家们已经验证了如下三种生物节奏周期:身体生物节奏周期,情感生物节奏周期和智力生物节奏周期。每种周期大约持续28天,并分成时间跨度一样的高能期与低能期两个时期。在身体生物节奏的高能期,我们有较强的抗病能力,身体各部分更协调自如,精力更旺盛;在低能期,我们的抗病能力减弱,身体各部分不太协调一致,而且容易感到疲劳。低能期是为下一个高能期"充电"积蓄能量。

[5] critical 危险的,临界的,决定的,关键性的/changeover 转变,转换/vice versa 反过来,反过来也是一样

"临界期"或最虚弱期是从高能期向低能期,或者从低能期向高能期转换的时期。这种"临界期"通常持续一天。在身体生物节奏"临界期"的那一天,发生事故或生病的可能性更大些。

[6] individual *adj.* 个别的,各个的,个人的,个体的;*n.* 个人,个体/enormous 巨大的,非常的/turbulence 骚动,骚乱/insurance companies 保险公司/to issue 发出,发行,发布/forecast *n. v.* 预测,预报/policy-holders 保险单持有人,意指投保人/to cut down 减少,削减,降低

人的经历都是个别的。我们每个人都有自己的生物节奏经历。有些人在他们"身体临界期"的日子里,经受着强烈的身体骚动以至于不得不上床睡觉。很多事故都频繁地发生在生物节奏骚动期,因此日本的一些汽车保险公司向投保人预报生物节奏的有关情况,以减少高损失事故的发生。

Exercises

I. Answer the following questions:

1. What did the medical scientists find at the beginning of last century?

2. What is the function of our internal "body clock"?

3. What are the biorhythms?

4. By what are our lives dominated?

5. What will happen if our 24-hour rhythm is interrupted?

6. Talk about other rhythms besides our daily rhythm of sleeping and waking.

7. What do "dry spells" mean?

8. What are the three biorhythmic cycles?

9. How many periods is each biorhythmic cycle divided into?

10. What does the "critical" time refer to?

11. What have car insurance companies in Japan done to cut down the number of accidents?

II. Translate the following words and phrases:

A. From Chinese into English.
 1. 生物节奏
 2. 生物钟
 3. 体能
 4. 副作用
 5. 时差反应
 6. 临界期
 7. 高能期
 8. 生物

B. From English into Chinese.
 1. medical scientists
 2. a surprising discovery
 3. to regulate the rise and fall of body energies
 4. to be dominated by
 5. as well as

6. time zones _____
7. work performance _____
8. to be all fingers and thumbs _____
9. accident-prone _____
10. resistant to illness _____
11. physical turbulence _____
12. insurance companies _____

III. Translate the following passage into Chinese:

Although insomnia is usually blamed on anxiety or depression, a new study reveals that physical ailments may also contribute. Researchers studied 3 445 adults with a chronic medical condition or depression and found the conditions most associated with severe insomnia were, inorder depression, hip problems, congestive heart failure, peptic ulcers, lung disease and back problems.

At the same time, our lives are dominated by the 24-hour night and day cycle. If the 24-hour rhythm is interrupted, many people feel tired or uncomfortable, thus resulting in insomnia. And some people will be ill after weeks of insomnia.

Well-known Sayings

△ *People do not lack strength, they lack will.*
△ *Have an aim in life, or your energies will all be wasted.*
△ *Life is a comedy to him who thinks, and a tragedy to him who feels.*

Lesson 23

The Age of Cloning

[1] The landmark paper published late last week in the journal *Nature* confirmed what the headlines had been screaming for days: researchers at the Roslin Institute near Edinburgh, Scotland, had indeed pulled off what many experts thought might be a scientific impossibility. From a cell in an adult ewe's mammary gland, embryologist Ian Wilmut and his colleagues managed to create a frisky lamb named Dolly, scoring an advance in reproductive technology as unsettling as it was startling. Unlike off-spring produced in the usual fashion, Dolly does not merely take after her biological mother. She is a carbon copy, a laboratory counterfeit so exact that she is in essence her mother's identical twin.

[2] What enabled the Scottish team to succeed where so many others have failed was a trick so ingenious, yet so simple, that any skilled laboratory technician should be able to master it—and therein lies both the beauty and the danger: once Wilmut and his colleagues figured out how to cross that biological barrier, they ensured that others would follow. And although the Roslin researchers had to struggle for more than 10 years to achieve their breakthrough, it took political and religious leaders around the world no time at all to grasp its import: if scientists can clone sheep, they can probably clone people too.

[3] Without question, this exotic form of reproductive engineering could become an extremely useful tool. The ability to clone adult mammals, in particular, opens up myriad exciting possibilities, from propagating endangered animal species to producing replacement organs for transplant patients.

[4] Agriculture stands to benefit as well. Dairy farmers, for example, could clone their champion cows, making it possible to produce more milk from smaller herds. Sheep ranchers could do the same with their top lamb and wool producers.

[5] But it's also easy to imagine the technology being misused, and as news from Roslin spread, apocalyptic scenarios proliferated. Journalists wrote seriously about the possibility of virgin births, resurrecting the dead and women giving birth to themselves. On the front page of the *New York Times*, a cell biologist from Washington University in St. Louis, Missouri, named Ursula Goodenough quipped that if cloning were perfected, "there'd be no need for men."

[6] Scientists have long dreamed of doing what the Roslin team did. After all, if starfish and other invertebrates can practice asexual reproduction, why can't it be extended to the rest of the animal kingdom? In the 1980s, developmental biologists in Philadelphia at what is now Allegheny University of the Health Sciences came tantalizingly close. From the red blood cells of an adult frog, they raised a crop of lively tadpoles. These tadpoles were impressive creatures, remembers University of Minnesota cell biologist Robert McKinnell, who followed the work closely. "They swam and ate and developed beautiful eyes and hind limbs," he says. But then, halfway through metamorphosis, they died.

[7] Scientists who have focused their cloning efforts on embryonic tissue have met with greater success. In 1952 researchers in Pennsylvania successfully cloned a live frog from an embryonic cell. Three decades later, researchers were learning to do the same with such mammals as sheep and calves. "What's new," observes University of Wisconsin animal scientist Neal First, "is not cloning mammals. It's cloning

mammals from cells that are not embryonic."

[8] The disadvantage of embryonic cloning is that you don't know what you are getting. With adult-cell cloning, you can wait to see how well an individual turns out before deciding to clone it. Cloning also has the potential to make genetic engineering more efficient. Once you produce an animal with a desired trait—a pig with a human immune system, perhaps—you could make many copies.

[9] To create Dolly, the Roslin team concentrated on arresting the cell cycle—the series of choreographed steps all cells go through in the process of dividing. In Dolly's case, the cells the scientists wanted to clone came from the udder of a pregnant sheep. To stop them from dividing, researchers starved the cells of nutrients for a week. In response, the cells fell into a slumbering state that resembled deep hibernation.

[10] At this point, Wilmut and his colleagues switched to a mainstream cloning technique known as nuclear transfer. First they removed the nucleus of an unfertilized egg, while leaving the surrounding cytoplasm intact. Then they placed the egg next to the nucleus of a quiescent donor cell and applied gentle pulses of electricity. These pulses prompted the egg to accept the new nucleus—and all the DNA it contained—as though it were its own. They also triggered a burst of biochemical activity, jump-starting the process of cell division. A week later, the embryo that had already started growing into Dolly was implanted in the uterus of a surrogate ewe.

[11] An inkling that this approach might work, says Wilmut, came from the success his team experienced in producing live lambs from embryonic clones. "Could we do it again with an adult cell?" wondered Wilmut.

[12] It was a high-risk project, and in the beginning Wilmut proceeded with great secrecy, limiting his core team to four scientists. His caution proved to be justified; the scientists failed far more often than they succeeded. Out of 277 tries, the researchers eventually produced only 29 embryos that survived longer than six days. Of these, all died before birth except Dolly, whose historic entry into the world was witnessed by a handful of researchers and a veterinarian.

[13] Rumors that something had happened in Roslin started circulating in scientific circles a few weeks ago. It was only last week, when the rumors were confirmed and the details of the experiment revealed, that the real excitement erupted. Cell biologists, like everybody else, were struck by the simple boldness of the experiment. But what intrigued them even more was what it suggested about how cells work.

[14] Like most scientists who score major breakthroughs, Wilmut and his colleagues have raised more questions than they have answered. Among the most pressing are questions about Dolly's health. She is seven months old and appears to be perfectly fine, but no one knows if she will develop problems later on. For one thing, it is possible that Dolly may not live as long as other sheep. After all, observes NCI's Stewart, "she came from a six-year-old cell. Will she exhibit signs of aging prematurely?" In addition, as the high rate of spontaneous abortion suggests, cloning sometimes damages DNA. As a result, Dolly could develop any number of diseases that could shorten her life.

[15] Indeed, cloning an adult mammal is still a difficult, cumbersome business—so much so that even agricultural and biomedical applications of the technology could be years away. PPL Therapeutics, the small biotechnical firm based in Edinburgh that provided a third of the funding to create Dolly, has its eye on the pharmaceutical market. Cloning, says PPL's managing director Ron James, could provide an efficient way of creating flocks of sheep that have been genetically engineered to produce milk laced with valuable enzymes and drugs. Among the pharmaceuticals PPL is looking at is a potential treatment for

cystic fibrosis.

[16] Nobody at Roslin or PPL is talking about cloning humans. Even if they were, their procedure is obviously not practical—not as long as dozens of surrogates need to be impregnated for each successful birth. And that is probably a good thing, because it gives the public time to digest the news—and policymakers time to find ways to prevent abuses without blocking scientific progress. If the policymakers succeed, and if their guidelines win international acceptance, it may take a lot longer than the editorial writers and talk-show hosts think before a human clone emerges—even from the shadows of some offshore renegade lab. "How long?" asks PPL's James. "Hopefully, an eternity."

Language Points and Chinese Translations

第23课 克隆时代

[1] landmark 里程碑/headline (报刊的)大字标题,头条新闻/to scream 令人震惊,大叫大嚷/to pull off 努力实现/ewe 母羊/mammary gland 乳腺/embryologist 胚胎学家/frisky 活泼的,欢跃的/to score 获得,取得/unsettling 扰乱的,使人不安的/startling 令人吃惊的,惊人的/off-spring 后代,产物/carbon copy 极相像的人或物/counterfeit 仿造品/in essence 本质上,实质上/identical 完全相同的,同一的,相等的/twin 孪生,双胎

上周末在《自然》杂志上发表的具有里程碑意义的论文,证实了数天以来令人震惊的报刊头条新闻:苏格兰爱丁堡附近的罗斯林研究所的研究人员们确实极尽努力实现了许多专家原来认为在科学上不可能做到的事情。胚胎学家 Ian Wilmut 和他的同事们用成年母羊乳腺的一个细胞培育出了一只活泼的羔羊,名叫多莉。在生殖技术上取得的这一进步既使人惊奇,又令人担忧。多莉与常规方式生产的后代不相同,她不只是酷似生母,她是一个复制品,一个实验室里的仿造物。她被仿制得如此精确,从本质上来说她就是其母亲的孪生姐妹。

[2] ingenious 巧妙的,精巧的,机灵的/to figure out 解决,计算出/import 意义,含意,重要性/to clone 克隆,指无性繁殖,无性生殖

使苏格兰小组在以前许多人失败之处获得成功的是一种诀窍,它既精巧又简单,任何有技巧的实验室技术员都能掌握它——而且它既美妙又有危险性:一旦 Wilmut 和他的同事们解决了如何跨越这个生物学上的障碍的问题,他们确信其他人就会跟着仿效。尽管罗斯林的研究人员们努力奋斗了十多年才取得了这一惊人的进展,但是全世界的政治和宗教领袖们很快就掌握了其重要的意义:如果科学家能克隆羊,那么他们也可能克隆人。

[3] exotic 异乎寻常的,奇异的,吸引人的/mammal 哺乳动物/myriad 无数的,极大数量的/to propagate 繁殖/species 物种,种类/organ 器官/transplant 移植

毫无疑问,这种异乎寻常的繁殖工程形式将成为非常有用的工具,特别是克隆成年哺乳动物的技能开创了无数令人兴奋的前景,从繁殖濒危动物的物种到为需要移植器官的病人生产可以替代的器官。

[4] dairy 牛奶场/champion 第一流的,优胜的/rancher 大牧场主或管理人

农业也一定受益。例如牛奶场的工人们能够克隆一流的奶牛,使较小的牛群能够生产出更多的牛奶。牧羊场主们也能以相同的方式克隆最好的产羔羊和产毛羊。

[5] apocalyptic 预示大动乱的,预示世界末日恐怖景象的/scenario 电影剧本,剧情说明/to proliferate 使激增,使扩散/to resurrect 使复活,使再现,复兴,恢复/to quip 讥讽,嘲弄

但是也很容易想象,该克隆技术会被滥用。当罗斯林研究所的消息传开时,出现了大量描写世界末日恐怖景象的电影剧本。新闻工作者们严肃认真地报道了种种可能性,如:处女生育,使死者复活,妇女自己生产自己等。华盛顿大学密苏里州圣路易斯分校细胞生物学家 Ursula Goodenough 在《纽约时报》的头版位置上讥讽说,假如克隆技术日趋完善,"则就不再需要男人了"。

[6] starfish 海星,海盘车/invertebrate 无脊椎动物/asexual reproduction 无性生殖/tantalizingly 惹弄人的,可

· 117 ·

望而不可即的,引起尚无法实现的希望/tadpole 蝌蚪/hind 后部的,后面的/limb 肢/metamorphosis 变形,变态,变状

好久以来科学家们就梦想做罗斯林小组所做成的事情。既然海星和其他无脊椎动物能进行无性生殖,为什么就不能扩大到其他种类的动物呢?在 20 世纪 80 年代,费城的发展生物学家在现在叫阿勒格尼医学科技大学里几乎接近了这个可望而不可即的目标。他们用成年青蛙的红细胞培育出了一群活跃的蝌蚪。明尼苏达大学的细胞生物学家 Robert McKinnell 以前密切跟踪过该项工作,现在回忆起来,那些蝌蚪给他留下了深刻的印象。他说,"它们游来游去,吃食,并长出了美丽的眼睛和后肢。"可是随后,它们在发育变形中途都死掉了。

[7] to focus on 使聚焦,集中,注视/embryorlic 胚胎的/tissue (生理细胞)组织/calf 小牛,复数形式:calves

那些把克隆的努力主要集中于胚胎组织的科学家们已经取得了较大的成功。1952 年宾夕法尼亚州的研究人员们成功地从胚胎细胞中克隆了一只活生生的青蛙。30 年后,研究人员们学会了在羊和牛等哺乳动物身上进行相同的克隆技术。威斯康星大学的动物科学家 Neal First 评论说,"新奇的事物并不是克隆出了哺乳动物,而是从非胚胎细胞中克隆出了哺乳动物"。

[8] genetic engineering 遗传工程/trait 品质,特性,性格/immune 有免疫力的

胚胎克隆的不利之处是你不知道通过克隆会得到什么。利用成年动物的细胞克隆,你在决定进行克隆之前能够预见到产生的个体是如何好,而且克隆还有可能使遗传工程更加有效。一旦你生产出了具有所期望的特性的动物——如一头带有人类免疫系统的猪,也许你就可以制造出许多复制品。

[9] to concentrate on 使集中于/to arrest 抑制,控制/choreographed 细心设计,筹划的/to go through 经历,经受,通过/udder (牛,羊等的)乳腺,乳房/pregnant 怀孕的,怀胎的/to starve 使挨饿,使饥饿/nutrient 营养物,滋养品/slumbering 微睡,处于休眠状态/hibernation 冬眠,越冬/to resemble 像,类似

为了培育出多莉羊,罗斯林小组重点是抑制细胞的发育周期——即在细胞分裂过程中所有细胞都经历的一系列仔细设计的步骤。就多莉羊这一实例而言,科学家们想要克隆的细胞是来自于一只怀孕母羊的乳腺。为了阻止其细胞分裂,研究人员们停止对细胞进行营养供应一个星期,这引起的反应是:细胞就像深度冬眠那样处于休眠状态。

[10] to switch to 转换,变换,转向/mainstream 主流,主要倾向/unfertilized 未受精的/cytoplasm 细胞质/intact 未受损的,完整的,未经触动的/quiescent 休眠的,静止期的/donor 供体,给予体/to prompt 促使,激起,引起/DNA=deoxyribonucleic acid 脱氧核糖核酸/to trigger 激发起,引起/embryo 胚胎,(受孕后的)胎儿/uterus 子宫(=womb)/surrogate 代用品,代理

在这一时刻,Wilmut 和他的同事们转而采用被称为核转移方式为主的克隆技术。首先他们在一个未受精卵中去掉其细胞核,使周围的细胞质完整无损,然后把该卵细胞放置在休眠的供体细胞的旁边,并给以轻微的电脉冲。这些电脉冲激发卵细胞接受该新细胞核——以及它所包含的所有 DNA——就好像是它自己的那样。电脉冲同时激发了生物化学活度,触发细胞分裂的过程。一周后,已开始生长成多莉的胚胎被移植进代孕母羊的子宫中。

[11] inkling 略知,模糊的想法,暗示/approach 方法,处理

Wilmut 说,他的小组从胚胎克隆产生出活羊所获得的成功中得到启示,这种克隆方法可能行得通。Wilmut 想知道,"我们是否也能用成年体细胞进行克隆?"

[12] to survive 活下来,幸存/to witness 目击,目睹,经历/veterinarian 兽医

这是一项高风险的计划。开始阶段,Wilmut 进行得非常秘密,把他的核心小组限定为 4 位科学家。他的小心谨慎证明是完全正确的,科学家们的失败要比成功多得多,这是常事。研究人员们在 277 次试验中最终仅生产出了 29 个胚胎,而且仅存活了六天多,其中,除了多莉外,其余的都在出生前就死掉了。几位研究人员和一位兽医目睹了多莉来到世上这一具有历史性意义的过程。

[13] to erupt 爆发,迸发/to strike 打动,感动,给……以印象,其过去分词是 struck/to intrigue 引起……的兴趣,好奇心

数周前,在罗斯林小组所发生的事就在科学界传开来了。直到上周,这些传说才得到证实,实验的详细情况也随之透露出来。这时,人们才感到真正地兴奋与激动。细胞生物学家像大家一样,被进行这种实验的果断和勇敢精神深受感动。但是更加引发他们兴趣的是该项实验揭示了细胞活动的方式。

[14] NCI=National Cancer Institute 美国国家癌症研究所/to exhibit 显示,显出,表示/aging 老化,变陈/prematurely 过早地,不到期的,早熟地/spontaneous 自发的,自动的/abortion 流产,小产,早产

Wilmut 和他的同事们像大多数取得重大突破的科学家一样,提出的问题多于解答的问题。目前最迫切的问题是关于多莉的健康。她仅七个月,看起来已长得很好,但是人们谁也不知道她今后会发生什么问题。首先,多莉很可能没有其他羊活得长。美国国家癌症研究所的 Stewart 评论说,"她来自于一个六岁羊的细胞,她是否会过早地显示出衰老的迹象呢?"而且正像高比率自然流产所显示的那样,有时候克隆技术会损伤 DNA。最终,多莉羊可能将会患上一些疾病从而导致缩短寿命。

[15] cumbersome 麻烦的,拖累的/therapeutics 治疗学/to have one's eye on 密切注视着/pharmaceutical adj. 医药的,药物的,药用的,n. 药品,药物/to lace 使带有活气,风味,用带子束紧/enzyme (生化)酶/cystic fibrosis 囊性纤维变性

确实,克隆成年的哺乳动物仍然是一件如此困难而又麻烦的事——以至于该技术在农业和生物医学上的应用还得等上好几年。PPL 治疗研究公司是位于爱丁堡的一家小型生物技术公司。该公司为研制多莉羊提供了三分之一的资金,它现在正密切注视着医药市场。该公司总裁 Rorl James 说,克隆技术能够以有效的方法培育成批的羊群,并使这些羊经过遗传工程处理而生产出含有有用的酶和药物成分的奶。而对囊性纤维变性具有潜在治疗作用的药物正是 PPL 公司所关注的众多药物之一。

[16] to impregnate 使怀孕,使妊娠/to digest 消化,领会,领悟/guideline 指导路线,方针,准则,指标/offshore 离岸的,向海的,国外的/renegade 背叛的,背教的,反抗传统习惯的/eternity 永恒,无穷,永无尽期

在罗斯林小组和 PPL 公司里还无人谈及克隆人的事。即使他们谈论了,他们的做法也很明显是不切实际的——对于每一次成功的生育,并不是只要几十名代孕妇代为怀孕就算了事。当然这也许是件好事,因为它可以让公众有时间去领悟这一消息——也可以让制定政策的人有时间找到预防滥用的方法而又不阻碍科学的发展。如果制定政策的人成功了,他们的指导方针也在国际上获得认可,则在海外某个背离传统道德观念的实验室的隐蔽地方出现了克隆人,其花费的时间要比社论撰写人和电视访谈节目主持人所预想的要长得多。PPL 公司的 James 问,"到底要多久?""很有希望,但永无尽期。"

Exercises

I. **Answer the following questions:**

1. According to the text, what happened at the Roslin Institute?

2. Why is Dolly different from offspring produced in the usual fashion?

3. Why does the author say that the form of reproductive engineering will become a very useful tool?

4. How do you know that scientists have long dreamed of doing what the Roslin team did?

5. What is the disadvantage of embryonic cloning? And what is the advantage of adult-cell cloning?

6. How did the Roslin team create Dolly?

7. According to the text, what is the most pressing question about Dolly?

8. Is cloning an adult mammal very difficult?

9. Why is cloning humans not practical according to the text?

10. Do you think that scientists can be allowed to clone animals? How about cloning humans?

II. Translate the following words and phrases:

A. From Chinese into English.
1. 胚胎生物学家
2. 乳腺
3. 生殖技术
4. 酶
5. 濒危动物物种
6. 红细胞
7. 哺乳动物
8. 生化活度
9. 休眠状态
10. 核转移
11. 供体细胞
12. 人类免疫系统

B. From English into Chinese.
1. offspring produced in the usual fashion
2. to take after
3. a laboratory counterfeit
4. in essence
5. to cross the biological barrier
6. breakthrough
7. asexual reproduction
8. metamorphosis
9. embryonic tissue
10. to arrest the cell cycle
11. a mainstream cloning technique
12. pulses of electricity
13. a high-risk project
14. to exhibit signs of aging prematurely
15. the pharmaceutical market
16. a potential treatment
17. policymakers
18. talk-show hosts

III. Translate the following passage into Chinese:

"Cloning is a tool for achieving a new understanding of biology at the most fundamental level. Our objective is not to clone a human being, but to cure human disease." said Beatrice Mintz of Fox Chase Institute for Cancer Research.

Already biologists studying the cell's inner workings and the various methods of cloning have made discoveries that may ultimately lead to breakthroughs in the fight against cancer, control of the aging process, and the conquest of more than 100 presently incurable human genetic diseases. Cloning may also bring about new strains of livestock. At Yale, for example, Markert is working toward the cloning of such animals as cattle and pigs.

To restrict cloning-related research would mean closing the door on an important area of knowledge. To continue to probe the secrets of the cell, however, is perhaps to uncover the secret of human cloning. And, given the nature of man, if it can be done it will be done.

[aging process 老化过程/genetic diseases 遗传疾病/new strains of livestock 牲畜的新品种/closing the door on 关闭……的大门,意指拒绝利用/given 鉴于,考虑到]

---- ***Well-known Sayings*** ----

△ *The reason that men oppose progress is not that they hate progress but that they love inertia.*

△ *The art of progress is to preserve order amid change, and to preserve change amid order.*

△ *There are two kinds of men who never amount to much—those who cannot do what they are told and those who can do nothing else.*

Lesson 24

Scientific Researches on Body's Rhythms

[1] Have you ever suffered from jet-lag, the fatigue and depression that comes from long hours spent in a jet aircraft travelling across the world over many time zones? Or like many people in northern European countries, have you ever suffered the dark depression of winter blues, the feelings of gloom that comes from facing the sombre December and January winter days under dark, cloudy skies? Maybe all you need is a little light—and merely on a small patch of your skin. In fact, in experiments investigating the effect of light in raising our spirits, American scientists have done all their research using light played on the back of the subjects' knees.

[2] What could be a key to jet-lag and winter blues is the hormone melatonin, which is known to regulate body rhythms. It is secreted as night falls and it can be used to help to overcome jet-lag and some sleep disorders. The low level of melatonin we experience in winter when light is dull and daylight hours are shorter is said to be a cause of that common feeling many people get in dull weather—winter depression.

[3] For years experts have experimented with treating jet-lag and seasonal affective disorder("winter depression") with light. They counsel victims to sit in front of lights simulating the sun's natural wavelengths to restore melatonin. In 1996, Diane Boivin and colleagues at Harvard Medical School found even dim reading lamps worked in this way.

[4] Exposure to light sets off a complex response inside the bodies of animals and humans. A university team in New York said they had found that shining light on the skin could re-set the body's internal clock. They chose the back of the knee because it was easy to reach and away from the eyes, which is where many scientists had believed circadian rhythm is determined. Circadian rhythms are the biological rhythms (or biorhythms) that occur in organisms regularly about once a day, such as sleeping and waking. These circadian rhythms have been shown to be altered by external factors in the environment such as light and noise which affect areas of the brain such as the pineal gland.

[5] New York scientists Dr Scott Campbell and Dr Patricia Murphy wanted to see if they could alter the body's internal rhythms by shining light on the skin. They were building on research indicating that, while light is important in setting the body clock, actually seeing it may not be the key factor. Blind people get jet-lag, too. And no cells have been found in the eyes of mammals that react to light in such a way.

[6] So Dr Murphy and Dr Campbell set up an experiment in which they shone light on the backs of some volunteers' knees. The 15 volunteers did not know whether or not they had been exposed to light thanks to thick blankets draped over their bodies. Measuring temperature changes, the researchers managed to shift the internal body rhythms of the volunteers who were exposed by up to three hours. They were unable to fully explain the results, but cited research showing that light can affect chemicals such as nitrous oxide, known to play a range of roles in body chemistry.

[7] "Timed bright-light exposure is an effective treatment for sleep and circadian rhythm disorders including jet-lag, shift work sleep disturbance, age-related insomnia and advanced-and delayed-sleep phase syndromes," the researchers said. Their findings could offer a way to treat these problems more

conveniently—perhaps even while the patient is asleep.

[8] The complexity of the body's internal clock is becoming increasingly clear to researchers, with light only one factor under investigation. Other research has indicated that a gene may help to govern the sleep cycle in mammals.

[9] Dr Murphy and Dr Campbell said daily small adjustments of the body's circadian rhythm clock is needed—and they may have shown that a little light on the skin is all it takes.

Language Points and Chinese Translations

第24课 对人体节奏的科学研究

[1] gloom 郁闷,忧闷/sombre 阴沉的,黯淡的/subject 被试验者

你是否得过时差综合征,也就是乘坐飞机长时间地在世界各地旅行跨越许多时区所产生的疲劳与抑郁? 或者你是否像北欧国家的许多人一样患过冬季忧郁症,也就是在12月和1月阴沉的冬季,面对着黯淡多云的天空所产生的郁闷情绪? 也许你所需要的是一点儿光线——仅照射在你的一小块皮肤上。实际上,美国科学家已经作了研究,用光线照射在被试验者的膝盖的后部,调查试验光线提高精神情绪的作用。

[2] hormone melatonin 荷尔蒙褪黑激素/rhythm 节奏,律动/to secrete 分泌/disorder 紊乱,凌乱,失调

能解除时差综合征和冬季忧郁症的关键是荷尔蒙褪黑激素,人们知道这种激素能够调节人体节奏。它在夜晚分泌,有助于治疗时差综合征和睡眠紊乱。在光线黯淡、日照短暂的冬季我们的褪黑激素分泌较少,据说这就是许多人在阴沉的天气普遍感觉到沉闷——冬季忧郁的一个原因。

[3] to counsel 劝告,忠告/victim 遭难者,受害者/to simulate 模拟,模仿/dim 黯淡,昏暗的

几年来专家们试验着用光线医治时差综合征和季节性情绪失调症(即冬季忧郁症)。他们劝告病患者坐在类似于太阳光自然波长的光线前以便恢复褪黑激素。1996年哈佛大学医学院的Diane Boivin和同事们发觉甚至黯淡的台灯也能起这样的作用。

[4] to set off 发动,推动,使……爆发/circadian 昼夜节奏的(24小时)生理节奏/biological 生物学的/organism 机体

动物和人体受到光的照射会引发复杂的反应。纽约一个大学的研究小组提出他们已经发现光照射在皮肤上能重新调整人体内的生物钟。他们之所以选择膝盖的后部做试验是因为光线容易照射到而眼睛又看不到。很多科学家相信在该部位可以确定人体的周期性节奏。周期性节奏是生物学节奏(或生物节奏),就像睡眠和苏醒一样,在人的机体内有规律地每天发生一次。研究表明这些周期性节奏随着外部环境因素的变化而改变,例如光和噪声就影响着松果体等一些大脑部位。

[5] 纽约的科学家Scott Campbell博士和Patricia Murphy博士想了解把光照射在皮肤上是否能改变人体的内部节奏。他们所作的研究表明,虽然光线在调节人体生物钟方面很重要,但是实际上并不是主要因素。盲人也会得时差综合征。现在尚未发现在哺乳动物的眼睛中有任何细胞能对光线作出这样的反应。

[6] to cite 引用,引证/nitrous oxide 一氧化二氮,氧化亚氮

所以,Murphy博士和Campbell博士进行了一次试验,他们把光照射在一些志愿受试者的膝盖后部,15个志愿受试者由于全身盖着厚厚的毛毯,并不知道是否被照射了光线。研究人员通过测试体温变化,成功地改变了受到光照射达三个小时的志愿受试者们体内的生物节奏。研究人员们不能充分解释这些结果,但是研究显示光能影响人体内像一氧化二氮这样的化学物质。人们已经知道这些化学物质在人体化学变化中能发挥一系列的作用。

[7] disturbance 失调,障碍,纷乱/syndrome 综合病症,症候群/conveniently 便利地,方便地

"定时的强光接触能有效地治疗睡眠失调和人体周期节奏紊乱,它们包括时差综合征,轮班工作所引起的睡

眠障碍,与年龄有关的失眠症,睡眠阶段提前和推迟引发的综合征等,"研究人员这样说。他们的调查结果为处理这些问题提供了一种更为方便的手段——甚至在患者熟睡期间也可以进行治疗。

[8] to govern 支配,调节

研究人员们已经越来越清楚地意识到了人体内部生物钟的复杂性,而光线仅是调查研究中的一个因素。其他的研究已表明基因可能有助于调节哺乳动物的睡眠周期。

[9] adjustment 调整,调节

Murphy 博士和 Campbell 博士说每天都需要对人体的生物钟进行微调——他们可能已经显示,在皮肤上照射少量的光线就足以进行微调了。

Exercises

I. **Answer the following questions:**

1. What is jet-lag?

2. What is the dark depression of winter blues?

3. What does the word "blues" refer to in the text?

4. What is the key to jet-lag and winter blues?

5. What is the function of the hormone melatonin?

6. What are the biological rhythms?

7. What is important in setting the body clock according to New York scientists?

8. What experiment did scientists do to show that light can shift the internal body rhythms?

9. What is an effective treatment for sleep and circadian rhythm disorders?

10. What helps to govern the sleep cycle in mammals according to researchers?

II. **Translate the following words and phrases:**

A. From Chinese into English.

1. 人体节奏
2. 时差综合征
3. 时区
4. 荷尔蒙褪黑激素
5. 受试验者
6. 有效的治疗方法
7. 基因

8. 睡眠周期 _____

B. From English into Chinese.

1. winter blues _____
2. a small patch of _____
3. to raise one's spirits _____
4. on the back of _____
5. to regulate body rhythms _____
6. victims _____
7. to simulate the sun's natural wavelengths _____
8. to set off a complex response _____
9. circadian rhythms _____
10. external factors _____
11. shift work sleep disturbance _____
12. complexity _____
13. investigation _____
14. small adjustment _____

Ⅲ. Translate the following passage into Chinese:

Your brainwaves may be used to check out whether you are busy, tired or doing your work properly.

Psychologist Arthur F. Kramer, at the University of Illinois, tested volunteers working on arithmetic problems. He found that he could predict their performance from the strength of the brain's electrical activity. This is measured through the scalp.

The future? Bosses could measure brain activity through the scalp and tell whether a worker is performing well, working hard, or too tired to do the job properly. Ongoing computer analysis could tell whether a worker, such as an air traffic controller, is seeing all the activity they have to monitor clearly enough.

[the brain's electrical activity 脑电波运动/scalp 头皮/an air traffic controller 空中飞行调度员/monitor *v.* 监控]

Well-known Sayings

△ *Never stop reaching for more.*

Do more than exist——live.

Do more than touch——feel.

Do more than look——observe.

Do more than read——absorb.

Do more than listen——understand.

Unit 7　Robots

第7单元　机器人

　　——— Robots are generally defined as devices or machines which can automatically perform repetitive tasks, and replace human efforts (as in industrial assembly lines). They can be operated by remote control or computer program. Their abilities include operating mechanical limbs, sensing and manipulating their environments and moving around.

　　——— Many people assume that all robots are characters in science fiction movies. In fact, robots are used all over the world, right now! They can build cars, clean houses, navigate Mars, help soldiers and doctors, entertain and care for children, feed and bathe the elderly and incapacitated, explore other planets, and even make a scientific discovery.

　　——— The artificial intelligence of the robots is projected to go up in the future and they will be able to think on their own. So, while current robots are intelligent, they must be closely monitored.

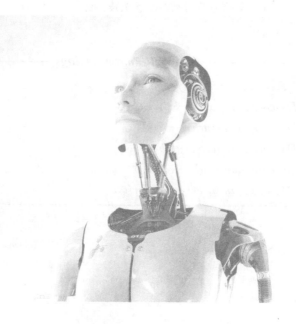

Lesson 25

Robot Wars: The Rise of Artificial Intelligence

[1] The robots are not so much coming; they have arrived. But instead of dominating humanity with superior logic and strength, they threaten to create an underclass of people who are left without human contact. The rise of robots in the home, in the workplace and in warfare needs to be supervised and controlled by ethical guidelines which limit how they can be used in sensitive scenarios such as baby-sitting, caring for the elderly, and combat, a leading scientist warns today.

[2] Sales of professional and personal service robots worldwide were estimated to have reached about 5.5 million this year—and are expected to more than double to 11.5 million next year—yet there is little or no control over how these machines are used. Some help busy professionals entertain children; other machines feed and bathe the elderly and incapacitated.

[3] Professor Noel Sharkey, an expert on artificial intelligence based at the University of Sheffield, warns that robots are being introduced to potentially sensitive situations that could lead to isolation and lack of human contact, because of the tendency to leave robots alone with their charges for long periods.

[4] "We need to look at guidelines for a cut-off so we have a limit to the contact with robots," Professor Sharkey said. "Some robots designed to look after children now are so safe that parents can leave their children with them for hours, or even days."

[5] More than a dozen companies based in Japan and South Korea manufacture robot "companions" and carers for children. For example, NEC has tested its cute-looking personal robot PaPeRo on children: the device lives at home with a family, recognizes their faces, can mimic their behaviour and be programmed to tell jokes, all the while exploring the house. Many robots are designed as toys, but they can also take on childcare roles by monitoring the movements of a child and communicating with a parent in another room, or even another building, through wireless computer connection or mobile phone.

[6] "Research into service robots has demonstrated a close bonding and attachment by children, who, in most cases, prefer a robot to a teddy bear," Professor Sharkey said. "Short-term exposure can provide an enjoyable and entertaining experience that creates interest and curiosity. But because of the physical safety that robot minders provide, children could be left without human contact for many hours a day or perhaps several days, and the possible psychological impact of the varying degrees of social isolation on development is unknown." Less playful robots are being developed to look after elderly people. Secom makes a computer called My Spoon which helps disabled people to eat food from a table. Sanyo has built an electric bathtub robot that automatically washes and rinses someone suffering from movement disability.

[7] "At the other end of the age spectrum [to child care], the relative increase in many countries in the population of the elderly relative to available younger care-givers has spurred the development of elder-care robots," Professor Sharkey said.

[8] "These robots can help the elderly to maintain independence in their own homes, but their presence could lead to the risk of leaving the elderly in the exclusive care of machines without sufficient human contact. The elderly need the human contact that is often provided only by caregivers and people

performing day-to-day tasks for them."

[9] In the journal *Science*, Professor Sharkey calls for ethical guidelines to cover all aspects of robotic technology, not just in the home and workplace, but also on the battlefield, where lethal robots such as the missile-armed Predator drones used in Iraq and Afghanistan are already deployed with lethal effect. The US Future Combat Systems project aims to use robots as "force multipliers", with a single soldier initiating large-scale ground and aerial attacks by a robot droid army. "Robots for care and for war represent just two of many ethically problematic areas that will soon arise from the rapid increase and spreading diversity of robotics applications," Professor Sharkey said. "Scientists and engineers working in robotics must be mindful of the potential dangers of their work, and public and international discussion is vital in order to set policy guidelines for ethical and safe application before the guidelines set themselves."

[10] The call for controls over robots goes back to the 1940s when the science-fiction author Isaac Asimov drew up his famous three laws of robotics. The first rule stated that robots must not harm people; the second that they must obey the commands of people provided they do not conflict with the first law; and the third law was that robots must attempt to avoid harming themselves provided this was not in conflict with the two other laws.

[11] Asimov wrote a collection of science fiction stories called *I, Robot* which exploited the issue of machines and morality. He wanted to counter the long history of fictional accounts of dangerous automatons—from the Jewish Golem to Mary Shelley's Frankenstein—and used his three laws as a literary device to exploit the ethical issues arising from the human interaction with non-human, intelligent beings. But late 20th-century predictions about the rise of machines endowed with superior artificial intelligence have not been realised, although robot scientists have given their mechanical protégés quasi-intelligent traits such as simple speech recognition, emotional expression and face recognition.

[12] Professor Starkey believes that even dumb robots need to be controlled. "I'm not suggesting like Asimov to put ethical rules into robots, but just to have guidelines on how robots are used." he said.

Language Points and Chinese Translations

第25课　机器人战争：人工智能的崛起

[1] 机器人不是很快就要来了，而是已经来了。但是它们不是在逻辑和力量上支配人类，而是造就一个完全被隔离没有人际接触的低下层人群而构成对人类的威胁。一个有影响力的科学家警告说，机器人在家庭、工作场所和战争中的兴起需要受到道德准则的监督和控制，对于机器人在诸如照看小孩、照料老人和战争等一些敏感处境中的应用要加以限定。

[2] 今年全世界专业机器人和个人服务型机器人估计已达550万台——并且有望在明年增长一倍多，达到1 150万台——然而，目前对任何使用这些机器人则很少或根本就没有控制。有些机器人帮助忙碌的职业人士陪孩子娱乐，另一些机器人则为老年人和残疾人喂食和洗澡。

[3] to leave…alone 不管，不理会/charges 这里指被托管或照顾的人或事物。如：The nurse took her charges to help in gleaning. 保育员带领她照管的孩子们去帮助拾麦穗。

谢菲尔德大学的人工智能专家诺埃尔·夏基教授警告说，机器人正在被引进潜在敏感的处境中，即可能导致人们孤独，以及相互间缺乏交流接触，因为被照管的人往往长时间只和机器人相处而无他人问津。

[4] 夏基教授说:"我们需要考虑用一些准则来规定一个终止点,以便使与机器人的接触有个限度。现在有些用来照管孩子的机器人设计得非常安全,以至父母可以让孩子们和机器人待在一起数小时,甚至好几天。"

[5] 在日本和韩国有10多家公司制造机器人"伙伴"和照管孩子的机器人保姆。例如,日本电气公司(NEC)就对专为儿童制造的外形漂亮可爱的个人机器人PaPeRo进行了测试:该款装置的机器人与家庭成员生活在一起,能辨识家庭成员的面孔,模仿他们的行为,被编制程序后还会讲笑话,并始终如一地照看着房屋。很多机器人被设计成玩具,但它们也能起到照看孩子的作用:监视孩子的一举一动,并且通过无线电脑连接或通过移动电话与处在另一个房间甚至另一幢大楼里的家长进行联络。

[6] 夏基教授说:"对服务型机器人的研究表明,孩子与机器人关系亲密,并对机器人有依恋感。在大多数情况下,孩子们更喜爱机器人而不是泰迪熊。与机器人短时间的接触能给人带来愉悦的感受,从而激发孩子的兴趣和好奇心。但是由于机器人保姆能给孩子们提供身体上的安全保护,这就使孩子们一天很多小时或者好几天都不与人接触,孩子们不同程度上与社会隔离对其成长可能造成的心理影响现在还不甚了解。"目前正在研发娱乐性较弱的机器人用以照顾老年人。日本西科姆集团(Secom)制造的一款名叫"My Spoon"的机器人,能帮助残疾人在桌边进食。三洋公司已经制造了一种电动浴缸机器人,能自动地为行动不方便的人擦洗身体。

[7] 夏基教授说:"需要照顾的既有小孩还有老年人。在很多国家,相对于可提供照料服务的年轻护工人来说,老年人口增长较快,这就刺激了对护理老年人的机器人的研发。"

[8] "这些机器人能够帮助老年人在自己家中自理,但是这些机器人的存在有可能导致这样的危险,即老年人完全处在机器人的照料之下而缺乏足够的人际接触。老年人需要有人际交往,而这常常只能由护工和照管他们日常生活的人提供。"

[9] 夏基教授在《科学》杂志上呼吁对机器人技术的各个方面进行道德规范,不仅是在家中和工作场所,而且还在战场上。例如在伊拉克和阿富汗所使用的装备导弹的"捕食者"无人机这类机器人杀手已经部署于战场,具有致命的杀伤力。美国未来战斗系统项目旨在把机器人用作"武力倍增器",单个士兵就可利用一支机器人部队发动大规模的地面和空中打击。夏基教授说:"照管型机器人和战斗型机器人只代表了伦理问题的诸多领域中的两个。这些领域不久就会随着机器人技术应用的迅速增加和日益多样化而呈现出来。从事机器人技术研究的科学家和工程师必须注意他们的工作可能带来的危险,同时公众舆论和国际讨论也是极其重要的,以便为合乎伦理和安全应用机器人技术制定政策规范,而不至于处于被动应付的局面。"

[10] 对机器人加以控制的呼吁可以追溯到上世纪40年代,当时科幻小说作家艾萨克·阿西莫夫提出了著名的机器人三定律。第一条规定机器人决不能伤害人类;第二条规定机器人必须服从人类的命令,但以这些命令不与第一条定律冲突为条件;第三条规定机器人必须尽力避免伤害自己,但不得违背前两条定律。

[11] automatons 自动装置,机械般动作的人或物/Golem(16世纪希伯来传说中)有生命的假人,机器人/Frankenstein 英国作家玛丽·雪莱于1818年所著小说中的生理学研究者(他创造了一个怪物,而自己被它毁灭),比喻自己所创造而无法控制的事物,作法自毙者,或指人形的怪物/to be endowed with 赋予,具有,赋有/protégés 被保护人,mechanical protégés 本文中意指被科学家赋予人工智能,能接受指令的机械装置,即机器人。

阿西莫夫写了一部科幻小说集,名叫《我,机器人》。该小说探讨了机器人和道德的问题。他想一反长期以来科幻小说把机器人描写成危险的形象——从犹太传说中有生命的假人到玛丽·雪莱笔下的人形怪物——而是利用他的三条定律作为一种文学手段,探讨有关人类与非人类的智能物体互动交流中所产生的伦理问题。但是20世纪后期有关具有高级人工智能的机器人将崛起的预言并没有实现,尽管机器人科学家已经赋予了这些受惠于他们的机械装置以准智能的特性,诸如简单的言语识别、情绪表达和面容识别等能力。

[12] 夏基教授认为,即使是哑巴机器人也必须受到控制。他说:"我并不像阿西莫夫那样提出建议为机器人制定伦理准则,而只是对如何使用机器人进行规范。"

Exercises

I. **Answer the following questions:**

1. What are the sensitive scenarios in which the robots are used?

2. What is the sales quantity of professional and personal service robots worldwide estimated this year? And how about the next year?

3. Why are robots being introduced to potentially sensitive situations that could lead to isolation and lack of human contact?

4. Why did Professor Sharkey say: "We need to look at guidelines for a cut-off so we have a limit to the contact with robots."?

5. Say something about the personal robot PaPeRo made by NEC.

6. What has the research into service robots demonstrated?

7. What has spurred the development of elder-care robots?

8. Where does Professor Sharkey call for ethical guidelines to cover robotic technology in the journal *Science*?

9. Why does the US Future Combat Systems project aim to use robots as "force multipliers"?

10. When did Issac Asimov put forward his famous three laws of robotics?

11. What did the science fiction stories *I, Robot* exploit?

12. Why should we put ethical rules into robots and also have guidelines on how robots are used?

II. **Translate the following words and phrases:**

A. From Chinese into English.
1. 人工智能
2. 道德准则
3. 敏感处境
4. 专业机器人和个人服务型机器人
5. 外形漂亮可爱的机器人
6. 兴趣和好奇心
7. 心理影响

8. 老龄人口 _____
9. 无人驾驶飞机 _____
10. 致命的杀伤力 _____
11. 照管型机器人和战斗型机器人 _____
12. 伦理问题 _____
13. 言语识别、情绪表达和面容识别 _____

B. From English into Chinese.
1. with superior logic and strength _____
2. the elderly and incapacitated _____
3. isolation and lack of human contact _____
4. to leave…alone _____
5. to mimic one's behaviour _____
6. in most cases _____
7. an enjoyable and entertaining experience _____
8. to be in the care of _____
9. without sufficient human contact _____
10. to call for _____
11. to initiate large-scale ground and aerial attacks _____
12. to go back to _____
13. science-fiction author _____
14. to conflict with _____
15. to be endowed with _____
16. quasi-intelligent traits _____
17. to put ethical rules into robots _____

Ⅲ. Translate the following passage into Chinese:

Foster-Miller is a company fielding Armed Unmanned Ground Vehicles (AUGVs). Three Swords robots-tracked devices the size of a chest of drawers fitted with light machine guns—were tested in Iraq last summer by the US army. Apparently they were a success. The company is now promoting a heavily armed version called Maars, which, according to the brochure, can be programmed to recognise no-fire zones.

"The robot hasn't fallen over once," says David Byers, assistant program manager for the Mule. "In fact, last summer in testing, it was being used to pull soldiers out of a ditch."

In the past five years, military use of robotic systems has increased dramatically. The US army alone has fielded more than 6,000, many of them in Iraq and Afghanistan. They are mostly used to conduct reconnaissance and disarm explosives, but there are regular news reports of Uncrewed Aerial Vehicles (UAVs) performing missile strikes on insurgents they were monitoring.

"A lot has been learned from UAVs," says David Chang at West Point Military Academy. "UGVs are almost a decade behind UAVs in development and the technological challenges are far greater. Picture the difference for a UAV at 20,000 feet with no obstacles, and contrast that with a UGV, which must navigate in a dense urban environment. Sensors, fusion of information, detecting negative obstacles and real-time control is imperative to ensure safety."

Byers says autonomous convoy experiments with the Mule, where the UGVs follow each other in a flocking pattern, have been going well. "If the robot is lost, inertial navigation systems can put it out of harm's way. If the operator is taken out—injured, killed or loses contact—then control can be transferred to another authorised party." The reaction from the US army has been overwhelmingly positive.

The British army would not comment on whether it plans to use armed robots, but it already incorporates many of the unarmed models in its operations. Stefan Kern, one of the organizers of the European Land Robot Trial, says."The German army is strongly investigating the use of unmanned ground vehicles, but armed robots are not the focus of this process. Short-term realisable robots are the major challenge at the moment."

No one thinks the robots will be completely autonomous any time soon. Chang says."There are still challenges to be overcome in situational awareness and tactical behaviours. When these units are eventually fielded, there will always be a human in the loop to make the tough decisions." Byers adds:"There will always be a soldier involved, at least part-time."

[Armed Unmaned Ground Vehicles 武装无人地面车辆/Swords robots-tracked devices "剑"式侦察机器人战车/the Mule 这里指"骡"式战车/Uncrewed Aerials Vechicles 无人飞机/West Point Military Academy 西点军校/detecting negative obstacles 判明壕沟/realtime control 实时控制]

Well-known Sayings

△ *Intellectuals solve problems, geniuses prevent them.*

△ *Obstacles are those frightful things you see when you take your eyes off the goal.*

△ *What you get by achieving your goals is not as important as what you become by achieving your goals.*

Lesson 26

Robot Scientist "Adam" Solves Genetic Problems

[1] A robot has become the first of its kind to make a scientific discovery by solving a problem that human researchers have failed to crack for decades.

[2] The robot, called Adam, was able to work out where an important gene would be located and to develop experiments to prove its theory. It had been challenged to identify a gene in yeast for which its human counterparts had been searching since at least the 1960s. The robot, devised at Aberystwyth University, was able to identify the gene, which controls an enzyme crucial to the production of lysine, an amino acid essential to growth.

[3] It is thought that robots like Adam, and its successor, Eve, which is soon to be switched on at Aberystwyth, offer new hope in the battle against disease.

[4] Professor Ross King, who led the project, said that malaria and schistosomiasis, an infection caused by a parasitic worm, were among the diseases that robots should be able to help to defeat. Adam's discovery, he said, was likely to play an important role in developing new treatments for fungal diseases such as athlete's foot.

[5] Fungi have a different mechanism from that of animals to produce lysine, so if a drug can be developed that can disable the gene it should be possible to treat people for fungal diseases without affecting their ability to make lysine.

[6] Robots are proving increasingly valuable because they can carry out large numbers of repetitive tests that in a person would induce boredom and loss of concentration. To take Adam a step farther than simple automation the research team, which reported its findings in the journal *Science*, developed software that enabled the machine to search for the lysine gene in yeast.

[7] Professor King said that teaching the robot to develop a hypothesis was "the easy part". The biggest challenge was for Adam to put together a series of experiments that were sensitive enough to detect tiny changes in the yeast related to the gene. The changes measured by Adam enabled it to pinpoint the gene. Adam was equipped with a database on genes that are known to be present in bacteria, mice and people, so it knew roughly where it should search in the genetic material for the lysine gene in baker's yeast, Saccharomyces cerevisiae.

[8] Professor King said: "We hope to have teams of human and robot scientists working together in laboratories. Because biological organisms are so complex it is important that the details of biological experiments are recorded in great detail. This is difficult for human scientists, but easy for robot scientists. Yeast is well understood. It's been studied for over 100 years. We knew this enzyme must be there, but we didn't know where."

[9] Douglas Kell, of the Biotechnology and Biological Sciences Research Council, which funded the project, said: "Robot scientists could provide a useful tool for managing such data and knowledge, making scientific procedures easier and more efficient."

[10] —Researchers at Cornell University in the United States have developed a program that enables

computers to work out natural laws. In tests a computer observing a pendulum worked out the laws of motion developed by Isaac Newton. The success raises hope a computer will be able to identify natural laws that as yet are unknown.

[11] **Machines on the move**

[12] —The word "robot" was invented by Josef Capek. It was first used in the 1921 play *R.U.R.*, written by his brother, Karel, about a factory producing human-like machines.

[13] —Leonardo da Vinci made sketches of a "mechanical knight" now known as Leonardo's Robot.

[14] —The Elektro robot at the New York World Fair in 1939 was led by voice commands. It could move its head and arms and even smoke.

Language Points and Chinese Translations

第 26 课 机器人科学家"亚当"解决基因难题

[1] 一个机器人解决了人类研究员几十年都没有攻克的难题,因而成为第一个完成科学发现的机器人。

[2] 这个称作亚当的机器人能够判断出某一个重要基因所处的位置,同时展开实验以证实其理论。它已经接受过试验,识别酵母中的一个基因,而人类科学家至少从上世纪 60 年代起就一直在搜寻这个基因。阿伯里斯特维斯大学设计的这个机器人能够识别这个基因。该基因控制着对产生赖氨酸非常关键的一种酶,而赖氨酸对于生长发育来说是一种必不可少的氨基酸。

[3] 人们认为,像亚当和它的继任者夏娃这样的机器人,将不久就要在阿伯里斯特维斯大学开始运作,为人们与疾病斗争带来新的希望。

[4] to play an important role in 在……方面发挥重要作用/athlete's foot 脚癣,香港脚

领导这个项目的罗斯·金教授说,疟疾和血吸虫病这种由寄生虫引起的传染病,都在机器人能够帮助治愈的疾病之列。他说,亚当的发现很可能在针对脚癣这类真菌性疾病研发新的治疗方法中发挥重要的作用。

[5] to be different from 与……不同/to disable 使失效,使无能

真菌产生赖氨酸的机制和动物不同,所以,如果能研发出一种药物使这种基因失效,则就有可能治疗人们的真菌性疾病而又不影响他们产生赖氨酸的能力。

[6] 机器人的价值已越来越得到证明,因为它们能够进行大量的重复性测试,而由人来做的话,就会引起厌烦,而且注意力也不易集中。为了使机器人亚当比简单的自动化操作更胜一筹,研究小组研发了能使其搜寻酵母中赖氨酸基因的软件,并在《科学》杂志上报道了其研究成果。

[7] to pinpoint 为……准确定位,确认,查出,指出/to be equipped with 配备,装备

金教授说,教机器人提出假设是"非常容易的"。最大的挑战是让亚当整合一系列极为敏感的实验,以便探查出酵母中与基因相关的细微变化。亚当测量到的这些变化能使其准确定位该基因。亚当配备有基因数据库,即那些已知存在于细菌、小鼠和人们身上的基因信息,因此它大致上能识别在基因材料中的何处去搜寻面包酵母,即酿酒酵母中的赖氨酸基因。

[8] 金教授说:"我们希望让人类和机器人科学家一起参与实验室工作。因为生物体非常复杂,所以将生物实验的细节详尽地记录在案很重要。这对人类科学家来说非常困难,而对机器人科学家却很容易。酵母是人们所熟知的,对它的研究已有 100 多年了。我们知道肯定有这种酶存在,但就是不了解它存在于哪里。"

[9] 资助该项目的生物技术和生物科学研究委员会成员道格拉斯·凯尔说:"机器人科学家能够提供一种有用的工具,用以管理这类数据和知识,从而使科研过程更加容易、更加有效。"

[10] ——美国康奈尔大学的研究人员已经研发出了一种程序,能使计算机推算出自然定律。在测试中,一

台观察摆捶的计算机推算出了艾萨克·牛顿创建的运动定律。这种成功使人们期待计算机将会发现迄今为止仍未知晓的一些自然定律。

[11] **发展中的机器人**

[12] *R.U.R.*《罗索姆的万能机器人》是剧作 *Rossum's Universal Robots* 的缩写。

——"robot"这个词是由约瑟夫·恰佩克发明的,该词在 1921 年由其弟卡雷尔在所写的剧作《罗索姆的万能机器人》中第一次被使用,该剧描写了一家工厂制造类人机器的故事。

[13] ——列昂纳多·达·芬奇绘制了"机械骑士"的素描图,现在以"列昂纳多机器人"而闻名。

[14] ——1939 年在纽约世界博览会上展示的 Elektro 机器人可以进行声控。它能活动其头和手臂,甚至还会抽烟。

Exercises

I. Answer the following questions:

1. Who is Adam? And what was it able to do?

2. What is lysine?

3. What diseases were robots able to help to defeat?

4. Why are robots proving increasingly valuable?

5. What was the biggest challenge for Adam?

6. What was Adam equipped with?

7. Why did Professor King hope to have teams of human and robot scientists working together in laboratories?

8. What kind of tool could robot scientists provide?

9. Who invented the word "robot"? And when was it first used?

10. Say something about the Elektro robot.

II. Translate the following words and phrases:

A. From Chinese into English.
1. 解决基因难题
2. 赖氨酸
3. 与疾病作斗争
4. 真菌性疾病

5. 在……方面发挥重要作用 _____
6. 机制，机理 _____
7. 重复性测试 _____
8. 提出假设 _____
9. 为……准确定位 _____
10. 基因数据库 _____
11. 生物实验 _____
12. 生物科学研究 _____
13. 自然定律 _____

B. From English into Chinese.

1. to be crucial to _____
2. to be essential to _____
3. successor _____
4. athlete's foot _____
5. loss of concentration _____
6. simple automation _____
7. the lysine gene in yeast _____
8. a series of experiments _____
9. to be related to _____
10. in great detail _____
11. to develop a program _____
12. to be led by voice commands _____

Ⅲ. Translate the following passage into Chinese:

Few concepts capture the human imagination more than robots, undoubtedly because they are often designed to mimic us. Even their technological development seems to parallel our advances. We can judge the progress of our ability to harness scientific achievement simply by looking at a robot and asking this question: Exactly how much is this machine like a human? Or as Matt Mason, head of the Robotics Institute at Carnegie Mellon University, says, "In studying robotics we're really just studying ourselves." To take a measure of our progress, *Discover* offers a look in that mirror as we analyze some great stepping-stones in robotics, points in time where science fiction meshes with science fact.

Robby the Robot(机器人罗比)

The term *robot* comes from Karel Capek's 1920 play *R. U. R.* (*Rossum's Universal Robots*). Robot is derived from the Czech word *robota*, meaning "forced labor", but it didn't creep into common usage until 1956, when MGM released the film *Forbidden Planet*, featuring Robby the Robot. So complicated was his design that engineers spent two months thermo-forming plastics into shapes previously thought impossible. They then added 2,600 feet of electrical wiring to make Robby's parts whirl and blink. Because MGM spent $1.9 million on the film, a blockbuster budget then, Robby became the iconic face of a burgeoning field. He even earned a spot as an inductee in Carnegie Mellon's Robot Hall of Fame.

Standford Arm(斯坦福机器臂)

Stanford engineering student Victor Scheinman designed one of the first successful electrically powered, computer-controlled robotic arms. It led directly to the Programmable Universal Machine for Assembly series of industrial robots, still an industry mainstay.

ASIMO(机器人阿西莫)

Honda's humanoid robot was the first one capable of true dynamic walking. It could climb stairs, navigate uneven surfaces, change its gait midstep, and even change direction midstride.

Roomba(居室地面清扫机器人)

The first affordable fully automatic floor vacuum and the first robot to sell a million units.

Gladiator(机器人角斗士)

This joint project between BAE Systems and Carnegie Mellon will soon become the first semiautonomous tactical unmanned ground vehicle. Designed to replace a Marine during the first wave of an attack, Gladiator can withstand small-arms fire, grenades, and antipersonnel mines. The robotic soldier is equipped with thermal imaging, GPS and laser range finders, day and night cameras, an acoustic and chemical detection system, a light-vehicle obscuration smoke system, and a mounted weapons system.

Well-known Sayings

△ *Knowledge is power.*
△ *Never put off till tomorrow what you can do today.*
△ *Nothing in the world is impossible if you set your mind to do it.*

Lesson 27

Robots of the Future

[1] Does the future of robotics hold the promise of a dream come true to lighten the workload on humanity and provide companionship? Or the murder and mayhem of Hollywood movies?

[2] When the Czech playwright Karel Capek sat down in 1920 to write a play about humanoid machines that turn against their creators, he decided to call his imaginary creations "robots", from the Czech word for "slave labour". Ever since then, our thinking about robots, whether fictional or real, has been dominated by the two key ideas in Capek's play. Firstly, robots are supposed to do the boring and difficult jobs that humans can't do or don't want to do. Secondly, robots are potentially dangerous.

[3] These two ideas remain influential, but not everyone accepts them. The first dissenting voice was that of the great Russian-American science-fiction writer, Isaac Asimov, who was born the same year that Capek wrote his notorious play. In 1940, barely two decades later, while others were still slavishly reworking Capek's narrative about nasty robots taking over the world, Asimov was already asking what practical steps humanity might take to avoid this fate. And instead of assuming that robots would be confined to boring and dangerous jobs, Asimov imaged a future in which robots care for our children, and strike up friendships with us.

[4] From the perspective of the early twenty-first century, it might seem that Capek was right and that Asimov was an idealistic dreamer. After all, most currently-existing robots are confined to doing nasty, boring and dangerous jobs, right? Wrong. According to the 2003 World Robotics Survey produced by the United Nations.

[5] Economic Commission for Europe, over a third of all the robots in the world are designed not to spray-paint cars or mow the lawn, but simply to entertain humans. And the number is rising fast. It is quite possible, then, that the killer app for robots will turn out to be not the slave labour envisaged by Capek, but the social companionship imagined by Asimov.

[6] The most impressive entertainment robot currently on the market is undoubtedly the Aibo, a robotic dog produced by Sony. According to Onrobo. com, a website devoted to home and entertainment robotics, Aibo is the standard by which all other entertainment robots are measured. Special software allows each Aibo to learn and develop its own unique personality as it interacts with its owner. But at over a thousand pounds a shot, they aren't cheap.

[7] Commercial products like the Aibo still have some way to go before they have the quasi-human capacities of "Robbie", the child-caring robot envisaged by Asimov in one of his earliest short-stories, but the technology is moving fast. Scientists around the world are already beginning to develop the components for more advanced sociable robots, such as emotional recognition systems and emotional expression systems.

[8] Emotions are vital to human interaction, so any robot that has to interact naturally with a human will need to be able to recognise human expressions of emotion and to express its own emotions in ways that humans can recognise. One of the pioneers in this area of research (which is known as "affective

computing") is Cynthia Breazeal, a roboticist at the Massachusetts Institute of Technology who has built an emotionally-expressive humanoid head called Kismet. Kismet has moveable eyelids, eyes and lips which allow him to make a variety of emotional expressions. When left alone, Kismet looks sad, but when he detects a human face he smiles, inviting attention. If the comer moves too fast, a look of fear warns that something is wrong. Human parents who play with Kismet cannot help but respond sympathetically to these simple forms of emotional behaviour.

[9] Another emotionally-expressive robot called WE-4R has been built by Atsuo Takanishi and colleagues at Waseda University in Japan. Whereas Kismet is limited to facial expressions and head movements, WE-4R can also move its torso and wave its arms around to express its emotions.

[10] The gap between science fiction and science fact is closing, and closing fast. In fact, the technology is advancing so quickly that some people are already worried about what will happen when robots become as emotional as we are. Will they turn against their creators, as Capek predicted? In the new Hollywood blockbuster, *I, Robot* (which is loosely based on an eponymous collection of Asimov's short stoties), Will Smith plays a detective investigating the murder of a famous scientist. Despite the fail-safe mechanism built into the robots, which prevents them from harming humans, the detective suspects that the scientist was killed by a robot. His investigation leads him to discover an even more serious threat to the human race.

[11] *I, Robot* is set in the year 2035, twenty-seven years in the future. To get an idea of how advanced robots will be by then, think about how far videogames have come in the last twenty-seven years. Back in 1973, the most advanced videogame was Pong, in which a white dot representing a tennis ball was batted back and forth across a black screen. The players moved the bats up and down by turning the knobs on the game console. By today's standards, the game was incredibly primitive. That's how today's robots will look to people in the year 2035.

[12] Will those future people look back at the primitive robots of 2008 and wish they hadn't advanced any further? If we want to avoid the nightmare scenario of a battle between humans and robots, we should start thinking about how to ensure that robots remain safe even when they are more intelligent. Isaac Asimov suggested that we could make sure robots don't become dangerous by programming them to follow the following "Three Robot Laws":

1) A robot may not injure a human being or, through inaction, allow a human being to come to harm.

2) A robot must obey orders given by human beings except where such orders would conflict with the First Law.

3) A robot must protect its own existence as long as such protection does not conflict with the First or Second Law.

[13] At first blush, these three laws might seem like a good way to keep robots in their place. But to a roboticist they pose more problems than they solve. Asimov was well aware of this, and many of his short stories revolve around the contradictions and dilemmas implicit in the three laws.

[14] The sobering conclusion that emerges from these stories is that preventing intelligent robots from harming humans will require something much more complex than simply programming them to follow the three laws.

Language Points and Chinese Translations

第27课 未来机器人

〔1〕未来机器人能使减轻人类工作负担并成为人类伴侣的梦想成真吗？还是会带来像好莱坞电影里的那种谋杀和大灾难呢？

〔2〕1920年,当捷克剧作家卡莱尔·恰佩克着手写一部关于具有人类特点的机器人反抗其制造者时,他决定将他所想象的创造物称为"机器人"。"机器人"一词来源于捷克语中的词汇"奴隶劳动"。从那时起,我们对机器人的概念无论是虚构的,还是真实的,都受到了恰佩克剧作中两个主要观点的影响。第一,机器人必须做人类不能做或不想做的单调乏味和困难的工作;第二,机器人具有潜在的危险性。

〔3〕to take over 接管,接收/to strike up friendships with sb. 开始与某人友好相处,开始与某人建立起友谊,to strike up 是"开始,建立起"之意。

这两种观点至今仍有影响力,但也并不是每个人都能接受。第一个发出不同声音的是伟大的俄裔美国科幻作家艾萨克·阿西莫夫。他在恰佩克写作那部众所周知的剧作的那一年出生。1940年,即整整20年后,当别人还在依样画葫芦地重复着恰佩克的叙述手法,描写可恶的机器人接管世界的故事时,阿西莫夫则已经在探索人类可能采取什么切实可行的措施来回避这种厄运。阿西莫夫并没有想当然地假设机器人仅限于做些乏味、危险的工作,在他关于未来的想象中,机器人能够照看我们的孩子,并与我们开始友好相处。

〔4〕从21世纪初的观察视角来看,恰佩克似乎是正确的,而阿西莫夫仅是个理想主义的梦想家。毕竟,现在大多数的机器人都只限于做一些肮脏、单调和危险的工作,是这样吗？依据联合国所作的2003年世界机器人技术调查,这种说法是错误的。

〔5〕killer app 是 killer application 的简写,意指:杀手应用软件,克敌制胜的方法或法宝。/to turn out 结果,原来,证明(是)

根据欧洲经济委员会所称,全世界超过三分之一的机器人其设计目的并不是用来给汽车喷漆或者修剪草坪,而仅仅是为人类提供娱乐。这类机器人的数量正在迅速增长。到将来某个时候,机器人克敌制胜的方法很可能不再是恰佩克所设想的奴隶劳动,而是阿西莫夫所想象的社会伙伴。

〔6〕目前,市场上给人印象最深的娱乐机器人无疑是"艾博",它是由索尼公司生产的一种机器狗。根据Onrobo.com网站(一个专业从事家用和娱乐机器人技术的网站)声称,"艾博"已成为所有其他娱乐机器人的依据标准。已有专门的软件使每个"艾博"机器人与其主人交流互动时都能学习和发展其自身的独特个性。但是其价格并不便宜,要1 000英镑。

〔7〕阿西莫夫在其早期的一部短篇小说中构想了能照看孩子的"罗比"机器人。现在像"艾博"机器人这样的商业产品要具有"罗比"那样类似于人的能力,依然任重而道远,但是该项机器人技术正在快速发展。世界各地的科学家们已经正在着手研制更加先进的能与人交往的机器人组件,如情感识别系统和情感表达系统。

〔8〕各种各样的情感在人类交际互动中非常重要,所以,任何必须与人进行自然交流的机器人都要能够辨别人类的各种情感表达,同时也要能够以人类可以识别的方式表达其自己的情感。这一研究领域(通常称作"情感计算")的开拓者之一是辛西娅·布雷齐尔。她是麻省理工学院的一位机器人专家,已经研制出了具有情感表达能力类似于人的机器人头脑"命运"。"命运"有能活动的眼睑,眼睛和嘴唇,这就使它能作出各种各样的情感表达。"命运"在独处时,看起来忧愁悲哀,但当它探测到有人的面孔时,就会微笑起来,以引起别人对它的关注。如果接近者动作太快,它就会显露出一种害怕的神色,警示哪里出了差错。和"命运"一起玩耍的人类父母会情不自禁地对这些简单的情感表达行为作出同情的反应。

〔9〕日本早稻田大学的高西教授和同事们已经研制出了另一个具有情感表达功能的机器人,叫WE-4R。"命运"的情感表达只限于面部表情和头部的活动,而WE-4R除此之外还能够活动其身体躯干和挥动双臂来表达各

种情感。

　　[10] 科幻小说和科学现实之间的鸿沟正在弥合，而且是在快速地弥合。事实上，机器人技术正在飞速发展，以至于有些人已在忧虑，当机器人与我们人类具有一样的情感时，将会发生什么样的事。它们会像恰佩克所预言的那样会转而反对它们的制造者吗？《我，机器人》是大体上依据阿西莫夫所写的同名短篇小说集改编的新的好莱坞大片，威尔·史密斯在该片中扮演了一名侦探，对一位著名科学家被谋杀的案件进行调查。尽管机器人内置的防止故障安全装置可以预防它们伤害人类，但这位侦探仍怀疑是一个机器人杀害了这位科学家。该调查使他发现了机器人对人类甚至更为严重的威胁。

　　[11]《我，机器人》的时间背景设定于2035年，即从现在起27年后的未来。要了解那时候机器人达到的先进程度如何，只要想一下在过去的27年里视频游戏发展的快速程度如何就行了。回想一下1973年，当时最高级的视频游戏是"乓"。在这个视频游戏中，代表网球的白点在黑色的屏幕上被来来回回地交叉击打。游戏者通过旋转游戏机上的球形捏手上上下下地移动球拍。用今天的标准来看，这款游戏原始简单得令人难以置信。到了2035年人们也将会以相同的眼光来看待今天的机器人。（本句意指到了2035年时人们所制造的机器人同样会比今天的机器人更先进更优越。）

　　[12] 将来当人们回顾2008年的早期机器人时是否会希望机器人不该进一步发展呢？如果我们想要避免人类与机器人之间发生战争的可怕场面，我们现在就要开始考虑到如何确保未来更加聪明的机器人对人类仍然具有安全性。艾萨克·阿西莫夫提出，我们可以通过给机器人编制程序，使它们遵循以下"机器人三定律"，以确保机器人不会变得具有危险性：

　　1）机器人不得伤害人类，或者任由人类遭受伤害而无所作为。
　　2）机器人必须服从人类的命令，除非这些命令与第一条定律发生冲突。
　　3）机器人应保护自己的生存，只要这种保护不违反第一和第二条定律。

　　[13] 乍看时，这三条定律似乎像是避免机器人的危险性的好方法。但是对于机器人专家来讲，这三条定律所产生的问题要比它们解决的问题更多。阿西莫夫完全意识到这一点，他写的许多短篇小说都是以机器人三定律所隐含的许多矛盾和困境为主要内容的。

　　[14] 从这些小说中可以作出这样合理的结论，即防止智能机器人伤害人类比简单地编制程序让机器人遵循三定律要复杂得多。

Exercises

Ⅰ. Answer the following questions:

1. What are the two key ideas in Capek's play?

2. What will the robots do in the future according to Asimov's imagination?

3. What are the robots designed to do in the world today according to the Economic Commission for Europe?

4. What will be the killer app for the robots of the future?

5. What is the unique personality of the robot Aibo? And how much is it?

6. What are the function of the components for more advanced sociable robots?

7. How does Kismei express its own emotions? And how about WE-4R?

8. What is happening to the gap between science fiction and science fact?

9. Please describe the videogame of Pong.

10. What are the "Three Robot Laws" put forward by Isaac Asimov?

11. What is your own idea of the three laws?

II. Translate the following words and phrases:

A. From Chinese into English.
1. 智能机器人
2. 潜在的危险性
3. 与某人开始友好相处
4. 科幻作家
5. 独特个性
6. 情感识别系统
7. 科幻小说
8. 视频游戏
9. 给机器人编程
10. 与……发生冲突

B. From English into Chinese.
1. to lighten the workload
2. to do the boring and difficult jobs
3. to remain influential
4. to take over the world
5. to be confined to doing sth.
6. from the perspective of
7. an idealistic dreamer
8. to spray-paint cars
9. to entertain humans
10. to look back
11. to protect one's own existence
12. contradictions and dilemmas

III. Translate the following passage into Chinese:

In Australia, a company called Metal Storm has adapted the Packbot, produced by its American partner iRobot. The Packbot is usually used to gather sensory data on dangerous locations, and has been adapted into a semi-autonomous killing machine called the Warrior: it can automatically acquire and fire at three targets in approximately 1.2 seconds, selecting the appropriate munition for each target. Stationary versions of Metal Storm weapons are already used for perimeter security. According to Joe Dyer of iRobot, the real benefit of the system is its resilience. As he succinctly puts it:"A robot can shoot second."

Nimblett of Lockheed is confident that army units with robotic capabilities will have a clear advantage over their enemies. "Battlefield perception is much better with the robots," he says. "So the real advantage is in our situational understanding." You only have to watch the video of a Swords cruising into a potential combat zone, its gun turret rotating, to get the idea.

The only force outside the US with plans to deploy armed robots is the South Korean army. Last year Samsung announced it had built an armed sentry to be deployed at the border with its northern neighbour. The robot is essentially a machine gun turret, without the manoeuvreability or firepower of its US rivals. It doesn't interact with other battle units in the way the American, network-centric, models do.

For now, the US army has the clear advantage in armed robotics. The technology it is developing gives them and their allies the ability to outmanoeuvre and outgun enemy combatants with unprecedented ease.

[Packbot 这里指"帕克博特"机器人战车/to gather sensory data 收集传感数据/semi-autonomous 半自主式/shoot second 这里意指：进行反复射击/batterfield perception 战场感知能力/interact with 与……配合，互相作用]

Well-known Sayings

△ *Pursue your object, be it what it will, steadily and indefatigably.*

△ *To study and not think is a waste. To think and not study is dangerous.*

△ *Don't believe what your eyes are telling you. All they show is limitation; look with your understanding.*

Unit 8　Application of Electronic Technology
第8单元　电子技术应用

—— Electronics is a field of engineering and applied physics dealing with the design and application of devices, usually electronic circuits, the operation of which depends on the flow of electrons for the generation, transmission, reception and storage of data and information.

—— Electronic technology, based on the principle of electronics, covers two branches: information electronic technology and power electronic technology; the former includes analog and digital electronic technologies, and the latter focuses on the electronics applied to conversion and control of electric power and its primary task is to process and control the flow of electric energy.

—— Generally speaking, electronic technology is the design, manufacturing and application of electronic components, devices and equipments. It is now widely applied in automatic control, operating system, communication, computer hardware and software, video equipment and multimedia products, office products such as photocopiers and fax machines, home appliances and some other fields.

Lesson 28

A Brave New Olfactory World
——Applications for Electronic Noses

[1] The human senses are all being automated. Electronic eyes and ears have been available for several years, and some robots have a rudimentary sense of touch. Now the electronic nose is here.

[2] Indeed, two rival noses have emerged within the past year from companies in the UK, the world leader in olfactory technology, and a third is due out next year. They share the same basic design as the human version—an array of sensors to detect molecules in the air linked to an electronic brain that makes sense of their signals.

[3] The electronic noses cannot yet match the sensitivity of human smell, any more than computerized voice recognition can compete with our ears. But for industrial purposes they have other advantages which are drawing potential users from the food, drink and fragrance industries worldwide to the first two British manufacturers, AromaScan and Neotronics.

[4] The third company, Bloodhound Sensors, expects to launch a nose next year. Its first application is rather different—a security device to distinguish between individuals by means of their characteristic, genetically determined body odours—though Bloodhound too will compete in the wider food, drink and cosmetics market.

[5] The human sniffing panels traditionally employed to assess complex odours do not perform consistently over time; their noses may become tired or sensitized to particular smells, or they may be affected by colds, allergies or spicy food.

[6] The electronic versions, in contrast, give repeatable and "objective" results—digital records of the odour—which can be displayed graphically in various ways.

[7] And the electronic noses are suitable for long-term pollution monitoring, 24 hours a day, in hazardous environments. For example an AromaScan instrument will be installed on Russia's Mir space station later this year, as part of a co-operative mission with the European Space Agency, to sniff out pollutants that might harm the cosmonauts.

[8] A far larger terrestrial application would be an intelligent smoke detector, which could distinguish between an accidental fire and smoke from a frying pan.

[9] A mass market beckons. If the electronic noses can be made small and cheap enough—and the three companies believe they can—there will eventually be one inside every refrigerator to warn when something perishable is going off and inside every microwave oven to switch it off when the food is cooked. They will turn on bathroom extractor fans when a smell needs clearing… Potential uses are limited only by the imagination.

[10] But consumer applications lie several years in the future. The first generation of noses, which cost about $25 000 each, are being used mainly for quality control in the food and drink industry—checking raw materials, processing and final products. Early applications by AromaScan and Neotronics include:
- Classifying the freshness of fish and seafood;
- Detecting off-smells and taints in pork;

- Monitoring the freshness and ripeness of fruit;
- Identifying different types of coffee bean before blending;
- Assessing instant coffee aromas during processing;
- Ensuring the consistency of branded beers in different breweries;
- Authenticating blended whisky.

[11] Bloodhound's first product will be an access control device called Scentinel. When someone wants to enter a high-security area, Scentinel sniffs the back of his or her hand, obtains an odour profile and compares this with the profile in its memory. If the two match, the door will open.

[12] The device can detect and differentiate between genetically linked body odours which are undetectable to the human nose. It is designed to ignore the smell of perfumes, soaps and cosmetics. Scentinel will be more reliable and convenient than other biometric security devices based, for example, on voice recognition or hand-prints.

[13] AromaScan is developing applications in a quite different area—health-care. Doctors have long known how to diagnose a few conditions by smell; for example the breath of someone in a diabetic coma has the aroma of acetone. But many diseases generate characteristic mixtures of volatile molecules, which could be used for diagnostic purposes with an electronic nose.

[14] Trials at Withington Hospital in Manchester have shown that an AromaScan instrument can detect wound infections at a very early stage and distinguish between different bacterial infections.

[15] The technology is expected to advance rapidly, as the three UK companies continue research with their university partners. They are discussing possible licensing deals and joint ventures with international electronics and instrumentation companies, which would bring in more development funds.

[16] The number and sensitivity of artificial sensors in the electronic nose will increase, and the whole thing will shrink in size. It may even be possible to supplement the polymer sensors with cloned versions of the human odour receptors.

[17] Scientists have long known that deep friendships and romantic alliances depend on "olfactory bonding". By the middle of the next century, people may want to confirm instincts by taking miniature electronic noses to parties, to assess the compatibility of potential partners.

Language Points and Chinese Translations

第28课 繁华的嗅觉新世界
——电子鼻的广泛用途

[1] available 可用的,可供的,可取得的/rudimentary 初步的,基本的

人类的感觉器官都可以用自动化技术进行制造。电子眼睛和电子耳朵已问世好几年了,一些机器人也具有初步的触觉,现在又有了电子鼻。

[2] rival 匹敌者,比拟物,对抗的/to emerge 出现/olfactory 嗅觉的,嗅觉器官的/array 排列,列阵

在嗅觉技术方面,占有世界领先地位的英国两家公司在去年研制了两种可以互相匹敌的电子鼻,第三种电子鼻预计在明年问世。它们的基本结构与人的鼻子相同——一排能检测空气中分子的传感器与电脑连接在一起,由电脑鉴别它们传递的信号。

[3] sensitivity 灵敏度,灵敏性,敏感性/recognition 识别,辨别/fragrance 香料,香气

电子鼻的灵敏度目前还不能和人的嗅觉媲美,正像计算机的辨音能力还比不上人的耳朵。但用于工业目的,它们还是有其他一些优势,英国最初的两家制造商:AromaScan 和 Neotronics 公司制造的电子鼻引起了世界各地

食品、饮料和香料工业潜在用户的注意。

[4] to launch 创办,开办,发起/security device 安全装置/odour 气味/cosmetics 化妆品

第三家公司 Bloodhound Sensors 预计在明年开发出一种电子鼻。其首要用途就与众不同——作为一种安全装置识别由遗传决定的人体体味的特征——当然,Bloodhound 公司也将会在更广阔的食品、饮料和化妆品市场参与竞争。

[5] to sniff v. 嗅,闻,用鼻子吸/panel 专家小组,专门人员/to assess v. 评估,评定,估量/allergy 变应性

以前历来是请一些专门人员对复杂的气味进行闻、嗅、评估,但是他们不能长时间始终如一地进行这样的工作;他们的鼻子对一些特别的气味会产生过敏,或者因感冒、过敏症或辛辣食品而受到影响。

[6] in contrast 对比,对照/graphically adv. 用图解,用图示

而相比之下,电子鼻可以提供反复测试的"客观"的结果——对气味进行数字式的记录——用各种不同的图解显示出来。

[7] to monitor 监视,监控/hazardous 危险的/cosmonauts 宇航员,宇宙飞行员

电子鼻适用于在危险的环境中,进行一天 24 小时长时间的污染监测。例如:作为与欧洲宇航局合作任务的一部分,今年晚些时候 AromaScan 仪器将安装在俄罗斯的和平号空间站上,以便检测可能对宇航员造成危害的污染物质。

[8] terrestrial 地球上的,陆地的

一种智能烟雾探测器可以在地球上进行更大范围的应用,它可以分辨出是偶然的火灾还是煎锅冒出的烟雾。

[9] to beckon 招呼,召唤/perishable 易腐败的,易死的/to go off 变坏/potential 潜在的

一个巨大的市场在召唤。如果电子鼻能够做得足够的小,又很便宜——这三家公司相信他们能够做到——这样最终当冰箱里腐败的食物变味时,安装在内的电子鼻就能发出警告,当微波炉里的食物煮熟时,安装在内的电子鼻就能将微波炉关掉,当浴室里的异味需要清除时,电子鼻就能启动浴室里的排风扇⋯⋯电子鼻的潜在用途很多,只是受到人们想象力的限制而已。(即人们怎样想象,就能开发出这种想象用途的电子鼻)。

[10] taint 腐败,沾染/aromas 香气,香味

但是消费者应用电子鼻还要再过几年。第一代电子鼻,每个造价要花 25 000 英镑,现在主要应用于食品和饮料工业方面的质量监控——检测原材料,检测加工过程和最终产品。AromaScan 和 Neotronics 两家公司制造的电子鼻的早期应用包括:

- 对鱼和海鲜食品的新鲜度进行分级;
- 对猪肉的变味和腐败进行检测;
- 对水果的新鲜度和成熟度进行监控;
- 对配料前的各种咖啡豆进行分辨;
- 对加工过程中的速溶咖啡香味进行评估;
- 保证不同酿酒厂生产的品牌的啤酒质量稳定;
- 鉴定威士忌酒的配方。

[11] Bloodhound 公司的第一个电子鼻产品将是一种称作气味哨兵的门禁装置。当某人要进入一个高度保密区域时,气味哨兵就闻其手背,取得气味类型,并与其储存库中的气味类型相比较,如果两种气味类型一致,门就开了。

[12] 这种装置能探测、分辨出人类鼻子察觉不出的与遗传有关的人体气味。它不受香水、肥皂和化妆品气味的干扰。与其他依靠辨认声音或手印等生物特征的安全装置相比,气味哨兵将更为可靠方便。

[13] to diagnose 诊断/diabetic 糖尿病的/coma 昏迷/acetone 丙酮/volatile 挥发性的

AromaScan 公司正在一个完全不同的领域——保健方面进行开发应用。医生们早就知道如何通过气味进行一些疾病的诊断。例如,处于昏迷状态的糖尿病患者的呼吸中含有丙酮的气味。但是许多疾病散发出特有的挥发性混合气味,电子鼻可以利用这些混合气味进行疾病诊断。

[14] trial 试验,试用,尝试/infection 感染/bacterial 细菌的

在曼彻斯特的 Withington 医院里进行的试验表明:AmoraScan 仪器能够在早期阶段检测出伤口感染,而且能够分辨出不同类型的细菌所引起的感染。

[15] 由于英国的三家公司继续和他们的大学合作伙伴进行研究,电子鼻技术可望得到快速发展。他们正在洽谈申请许可证以及和国际电子仪器仪表公司成立合资企业的事项,这将引进更多的发展基金。

[16] to shrink 收缩,缩小,缩减/to supplement 增补,补充

电子鼻中的仿真传感器的数量和灵敏度都将增加,整体尺寸将缩小,甚至有可能克隆人的嗅觉器官而增添聚合传感器。

[17] romantic 浪漫主义的,虚构的,离奇的/alliance 联盟,同盟/instinct 本能,直觉,天性/miniature 小型/compatibility 和谐,相容,共存,适合

科学家们早就知道深厚的友谊和浪漫的联盟取决于"嗅觉联结",在下个世纪中叶,人们可能会带着小型的电子鼻参加聚会来确认本能感觉,评估与潜在伙伴的和谐相容性。

Exercises

Ⅰ. **Answer the following questions:**

1. Why do electronic noses share the same basic design as the human version?

2. In what industries do electronic noses have advantages?

3. Why don't the human sniffing panels perform consistently while assessing complex odours? How about electronic noses?

4. Can you give an example to show the fact that electronic noses are suitable for long-term pollution monitoring in harmful environments?

5. What are the consumer applications for electronic noses? Can you imagine them?

6. How much are electronic noses of the first generation? And what are they used for?

7. What are the early applications for electronic noses?

8. What are the applications for electronic noses in the area of health-care?

9. Why is the electronic nose technology expected to develop fast?

10. How will people assess the compatibility of their potential partners in the near future?

Ⅱ. **Translate the following words and phrases:**

A. From Chinese into English.

1. 电子鼻 _____
2. 嗅觉技术 _____
3. 香料工业 _____
4. 长期污染控制 _____

5. 智能烟雾探测器 _____
6. 质量监控 _____
7. 仿真传感器 _____

B. From English into Chinese.
1. human senses _____
2. an array of sensors to detect molecules in the air _____
3. sensitivity _____
4. computerized voice recognition _____
5. to compete with _____
6. potential users _____
7. a security device _____
8. to bring in more development funds _____
9. joint ventures _____
10. to assess the compatibility of potential partners _____

Ⅲ. Translate the following passage into Chinese:

You can't tell a package of sandwich meat is spoiled until you open it and sniff. Now, artificial intelligence may put an end to that unpleasant surprise. An electronic nose developed at the University of Washington may help the food-processing industry detect possible odors long before foods are packaged. The device draws in air that is analyzed by arrays of sensors designed to identify specific odor-causing chemicals. It can scan four distinctive aroma groups prevalent in food processing. The nose is sensitive enough to detect a single odor-producing molecule among a million other molecules in an air sample, according to project leader Pat Carey.

Well-known Sayings

△ *One loses by pride and gains by modesty.*
△ *Deeds are fruits, and words are but leaves.*
△ *Ability is what you are capable of doing. Motivation determines what you do. Attitude determines how well you do it.*

Lesson 29

Digital Storage Oscilloscopes

[1] Digital storage oscilloscopes (DSOs) do more than just digitize and display waveforms. With a DSO, you can store data to disk, print them, and perform calculations on them right in the instrument. DSOs are useful to engineers who measure electromechanical properties such as vibration, acceleration, angle, displacement, power, and pressure by using sensors such as strain gauges, pressure transducers, shaft encoders, linear variable differential transformers (LVDTs), accelerometers, and magnetic position sensors. Some DSOs are complete data-acquisition systems that often don't require an external computer to process data.

[2] DSOs often have an entire suite of math functions that include

- min and max;
- peak-to-peak;
- statistics;
- overshoot;
- risetime and falltime; and
- frequency and spectrum.

[3] In many applications, you'll need to convert voltage measurements from your sensors to engineering units. Many DSOs can perform that scaling using multiplication and addition (the $mX+b$ function). Some DSOs carry scaling further and have a polynomial feature for linearizing nonlinear scales. Other math functions include differentiation and integration. Differentiation lets you calculate acceleration or deceleration from vibration measurements. Integration lets you measure flow totals or calculate area or power.

[4] Frequency is also important in making rotational measurements. You may be using a DSO to measure the output from a shaft encoder. If you care about the shaft's rotation speed, you'll need a DSO that provides a built-in frequency-measurement function. Just keep in mind that instruments usually display frequency measurements in hertz, but you may want your measurements in rpm. Assume that a shaft encoder produces 4 000 pulses per revolution. To convert frequency in hertz to rpm for this encoder, you'll have to multiply the frequency by 0.015 (60/4 000).

[5] Shaft encoders produce pulse outputs that are easy for a DSO to capture. Many transducers, however, produce output voltages that are too small for DSOs to measure accurately. For example, a typical strain gauge with an output of 3 mV/V using a 10-V excitation voltage will have an output of ±30 mV. Most DSOs don't have a 30-mV full scale, though, so if you use the next higher full scale(50 mV), you'll lose resolution. You may need to amplify the transducer's output to make better use of a scope's analog-to-digital converter. Also, a strain gauge produces a differential output, but a scope's input is single-ended. To eliminate ground loops caused by the scope's ground lead, you should use a differential amplifier. Usually, this amplifier will be external to the scope.

The Speed You Need

[6] Engineers making electromechanical measurements generally don't need the fastest DSOs. DSOs with sampling rates up to 100 Msamples/s or 200 Msamples/s cover most electromechanical applications.

[7] No discussion of sample rates is complete without mentioning memory depth. Because electromechanical measurements are slower than electronic measurements, you don't need the high sample rates available in more expensive DSOs. But, electromechanical tests may produce signals that you'll have to measure for milliseconds or even seconds. Therefore, you may need a combination of sampling rate and memory depth that lets you capture enough of the signal to give you a complete picture of the test data, yet provides enough time resolution for you to view details. Assume that you need to sample at 200 ksamples/s but need to capture 0.5-s worth of signal. To do that, you'll need a scope with 100 ksamples of memory.

[8] While DSOs can store data and perform calculations, you may find that their displays don't update as fast as those on analog scopes. A DSO must first digitize a waveform, move that data to memory, then select the points for display—DSOs typically display only about 500 points at one time. That digitizing and moving of data take time, so DSOs typically update their displays at 100 update/s or 200 updates/s. Therefore, if the waveform you're viewing changes rapidly from one repetition to the next, the DSO won't appear to be as fast as an analog scope at updating its display.

[9] Electromechanical measurements usually require some signal processing to present the information you need. If you're making vibration measurements, for example, you'll likely want to know a signal's frequency components. While having a DSO that measures the fundamental frequency of a signal is useful, you'll probably want a DSO that calculates fast Fourier transforms (FFTs). FFTs—a DSO software option—let you view the frequency content of your signal. With an FFT, you can find the harmonic content in a vibration or identify resonant frequencies in a mechanical design.

Time and Frequency

[10] DSOs measure signals by first sampling points of a time-domain waveform and digitizing them. An FFT's frequency resolution depends on the number of points that the DSO uses in its calculations. The number of frequency points can't exceed one half of the number of samples in a time-domain waveform; the maximum frequency attainable from an FFT is one half of the sample rate.

[11] Not all DSOs process all of the sampled points in a waveform. On some DSOs, the number of time-domain points used to calculate an FFT is fixed, while on others you can select the number of points to process. Our survey table shows that many DSOs produce FFTs that do not use all of the points in a measurement.

Language Points and Chinese Translations

第29课 数码存储式示波器

[1] oscilloscope 示波器(在阴极射线管屏幕上,如电视机的荧光屏,或计算机的屏幕显示出波动曲线以表示电流变动的仪器)/to digitize 使数字化/electromechanical property 电气机械特性/angle 角,角度/displacement 位移,移置/strain gauge 应力计量器/pressure transducer 压力传感器/shaft encoder 转轴编码器/linear variable differential transformer 线性可变差动变压器/accelerometer 加速度计量器/magnetic position sensor 磁性方位传

感器

数码储存式示波器(DSOs)不仅仅是把被测信号数字化并显示出波形。有了DSO,你就能把数据存入磁盘,打印出来,并且直接在示波器上进行数据计算。数码储存式示波器对工程师来说很有用。他们可以使用应力计量器、压力传感器、转轴编码器、线性可变差动变压器(LVDTs)、加速度计量器和磁性方位传感器等各种传感器对电气机械特性,如振动、加速度、角度、位移、功能、压力等进行测量。有些DSO本身就是完整的数据收集系统,它们通常并不需要外接计算机就能处理数据。

[2] DSO通常具有全套的数学运算功能,包括:

- 计算最小值与最大值;
- 计算峰值;
- 统计运算;
- 超调计算;
- 计算上升和下降时间;
- 计算频率和频谱。

[3] to scale 按比例(运算,绘制或增减)/polynomial 多项式/to linearize 使成线状的,线性化

在很多实际应用中,需要把传感器的电压测量值转换成工程的单位读数。许多DSO能够运用乘法和加法进行按比例运算(mX+b方程)。有些DSO还能作进一步的计算,进行多项式运算,使非线性标度特性线性化。示波器的其他数学运算功能还包括微分与积分。微分功能可以从振动测量值计算出加速度或减速度。积分功能可以测量总流量,计算面积或功率。

[4] rotational 转动的,旋转的,名词为rotation/hertz赫兹(每秒周波数)/rpm是一缩略语,转数/分,指每分钟旋转数,即revolutions per minute的缩略形式

频率数据在旋转测量中也很重要。你可能使用DSO对转轴编码器的输出进行测量。如果你关注转轴的旋转速度,你就需要带有频率测量功能的DSO。只是要记住,示波器通常以赫兹显示频率测量值,但是你可能想要用转数/分来表示测量值。假定转轴编码器每旋转一次产生4 000次脉冲,为了要把该编码器的频率赫兹数转变成转数/分,你就得把频率乘以0.015 (60/4 000)。

[5] to capture 捕获,巧取/excitation voltage 激发电压/to amplify 放大,扩大/to eliminate 除去,剔除,消除/ground loop 接地回线,回路/ground lead 接地导线,地线

转轴编码器所产生的脉冲输出很容易被DSO采集到。但是,很多传感器所产生的输出电压太低以致DSO不能给以准确的测量。例如,使用10-V激发电压具有3mV/V输出的典型的应力计量器仅产生±30 mV的输出。而大多数DSO并没有30-mV的满档测度。因此你如果使用下一个较高的满档测度(50 mV),你就失去了分辨率。你可能需要把传感器的输出进行放大以便更好地利用示波器的模数转换器。应力计量器还产生差动输出,但是示波器的输入是单极的。为了消除示波器地线所造成的接地回路,就应该使用差动放大器。这种差动放大器通常是外接于示波器的。

你所需要的速度

[6] sampling rate 取样速率,采样速率/Msamples/s 兆采样/秒,M:mega(=million)兆,百万(=10^6)

进行电气机械测量的工程师一般并不需要最快速的DSO。采样速率达100兆采样/秒或200兆采样/秒就能满足大多数电气机械测量的实际应用。

[7] memory depth 储存深度/combination 结合,组合,联合/Ksamples/s 千采样/秒,K:kilo 一千(1 000)

如果不提及储存深度,则对采样速率的讨论就不完全。因为电气机械测量要比电子测量的速度慢,所以并不需要具有高速采样率的更昂贵的DSO。但是,电气机械测试可能会产生你所必须测量的几毫秒甚至几秒的信号,因此你需要把采样速率和储存深度结合起来以便获取足够的信号,获得测试数据的完整图像,并提供足够的时间分辨率观察细节。假设你需要按200千采样/秒的速率进行采样,但是又需要获取0.5秒长的信号,那么你就将需要有100千采样储存容量的示波器。

[8] to update 更新,使现代化,修正/repetition 重复,复现,再发生

虽然 DSO 能够储存数据并进行计算,但是你会发现其展示图像的更新速度不像模拟式示波器的那样快速。DSO 首先必须使波形数字化,将数据移送至储存器,然后选择展示点——DSO 一般一次只展示大约 500 点。数字化和移动数据需要花费时间,所以 DSO 一般按每秒 100 次或 200 次的速度更新其展示的图像。因此,如果你正在观看的波形从一次重复展示迅速变化到下一次,DSO 就不会像模拟式示波器那样快速地更新其展示的图像。

[9] component 成分/option 选择,选项,可选择之事物/harmonic content 谐波成分/resonant frequency 共振频率

电气机械测量通常要进行某种信号处理以便提供你所需要的信息。例如,如果你正在作振动测量,你很可能想知道信号的频率成分。虽然你有一台能测量信号基本频率的示波器很有用处,你很可能也会想要一台能计算快速傅立叶转换(FFTS)的示波器。FFTS——示波器的软件选项——使你观看到信号的频率成分。有了 FFT,你就可以找到振动信号的谐波成分或认出一种机械配置的共振频率。

时间和频率

[10] time-domain waveform 时域波形,domain 领域,范围/to exceed 超过/attainable 可得到的,可达到的

DSO 测量信号时首先对时域波形的测点进行采样,并将其数字化。FFT 的频率分辨率取决于 DSO 在计算中所使用的采样测点数。频率测点数不能超过时域波形采样数的一半;从 FFT 可得到的最高频率是采样速率的一半。

[11] 并不是所有的 DSO 都能处理某一波形的所有采样点。在一些 DSO 上,用来计算 FFT 的时域点数是固定不变的,而在另一些 DSO 上,对要处理的时域点数可以进行选择。我们的测量一览表显示:许多 DSO 在计算 FFT 时并不使用所有的测点。

Exercises

Ⅰ. Answer the following questions:

1. What are the functions of DSOs?

2. What are the electromechanical properties?

3. What sensors do engineers use when they make electromechanical measurements?

4. What math functions do DSOs have?

5. What are the uses of differentiation and integration in electromechanical measurements?

6. Do DSOs usually display frequency measurements in hertz or in rpm? How do you convert frequency in hertz to rpm?

7. Why do engineers not need the fastest DSOs?

8. Why do we need a combination of sampling rate and memory depth?

9. At what speed do DSOs typically update the displays?
   _____
10. What is the use of FFT?
    _____
11. How do DSOs measure signals?
    _____
12. What is the maximum frequency attainable from an FFT?
    _____

II. Translate the following words and phrases:

A. From Chinese into English.
1. 数码储存式示波器 _____
2. 电气机械特性 _____
3. 位移 _____
4. 加速度 _____
5. 转轴编码器 _____
6. 压力传感器 _____
7. 微分和积分 _____
8. 脉冲 _____
9. 基本频率 _____
10. 共振频率 _____
11. 最小值与最大值 _____
12. 时域波形 _____
13. 转速 _____
14. 赫兹 _____

B. From English into Chinese.
1. digitize _____
2. to store data to disk _____
3. magnetic position sensors _____
4. complete data-acquisition systems _____
5. statistics _____
6. engineering units _____
7. to measure flow totals or calculate area or power _____
8. to care about _____
9. a built-in frequency-measurement function _____
10. to convert… to… _____
11. a differential amplifier _____
12. milliseconds _____
13. to update the displays _____
14. signal processing _____
15. a signal's frequency components _____
16. software option _____

III. Translate the following passage into Chinese:

The conversion of analog signal into a more manipulate bit stream is hardly a novel concept. The technology's mass appeal, though, is of more recent date. Economics is only part of the reason. Within the past few years, various semiconductor devices and software tools have conjoined to make digital signal processing not just cost-effective for commercial and consumer applications, but so attractive as to have inspired a hundred new uses.

Today, digital signal processor(DSP) chips are central to products ranging from cellular phones, modems, and personal digital assistants to disk drives and security and identification systems. The devices even show up in automotive systems.

So rapidly have these applications grown, some might assume that their key enabler—the single-chip digital signal processor—was invented only yesterday. In fact, it has been around for almost 15 years. For the most that time, however, a lack of software support and a marginal price/performance ratio limited its acceptance. Even today many potential users are loath to embrace the technology because of its "difficulty" reputation.

[a more manipulate bit stream 更易操作处理的数据流/mass appeal 对公众的吸引力,引起大众的兴趣/digital signal processor(DSP) 数码信号处理器/personal digital assistants 个人数码辅助设备/identification systems 识别系统/key enabler 主要部件,关键部件/single-chip 单片/a marginal price/performance ratio 勉强可接收的价格/性能比]

Well-known Sayings

△ Whatever is worth doing at all is worth doing well.

△ Man's youth is a wonderful thing: it is so full of anguish and of magic and he never comes to know it as it is, until it has gone from him forever.

△ Happiness isn't about what happens to us—it's about how we perceive what happens to us. It's the knack of finding a positive for every negative, and viewing a setback as a challenge. It's not wishing for what we don't have, but enjoying what we do possess.

Lesson 30

E-mail Phones

[1] Do you send and receive more phone calls or e-mails?

[2] When you're looking for information, do you reach for the *World Book Encyclopedia* or the World Wide Web? If your answers are e-mail and the Web, or you wish they were, then a new breed of telecommunication device variously called an e-mail phone or Internet phone may soon find its way into your kitchen or living room.

[3] What's an e-mail phone, or e-phone for short? Essentially, it's the merger of telephone and computer—or at least a tantalizing slice of what a computer provides. With most of these new screen phones, that means being able to read and reply to electronic mail directly from the phone, without booting up (or even owning) a PC. With some, it also means being able to scour the Web to make vacation plans or research homework assignments, albeit at slow speeds and on a rather small screen. And, oh yes, you can still make phone calls, too.

[4] Why an e-phone? This is one invention that seems to be following our lead. Millions of us already exchange e-mails routinely with family and friends at home, not just business colleagues and customers at the office. And the kitchen or the family room is often more conducive to these personal missives than wherever the computer sits, assuming there is one.

[5] No computer experience is required to use an e-phone. Most let you sign up with your choice of Internet service provider (ISP), which typically charges about $20 per month. Some phones offer a preselected menu of ISPs, which can make getting started even easier. Ironically, it's harder to set up an Internet phone if you already have an e-mail account. You'll need to get a battery of arcane information from your current ISP.

[6] Once you're past this tedious hurdle and enter the account information into the phone, you can check your e-mail from either your computer or phone.

[7] To access your e-mail account from one of these phones, you typically have to select e-mail service from a menu. Phones with touch-screens have an icon for that on the opening screen. For other phones, you press one of the buttons lining the bottom or sides of the display, much as with an ATM machine. The phone then calls your ISP. When the ISP picks up, the phone automatically transfers your account name and password. Once accepted, the ISP will start sending the phone your messages. They appear in a list with the name of the sender, the subject of the message, and the date the message was sent. By touching the item you want to read or hitting a button next to it, the message will be displayed. Once you've read it, you can reply to the message, move on to the next one, or, with most phones, delete the message from your account. You can check your e-mail manually, but most e-phones can also be set to check several times a day automatically. In automatic mode, the phone flashes to tell you mail is waiting. If you happen to be using the phone when it is scheduled to check for e-mail, the phone will automatically try again when the line is free.

[8] E-mail by any means can be habit-forming, so it's worth paying close attention to your keyboard

options with these phones. Some have full-size, wireless key-boards that can be stashed elsewhere when not in use. The others have key-boards built into their units, or tucked away in a slide-out drawer. The wireless variety are by far the easiest to type on. The slide-out keyboards are considerably smaller and more cramped, and a keyboard drawer adds to the overall size of the phone. But you can't lose the keyboard, and you will never have to replace the keyboard's batteries, as you do with the wireless models.

[9] One serious drawback to e-mail by phone is that none of these models can receive (or send) attached files, whether they contain documents or graphics. And since swapping pictures of the kids or grandkids via e-mail appendages has become one of the more appealing aspects of electronic messaging, that's real loss. Some phones will attempt to display simple text files as part of the message, but other types of files will appear as gibberish, or not at all. If you share the e-mail account with a PC and don't delete the message, however, you can usually retrieve the message and file on your computer.

[10] Screen size matters, too, especially on e-phone designed to cruise the Web as well as park your e-mail.

[11] Starting a Web browsing session is similar to retrieving your e-mail. You touch a button or screen icon and the phone dials your ISP. Once connected the default page (often a Web search page like Yahoo or Excite) is displayed. The quality of the graphics is surprisingly good on these phones, but the images are not as big or as sharp as on desktop PCs. And the Web browsers built into these phones are more limited than on their PC counterparts. Often, the software doesn't recognize some formatting codes, so pictures can pop up in odd locations.

[12] For retrieving basic information, checking stock quotes, and so on, the phones are adequate Web surfers.

[13] They are not especially fast surfers, however. The modems integrated into these phones are usually 28.8 or 33.6 kbps models, and you can't trade up later to a higher-speed model, as you can with PCs. They are up-to-date in most phone features. Early next year, Samsung and others expect to sell e-phones that will offer even more features and services. In particular, electronic banking and shopping services are expected to be a part of that expanded menu of options.

[14] Are e-phones really ready for the kitchen? Maybe. Certainly, many of these models cost more than we're used to spending on phones, and they offer something less than the kind of full e-mail and Web browsing capabilities we're used to with computers. But the notion of a universal message center has at least been spawned into the real world, and the kitchen may never quite be the same again.

Language Points and Chinese Translations

第 30 课　电子邮件电话

[1] 你平时打电话多还是收发电子邮件多？

[2] encyclopedia 百科全书/breed 品种，种类/telecommunication 电信/to find one's way into 到达，设法到达

当你查询信息时，你是借助于《世界图书百科全书》还是进入环球网？如果你回答是通过电子邮件和环球网寻找信息或者你希望能通过它们查询信息，那么一种新型的电信装置不久就可能进入你的厨房和起居室，这种装置叫作电子邮件电话或网络电话。

[3] merger 合并,并吞/tantalizing 逗人的,诱人的/to scour 搜索,急速穿行,追寻/albeit 尽管,虽然

电子邮件电话(或者简称为电子电话)是什么？实质上,它是电话和计算机的结合——或者至少是计算机所拥有的功能中颇有吸引力的。这种新型的电话,大部分都带有屏幕,即意味着能够直接从电话上阅读和回答电子邮件,不需要打开(甚至不必要自己拥有)一台个人电脑。有了这样的电话,虽然速度较慢,电话上的屏幕较小,但是它意味着可以在环球网上搜索,制定度假计划或者研究家庭作业。当然,你仍然可以打电话。

[4] to follow one's lead 效法某人/routinely 日常地,例行地,常规的/conducive to 有助于,有益于/missive 信件,公文,公函/assuming 假定

为什么叫电子电话？这似乎是在效仿人们打电话的一种发明创造。在日常生活中,我们不仅在办公室与同事和客户互相收发电子邮件,而且也与家中的家庭成员或朋友们收发电子邮件。假定有一台电子邮件电话,那么人们就可更方便地在厨房或房间里处理各种信函了,即使这些地方都摆上电脑也没有这样方便。

[5] to sign up 签约雇用/ironically 讽刺地,令人可笑地/arcane 秘密的,神秘的

使用电子邮件电话无需有使用过计算机的经验。大多数电子邮件电话可让你自己选择因特网服务提供商(ISP),一般每月收取大约20美元的费用。一些电子邮件电话可以提供ISP的预选菜单,从而能够更容易地启动电话。然而如果你已经开立了电子邮件账户,就很难设立因特网电话。你将必须从现在的因特网服务提供商处获取一套秘密的资料。

[6] tedious 冗长乏味的,沉闷的,使人厌烦的/hurdle 障碍

一旦你通过了这令人厌烦的障碍,并将账户资料存入电话,你就可以从计算机或电话上检索你的电子邮件。

[7] icon 图标,图形,画像/to pick up 接受,获得,收到/ATM machine 自动取款机,ATM=automatic teller machine/to transfer 传递,传输/password 密语,指令,口令/to delete 删除

从这些电话进入你的电子邮件账户,你一般必须从菜单上选择电子邮件服务项目。带有触摸屏的电话在初始屏幕上有一个图标代表该菜单。而对另一些电话,你可在显示屏幕的底部或边上排列的许多键中,按一下其中的一个键,如同自动取款机上一样。然后电话呼叫你所选择的因特网服务提供商,当该网络接通后,电话就自动地传输你的账户名称和密码。因特网服务提供商一收到你传输的信息,就会立即在电话机上发送你的信件。信件上列出了发送人的名字,信件的接收人以及信件发送的日期。触摸一下你想要阅读的信息或者击一下旁边的键,该信件就显示出来了。一旦你读完了该信件,就可进行回答,然后再阅读下一封信件,或者从你的账户中删除该信件。你可以手动检查你的电子邮件,但是大多数电子邮件电话也可进行设置,以便每天能自动地检查数次。电话机处于自动模式时,能够不断地闪烁,告诉你有电子邮件在等着进来。如果在预定查阅电子邮件的时刻,你刚好正在使用电话,则电话将能在停止使用时再次自动地进行查阅。

[8] by any means 无论如何/to stash 贮藏,藏匿/to tuck 塞,使隐藏/cramped 狭窄的

无论如何,使用电子邮件可以养成习惯,因此要仔细注意这些电话机键盘的选择。有些电话机具有大小全套的无线键盘,不使用时可以贮藏起来。另一些电话机的键盘放在电话机的组件里,或者可以像滑动的抽屉那样隐藏起来。无线键盘最容易操作,像抽屉一样滑动的键盘相对较小较狭窄些,而且键盘抽屉也增加了电话机的总体积。但是你不能没有键盘,而且正像无线电话模式一样,你将永远不必替换键盘的电池。

[9] to swap 交换,物物交换/appendage 附加物,附属物/appealing 动人的,有吸引力的/gibberish 无意义的谈话,莫名其妙的话/to retrieve 重新得到,恢复,取回,收回

电子邮件电话的一个严重缺点是所有以上这些模式的电话都不能收发附加文件,不管它们是否包含图表。由于通过电子邮件附件收发孩子或孙儿孙女的照片已成为电子邮件更为吸引人的一个方面,这确实是一种损失。一些电话将尝试着显示简单的文本档案作为一部分信息,但是其他种类的档案文本则显得莫名其妙或毫无意义。但是,你如果把电子邮件和个人电脑合用一个账户,并且不删除信息,则你通常能在你的电脑上获取信息和文件。

[10] 电子邮件电话的屏幕大小也很重要,特别是设计用于在网上漫游和储存你的电子邮件的电话。

[11] to browse 浏览,随便翻阅/to dial 拨号码打电话/default 欠缺/graphic 图表、文字等/sharp 明显的,轮廓鲜明的,清晰,线条分明/counterpart 互相对应的人或物,配对者,相对物/formatting code 格式码/to pop up (突然,迅速地或意外地)出现

用电子邮件电话在网上浏览与回收电子邮件相类似。你敲一下键或触动一下屏幕图标,电话就打向因特网服务提供商。一旦接通后就显现出有些缺陷的网页(常常像雅虎或精彩网站上那样的网络搜索页)。电话屏幕上出现的图表的质量特别好,但是图像没个人电脑上的那样大而清晰。安装在这些电话里的网络浏览器要比个人电脑的浏览器受到更多的限制。通常,软件不会识别某些格式码,所以图像就会突然地出现在一些奇怪的位置上。

[12] quote 报价单/surfer 冲浪者,冲浪运动员,本文中指在网上搜索各种信息等/adequate 足够的,符合要求的,令人满意的

就检索基本信息,检查股票报价等等而言,这种电话完全可以满足在网上搜索查询的需求。

[13] to trade up 买更高价的东西/to integrate into 使并入,使一体化/up-to-date 时新的,新式的

然而,这些电话并不能特别快速地上网。这些电话中的调制解调器通常都是 28.8 或 33.6 千毕特/秒型号的,而且今后还不能够像个人电脑那样可以升级换代成更高速的。就电话的特点而言,这当属最新式的。明年初,韩国的三星公司和其他一些公司可望销售能提供更多特色与服务功能的电子邮件电话,特别是电子银行业务和购物服务可望成为可选菜单的一部分。

[14] notion 概念,想法,见解/to spawn 引起,产生,使发生

电子邮件电话是否确实为进入人们的厨房做好了准备?可能是这样。当然,许多这种型号的电子邮件电话的价格要比我们平时购买的电话更贵些,而且它们也不像我们习惯使用的电脑那样会提供完全的电子邮件和网上浏览能力。但是,全球信息中心这种观念至少已经进入了这个现实世界,人类的厨房可能再也不会是原来意义上的厨房了。

Exercises

Ⅰ. Answer the following questions:

1. What is an e-mail phone?

2. Why is the kitchen more conducive to personal missives than wherever the computer sits?

3. Why does the author say that no computer experience is required to use an e-mail phone?

4. How do you reach your e-mail account from an e-mail phone?

5. Say something about the keyboards of e-mail phones?

6. What is the drawback to e-mail by phone?

7. According to the author, what is also important on e-mail phones?

8. How to start a Web browsing session with an e-mail phone?

9. Why does the author say that the default page is displayed?

10. As to modems, what kind of model is now used in e-mail phones?

11. What will especially become a part of a menu?

12. Why does the author say that the kitchen may never quite be the same again?

II. Translate the following words and phrases:

A. From Chinese into English.

1. 环球网(万维网)
2. 电信
3. 电子邮件电话
4. 网络搜索页
5. 电子银行业务
6. 菜单
7. 图标
8. 密码(指令)
9. 键盘
10. 附加文件
11. 文本档案
12. 浏览器

B. From English into Chinese.

1. encyclopedia
2. to be conducive to
3. personal missives
4. preselected menu
5. phones with touch-screens
6. habit-forming
7. to delete the message
8. to cruise the Web
9. to retrieve e-mail
10. to trade up
11. up-to-date features
12. to offer full e-mail and Web browsing capabilities
13. to be used to
14. counterparts
15. notion
16. a universal message center

III. Translate the following passage into Chinese:

E-mail is a pipeline to meet friends and people with similar interests or problems. If logged on and hooked up to a national on-line information service, E-mailers can send the letters they compose at leisure on their computers by modem through the phone line to the subscribed service. E-mail addresses—either names or on-line service account numbers—automatically forward mail to the right place. A response can shoot back in no time as soon as the intended recipient checks in. And E-mailing is far cheaper than long-distance calling. But what makes E-mailing amazingly seductive is freedom from time and place. Telephone tag and different time zones are annoyances of the past once you have someone's E-mail address. Cost-effective optimum just spurs you to explore this "invisible world." Small wonder E-mailing is expanding exponentially.

[log on *v.* （电脑）启用/seductive 富有魅力的/tag *n.* 账单/cost-effective *adj.* 经济效益/optimum *n.* 最佳效果/exponentially 几何级数地]

Well-known Sayings

△ *That is a good book which is opened with expectation and closed with profit.*

△ *The books which help you most are those which make you think most.*

△ *Politeness is not always the sign of wisdom, but the want of it always leaves room for the suspicion of folly.*

Unit 9 Environmental Protection and Pollution Treatment

第 9 单元 环境保护和污染处理

—— Protection of the environment—the quality of air, water and the land around us—used to be the concern of groups on the edge of society. Now government and businesses realise that bad air and water pollution affects everyone, making it difficult for cities to survive and for businesses to make a profit.

—— Atmospheric carbon dioxide, or CO_2, has been increasing steadily for decades. This is thought to be caused by an expanded use of fossil fuels and by toppling of tropical forests. Scientists have linked the CO_2 rise to global warming, a phenomenon known as the greenhouse effect. Nations of the world now are drawing up plans to reduce fossil-fuel burning in hopes of reducing greenhouse gases in the atmosphere.

—— Modern man pollutes with everything he does, so total elimination would require drastic measures. We must employ determined public action. We can reduce pollution, even if we can't eliminate it altogether. But everyone must do his part.

Lesson 31

Environmental Protection and Pollution Treatment

[1] The rich world's arguments about the environment follow a pattern. Environmentalists say pollution is dire and getting worse. Businessmen retort that a real cleanup would cost too much. Joe Citizen believes both: the environment is indeed going down the plug-hole, but so might his job if anyone tries to stop that. All of them, it turns out, are wrong.

[2] Drawing on a wealth of statistics, many official reports show that, in rich countries at least, many of the worst pollution problems are far smaller than they used to be—and that the costs of this success have so far been small.

[3] Start with air pollution. The dreaded greenhouse gases are still flowing into the atmosphere. But output of gases that attack the ozone layer, another potentially serious problem, is well under control. Production of CFCS—chlorofluorocarbons, used in aerosols and refrigerators—has fallen by two-thirds since the mid-1980s.

[4] Worries about urban air pollution now centre on problems like ground-level ozone and microscopic particles. The output of nitrogen oxides, or NOX, which helps produce ground-level ozone, has remained stubbornly high. But many equally serious and more visible pollutants have been beaten back. The flow of oxides of sulphur (or SOX), which contributes to evils such as acid rain and the pea-soup fogs that were apt to shroud London until the 1950s, has fallen by around a third in rich countries since 1980. Emissions of lead, soot and carbon monoxide—each hazardous to human health—have tumbled. In America, legislation has brought lead pollution down by 98% since 1970.

[5] Water quality has improved in many ways. There is still worry about chemicals, such as fertilizers and heavy metals, draining off the land. But many of the organisms that once infested rich-world waterways—and which still kill millions in poor countries—are retreating steadily. Such "organic" pollution is often caused by the dumping of raw sewage. Progress is largely due to the spread of waste-water treatment.

[6] Even land in rich countries is better protected than it was. Though many rich countries are generating more rubbish (the all-OECD volume of municipal waste has risen by more than 40% since 1980), restraints on the disposal of potentially dangerous substances have become much stricter. Current worries often centre on old industrial sites built when rules were lax. Recycling has spread fast; around half of all glass used in OECD countries is now recycled, twice as much as ten years ago.

[7] Land conservation is far from perfect, but at least the rules are spreading. About 10% of land in OECD countries is subject to tough restraints on development—in parks and nature reserves, for instance—up from 4% in 1980. Even the amount of forest cover has increased a little since 1980, though not enough to make up for the rich countries' depredation of forests in poor ones.

[8] Has this cost jobs? OECD officials have found no evidence for that. Spending on pollution control amounts to 1%~2% of GDP in most rich countries, but that has not cut jobs overall. True, certain industries such as mining have lost jobs, and some companies have moved to less strict thirdworld countries. But greenery, like any new market, has also created jobs: the market worldwide (which in

practice means largely in OECD countries) was worth some $200 billion in 1990.

[9] Much of this progress was due to market forces, not regulation. It took rules to keep lead out of petrol and pea-soup fog away from London. But much of the fall in SOX and soot emissions, for example, springs from the decline of coal-burning industries. Except for waste-water treatment, most improvements have come fairly cheap. Either inexpensive alternatives already existed, as with CFCS, or cheap gadgets could be added to existing machinery, such as catalytic converters for cars.

[10] Some regulation has gained support because it protects vested interests. German recycling laws, obliging brewers to use refillable bottles, helps small brewers, with local distribution networks already in place, against incoming foreigners. The rich countries' ban on CFCS is backed by big chemical firms eager to create a market for their substitutes. Britain's National Trust, which conserves a growing proportion of its countryside, also helps to conserve its less-rich-than-they-were land-owning aristocrats in the homes to which they have become accustomed.

[11] The remaining problems will be harder and more expensive. Alternatives to fossil fuels, which give off greenhouse gases, are mostly expensive. Enforcement will be trickier. The pollution from large, identifiable outlets such as municipal sewage works is easy to spot and stop; the run-off of nitrates from some small holder's use of fertilizers is neither.

[12] Moreover, solving current pollution problems will often mean attacking powerful interests. Fossil fuel is a $1 trillion-a-year industry. The best way to improve urban air may be to curb the use of cars, even though modern cars are far cleaner than earlier ones. But most voters use cars. The OECD environment ministers may be feeling pleased with themselves. But from here on the going will get tougher.

Language Points and Chinese Translations

第 31 课　环境保护和污染治理

[1] dire 可怕的,悲惨的/to retort 反驳,还击,报复/Joe（美俚）adj. 知性的,消息灵通的/plug-hole 塞孔,插孔

世界上的富裕国家有关环境问题的争论遵循着一种模式。环境问题专家说污染状况很可怕而且正日益恶化。商界人士反驳说要彻底消除污染代价太大。知性的人们认为两者都对:环境状况确实很糟糕,但是谁要试图阻止这种恶化状况,工作量又是如此之大,结果证明这些都错了。

[2] to draw on 利用,吸收,凭,靠/a wealth of 大量,许多/statistics 统计,统计表

许多官方报道引用大量的统计资料表明:至少在富裕国家,许多严重的污染问题要比以前小得多,而且到目前为止治理污染取得成功所花的费用很小。

[3] to start with 作为开始,首先/dreaded 令人担心,畏惧/ozone 臭氧/under control 被控制住/chlorofluorocarbons 含氯氟烃/aerosol 烟雾剂,气溶胶

首先从空气污染谈起。令人担心的温室气体还在继续不断地排入大气层。但是另一个潜在的严重问题,即侵袭臭氧层的气体总量已得到了很好的控制。自从80年代中期以来,在制造烟雾剂和电冰箱时所使用的含氯氟烃化学物质(CFCS)的生产已经下降了三分之二。

[4] to centre on… 把……集中在……/ground-level 基态,地平面/nitrogen oxides(NOX) 氮氧,氧化氮/stubbornly 顽固,顽强,坚持的,棘手的/sulphur 硫,硫黄/oxides of sulphur(SOX) 氧化硫/pea-soup 黄色浓雾/to be apt to 易于……的,有……倾向的/to shroud 覆盖,掩蔽/lead 铅/soot 煤烟,烟灰/to tumble 下跌,倒坍

· 164 ·

现在对于城市空气污染的担忧主要集中在地面臭氧和微粒等问题上。促使形成地面臭氧的氧化氮(NOX)的排放量还相当高。但是许多一样严重和更为明显的污染物质已受到了控制。氧化硫(SOX)的排放促成了像酸雨和黄色浓雾这样的灾害。在 50 年代之前,黄色烟雾总是笼罩在伦敦上空。但是自从 1980 年以来在富裕国家里硫氧化物的排放量已下降了大约三分之一。铅、煤烟和一氧化碳的散发量——它们均对人类健康有害——已经大大下降。在美国,自从 1970 年以来,立法已经使铅污染下降了 98%。

〔5〕to drain off 排出……的水或液体/to infest 大批出没于,大批的/raw sewage 未经过处理的污水,污物

水质也已在多方面得到了改善。但是人们仍然担心从土壤里渗出的像化肥和重金属这样的化学物质。原先在富裕国家的河道里大量存在的多种有机物——现在在贫穷国家仍然在夺取数以百万计人的生命——正在持续不断地下降。这种"有机物"污染通常是因排放未经处理的污水而造成的。治污的进步主要是由于普遍开展了污水处理。

〔6〕OECD 经济合作与发展组织(Organization for Economic Cooperation and Development)/restraint 抑制,遏制/disposal 处理,处置/recycling 回收利用,再循环

在富裕国家甚至土地也比以前受到了更好的保护。虽然许多富国正在产生更多的垃圾(1980 年以来所有经济合作与发展组织国家的城市废物已经增加了 40%多),但是对潜在危险物质处理的种种限制更加严格。目前人们担心的焦点常常集中于以前一些法规不严密时所建造的老工业基地。废物回收利用已得到了迅速而普遍的推广。在经济合作与发展组织国家使用过的玻璃制品现在大约有一半左右得到了回收利用。这几乎是十年前的两倍。

〔7〕to be far from 远远不够,远离/depredation 掠夺,劫掠,毁坏

土地资源保护工作还远远不够完善,但是至少各种法规制度正在实施。在经济合作与发展组织国家中大约有 10%的土地在开发方面受到了严格的管制——例如公园和自然保护区——而在 1980 年仅为 4%,自 1980 年以来甚至连森林覆盖面积也增加了一些,虽然这远不够弥补富国对穷国森林资源的掠夺。

〔8〕GDP 国内生产总值(Gross Domestic Production)

保护环境是否会使人们失去工作机会?经济合作与发展组织的官员们说还未发现这方面的迹象。在大多数富裕国家用于控制污染的费用达国内生产总值的 1%~2%,但是总体上未曾削减工作机会。确实,像采矿业等某些产业已减少了一些工作机会,一些公司已经搬迁到了对环保不太严格的第三世界国家。但是像任何新兴的市场那样,温室栽培也创造了就业机会。1990 年全世界范围内该市场价值大约 2 000 亿美元(实际上主要是指经济合作与发展组织国家)。

〔9〕gadget 小装置,小配件,小机件/catalytic converter 催化式转化器

这些进步主要是由于市场的力量,而不是靠规章制度。过去利用法规使汽油脱铅和消除伦敦上空的黄色烟雾,但是硫的氧化物和煤烟排放的下降主要是由于减少了燃煤工业。除了废水处理外,大多数环保改进措施费用相当低廉,或者是已有了价格较便宜的含氯氟烃化学物质的替代物,或者是在现有的机器上增添了较便宜的小装置,如用于汽车的催化式转化器等。

〔10〕vested 既得的,既定的,法律规定的/brewer 酿酒商,酿酒人/aristocrat 贵族

一些规章制度由于保护了既得利益者而得到了人们的支持。德国的废物回收利用的法规要求酿酒商使用可反复灌装的瓶子,这使小型的酿酒商利用在本地已建成的销售网络,抵制外来酿酒业主的进入。富裕国家禁止使用含氯氟烃化学物质,得到了一些热切希望开发替代品市场的大的化学公司的支持。英国的全国信托基金会,日益重视农村土地的环保,也有助于那些拥有土地的没落贵族们继续留在他们已经习惯了的家园里。

〔11〕enforcement 执行,实施/tricky 复杂的,微妙的,棘手的/identifiable 可以辨认的/nitrate 硝酸盐

剩余的问题将更困难,费用也更高。排放温室气体的矿物燃料的替代品大多数都很昂贵,要实施这种替代将更错综复杂。对于像城市污水处理厂这样大而又容易识别的污染源容易确定和加以控制,而对一些农民使用化肥而导致硝酸盐的渗逸就很难发现与制止了。

〔12〕trillion 万亿,兆/to curb 控制,抑制,约束

此外,要解决目前的污染问题也将常常有损强势利益集团的利益。矿物燃料就是年产值达一万亿美元的产业。提高城市空气质量的最佳办法可能还是对汽车的使用加以控制。虽然现代化的汽车比早期的汽车造成的污

染要少得多，但是大多数选民仍使用汽车。经济合作与发展组织的环境部长们可能对环保工作自感满意，但是今后的进展将越来越艰难。

Exercises

I. Answer the following questions:

1. What pattern do the rich world's arguments about the environment follow?
2. What has been well under control and what has fallen by two-thirds?
3. What problems do worries about urban air pollution now centre on?
4. Why has water quality improved?
5. What has resulted from recycling in OECD countries?
6. Say something about land conservations in OECD countries?
7. Does the environmental protection cost jobs? Why?
8. Why does the author say that much of the progress in the environmental protection is due to market forces?
9. Why has some regulation gained support?
10. In the environmental protection, we still have a long, long way to go. Do you think so? Give your reasons.

II. Translate the following words and phrases:

A. From Chinese into English.
1. 环境问题专家
2. 空气污染
3. 臭氧层
4. 温室气体
5. 酸雨
6. 废水处理
7. 回收利用
8. 土地资源保护
9. 自然保护区
10. 矿物燃料

B. From English into Chinese.
1. to follow a pattern
2. to draw on a wealth of statistics

3. to start with _____
4. under control _____
5. ground-level ozone _____
6. microscopic particles _____
7. visible pollutants _____
8. to be apt to _____
9. hazardous to human health _____
10. restraints on the disposal of potentially dangerous substances _____
11. GDP _____
12. OECD _____
13. coal-burning industry _____
14. local distribution networks _____
15. to be accustomed to _____
16. to create a market for substitutes _____

III. Translate the following passage into Chinese:

Protection of the environment—the quality of air, water and the land around us—used to be the concern of groups on the edge of society. Now governments and businesses realise that bad air and water pollution affects everyone, making it difficult for cities to survive and for businesses to make a profit.

London, England's biggest city, often suffers from air pollution. More than 1 000 people a year in London die because of this poor air quality, especially the very young, the old and cigarette smokers who are at high risk.

Many European countries and the United States check vehicles for gas and smoke emissions. This is to make sure the levels are below the permitted output. Germany has 600 sites that monitor carbon monoxide. Some 99 percent of the world's carbon monoxide released into the atmosphere comes from motor vehicles.

[edge *n.* 边缘,边线,本句中意指在过去,社会上很少人关注环境保护这个问题/emissions 排放,散发物]

Well-known Sayings

△ *Understand yourself in order to better understand others.*

△ *Quitters never win, and winners never quit.*

△ *There are no secrets to success. It is the result of preparation, hard work, and learning from failure.*

Lesson 32

A Clean World or a Polluted World?

[1] Consume, consume, consume! Our society is consumer oriented—dangerously so. To keep the wheels of industry turning, we manufacture consumer goods in endless quantities, and, in the process, are rapidly exhausting our natural resources. But this is only half the problem. What do we do with manufactured products when they are worn out? They must be disposed of, but how and where? Unsightly junk-yards full of rusting automobiles already surround every city in the nation. Americans throw away 80 billion bottles and cans each year, enough to build more than ten stacks to the moon. There isn't room for much more waste, and yet the factories grind on. They cannot stop because everyone wants a job. Our standard of living, one of the highest in the world, requires the consumption of manufactured products in ever-increasing amounts. Man, about to be buried in his own waste, is caught in a vicious cycle. "Stop the world, I want to get off," is the way a popular song put man's dilemma.

[2] It wasn't always like this. Only 100 years ago man lived in harmony with nature. There weren't so many people then and their wants were fewer. Whatever wastes were produced could be absorbed by nature and were soon covered over. Today this harmonious relationship is threatened by man's lack of foresight and planning, and by his carelessness and greed. For man is slowly poisoning his environment.

[3] Pollution is a "dirty" word. To pollute means to contaminate—to spoil something by introducing impurities which make it unfit or unclean to use. Pollution comes in many forms. We see it, smell it, taste it, drink it, and stumble through it. We literally live in and breathe pollution, and, not surprisingly, it is beginning to threaten our health, our happiness, and our very civilization.

[4] Once we thought of pollution as meaning simply smog—the choking, stinging, dirty air that hovers over cities. But air pollution, while it is still the most dangerous, is only one type of contamination among several which attack the most basic life functions.

[5] Through the uncontrolled use of insecticides, man has polluted the land, killing the wildlife. By dumping sewage and chemicals into rivers and lakes, we have contaminated our drinking water. We are polluting the oceans, too, killing the fish and thereby depriving ourselves of an invaluable food supply.

[6] Part of the problem is our exploding population. More and more people produce more wastes. But this problem is intensified by our "throw-away" technology. Each year Americans dispose of 7 million autos, 20 million tons of waste paper, 25 million pounds of toothpaste tubes and 48 million cans. We throw away gum wrappers, newspapers, and paper plates. It is no longer fashionable to reuse anything. Today almost everything is disposable. Instead of repairing a toaster or a radio, it is easier and cheaper to buy a new one and discard the old, even though 95 percent of its parts may still be functioning. Baby diapers, which used to be made of reusable cloth, are now paper throw-aways. Soon we will wear clothing made of paper:"Wear it once and throw it away" will be the slogan of the fashion conscious.

[7] Where is this all to end? Are we turning the world into a gigantic dump, or is there hope that we can solve the pollution problem? Fortunately, solutions are in sight. A few of them are positively ingenious.

[8] Take the problem of discarded automobiles for instance. Each year over 40 000 of them are abandoned in New York City alone. Eventually the discards end up in a junkyard. But cars are too bulky to ship as scrap to a steel mill. They must first be flattened. This is done in a giant compressor which can reduce a Cadillac to the size of a television set in a matter of minutes. Any leftover scrap metal is mixed

with concrete and made into exceptionally strong bricks that are used in buildings and bridges. Man's ingenuity has come to his rescue.

[9] What about water pollution? More and more cities are building sewage-treatment plants. Instead of being dumped into a nearby river or lake, sewage is sent through a system of underground pipes to a giant tank where the water is separated from the solid material, purified, and returned for reuse to the community water supply. The solid material called sludge, is converted into fertilizer. The sludge can also be made into bricks.

[10] Controlling air pollution is another crucial objective. Without food, man can live about five weeks; without water about five days. Without air, he can only live five minutes, so pure air is a must. Here the wrong-doer is the automobile. Where there is a concentration of automobiles, as in our big cities, air pollution is severe. It is important to see that our cars are equipped with pollution-control devices. Such devices effectively reduce the harmful gases emitted from the engine.

[11] Power plants, factories, and apartment buildings can also avoid air pollution. When possible they should use clean fuels like gas and oil. And the smokestacks of these buildings should be equipped with filters and other smoke-reduction devices.

[12] Can we eliminate pollution altogether? Probably not. Modern man pollutes with everything he does, so total elimination would require drastic measures. Every power plant would have to shut down. Industries would have to close. We would have to leave all our automobiles in the garage. Every bus and truck and airplane would have to stop running. There would be no way to bring food to the cities. There would be no heat and no light. Under these conditions, our population would die in a short time.

[13] Since such a drastic solution is impossible, we must employ determined public action. We can reduce pollution, even if we can't eliminate it altogether. But everyone must do his part. Check your car to see if the pollution-control device is working. Reduce your use of electricity. Is air conditioning really necessary? Don't dump garbage or other waste on the land or in the water. Demand that government take firm action against polluters. We can have a clean world, or we can do nothing. The choice is up to you.

Language Points and Chinese Translations

第32课 我们要一个清洁的世界还是污染的世界？

[1] consumer oriented 以消费者为导向的/consumer goods 消费品/natural resources 自然资源/manufactured products 制造品，产品/worn out 用坏的，用旧的，不能再用的/to dispose of 处理，处置/junkyards 废旧物堆置场/room 空间/to grind on 继续不断地苦干/about to do sth. 即将，将要，正要，相当于 on the point of doing sth. /vicious cycle 恶性循环/dilemma 困境，窘境，进退两难

消费，消费，再消费！我们的社会是以消费者为导向的——已到了十分危险的程度。为了使工业继续不断地发展，我们制造出无穷无尽的消费品，同时在这一过程中快速地耗尽自然资源。但是这还只是问题的一半。当产品淘汰后，我们怎么办？它们必须被处理掉，但问题是如何处理并在什么地方处理它们呢？全国（这里指美国）每个城市都已被废旧生锈的汽车堆置场所包围，很不雅观。美国人每年扔掉800亿个瓶子和罐头，足以堆放高达至月球的十多堆。已没有空间容纳更多的废弃物，然而工厂还在继续不停地拼命生产。因为大家都需要工作，所以工厂不会停止生产。我们的生活水平在世界上名列前茅，对制成品的消费量日益增长，人类已陷入恶性循环，即将被自己制造的废物所埋葬。"让世界停一下，我要活（或者生存）下去。"一首流行歌曲就是这样来描述人类进退两难的尴尬境地。

[2] in harmony with 相配，与……一致，协调/wants n. 需求，欲望/foresight 远见，先见，深谋

过去并不是这种状况。仅100年前人类还和大自然相处得十分和谐、协调。那时候没有这么多人,人们的需求也极少,不管产生了什么废物都能被自然界吸纳并且很快就被遮盖了。今天,由于人类缺乏远见、没有计划、粗心疏忽和贪得无厌,这种和谐关系受到威胁,因为人类正在慢慢毒害自己的环境。

[3] to contaminate 弄脏,玷污,污染/to stumble 绊跌,绊倒

污染是一个"肮脏"的字眼。污染意指弄脏——因带进杂质而使某个东西不清洁或不适合使用,因而毁坏了这东西。污染以多种多样的形式存在。我们对其看得见,闻得出,尝得着,喝得到,甚至被其绊倒。我们简直就是在污染中生活和呼吸,而且不足为怪的是,污染正在开始威胁我们的健康、幸福和文明。

[4] smog:mixture of fog and smoke 烟雾/choking 令人窒息的/stinging 刺激的,刺痛的/to hover 盘旋,徘徊,that hovers over cities 笼罩在城市上空,这是一定语从句,修饰前面的 air。

我们曾经认为污染只是意指烟雾——笼罩在城市上空的令人窒息、带有刺激性的肮脏空气。但是,空气污染虽然最具有危害性,却只是侵袭最基本生命机能的几种污染物之一。

[5] to deprive sb. of sth. 使丧失,剥夺,使不能享用

由于滥用杀虫剂,人类已污染了土地,毒杀了野生动物。我们向江河与湖泊排放污水及化学物质,污染了饮用水。我们也在污染海洋,毒死了鱼类,从而使自己失去了宝贵的食物供应来源。

[6] to intensify 加剧,使更剧烈/toaster 烤面包器/to discard 丢弃,抛弃/conscious 察觉的,明白的,知道的,自觉的

问题的一部分是由于我们日益爆炸的人口,越来越多的人产生越来越多的废物。但是,"一次性使用"技术加剧了该问题的严重性。美国人每年要清除700万辆汽车,2 000万吨废纸,2 500万磅牙膏管和4 800万只罐头盒。我们丢弃口香糖包装纸、报纸和纸盘。任何物品的再利用即已不再时髦。今天几乎一切东西都可以随意处置。人们不再修理烤面包器或收音机,买个新的、扔掉旧的更为方便和便宜,虽然其95%的部件可能还有使用功能。婴儿尿布,过去是用布做的,并可以重复使用,而现在是用纸做的,用过即扔。不久我们将穿用纸做成的衣服:"穿一次即扔",这将是具有时尚意识的人们的口号。

[7] gigantic:of immense size 巨大的,庞大的/ingenious adj. 有独创性的,精巧的

所有这一切将在何处终了?我们是在把世界变成一个巨大的垃圾场,还是有希望能够解决污染问题?幸运的是,解决办法已经在望,其中一些办法确有独创性。

[8] to abandon 抛弃,放弃,丢弃/to end up 结束,告终/bulky 庞大的,笨大的/to flatten 把……弄平/Cadillac 小汽车的牌号,凯迪拉克轿车/concrete 混凝土/ingenuity 独创,独出心裁/rescue v., n. 援救,营救,come to sb's rescue 来援救某人

例如,就拿丢弃的汽车问题来说吧。每年仅纽约市丢弃的汽车就有40 000多辆。这些废弃的汽车最终被拖送到垃圾场。但是汽车太笨重不能当做废铁运往钢铁厂,首先要将它们压扁,这一工作是由一个巨大的冲床来完成的。冲床可以在几分钟的时间里把一辆"Cadillac"牌小汽车挤压成一台电视机那么大小,剩下的废金属和混凝土混合在一起被制成特别坚硬的砖块,用来建造大楼和桥梁。人类的独创精神已经开始用于拯救人类本身。

[9] sewage-treatment plants 污水处理厂/to dump into 把……倾倒进……/Sludge 泥状沉积物,淤渣/convert into 把……转变,变换成……

水污染如何处理呢?越来越多的城市正在建造污水处理厂,污水不再被排放到附近的江河、湖泊,而是通过地下管道系统被送至一个巨大的储水池,在那里水与固体物质进行分离、净化后,作为供水送往社区被再次利用。固体物质被称作淤渣,可以转化为肥料,也可以制成砖块。

[10] crucial objective 重要的目标/must n. 指 something that must be done 必不可少,必需的事物/to see that …也可说 to see to it that… 务必做到,注意做到。该动词不定式短语在本句中作主语,句首的 it 是形式主语。

控制空气污染是另一个重要目标。没有食物,人类能够生存大约五周;没有水大约生存五天;没有空气,人类只能生存五分钟,所以纯净的空气是必不可少的。造成空气污染的祸首是汽车。就像在我们的大城市,汽车大量集中的地方,空气污染就十分严重。为此我们的汽车都务必要安装上控制污染的装置,这很重要。这些装置可以有效地减少发动机排放出来的有害气体。

[11] When (it is) possible… 本句中 it is 已省略了/smokestack 大烟囱/filter 过滤器

发电厂、工厂和公寓大楼也能够避免空气污染。如果可能的话,它们都应该使用像可燃气和油类这样的清洁燃料。这些建筑物的烟囱应该安装过滤设备和其他减少烟雾的装置。

[12] to eliminate 清除,消除,其名词形式为 elimination/modern man 现代人类/drastic 严厉的,极端的/garage 车库

我们能够完全地清除污染吗？可能不会。现代人类所做的一切都会有污染,所以完全彻底地清除污染需要有严厉的措施。每个发电厂都必须关闭,所有工厂企业都必须停工,我们必须把所有的汽车都停放在车库里不用,所有的汽车、卡车和飞机都必须停止运行。这样就无法把食物运送到城市,也没有供热和照明。在这种状况下,我们人类就会在短时间内死亡。

[13] to do one's part 尽某人的职责,尽力/to take firm action against 对……采取坚决的行动或有力的措施/to be up to sb. 应由某人……,视为某人的职责

由于不可能采取这种激进的措施,我们就必须坚决地呼唤起公众的行动。即使我们不能完全地清除污染,但只要大家尽力,我们就能减少污染。检查汽车的污染控制装置是否工作正常。节约用电。空调确实很必要吗？不要把垃圾或其他废物排放到土壤和水里。要求政府对那些制造污染者采取坚决的行动。我们或者拥有一个清洁的世界,或者无能为力,一切取决于你。

Exercises

I. Answer the following questions:

1. What do people have to do in order to keep the wheels of industry turning?

2. Why does the author say that man is about to be buried in his own waste?

3. Why is the harmonious relationship between man and nature threatened today?

4. What does "to pollute" mean?

5. Why is air pollution the most dangerous?

6. How does man pollute with everything he does?

7. How many cars are abandoned in New York City every year and how are they disposed of?

8. How do people prevent water pollution?

9. How do people prevent air pollution?

10. Can man eliminate pollution altogether? Why?

11. How should we do to prevent pollution?

12. Are you sure that we can have a clean world? Give your reasons.

II. Translate the following words and phrases:

A. From Chinese into English.

1. 消费品

2. 自然资源 _____
3. 生活水平 _____
4. 恶性循环 _____
5. 最基本的生命机能 _____
6. 污水处理厂 _____
7. 污染控制装置 _____
8. 清除污染 _____
9. 非常措施 _____
10. 公共行动 _____

B. From English into Chinese.
1. consumer oriented _____
2. to dispose of _____
3. to live in harmony with nature _____
4. lack of foresight and planning _____
5. to deprive of _____
6. the fashion conscious _____
7. in sight _____
8. to convert…into… _____
9. to be equipped with _____
10. to see (to it) that… _____
11. to take firm action against _____
12. to be up to sb. _____
13. smog _____
14. ingenious _____

Ⅲ. Translate the following passage into Chinese:

China has the world's longest meteorological records, going back over 500 years. They help us clearly to understand the problem of global warming. The five warmest years since the 15th century have all been in the 1990s; 1997 was the warmest year ever recorded. We know that if this trend continues, it will bring more and more severe weather events and it will disrupt the lives of hundreds of millions of people in the world during the coming century. China is already taking impressive steps to protect its future. Leaded gasoline is being banned. Inefficient stoves have been upgraded. People can find out about air quality from newspapers. Communities and provinces and the national government are doing more to clean up rivers. Chinese scientists are fighting deforestation and soil erosion. And citizens are doing more to promote public education about the environment, among families and especially among children.

Well-known Sayings

△ *If you cannot have the best, make the best of what you have.*

△ *Success seldom comes easily on the first try. Persistence is the ultimate key to success. What separates the successful and the unsuccessful is persistence.*

△ *Successful people also fail occasionally, but they do not let their failures defeat their spirit. They learn from defeats, revise their strategy as needed and try again until they succeed.*

Lesson 33

Good Effects of El Nino

[1] The climate phenomenon that is being blamed for floods, hurricanes and early snowstorms also deserves credit for invigorating plants and helping to control the pollutant linked to global warming, a new study shows.

[2] El Nino—the periodic warming of eastern Pacific Ocean waters—causes a burst of plant growth throughout the world, and this removes carbon dioxide from the atmosphere, researchers have found.

[3] Natural weather events, such as the brief Warming caused by El Nino, have a much more dramatic effect than previously believed on how much carbon dioxide is absorbed by plants and how much of the gas is expelled by the soils, said David Schimel of the National Center for Atmospheric Research. He is co-author of a study to be published in the journal Science.

[4] Atmospheric carbon dioxide, or CO_2, has been increasing steadily for decades. This is thought to be caused by an expanded use of fossil fuels and by toppling of tropical forests. Scientists have linked the CO_2 rise to global warming, a phenomenon known as the greenhouse effect. Nations of the world now are drawing up plans to reduce fossil-fuel burning in hopes of reducing greenhouse gases in the atmosphere.

[5] Those determining how much to reduce fossil-fuel burning, said Schimel, should consider effects of natural climate variability on the ability of plants to absorb CO_2.

[6] Schimel said satellite measurements of CO_2, plant growth and temperature show that natural warming events such as El Nino at first cause more CO_2 to be released into the atmosphere, probably as the result of accelerated decay of dead plant matter in the soil.

[7] But later, within two years, there is an explosion of growth in forests and grasslands, causing plants to more vigorously suck carbon dioxide out of the atmosphere.

[8] "We think that there is a delayed response in vegetation and soils to the warming of such things as El Nino, and this leads to increased plant growth," said Schimel.

[9] However, it is not clear whether the warming by El Nino causes a net decrease in the buildup of CO_2 over the long haul. "We don't really know that yet," said Schimel.

[10] What the study does show, however, is that the rise and fall of CO_2 in the atmosphere is strongly influenced by natural changes in global temperature, said B. H. Braswell of the University of New Hampshire, a co-author of the study.

[11] Braswell said that in years when the global weather is cooler than normal, there is a decrease in both the decay of dead plants and in new plant growth. This causes an effect that is the opposite of El Nino warming. CO_2 atmosphere levels first decline and later increase.

[12] "I think we have demonstrated that the ecosystem has a lot more to do with climate change than was previously believed," said Braswell.

[13] The researchers used satellite measurements taken from 1980 to 1991. This period included a major El Nino in 1982 to 1983 and warm years later in the 1980s.

[14] Each of these events, said the authors, had a direct, but often delayed, effect on the CO_2 levels in the atmosphere.

Language Points and Chinese Translations

第33课 厄尔尼诺现象的正面效应

〔1〕一项新的研究表明,虽然水灾、飓风和提前来临的暴风雨等气候现象使人们怨声载道,但是由于地球转暖也促使植物生长旺盛且有利于控制污染。

〔2〕研究人员已经发现,厄尔尼诺现象——太平洋东部水域周期性升温——引起全球范围内植物突发生长,从而清除大气中的二氧化碳。

〔3〕国家大气研究中心的David Schimel,作为参加编写者之一,将在《科学》杂志上发表他们的一个研究成果。他说:厄尔尼诺现象引起大自然气候短暂转暖,对植物吸收二氧化碳和土壤排出气体量的多少有着微妙的作用,而在以前人们对此知之甚少。

〔4〕to topple 推倒,倒塌,这里意指对热带森林的砍伐。/to draw up 起草,拟定

几十年来,大气中的二氧化碳(CO_2)含量一直在稳定增加。人们认为这是由于大量使用矿物燃料和砍伐热带森林所造成的。科学家们已把CO_2含量升高与地球转暖联系起来,也即人们所认为的温室效应现象。现在世界各国都在制订计划减少燃烧矿物燃料,以期降低大气中温室效应所产生的各种气体含量。

〔5〕to determine 决定,本句中为现在分词作定语,修饰前面的 those/variability n. 多变性,变异性

Schimel说,决定减少燃烧矿物燃料使用量的那些诸多因素应该考虑到自然气候的多变性对植物吸收二氧化碳能力所产生的作用。

〔6〕to release 释放/as the result of 由于……的结果

Schimel说,卫星对二氧化碳气体、植物生长和气温的监测结果表明:像厄尔尼诺这种使自然变暖的现象,很可能由于土壤里死亡植物的加速腐烂而首先导致向大气层中释放出更多的二氧化碳。

〔7〕to suck 吸收,与absorb意思相同

但是在此后的两年中,森林和草地植物勃发生长,大量吸收大气层中的二氧化碳。

〔8〕response n. 反应,应答,答复/to lead to 导致,引起

Schimel说,"我们认为植被和土壤对厄尔尼诺这种变暖现象虽然反应迟缓,但这必然会导致植物加速生长。"

〔9〕net decrease 净减少/buildup 逐渐形成或建立/haul n. 拖拉/over the long haul 意指在长期过程中

然而,现在还不清楚,由厄尔尼诺引起的气候转暖现象是否能在长时间过程中使二氧化碳气体的形成量净值减少。Schimel说,"我们目前对此还确实不知道。"

〔10〕该研究项目的合作者,新罕布什尔州立大学的B. H. Braswell说,研究结果确实表明大气中二氧化碳气体含量的增加和减少受到全球气温自然变化的影响很大。

〔11〕Baswell说,几年后当全球气温低于正常值时,死亡植物的腐烂和新植物的生长速度均会降低。这导致与厄尔尼诺的效应完全相反,大气中二氧化碳含量也先下降后上升。

〔12〕to demonstrate 证明,论证,表明/ecosystem=ecology+system 生态系统,生态环境

Braswell说,"我认为我们已经证明:生态环境和气候的变化密切相关,这大大超越了人们以前对此的认识。"

〔13〕研究人员使用了卫星从1980年至1991年期间记录下的监测结果。这段时期包括了1982年至1983年期间主要的厄尔尼诺现象和80年代后期几年的气候转暖现象。

〔14〕该项研究成果的作者们说,每种现象都对大气层中二氧化碳含量产生直接的影响,但其效应常常是迟缓的。

Exercises

I. Answer the following questions:

1. What is the climate phenomenon being blamed for and what does it deserve credit for?

2. What have researchers found?

3. What does the brief warming caused by El Nino have an effect on?

4. Why has atmosphere carbon dioxide been increasing steadily for decades?

5. What is the greenhouse effect?

6. Why are many countries now making plans to reduce fossil-fuel burning?

7. What do satellite measurements show?

8. According to Schimel, what is not clear at present?

9. According to Braswell, what does the study show?

10. Why does the ecosystem have something to do with climate change?

II. Translate the following words and phrases:

A. From Chinese into English.
1. 厄尔尼诺现象 ___
2. 气候现象 ___
3. 周期性升温 ___
4. 二氧化碳 ___
5. 矿物燃料 ___
6. 温室效应 ___
7. 自然气候的变异性 ___
8. 生态环境 ___

B. From English into Chinese.
1. global warming ___
2. to have a dramatic effect on ___
3. an expand use of ___
4. to draw up plans ___
5. in hopes of ___
6. a delayed response ___
7. over the long haul ___

8. to have a lot to do with _____

III. Translate the following passage into Chinese:

El Nino is the Spanish name for the baby Jesus. The phenomenon is so-called because warm water moving across the Pacific traditionally reaches South America around Christmas. Scientists have now applied the term El Nino to the major warming episodes over large South American coastal areas and westernly along the equator and the Dateline area. Scientists noted the El Nino has a return period of four to five years and lasts between 12~18 months.

The strongest El Nino last century occurred in 1982 to 1983 and resulted in droughts and disastrous forest fires in Indonesia and Australia, wreaking economic damage of at least $US 8 billion.

Well-known Sayings

△ *The secret of success is the consistency to pursue.*
△ *Great opportunity is usually disguised as unsolvable problems.*
△ *The talent of success is nothing more than doing well whatever you do without a thought of fame.*

Unit 10 Space Station and Space Technology

第 10 单元 太空站和空间技术

—— The International Space Station, as one of the most ambitious space projects ever and a key launching board for exploration of the solar system, features unprecedented technical, managerial, and international complexity. The ISS is the largest ever experiment in international technological cooperation. It is a necessary stepping stone to long-term human activities in new areas of operations. The station is off the planet and it's the first step outward—not an end in itself, but a step along the way.

—— Space science, applications and technology are crucially important strategic fields. The utilization of earth observation is an important part of space applications that maintains a strong connection with human society, noting that it offers fundamental means for sustaining a stable coexistence between man and nature as well as improving the quality of human life. On the other hand, space technology provides strong support for the achievement of the goals of space science and applications.

—— Space flight may be about to undergo a transformation far more radical than anything planned by national or international space agencies. In the next fifteen years or so, there could be a fleet of fifty spaceplanes carrying a million people into orbit about the earth each year.

Lesson 34

The International Space Station

[1] Late June in Kazakhstan, a Russian Proton rocket sits poised for launch at the once-secret Baikonul space base. Observers from NASA and other space agencies have crowded into the vintage control room and journalists from around the world are monitoring the countdown. At zero, the Proton's engines thunder, it lifts away from Earth and quickly disappears from sight. The first module of the long-awaited International Space Station is headed for orbit.

[2] If all goes well, that will be the scene just a month from now, when one of the world's most ambitious engineering projects finally gets off the ground. In January 1999, after six launches by U. S. space shuttles and Russian boosters, a three-man crew will take up residence. From that moment onward, the space station will be a permanent off-planet extension of human civilization.

[3] When the station is completed, around the end of 2003 if NASA sticks to its schedule, it will be a multi-room hotel and research facility orbiting the Earth every 90 minutes. Its permanent population will be six or seven, with the mix shifting as Americans, Russians, Europeans, and Japanese move in and out over the months and years. By that time, resupply and assembly flights by shuttles or Russian rockets will have become so routine that today's breathtaking series of space rendezvous is certain to become tomorrow's humdrum.

[4] You'll know the ISS is there. Five times the size of the Russian space station Mir, it will have solar wings and radiators sprouting from trusses spanning 356 feet. Its central core will be a collection of motor-home-size labs, living quarters, and supply canisters plugged together like a supersize Lego set. Together they'll fill a fore-to-aft length of 290 feet, almost as long as a football field.

[5] The final configuration, requiring 45 separate space launches over at least six years and many long days of spacewalks by astronaut construction workers, will track diamond-bright across the night sky. Only the moon and Venus will be bigger and more visible.

[6] "It takes a while to get perspective on how big this thing is," says Kevin Chilton, the station's operations manager at the Johnson Space Center in Houston. To demonstrate, he stretches his arms across a model of the station without reaching either end. The space shuttle docked to the station is only the size of a football and almost lost in the labyrinth of trusses, panels, and modules.

[7] The station's complexity is as awesome as its size. Built by a partnership of 16 nations, ISS will consist of hundreds of individual elements that come from all over the world. "Most of the elements will never be physically mated until they come together in orbit," explains Randy Brinkley, NASA's Houston-based program manager for the space station. "But we're confident that when we turn on the lights, it will all work."

[8] But even if all the pieces fit perfectly, the assembly process itself will be risky. Unlike an airplane, the space station is flown while it's being built, and each new piece that is added may change the way the station behaves in flight.

[9] Computer software problems are also a concern. "Probably the biggest single risk that we face on this project," says Stone. Like the hardware elements, the software components come from all over the

world and must mesh smoothly. The astronauts won't even be able to turn on the station's lights without help from a computer, because all of the electric power switching will be controlled by software.

[10] The station is divided roughly into two sections, one built primarily by the United States and the other built by Russia. "In some ways, it looks like two different spacecraft in close proximity," says Stone, "but to the crew, it will all be one vehicle."

[11] The other nations participating in the project are also contributing hardware: Japan's space agency, NASDA, is supplying a laboratory module that includes a "back porch" where experiments can be exposed to space; astronauts will use a robotic arm to lift experiments onto the porch from an air lock. The European Space Agency is also providing a lab module. The Canadians are building a robotic arm and hand that will be invaluable for assembly work and heavy lifting. And Brazil is contributing a window facility, astronauts can use it to study changes in the Amazonian rainforest, among other things.

Language Points and Chinese Translations

第34课 国际空间站

[1] Kazakhstan 哈萨克斯坦(共和国)/proton 质子,proton rocket 质子火箭/to poise 使平衡,保持平衡,作好姿势,本句中 poised for launch 是一过去分词短语作前面动词 sits 的表语,译成"等待发射,准备发射"。/Baikonul 拜科努尔,地名,在哈萨克斯坦共和国境内,是航天器发射场/space base 航天基地,太空基地/NASA (美国)国家航空航天局,是 National Aeronautics and Space Administration 的缩写形式/vintage 老式的,旧式的/to monitor 监视,监听/countdown 倒计时/module n. 模组,单体,本文中指舱室/to head for 向……前进,进发

6月下旬,哈萨克斯坦境内,在一度秘密的拜科努尔航天基地,一颗俄罗斯的质子火箭正在等待发射。来自美国航空航天局和其他航天局的观察人员已聚集在老式的控制室里,与此同时,来自世界各地的新闻记者们正注视着倒计时。当倒数至零秒时,质子火箭的发动机发出雷鸣般的响声,质子火箭升腾着离开了地球,很快就消失得无影无踪。人们等待已久的国际空间站的第一个太空舱向轨道进发。

[2] ambitious 雄心勃勃的/to get off 离开,起飞,飞离/space shuttle 航天飞机//booster 运载火箭/off-planet 离开地球的,地球以外的,这里的 planet 指地球

如果一切都进展顺利的话,从现在算起只要一个月就会看到以上这一场景。世界上最雄心勃勃的一个工程项目终于离开了地面。在1999年1月,即在美国的航天飞机和俄罗斯的运载火箭进行六次发射后,由三人组成的宇航工作人员将住在那里。从那时起,国际空间站将是人类文明向地球以外扩展的一个永久性窗口。

[3] to stick to 坚持/schedule 预定计划表,时间表/multi-room hotel 多个房间的旅馆/facility 设施,设备,场所/orbiting the Earth every 90 minutes 每90分钟围绕地球运行一周,该现在分词短语作定语修饰前面的 hotel 和 facility。/permanent population 常住人口/mix shifting 在本句中指各国的宇航员在该空间站进进出出,轮流交换。/resupply n. 给养,供应品/assembly n. 组装件,配件/routine 平常的/breathtaking 惊险的,紧张刺激的/rendezvous 会合点,集会地点/humdrum 单调乏味的

如果美国航空航天局坚持执行预定的计划,那么到2003年年底左右,国际空间站就将完全建成。它将是一个有多个房间的旅馆和研究场所,每90分钟围绕地球运行一周。它的常住人口将是六七人,由美国、俄罗斯、欧洲和日本的宇航员数月或数年一次地迁进迁出,轮换居住。到那时,航天飞机或俄罗斯的火箭运送给养供应品和配件的飞行将会变得十分普通、平常,今天宇宙飞行器在太空一次又一次连续而又惊险的会合,到明天一定会变得单调乏味。

[4] ISS 国际空间站,是 International Space Station 的缩写形式/Mir(俄罗斯的)"和平号"(空间站)/truss (太空舱)构架,桁架/to span 跨过,从一边至另一边,指 to extend across from side to side/motor-home-size 像活动房

子大小的/canister 小罐,舱储室/plugged together 相互紧密连接在一起的,在本句中作定语修饰前面的名词。/fore-to-aft 从舱首到舱尾,从前部到后部

你将会认出国际空间站就在那里,它的大小是俄罗斯的"和平号"空间站的五倍,太阳能电池板翼和散热器从太空舱构架向外伸展,跨度长达356英尺。它的中心部位是由活动房大小的实验室、生活区和供应储舱组成的一个集合体,它们互相紧密连接在一起就像一组特大型的积木玩具,首尾共长290英尺,几乎像一个足球场那么长。

[5] configuration n. 规模,形态,构形,结构/spacewalks 太空行走/Venus 金星

国际空间站的最终结构形态需要在至少六年的时间里进行45次有间隔的太空发射,并且由宇航建设工作人员长时间的太空行走进行组建才能完成,其轨迹将在夜空中留下钻石般的亮丽光彩。只有月亮和金星比它更大,看得更清楚。

[6] perspective n. 透视,透视法/to demonstrate 演示,论证,表明/to dock 停靠,入场/labyrinth n. 迷宫,迷路,曲径/panel 指太空舱的电池板

休斯顿约翰逊航天中心的国际空间站地面操作部经理 Kevin Chilton 说:"这个物体到底有多大,要过一段时间才能看到全貌。"为了演示其大小,他伸出双臂,横跨这空间站的一个模型而两手互相够不着。停靠在空间站的航天飞机只有一个足球那么大小,在太空舱构架、电池板和舱房的簇拥中几乎都看不到其存在。

[7] awesome adj. 令人敬畏的,可畏的/to consist of 由……组成/individual adj. 个别的,独特的,个体的

像其规模那样,该空间站的复杂程度也异常惊人。它由16个国家合作构建,由来自世界各地数以百计的各种独特部件构成。美国航空航天局休斯顿基地的空间站项目经理 Randy Brinkley 解释说,"大多数部件要一起进入运行轨道后才能互相匹配组装。但是我们有信心,当我们开灯时,一切都会运作起来。"

[8] 但是即使所有的组件都匹配得很完美,装配过程本身也将十分危险。空间站不像飞机,它是在飞行中组建,每安装上一个新部件就有可能改变空间站的运行方式。

[9] to mesh 吻合,相啮合,协调,和谐

计算机的软件问题也是一件值得关切的事。Stone 说,"这也许是我们在这一项目中所面临的最大的单个风险"。像硬件组件一样,软件部分也来自于世界各地,必须十分协调兼容。如果没有计算机的帮助,宇航员甚至打不开空间站的灯,因为所有电源开关都将由软件控制。

[10] in close proximity 非常接近,相当于 very near

空间站大致分成两个部分,一部分主要由美国制造,另一部分则由俄罗斯制造。Stone 说,"以某种方式来说,它看起来就像是两个不同的太空船紧密连接在一起,但是对于宇航员全体人员来说,它又将是一个完整的运载工具。"

[11] NASDA(日本)国家宇宙开发事业团,是 National Space Development Agency of Japan 的缩写形式/air lock: compartment with air-tight doors at each end 气密室/invaluable 无价的,珍贵的/rainforest(热带)雨林/among other things 除了别的以外,还……,格外,尤其

参加该项计划的其他国家也提供了硬件:日本航天局——国家宇宙开发事业团提供了一个实验舱,该舱包括一个"后廊",在那里可以直接暴露在太空条件下进行各种实验。宇航员将使用机械臂从气密室提起实验物品放置到后廊上。欧洲航天局也提供了一个实验舱。加拿大人正在建造一个机械臂和机械手,这对于安装工作和提升重物来说将是非常宝贵的。巴西提供了一个窗式装置,宇航员们可以用它来研究亚马逊河流域的热带雨林的变化以及其他一些情况。

Exercises

I. Answer the following questions:

1. What will happen in late June?

2. What will get off the ground if all goes well?

3. Beginning in January 1999, what will the International Space Station be according to the author?

4. When will the station be completed and what will it be?

5. Can you say something about the permanent population in the station?

6. Please describe the size and the length of the station.

7. What will the final configuration require?

8. How many countries will take part in the construction of the station?

9. Why are computer software problems a concern?

10. How many sections is the station divided into and what does it look like?

II. Translate the following words and phrases:

A. From Chinese into English.
1. 国际空间站
2. 航天中心
3. 太空基地
4. 太阳能电池板翼
5. 散热器
6. 轨道
7. 计算机软件
8. 宇航员

B. From English into Chinese.
1. a proton rocket
2. NASA
3. to crowd into
4. to monitor the countdown
5. to head for
6. the most ambitious engineering projects
7. a permanent off-planet extension of human civilization
8. space walks
9. in close proximity
10. to participate in
11. to be exposed to
12. among other things
13. a lab module
14. a robotic arm and hand

III. Translate the following passage into Chinese:

"The future ain't what it used to be" may be the thought in 2001 when people compare the International Space Station with the huge orbital base suggested in the 1967 movie, 2001: *A Space Odyssey*. Just designing the station has been an odyssey, taking two years longer than getting the first humans to the moon (1961—1969) with Project Apollo.

Now, Years after it was initially proposed, major parts of ISS, the station's acronym, are at last being built, and the first of these should be launched in late 1997. When completed, ISS will be the most expensive international space project ever, with current estimates at more than $US 100 billion for launch, construction, and operation for a 10-year period. The gigantic tinker toy-like structure will be the largest man-made object in orbit, spanning 109.1 meters from tip to tip and weighing 423 000 kg. Its six-person crews will be able to float through interconnected modules that give them twice the working volume of a Boeing 747 jetliner.

Two key benefits ISS will offer, NASA and other manned-space supporters expect, will be allowing fundamental research in materials and life sciences to go on for longer periods than the U.S. Space Shuttle allows, and helping set the stage for manned missions to the planets.

［odyssey《奥德赛》古希腊史诗，相传为荷马所作，本文中转意为长期的探索过程／tinker toy-like structure 像拼接式玩具结构］

Well-known Sayings

△ *The magnitude of a "progress" is gauged by the greatness of the sacrifice that it requires.*

△ *The reason that men oppose progress is not that they hate progress but that they love inertia.*

△ *The art of progress is to preserve order amid change, and to preserve change amid order.*

Lesson 35

A New Concept for Spacecraft Tiles

[1] A new concept for spacecraft tiles also can be used on Earth to make efficient, vacuum-like insulation for refrigerators, furnaces and automobile catalytic converters.

[2] The new material is similar to that used for the tiles on the Space Shuttle to protect the vehicle from the heat generated during re-entry into Earth's atmosphere. However, the new tiles have a layer of aerogel, or "solid smoke," mixed into the tile's air spaces.

[3] "Solid smoke, or aerogel, works like a vacuum layer because it's a great insulator," said aerogel tile co-inventor Dr. Susan White of NASA's Ames Research Center, Moffett Field, California. "The new aerogel tiles can insulate spacecraft from ten to 100 times better than today's tiles."

[4] Aerogel is made of silica, alumina and carbon as well as other materials, and can weigh less than the same volume of air. "The aerogel used to fill the air spaces inside the tiles is like strings of nanosized pearls, all tangled up," White said. A nanometer is a billionth of a meter.

[5] The fibres that form the tiles are mostly a mixture of silica and alumina oxides, according to co-inventor Dr. Daniel Rasky, also of Ames. The spaces inside the untreated spacecraft tiles are less than a millimetre wide.

[6] "The reason the aerogel tile composite will act as a great insulator for keeping freezers cold, or automobile catalytic converters hot, is that the air flowing through the tile is almost completely blocked by aerogel," White said. "It is like having a chunk of solid vacuum where you need it."

[7] "Aerogel is very brittle and can't be machined, but spacecraft insulation tiles filled with a layer of aerogel can be cut, machined, drilled and attached to a surface," White said. "Aerogel-tile insulation can be made into different shapes for many uses here on Earth."

[8] The aerogel space-tile material could be used in commercial products that require mechanically tough super-insulation, such as catalytic converters for cars or specialty refrigeration units. In addition, the new material potentially could be used for furnaces; for liquefied gas transport trucks; or for liquid carbon dioxide, special nitrogen and oxygen containers.

[9] The new aerogel tiles could also be used to insulate future spacecraft from the heat of re-entry into the atmosphere. The materials will also protect spacecraft better from ice formed on the extremely cold fuel tanks when the vehicle is waiting on the pad for launch.

[10] High temperature and environmental testing of aerogel space tiles was conducted at Ames for seven years. A patent is pending for the new material.

Language Points and Chinese Translations

第35课 航天器护瓦的新观念

[1] vacuum 真空/insulation 绝缘,隔离

航天器护瓦的新观念也可用于人类世界,为电冰箱、锅炉和汽车触发转换器制造有效的真空绝缘体。

[2] to be similar to… 与……相似/to protect…from 保护……免受……/aerogel 气凝胶

这种新型的材料与航天飞机上使用的护瓦材料相似。这种护瓦可以保护航天飞机免受在重返地球大气层时所产生的高温,不过,这种新型的护瓦,在其空气夹层中填有一层气凝胶,或叫"固态烟雾"的物质。

[3] insulator 绝缘体,隔离物/co-inventor 合作发明人,即发明者之一

在美国加利福尼亚州莫菲特费尔德的国家航空航天局艾姆斯研究中心的Susan White博士是气凝胶瓦的发明者之一。她说:"固态烟雾,或气凝胶,由于本身就是一种良好的绝缘体,所以其作用相当于一个绝缘层。这种新式的气凝胶瓦可以使航天器的绝缘性能比现在所使用的防护瓦强十至一百倍。"

[4] nanosized 纳米尺寸的,nano 表示"纤(毫微,10^{-9})"/to tangle 缠结,纠缠,tangled up 缠结在一起的

气凝胶是由二氧化硅、氧化铅、碳以及其他材料制成,比重比空气小。White 说,"用以填充在瓦内空气夹层里的气凝胶好像成串的纳米尺寸的微小珍珠,互相缠结在一起"。一纳米是一米的十亿分之一。

[5] fibre 纤维/mixture 混合物/millimetre 毫米

根据艾姆斯研究中心的另一位参与发明者 Daniel Rasky 博士所说,构成护瓦的纤维主要是二氧化硅和氧化铝的混合物。未经处理的航天器护瓦的内层空隙不到一毫米宽。

[6] composite 合成物,混合物/to block 阻挡,阻滞,封锁/chunk 一大块,厚块

White 说:"气凝胶瓦作为良好的绝缘体可以使冷却机保持低温,或使汽车触发转换器保持高温,其原因在于流经气凝胶瓦的空气几乎完全被气凝胶所阻滞。这就好像在所需要的地方都安置一大块固态真空物体。"

[7] brittle 易碎的,脆的/to machine 机械制造,机械加工

White 说:"气凝胶很脆弱,不能进行机械加工,但是填满了一层气凝胶的航空器绝缘瓦就可以被切割、加工、钻孔,并被贴附在物体的表面。气凝胶绝缘材料可制成各种不同的形状,适合于多种用途。"

[8] commercial 商业上的/potentially 潜在地,可能地,具有开发潜力地

气凝胶太空瓦材料可使用于一些要求机械强度高的超绝缘材料的商业产品,如:汽车触发转换器或者特种制冷部件。另外,这种新型的材料具有开发潜力,可以应用于高炉、液化气运输车和液态二氧化碳、特殊的装氮和氧的容器等。

[9] pad 衬垫,本文中指航天器的发射台/launch v. n. 发射,投射

新型气凝胶瓦还可以应用于未来的航天器,以阻隔其重返大气层时所产生的高热。当航天器在发射台等候发射升空时,这种材料也将能有效地阻止极冷的燃料箱表面结冰从而保护航天器。

[10] to conduct 处理,管理,指挥,引导/patent 专利,专利权/pending 悬而不决的

在艾姆斯研究中心,对气凝胶太空瓦的耐高温性以及环境模拟测试已经进行了七年。目前正在申请这种新型材料的专利权。

Exercises

I. Answer the following questions:

1. What is the function of spacecraft tiles?

2. What do the spacecraft tiles have?

3. According to the text, who are the inventors of aerogel tiles?

4. How about the insulation of aerogel tiles?

5. What is aerogel made of?

6. Why does the aerogel tile act as a great insulator?

7. Why can aerogel-tile insulation be made into different shapes for many uses?

8. What products can the aerogel space-tile material be used in? Can you name some of them?

9. How many years has Ames Research Centre conducted the test of aerogel space tiles?

II. Translate the following words and phrases:

A. From Chinese into English.
1. 航天飞机
2. 真空绝缘材料
3. 汽车触发转换器
4. 大气层
5. 纳米
6. 气凝胶
7. 机械加工
8. 专利权

B. From English into Chinese.
1. a new concept
2. to be similar to
3. to protect...from...
4. re-entry into Earth's atmosphere
5. a layer of
6. NASA
7. the same volume of air
8. a chunk of solid vacuum
9. commercial products

10. mechanically tough super-insulation _____
11. in addition _____
12. high temperature and environmental testing _____

III. Translate the following passage into Chinese:

1. Semiconductor lasers, which have been shrunk to an astonishing scale of nanometers (a nanometer is one billionth of a meter)—even smaller than the wavelength of the light they emit—are the answer. This technology will bring down the cost of bringing optic fibers to the homes.

2. Space Adventure presents a large series of brief topical articles on a variety of space and astronomical topics. Suitable for both students and adults, the articles cover everything from the history of astronomy, rockets, and the search for extra-terrestrial intelligence, to key personalities in astronomy and space exploration, information on the solar system and the universe, and scientific developments that aided astronomy. This page served as a great introduction to astronomy and space exploration. Access to Space Adventure: *http://raphael. freerange. com/WWW/reference-files/space/*

Well-known Sayings

△ *He that has a tongue in his head may find his way anywhere.*
△ *Initiative to success is what a lighted match is to a candle.*
△ *The executive of the future will be rated by his ability to anticipate his problems rather than to meet them as they come.*

Lesson 36

Space Travel in the Future

[1] Space flight may be about to undergo a transformation far more radical than anything planned by national or international space agencies. In the next fifteen years or so, there could be a fleet of fifty spaceplanes carrying a million people into orbit about the Earth each year, at $10 000 per head. A prototype of spaceplane could be up and flying within five or six years.

[2] Perhaps surprisingly the main obstacles to realising this dream are neither technical nor commercial. Space transportation is expensive and risky at present because all launchers so far have used large throwaway components that are based on ballistic missile technology. But the technology already exists for a prototype of a fully reusable, aeroplane-like launcher, and its development costs need only be equivalent to about two space shuttle flights (about $1 000 million). The cost per prototype spaceplane flight would be about 1 percent of that for the shuttle, and the cost per person carried into orbit in an enlarged version of such a spaceplane could be as low as $10 000, or 0.1 percent of the cost in the space shuttle.

[3] Costs this low will not be achieved without several years of operating experience and continuous development to create heat shields and rocket motors that meet the usual airliner standards of long life and low maintenance costs. According to recent market research in Japan, more than a million people a year would be prepared to pay such a price for a brief visit to a space station (*Journal of Space Technology and Science*, vol. 10, 1994). If correct, this level of space tourism would provide the sort of commercial incentive and operating experience needed to achieve airliner standards.

[4] However, space policy is so dominated by politics that more than sound engineering and commercial arguments will be needed to transform a high-cost industry into a low-cost one. Many aviation engineers considered spaceplanes to be feasible over thirty years ago. (My first job, starting in 1961, was as a member of a spaceplane design team.) They were not developed primarily because the main player in the field, NASA, became preoccupied with its part in the Cold War and locked into a ballistic missile mindset. As a result, NASA has not encouraged studies of spaceplanes that could be built using existing technology and tends to view predictions such as those outlined above as far-fetched.

[5] How then can the transformation be brought about? Four recent events should between them trigger the required overthrow of the mindset. The first components have been manufactured for the International Space Station and NASA, in conjunction with the Space Transportation Association, has begun the first official study of space tourism. And NASA awarded a contract in March 1995 to a team comprising the Orbital Science Corporation and the Rockwell International Corporation, for development of the X-34 launcher.

[6] The X-34 has a reusable lower stage and an expendable upper stage, and is designed to reduce the cost of launching small satellites. Unpiloted and looking rather like a large, fat fighter aeroplane, it is launched from a converted Boeing 747. Having released the upper stage at about one half satellite speed, the rocket-powered lower stage glides back to base and lands. Following inspection, maintenance and refuelling, the lower stage will be ready for the next flight a few days later. The first orbital test flight is

scheduled for just two and a half years from now. In April 1995, NASA placed competitive study contracts with Lockheed, McDonnell Douglas and Rockwell for the X-33 demonstrator, which is intended to lead to an unpiloted single-stage-to-orbit launcher.

[7] When the implications of such projects become widely appreciated, the case for a new and realistic way ahead for space will become overwhelming. While the X-34 cannot be described as a true spaceplane, since it has an expendable upper stage, if it is successful it will provide unassailable evidence for the feasibility of a true spaceplane. A piloted two-stage spaceplane using existing technology will then be seen as among the all-time best aerospace buys. Its development cost would be recovered by saving just three shuttle flights.

[8] It is not so much that the spaceplane would be especially efficient, but rather that the shuttles are especially inefficient, and that NASA has so far succeeded in playing down this fact. British companies have proposed designs that are more suitable than the X-33 and X-34, but they are handicapped by a government not prepared to invest in even seed corn studies of new launchers.

[9] The largest new space project planned at present is the International Space Station. The estimated cost is about \$20 billion plus about the same again in launch costs, including some 28 shuttle flights. A large part of the cost is due to the complexity of integrating the various modules from the US, Canada, Europe, Japan and Russia. If these modules were adapted to be flown separately as independent small space stations, not only would costs come tumbling down, but the science would be far better because each discipline—be it astronomy, atmospheric science, Earth observation or microgravity research—has a different optimum orbit. The resulting constellation of small space stations would require more frequent servicing and supply flights than the single large one. This would not be affordable using the shuttle but would be with the new spaceplane. The total cost could be reduced by at least 80 per cent to less than \$8 billion.

[10] Then all that is needed is for some entrepreneurs to realise that the best way to finance new spaceplanes and space stations is to carry tourists. And before too long a million people a year will be taking their once-in-a-lifetime, round-the-world cruise in orbit.

Language Points and Chinese Translations

第36课 未来的太空旅游

[1] to undergo 经历,经受/radical 根本的,基本的,彻底的/a fleet of 一队,一群,fleet 指船队,机群/prototype 原型,范例,样板,标准/up 本文中指事物的出现,发生

太空飞行将要经历一次根本性的变化,其程度要远远超过国家或国际太空机构所制订的任何计划。在未来的大约15年内,每年将要有50架太空飞机组成的机群搭载100万旅客进入地球轨道,每人收费1万美元。太空飞机的样机将能在五六年的时间内制成并升空飞行。

[2] ballistic missile 弹道导弹,ballistic 弹道的/reusable 可以重复使用的,可以再次使用的/launcher 指运载火箭等发射器,弹射器或发射装置/space shuttle 航天飞机

也许令人意外的是,要实现这一梦想的主要障碍并不是技术或商业上的问题。到目前为止,由于所有的运载火箭都是使用以弹道导弹技术为基础的大型一次性部件,因此目前太空运输既昂贵又有风险。但是现在已经开发出了技术可以用于制造能重复使用、像飞机一样的火箭样机,其研制费用仅相当于航天飞机在太空飞行两次的费用(大约10亿美元)。这种典型的太空飞机在太空飞行一次的费用大约是航天飞机飞行费用的1%,而乘坐一

架经过改装扩大的太空飞机进入轨道,每位旅客所花费用仅为1万美元,即为乘坐航天飞机所需费用的0.1%。

[3] heat shields 隔热装置,防热遮护板/maintenance 维修,保养/incentive 刺激,鼓励,激发

要达到这样低廉的费用,必须有数年的运作经验,以及持续不断的研制开发,制造出隔热防护装置和火箭发动机,从而达到普通飞机使用寿命长、维修保养成本低的标准。根据最近在日本进行的市场调研,每年将有100多万人准备支付这样的价钱,到太空站进行短暂的访问游览(《太空技术和科学杂志》1994年第10卷)。如果这一调研正确无误,则这一水平状况的太空旅游将为太空飞机达到普通客机标准提供必要的商业刺激和运作经验。

[4] to dominate 支配,控制,处于支配地位/sound 正确的,合理的,可靠的/argument 论据,理由,论证/to become preoccupied with 全神贯注于,专心于,一心想……/Cold War 冷战,指当时美苏两个超级大国在军事、外交等方面的对立/mindset 思想的形式,思想倾向/to tend to 倾向于,趋向,走向/to outline 概括,略述,画出……的轮廓/far-fetched 牵强的,不自然的,远不可及的

但是太空政策受到政治的支配,要把高成本的产业转变为低成本的产业,仅有正确合理的工程和商业方面的论证是远远不够的。许多航空工程师认为太空飞机在30多年前就具有可行性。(1961年,我第一次参加工作时是太空设计小组的一名成员。)当时没有开发太空飞机,其根本原因是该领域的主要参与者美国国家航空航天局一心投入冷战,倾心研制弹道导弹。结果,国家航空航天局不鼓励使用现有的技术进行建造太空飞机的研究,而把上述的预测看作牵强附会而远不可及。

[5] to bring about 带来,造成/to trigger 发射,激发起,引起/overthrow 推翻,打倒/in conjunction with 与……协力,连同/to comprise 由……组成,构成,包含,包括/orbital 轨道的

那么,这种转变是怎样产生的呢?最近的4件大事使国家航空航天局抛弃了原来的思想倾向。国际空间站的第一批部件已经制造出来了,国家航空航天局已与太空运输协会一起开始了对太空旅游的首次正式研究。1995年3月,国家航空航天局与由轨道科学公司和洛克韦尔国际公司组成的小组签署了一个合同,以便研制X-34运载火箭。

[6] expendable 可消费的,可消耗的/to convert 转变,改变,变换/to release 释放,放出,解除/to glide 滑行,滑翔,下滑/to refuel 给……加燃料/demonstrator 证明者,示范者,演示器

X-34运载火箭由上下两级火箭组成,上一级火箭是发射后即弃用的,下一级火箭可以重复使用,这样设计的目的是为了减少发射小型卫星的成本。X-34运载火箭看起来很像一架大型的战斗机,无人驾驶,它是从经过改装的波音747飞机上发射的。当以卫星的一半速度释放出上一级火箭后,火箭驱动的下一级就滑行返回基地着落。这下一级火箭经过检测,维修和再次填充燃料后,可以为数天后再次飞行做好准备。第一次轨道测试飞行计划于两年半后进行。1995年4月国家航空航天局与洛克希德,麦克唐奈·道格拉斯和洛克韦尔三家公司就研制X-33演示器签署了合同,以让三家公司竞争,制造出一种无人驾驶的单级入轨的运载火箭。

[7] implication 含意,含蓄/overwhelming 压倒的,势不可挡的,不可抗拒的/unassailable 不可攻破的,不容置疑的,无懈可击的/feasibility 可行性/all-time 空前的/to save 节省,省去,避免

当人们广泛地意识到这项航天计划的意义后,为了未来太空开发而运用全新和可行的方式将成为势不可挡的潮流。虽然X-34因带有可消耗性的上级火箭而不能被看做是真正的太空飞机,但是如果它被研制成功了,它将为真正太空飞机的可行性研究提供不容置疑的证据。利用现有技术开发的可由人驾驶的二级太空飞机将被看做是最便宜的太空航天器之一,其开发费用只要减少三次航天飞机的飞行即可收回。

[8] to play down 降低,贬低,减弱,缩小/to handicap 妨碍,使不利/seed corn 原意指谷种,本文中指开发一项新事物的起初阶段。

这里并不是要强调太空飞机是特别地有效,相反,倒是航天飞机的效率极低,而且国家航空航天局迄今一直在低调处理这一事实。英国的公司提出了比X-33和X-34更为适当的设计方案,但是由于政府甚至在这新型运载火箭的开始阶段的研究都不准备作任何投资,从而阻碍了设计方案的实施。

[9] complexity 复杂性,复杂的事物/to integrate 使结合,使一体化,使并入/module 组件,舱/to adapt 使……适应,改编/to tumble down 下跌/discipline 学科/optimum 最适合的/constellation 星座/affordable 能担负得起的,可以承受得起的

目前制订的最大最新的航天计划是建立国际空间站。建站费用估计大约为200亿美元,再加上大约200亿美元的发射费用,其中包括大约28次航天飞机飞行。由于要把美国、加拿大、欧洲、日本和俄罗斯所研制的各种

航天舱组合成一体的复杂性,这将要用掉大部分费用。如果这些航天舱都被改成独立的小型空间站进行单独飞行,则不仅可以大大减少费用,而且更具有科学性,因为每门学科——不管是天文学、大气学、地球观测或者微引力研究——都有各不相同的最适合的运行轨道。由小型空间站所组成的星座要比单一大型的空间站需要更加频繁的维修和供给飞行。使用航天飞机来完成这种飞行是不经济的,而使用新型的太空飞机就可行。其总费用至少可以降低80%,即不到80亿美元。

[10] entrepreneur 企业家,创业者/to finance 为……筹措资金,供资金给/cruise 巡航,巡游

这样,所需要做的事就是让一些企业家意识到为太空飞机和空间站筹措资金的最好方式就是运载游览观光者。不久的将来,每年将会有100万人进入地球轨道,经历终生只有一次的环球巡游。

Exercises

I. Answer the following questions:

1. According to the author, what will happen in the next fifteen years or so? And when will a prototype of spaceplane be built?
   _____
2. What are the main obstacles to realize the dream? Why? And how to overcome these obstacles?
   _____
3. Why does the author say that space policy is dominated by politics? Give an example.
   _____
4. Say something about X-34 launcher.
   _____
5. Say something about the International Space Station.
   _____
6. How many countries have worked together to build the International Space Station? And what are they?
   _____
7. Why does the author think that it is better to build small space stations?
   _____
8. According to the text, what is the best way to finance new spaceplanes and space stations?
   _____

II. Translate the following words and phrases:

A. From Chinese into English.
1. 太空飞行 _____
2. 运行轨道 _____
3. 运载火箭 _____
4. 弹道导弹技术 _____
5. 太空技术与科学 _____
6. 火箭发动机 _____
7. 微引力研究 _____
8. 无人驾驶的单级入轨火箭 _____

B. From English into Chinese.

1. spaceplane _____
2. space transportation _____
3. large throwaway components _____
4. to be based on _____
5. prototype _____
6. operating experience and commercial incentive _____
7. to be preoccupied with _____
8. a reusable lower stage and an expendable upper stage _____
9. unassailable evidence _____
10. feasibility _____
11. to play down _____
12. seed corn studies _____
13. complexity _____
14. module _____
15. astronomy and atmospheric science _____
16. round-the-world cruise _____

Ⅲ. Translate the following passage into Chinese:

An upcoming Japanese moon mission will make the first attempt in space exploration history to probe deep below the surface of another world. The Lunar-A mission, to be launched this summer by Japan's Institute for Space and Astronautical Science, will fire a trio of three-foot-long dartlike "penetrators" at the moon from an orbiting satellite. With two penetrators on the side facing Earth, and one on the far side, the three probes will form a simple instrument network.

A planetary scientist at the Japanese institute, says that combining the data from the three penetrators will give scientists a clearer picture of the moon's interior. This may yield clues about the formation of both the moon and Earth. Without better knowledge of the moon, we can't fully understand the very early history of Earth. If successful, the Japanese penetrator technique could be used on future missions to asteroids and Mars.

［penetrator 穿透探测器/asteroids 这里指火星轨道上的小行星］

Well-known Sayings

△ *Nothing is impossible to a willing heart.*
△ *The true value of life is not in what we get but in what we give.*
△ *The important thing in life is to have a great aim, and the determination to attain it.*

Unit 11   Nanotechnology

第 11 单元   纳米技术

—— *Nanotechnology is the science of making or working with things that are so small that they can only be seen by using a powerful microscope. It involves the manipulation of matter at the molecular scale and has the potential to fundamentally alter the way people live, by providing new drug delivery systems, faster and cheaper manufacturing processes, cleaner and more efficient energy generation, new materials, clean water and the next generation of computing devices.*

—— *Nanotechnology can address economic and social challenges relating to mining and agribusiness; health and environment; electronics; and information and communication technologies.*

—— *Nanotechnology—molecular manufacturing—will radically transform the world, and the people, of the early 21st century. Although nanotechnology carries great promise, unwise or malicious use could seriously threaten the survival of the human race.*

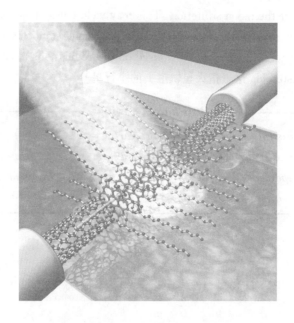

Lesson 37

Nanotechnology

[1] **What is nanotechnology, and do we put the world at risk by adopting it?**

[2] **Why are we asking this question now?**

[3] The Royal Commission on Environmental Pollution has just published a report on novel materials and has looked at the case of nanotechnology, which describes the science of the very small. Nanotechnology covers those man-made materials or objects that are about a thousand times smaller than the microtechnology we use routinely, such as the silicon chips of computers.

[4] Nanotechnology derives its name from the nanometre, which is a billionth of a metre. To get some measure of the scale of the materials and devices we are talking about, a human hair is about 80,000 nanometres wide.

[5] **Should we be concerned about nanotechnology?**

[6] The Royal Commission found no evidence of harm to health or the environment from nanomaterials, but this "absence of evidence" is not being taken as "evidence of absence". In other words, just because there are no apparent problems, this is not to say that here is no risk now or in the future. The Commission is concerned about the pace at which we are inventing and adopting new nanomaterials, which could result in future problems that we are ill-equipped to understand or even detect with current testing methods.

[7] The Commission's broad conclusion is that the speed of development in the field of nanotechnology "is beyond the capacity of existing testing and regulatory arrangements to control the potential environmental impacts adequately". In summary, not enough is known about the effect that these very small devices and materials will have on human health or the environment, and the tests that could tell us about them are either not available or not being used.

[8] **What is covered by the term nanotechnology?**

[9] There are about 600 consumer products already on the market that use nanotechnology. They include nanoparticles of titanium dioxide added to sun creams to make them transparent instead of white, or tiny fragments of silver that are added to sports equipment to make them odour-free—the silver acts as a powerful antibacterial agent. Nanomedicine are also being developed to fight cancer and other fatal diseases.

[10] So nanotechnology is not all bad, but the point is, the ability to make such fine particles and materials is getting better all the time. As a result, many companies are taking up the opportunity of using them in products with little or no knowledge of how they may have an impact on human health or the environment. The silver particles in sports clothing might end up killing off bacteria in sewage systems for example.

[11] **Is everything at the nano scale artificial?**

[12] No. A molecule of DNA is an example of a natural nanoscale substance with the diameter of its double helix structure measuring about one nanometre. A typical virus, meanwhile, is about 100 nanometres wide. This is the range of nanoscale objects in nature that roughly covers the field of synthetic nanotechnology. So the human body and nature at large is well used to nanoscale objects and materials.

[13] **Why might there be risks?**

[14] One of the chief concerns is that when you make something very small out of a well known material, you may actually change the functionality of that material even if the chemical composition remains the same. Indeed, the Commission emphasized this point: "It is not the particle size or mode of production of a material that should concern us, but its functionality."

[15] Take gold, for instance, which is a famously inert substance, and valuable because of it. It doesn't rust or corrode because it doesn't interact with water or oxygen, for instance. However, a particle of gold that is between 2 and 5 nanometres in diameter becomes highly reactive. This is not due to a change in chemical composition, but because of a change in the physical size of the gold particles.

[16] **How can this result in a change of function?**

[17] One reason is to do with surface area. Nanoparticles have a much bigger surface area-to-volume ratio than microparticles a thousand times bigger. It is like trying to compare the surface area of a basketball with the combined surface area of pea-sized balls with the same total weight of the single basketball.

[18] The pea-sized balls have a surface area many hundreds, indeed thousands of times bigger than the basketball, and this allows them to interact more easily with the environment. It is this increased interactivity that can change their functionality—and so make them potentially more dangerous to health or the environment.

[19] "As many chemical reactions occur at surfaces, this means that nanomaterials may be relatively much more reactive than a similar mass of conventional materials in bulk form," the Royal Commission said. This suggests that the emphasis on weight alone in terms of toxicity thresholds may not apply for nanomaterials, it added.

[20] **Are there precedents?**

[21] The Commission cites several examples of health problems caused by the introduction of novel materials. Asbestos, for instance, was an infamous example of a material that provided tremendous benefits as a fire retardant, but when asbestos fibres were inhaled, it resulted in highly malignant cancer mesothelioma.

[22] Lead additives in petrol have been linked with harmful effects on children's mental development, supposedly inert gases called chlorofluorocarbons in refrigeration are now known to have depleted the protective ozone layer of the atmosphere, and the antifouling agent tributyltin in paint has been found to change the sex of marine organisms. More recently, tiny particles called PM10s in exhaust fumes have been linked with lung and heart problems caused by pollution.

[23] **Where did the idea of these dangers emerge?**

[24] The first scientist to see the potential of nanotechnology was the American physicist Richard Feynman who gave a famous 1959 lecture to the American Physical Society entitled "there is plenty of room at the bottom".

[25] Although it was Feynman who first talked about the potential advantages of technology on the small scale, it was an American engineer and author called Eric Drexler who coined the term "nanotechnology" in his 1981 book *Engines of Creation*. It was also Drexler who first warned of the risk. He described a future in which tiny, self-replicating robots would take over the world—a view he has since-disowned. But that did not stop Michael Crichton building on the idea in his novel *Prey*, which portrayed a future threatened by minuscule, self-replicating machines that could devour the world in a form of "grey goo".

Language Points and Chinese Translations

第37课　纳米技术

[1] nanotechnology 纳米技术　纳米(nanometer, nm)是一种长度单位,1纳米等于10亿分之一米。纳米技术是指尺寸在100纳米以下的微小结构。纳米技术是专门研究结构尺寸在0.1~100纳米范围内材料的性质和应用的一门高新技术,其实是一种用单个原子、分子制造物质的技术。纳米技术是一门交叉性很强的综合学科,研究的内容涉及现代科学技术的广阔领域。纳米科学与技术主要包括:纳米物理学、纳米化学、纳米材料学、纳米生物学、纳米电子学、纳米加工学和纳米力学等七个分支学科。有资料显示,最近十多年内,纳米技术将成为仅次于芯片制造的第二大产业。

纳米技术是什么,我们采用纳米技术会使世界处于危险境地吗？

[2] 我们为什么现在提出这个问题？

[3] 皇家防制环境污染委员会刚刚发表了一份有关新型材料的报告,并已在关注描述细微科学的纳米技术事例。纳米技术包括了那些人工材料或比我们日常使用的比如计算机硅片那样的微电子技术还要小1 000倍的物体。

[4] to derive…from 起源,由来,衍生,派生/a billionth 10亿分之一,分数的英语表达方法是分子用基数词,分母用序数词;分子超过1,则分母的序数词要用复数形式,如2/3 two thirds

纳米技术的名称由纳米衍生而来,1纳米是10亿分之1米。为了对我们正在谈及的纳米材料和装置的尺寸有一个量的概念,一根人的头发的直径大概是8万纳米。

[5] to be concerned about 关心,关切,关注

我们应当关注纳米技术吗？

[6] 皇家委员会并未发现关于纳米材料有害于健康或环境的任何证据,但是"缺少证据"不能被看做是"没有证据"。也就是说,仅仅因为没有明显的问题,不等于说现在或将来就没有风险。该委员会所关切的是我们正在研发和采用新型纳米材料的进展情况,这些新型的纳米材料在将来可能会产生一些问题,只是目前条件不具备,使用现有的检测方法我们还难以理解或查不出来而已。

[7] 该委员会的主要结论是:纳米技术领域的发展速度"已超越了足以控制其对环境潜在影响的现有检测能力和规约方法。"简言之,我们对于这些微型装置和细微材料对于人类健康或环境所产生的作用知之甚少,同时能使我们了解其相关情况的检测手段或者是现在还没有,或者是尚未得到应用。

[8] 纳米技术这一术语涵盖了什么？

[9] 现在市场上已经有大约600种运用纳米技术的消费产品,其中有添加到防晒霜中使其由白色变为透明的二氧化钛纳米微粒;还有细微的银粉,这种银粉添加到体育器材中可使其免除异味——银具有强效的抗菌剂作用。现在还正在研发纳米药物用以治疗癌症和其他致命疾病。

[10] to end up doing sth. 以……结束,告终

所以,纳米技术并不是一无可取,重点是要有能力始终使这些细小微粒和材料得到更好的应用。结果是很多公司在对它们对人类健康或环境有何种影响知之甚少或者根本不了解的情况下利用时机将它们应用于产品中。例如,运动服中的银粒子可能最终会灭杀排污系统中滋生的细菌。

[11] 一切纳米级的物质全都是人造的吗？

[12] DNA是英文Deoxyribonucleic acid的缩写,汉译成脱氧核糖核酸,是染色体的主要组成成分,也是组成基因的材料。DNA分子的双螺旋结构(double helix)是相对稳定的/at large 总体上,整体上,整个的,普通的

不。DNA分子就是一个天然纳米级物质的例子,其双螺旋结构的直径大约为1纳米。同时,一个典型的病毒其宽度大约为100纳米。这是自然界中纳米级物质的大小范围,人造纳米技术领域也大致在此范围。所以人体和自然界总体上都能很好地习惯于纳米级的物质和材料。

［13］为什么可能存有风险呢？

［14］一个主要的担忧是，当你把一种非常熟悉的材料制成很细微的物质时，实际上你可能改变了那种材料的功能，即使其化学成分仍然相同。该委员会正是强调了这一点："我们关注的不是材料粒子的大小或其生产模式，而是其功能。"

［15］以金为例，它是一种典型的惰性物质，它也因此而贵重。它不与水或氧发生反应，所以不会生锈或腐蚀。然而，一个直径在 2 至 5 纳米之间的金子微粒具有很高的活性。这并不是由于其化学成分的变化，而是由金子微粒的物理尺寸的变化造成的。

［16］纳米粒子如何导致物质功能的改变？

［17］一种原因是与物质的表面积有关。纳米粒子的表面积与体积之比率要比大于其 1 000 倍的微米粒子大得多。这就好象试图把一个篮球的表面积和与其重量相等的许多豌豆大小的小球的总表面积相比较一样。

［18］这些豌豆大小的小球的总表面积比篮球的表面积大数百倍，甚至数千倍，这就使它们更容易与环境相互作用。正是这种增加的相互作用改变了它们的功能——从而使它们对健康和环境具有更多的潜在危险性。

［19］皇家委员会声称："由于很多化学反应都是在表面发生的，这意味着纳米材料要比类似质量的大块常规材料相对来说更容易起化学反应。"该委员会又称，这表明仅强调重量而设定毒性阈值的方法并不适用于纳米材料。

［20］是否有先例？

［21］该委员会引用了几个由于使用了新型材料而引发健康问题的例子。例如，石棉就是一种名声不好的材料，它作为一种阻燃剂可提供很多益处，但一旦吸入石棉纤维，就会引发高度恶性的间皮瘤癌。

［22］汽油中的铅添加剂被认为对儿童的智力发育具有伤害性；根据推测，用于制冷的惰性气体氟利昂现在已知破坏了起保护作用的大气臭氧层；油漆中的防污剂磷酸三丁酯已被发现改变了海洋生物体的性别。新近，废气中被称作 PM10 的细微颗粒与由污染引发的心肺疾病有关。

［23］对这些危险显现的认知来自何处？

［24］发现纳米技术潜在价值的第一位科学家是美国的物理学家理查德·费曼，他在 1959 年对美国物理协会作了题为"底层拥有大量空间"的著名演讲。

［25］to devour 毁灭，吞没，狼吞虎咽似地吃/in a form of 以一种……的形式/goo 黏性物质

虽然费曼是第一个谈论细微技术潜在的优越性，但是创造出"纳米技术"这个术语的是美国的工程师兼作家埃里克·德雷克斯勒。他在 1981 年所写的《造物引擎》一书中创造了这个术语。德雷克斯勒也第一次提出了风险警告。他描述了一个未来世界。在那个未来世界中，能够自我复制的微小的机器人接管了世界——他此后一直否认这一观点。但是这并未阻止迈克尔·克赖顿基于这个想法创作了小说《纳米猎杀》。该小说描绘了一个未来世界，受到了许多微小的能自我复制的机器的威胁，而这些机器能够以一种"灰色黏质"的形式毁灭世界。

Exercises

I. Answer the following questions:

1. What does nanotechnology cover?

2. Where does nanotechnology derive its name?

3. How wide is a human hair?

4. What is the Royal Commission's conclusion?

5. Why does the author say that nanotechnology is not all bad?

6. Why might there be some risks when we adopt nanotechnology?

7. How can the change in the physical size of the particles result in the change of function?

8. What are the benefits and harmful effects of asbestos, lead additives and chlorofluorocarbons?

9. Who was the first scientist to find the potential advantages of nanotechnology?

10. Who first warned of the risk of adopting nanotechnology?

II. Translate the following words and phrases:

A. From Chinese into English.
1. 纳米技术
2. 微电子技术
3. 计算机硅片
4. 10亿分之1米
5. 检测方法
6. 二氧化钛纳米微粒
7. 强效的抗菌剂
8. 化学成分
9. 生产模式
10. 惰性物质
11. 表面积与体积之比率
12. 对健康和环境潜在的危险性
13. 毒性阈值
14. 阻燃剂
15. 大气臭氧层
16. 海洋生物

B. From English into Chinese.
1. the Royal Commission on Environmental Pollution
2. man-made materials or objects
3. absence of evidence
4. to be concerned about sth.
5. to result in
6. the capacity of existing testing
7. to control the potential environmental impacts
8. in summary
9. to have effect on
10. odour-free
11. to fight cancer and other fatal diseases
12. to take up the opportunity of doing sth.
13. to end up killing off bacteria in sewage systems

14. to interact with water or oxygen _____
15. conventional materials in bulk form _____
16. harmful effects on children's mental development _____
17. self-replicating robots _____
18. in a form of… _____

III. Translate the following passage into Chinese:

Utilizing materials known in scientific circles as "piezoelectrics," Cagin, whose research focuses on nanotechnology, has made a significant discovery in the area of power harvesting—a field that aims to develop self-powered devices that do not require replaceable power supplies, such as batteries.

Specifically, Cagin and his partners from the University of Houston have found that a certain type of piezoelectric material can covert energy at a 100 percent increase when manufactured at a very small size—in this case, around 21 nanometers in thickness. What's more, when materials are constructed bigger or smaller than this specific size they show a significant decrease in their energy-converting capacity, he said.

His findings, which are detailed in an article published this fall in *Physical Review B*, the scientific journal of the American Physical Society, could have potentially profound effects for low-powered electronic devices such as cell phones, laptops, personal communicators and a host of other computer-related devices used by everyone from the average consumer to law enforcement officers and even soldiers in the battlefield. Many of these high-tech devices contain components that are measured in nanometers—a microscopic unit of measurement representing one-billionth of a meter. Atoms and molecules are measured in nanometers, and a human hair is about 100,000 nanometers wide.

Though Cagin's Subject matter is small, its impact could be huge. His discovery stands to advance an area of study that has grown increasingly popular due to consumer demand for compact portable and wireless devices with extended lifespans. Battery life remains a major concern for popular mp3 players and cell phones that are required to perform an ever expanding array of functions. But beyond mere consumer convenience, self-powering devices are of major interest to several federal agencies.

"Even the disturbances in the form of sound waves such as pressure waves in gases, liquids and solids may be harvested for powering nano-and-micro devices of the future if these materials are processed and manufactured appropriately for this purpose," Cagin said. Key to this technology, Cagin explained, are piezoelectrics.

Well-known Sayings

△ *Under the pressure of trial and responsibility we are often stronger than when there is no pressure.*

△ *The strongest of all warriors are these two—Time and Patience.*

△ *Our greatest glory consists not in never falling, but in rising every time we fall.*

Lesson 38

A New Treatment for Cancer——Nanoparticles

Nanospheres Leave Cancer No Place to Hide

[1] Gold-coated glass "nanoshells" can reveal the location of tumours and then destroy them minutes later in a burst of heat.

[2] Using these particles to detect and destroy tumours could speed up cancer treatment and reduce the use of potentially toxic drugs. It could also make treatment cheaper, says Andre Gobin of Rice University in Houston, Texas, who helped to create the particles.

[3] In 2003 Gobin's supervisor Jennifer West showed that gold-coated silica nanospheres could destroy tumours in mice, while leaving normal tissue intact. The blood vessels surrounding tumours are leakier than those in healthy tissue, so spheres injected into the bloodstream tend to accumulate at tumour sites. Illuminating the tumour with a near-infrared laser then excites a "sea" of loose electrons around the gold atoms via a process called plasmon resonance. This creates heat, killing all the nearby cells.

[4] However, before this can happen doctors first have to make sure they find all the tumour sites, which requires an MRI or CT scan. This extra stage can mean multiple hospital visits and more drags for the patient.

[5] Now the team has shown how to tweak the size of the nanoshells so that they also scatter some of the radiation. That means any cancer sites will "light up" under low-intensity infrared, so they can then be zapped with the laser. "We can use one single particle to accomplish two tasks and neither feature is diminished greatly," says Gobin.

[6] To achieve this, the team had to carry out a delicate balancing act. Smaller spheres convert more radiation to heat, which makes them better at destroying tumours, but larger ones scatter more radiation, which is vital for the imaging stage. Previously, the spheres were 120 nanometres in diameter, which meant they only scattered 15 per cent of the light shone on them, and converted the rest to heat. West's team increased their size to 140 nanometres, causing them to convert 67 per cent of the light to heat, and to scatter the remaining 33 per cent.

[7] The team injected the new particles into mice with colon carcinoma tumours and used a technique called optical coherence tomography to test their ability to act as an imaging agent. This involves shining low-power near-infrared light onto the tissue and then measuring where the scattered light bounces back. They found that the nanoparticles caused tumour tissue to light up 56 per cent more strongly than healthy tissue.

[8] The team then applied a higher-power infrared laser to each tumour site for 3 minutes to heat the tissue. After a few weeks, they found the tumours had been almost completely destroyed. Eighty per cent of the mice treated survived for more than seven weeks, while all the control mice, who did not receive the nanoshells, died after three weeks.

[9] Since optical coherence tomography only penetrates up to 2 millimetres, the imaging step will only be useful for locating tumours near the surface, such as cervical, mouth and skin cancers, says Gobin. However, the team plans to modify the nanoshells so that they work with more deeply penetrating

radiation, such as X-rays. Houston-based Nanospectra Biosciences, which West co-founded, will begin trials of the spheres in humans in the next two months.

Nanoparticles That Cancer Cells Just Can't Resist

[10] Turning cancer cells into mini magnets by using nanoparticles could make biopsies so sensitive and efficient that there will be no need to repeat these invasive tests.

[11] Biopsy results can be ambiguous: sometimes they can be negative simply because there are too few malignant cells in the sample to be detected—not because all trace of disease has gone. Now researchers from the University of New Mexico and the company Senior Scientific, both in Albuquerque, have come up with a solution that harnesses the power of magnetic attraction.

[12] The idea is to use magnetic iron oxide nanoparticles encased in a biocompatible material. These in turn can be coated with antibodies that bind to chemicals found only in cancerous cells. When injected into the body, thousands of the particles stick to cancer cells, turning them into miniature magnets. The cells can then be drawn towards magnets encased in the tip of a biopsy needle.

[13] A mathematical model of the system confirmed that significant numbers of cancer cells, laden with nanoparticles, could be attracted to a needle within two or three minutes. In the lab, the researchers showed that a magnetised needle could attract leukaemia cells surrounded by nanoparticles and suspended in blood or other synthetic materials designed to mimic bodily fluids. Nanoparticles have been used before to destroy diseased cells but this is the first time they have actually retrieved cells.

[14] The technique could benefit people with leukaemia, who must undergo regular bone marrow biopsies to check for signs of lingering disease. "Quite often, for example, in young children, doctors have to do several biopsies to get enough bone marrow," says Ed Flynn, president of Senior Scientific. It might also be possible to detect cells from breast, prostate, and ovarian cancers that have spread to other parts of the body in amounts too tiny to sample with an ordinary needle. The researchers are now seeking approval to test the method on human volunteers.

[15] Bruce Morland, a paediatric oncologist at Birmingham Children's Hospital in the UK says that the idea would have to compete with techniques that have recently made it easier to detect tiny amounts of leukaemia cells in biopsies. "I am tempted to think that this technique will not be any more sensitive," he says. It might be used, however, to detect low levels of cancer that have spread "silently" into the bone marrow, he adds.

Language Points and Chinese Translations

第38课 癌症新疗法——纳米粒子

纳米球粒让癌无藏身之处

[1] 镀金的玻璃"纳米炮弹"能够找到肿瘤的方位,并能在数分钟内用灼热摧毁这些肿瘤。

[2] 利用这些粒子探查和摧毁肿瘤,可以加速治疗癌症,并减少潜在有毒药物的使用。(美国)德克萨斯州休斯敦市莱斯大学的安德烈·戈宾说,这种治疗也能使医疗费用更加低廉。他曾经参与了这种纳米粒子的研发。

[3] 2003年,戈宾的导师詹妮弗·韦斯特指出,镀金二氧化硅纳米球粒能够摧毁小鼠的肿瘤,而同时不损伤正常组织。肿瘤周围的血管要比健康组织中的血管更具有渗漏性,因此注入血流中的纳米球粒往往积聚在肿瘤处。用近红外激光照射肿瘤就可经过一个称作等离子体共振的过程,在金原子周围激发起一片自由电子的"海洋"。由此产生灼热,杀灭附近所有的癌细胞。

[4] MRI 磁共振成像,是 magnetic resonance imaging 的缩略语/CT 计算机化 X 线体层照相术,是 computerized tomography 的缩略语

然而,在此之前,医生首先必须确保已找到了所有的肿瘤位置,这就需要进行磁共振成像术(MRI)或者计算机化 X 线体层照相术(CT)扫描。这个额外的过程意味着病人要多次去医院就诊,并且服用更多的药物。

[5] 现在该医疗研究团队已经揭示如何拉扭纳米炮弹的形体,以便使它们也散射出一些放射线。这意味着在低强度红外线照片下任何癌症患处都会"发亮",以便随后用激光进行灭杀。戈宾说:"我们可以采用单一粒子完成这两项任务,而且都不会明显削弱粒子的特性。"

[6] 为了达到这样的效果,该团队必须进行一项微妙的平衡术。较小的纳米球粒会把更多的辐射能转变为热,从而更有效地摧毁肿瘤,而较大的纳米球粒会散射出更多的辐射光,这在造影成像阶段至关重要。以前,纳米球粒的直径是 120 纳米,这意味着它们仅仅将照射其上的光散射出 15%,而把其余的光(85%)都转变成热。韦斯特团队将纳米球粒直径增加到 140 纳米,从而使它们把 67% 的照射光转变为热,同时散射出其余 33% 的光。

[7] 该团队把这种新的纳米粒子注入患有恶性结肠肿瘤的小鼠体内,并采用一种称作光学相干性 X 线断层照相术来测试它们作为造影成像剂的能力。这种操作过程包括把低能近红外光照射到组织上,然后测量出散射光在何处反射回来。他们发现纳米粒子可以使肿瘤的反光强度比健康组织高出 56%。

[8] 然后该团队采用更高能量的红外激光照射每个肿瘤处 3 分钟以加热该组织。几周后,他们发现这些肿瘤几乎完全被摧毁了。经过治疗的小鼠有 80% 存活了 7 周多,而所有未曾接受纳米炮弹的对照小鼠 3 周后就都死亡了。

[9] 戈宾说,由于光学相干性 X 线断层照相术的放射线仅仅穿透到皮下 2 毫米,这种造影成像手段只能应用于定位表皮的肿瘤,例如宫颈癌、口腔癌和皮肤癌。然而,该团队计划改进这些纳米炮弹,以使它们能配合穿透度更深的放射线进行工作,例如 X 射线。韦斯特和其他人在休斯敦市合作创建的纳米光谱生物科技公司将在以后两个月里开始这种纳米球粒在人体中的试验。

癌细胞确实不能抵抗纳米粒子

[10] 采用纳米粒子把癌细胞转化为微型磁体能使活组织检查非常灵敏与有效,因此不必重复这些侵入性检测。

[11] 活组织检查的一些结果可能并不清晰:有些呈阴性只是因为所取样品中的恶性肿瘤细胞太少而检测不出来——并不是因为疾病的所有征兆都已经消失。现今(美国)阿尔伯克基市的新墨西哥大学和高级科技公司的研究人员已经提出了一种利用磁引力的解决方法。

[12] 这个构想是把磁性氧化铁的纳米粒子包裹在一种不会引起排斥的材料里。这些纳米粒子又转而用抗体包扎,这些抗体与仅在癌细胞中发现的化学物质相结合。数以千计的这些纳米粒子被注入身体后就粘附在癌细胞上,把它们转化为微型磁体。这些癌细胞然后就被吸引至包裹在活组织检查针头里的磁体。

[13] 该体系的数学模型证实,满载纳米粒子的大量癌细胞在 2 或 3 分钟内就能被吸附到针头上。研究人员在实验室里证实,一个磁化针头能够吸附被纳米粒子包围的、悬浮在血液中或用于模拟体液的其他合成材料中的白血病细胞。以前是利用纳米粒子摧毁癌细胞,而这是首次它们竟然提取了癌细胞。

[14] 这项技术可能有益于白血病患者,这类病人必须进行定期的骨髓活组织检查以便检验出缠绵疾病的征兆。高级科技公司总裁埃德·弗莱恩说:"例如,医生们必须经常在少年儿童中做数次活组织检查才能获取足够的骨髓。"该项技术还可以检测出已经扩散到身体其他部位极微量而不能用常规针头取样的乳腺癌、前列腺癌和卵巢癌细胞。研究人员现在正在寻求获准在人类志愿者身上测试这种方法。

[15] 英国伯明翰市儿童医院的儿科肿瘤学家布鲁斯·莫兰德说,这种治疗理念必然会和最近更容易从活组织检查中检测微量白细胞的技术进行竞争。他说:"我冒昧地认为这项技术将是最为灵敏的了。"然而,他又补充说,可能会采用这项技术来检测已经"悄悄"地扩散到骨髓中的低量癌细胞。

Exercises

I. Answer the following questions:

1. What is the function of gold-coated glass "nanoshells"?

2. What did Jennifer West show in 2003?

3. What does it mean to tweak the size of the nanoshells to let them scatter some of the radiation?

4. What kind of balancing act did the team carry out?

5. Why will the imaging step only be useful for locating tumours near the surface?

6. Why can biopsy results be ambiguous?

7. Say something about the idea mentioned in Paragraph 12?

8. What did the researchers show in the lab?

9. Why does the author say that the technique could benefit people with leukaemia?

10. What does bruce Morland, a paediatric oncologist, say?

II. Translate the following words and phrases:

A. From Chinese into English.
1. 纳米球粒
2. 探查和摧毁肿瘤
3. 潜在有毒药物
4. 近红外激光
5. 磁共振成像术
6. 扫描
7. 把辐射能转变为热
8. 定位
9. 活组织检查
10. 侵入性检测
11. 数学模型
12. 与……竞争

B. From English into Chinese.
1. gold-coated glass nanoshells
2. a burst of heat
3. plasmon resonance

4. low-intensity infrared _____
5. colon carcinoma tumours _____
6. to act as an imaging agent _____
7. to come up with a solution _____
8. laden with _____
9. in the tip of a biopsy needle _____
10. suspended in blood _____
11. to mimic bodily fluids _____
12. to test the method on human volunteers _____

III. Translate the following passage into Chinese:

It has been reported that a Hong Kong gym is using the technology to convert energy from exercisers to help power its lights and music. While advances in those applications continue to progress, piezoelectric work at the nanoscale is a relatively new endeavor with different and complex aspects to consider, said Cagin. For example, imagine going from working with a material the size and shape of a telephone post to dealing with that same material the size of a hair, he said. When such a significant change in scale occurs, materials react differently. In this case, something the size of a hair is much more pliable and susceptible to change from its surrounding environment, Cagin noted. These types of changes have to be taken into consideration when conducting research at this scale, he said.

"When materials are brought down to the nanoscale dimension, their properties for some performance characteristics dramatically change," said Cagin who is a past recipient of the prestigious Feynman Prize in Nanotechnology. "One such example is with piezoelectric materials. We have demonstrated that when you go to a particular length scale—between 20 and 23 nanometers—you actually improve the energy-harvesting capacity by 100 percent. We're studying basic laws of nature such as physics and we're trying to apply that in terms of developing better engineering materials, better performing engineering materials. We're looking at chemical constitutions and physical compositions. And then we're looking at how to manipulate these structures so that we can improve the performance of these materials."

Well-known Sayings

△ *Obstacles are challenges for winners, and excuses for losers.*
△ *Failures are divided into two classes—those who thought and never did, and those who did and never thought.*
△ *There are only two forces in the world: the sword and the spirit. In the long run, the sword will always be conquered by the spirit.*

Unit 12 Scientific Theory and Scientific Research
第 12 单元 科学理论和科学研究

—— *Science refers to a system of acquiring knowledge based on scientific method, as well as to the organized body of knowledge gained through research. Science is the pursuit of truth, of explanation, prediction and control of a phenomenon.*

—— *Scientific theory is a mathematical or logical explanation, or a testable model of the manner of interaction of a set of natural phenomena, capable of predicting future occurrences or observations of the same kind, and capable of being tested through experiment or otherwise verified through empirical observation. Scientific theory has its vivid features of systematicness, logicality, truth, pluralism and reductiveness.*

—— *Scientific research involves a series of techniques meant to investigate a phenomenon, gather new knowledge and work on areas that have not gained a lot of focus yet. Scientific research calls for a lot of field work, analytical abilities and concentric observation. Specifically, scientific research is a systematic, controlled empirical and critical investigation of natural or social phenomena that either is guided by theory and hypotheses about the presumed relations among such phenomena, or results in theory and propositions about the possible relationship among such phenomena.*

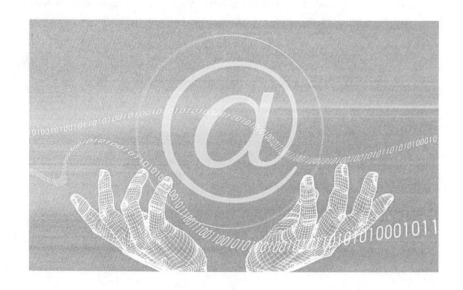

Lesson 39

What Is a Scientific Theory?

[1] In order to talk about the nature of the universe and to discuss questions such as whether it has a beginning or an end, you have to be clear about what a scientific theory is. I shall take the simple-minded view that a theory is just a model of the universe, or a restricted part of it, and a set of rules that relate quantities in the model to observations that we make. It exists only in our minds and does not have any other reality (whatever that might mean). A theory is a good theory if it satisfies two requirements: It must accurately describe a large class of observations on the basis of a model that contains only a few arbitrary elements, and it must make definite predictions about the results of future observations. For example, Aristotle's theory that everything was made out of four elements, earth, air, fire, and water, was simple enough to qualify, but it did not make any definite predictions. On the other hand, Newton's theory of gravity was based on an even simpler model, in which bodies attracted each other with a force that was proportional to a quantity called their mass and inversely proportional to the square of the distance between them. Yet it predicts the motions of the sun, the moon, and the planets to a high degree of accuracy.

[2] Any physical theory is always provisional, in the sense that it is only a hypothesis: you can never prove it. No matter how many times the results of experiments agree with some theory, you can never be sure that the next time the result will not contradict the theory. On the other hand, you can disprove a theory by finding even a single observation that disagrees with the predictions of the theory. As philosopher of science Karl Popper has emphasized, a good theory is characterized by the fact that it makes a number of predictions that could in principle be disproved or falsified by observation. Each time new experiments are observed to agree with the predictions the theory survives, and our confidence in it is increased; but if ever a new observation is found to disagree, we have to abandon or modify the theory. At least that is what is supposed to happen, but you can always question the competence of the person who carried out the observation.

[3] In practice, what often happens is that a new theory is devised that is really an extension of the previous theory. For example, very accurate observations of the planet Mercury revealed a small difference between its motion and the predictions of Newton's theory of gravity. Einstein's general theory of relativity predicted a slightly different motion from Newton's theory. The fact that Einstein's predictions matched what was seen, while Newton's did not, was one of the crucial confirmations of the new theory. However, we still use Newton's theory for all practical purposes because the difference between its predictions and those of general relativity is very small in the situations that we normally deal with. (Newton's theory also has the great advantage that it is much simpler to work with than Einstein's!)

[4] The eventual goal of science is to provide a single theory that describes the whole universe. However, the approach most scientists actually follow is to separate the problem into two parts. First, there are the laws that tell us how the universe changes with time. (If we know what the universe is like at any one time, these physical laws tell us how it will look at any later time.) Second, there is the question of the initial state of the universe. Some people feel that science should be concerned with only the first

part; they regard the question of the initial situation as a matter for metaphysics or religion. They would say that God, being omnipotent, could have started the universe off any way he wanted. That may be so, but in that case he also could have made it develop in a completely arbitrary way. Yet it appears that he chose to make it evolve in a very regular way according to certain laws. It therefore seems equally reasonable to suppose that there are also laws governing the initial state.

[5] It turns out to be very difficult to devise a theory to describe the universe all in one go. Instead, we break the problem up into bits and invent a number of partial theories. Each of these partial theories describes and predicts a certain limited class of observations, neglecting the effects of other quantities, or representing them by simple sets of numbers. It may be that this approach is completely wrong. If everything in the universe depends on everything else in a fundamental way, it might be impossible to get close to a full solution by investigating parts of the problem in isolation. Nevertheless, it is certainly the way that we have made progress in the past. The classic example again is the Newtonian theory of gravity, which tells us that the gravitational force between two bodies depends only on one number associated with each body, its mass, but is otherwise independent of what the bodies are made of. Thus one does not need to have a theory of the structure and constitution of the sun and the planets in order to calculate their orbits.

[6] Today scientists describe the universe in terms of two basic partial theories—the general theory of relativity and quantum mechanics. They are the great intellectual achievements of the first half of this century. The general theory of relativity describes the force of gravity and the large-scale structure of the universe, that is , the structure on scales from only a few miles to as large as a million million million million(1 with 24 zeros after it) miles, the size of the observable universe. Quantum mechanics, on the other hand, deals with phenomena on extremely small scales, such as a millionth of a millionth of an inch. Unfortunately, however, these two theories are known to be inconsistent with each other—they cannot both be correct. One of the major endeavors in physics today, is the search for a new theory that will incorporate them both—a quantum theory of gravity. We do not yet have such a theory, and we may still be a long way from having one, but we do already know many of the properties that it must have.

Language Points and Chinese Translations

第39课 什么是科学理论？

[1] the nature of the universe 宇宙的本质／the simple-minded view 率直的观点／to relate…to…（在思想或意义上）使有关联,相当于 to connect in thought or meaning/arbitrary 武断的,任意的／prediction 预言,预示／to be proportional to 与……成正比,相称的

为了谈论宇宙的本质,并讨论宇宙是否有开始或结束这样的问题,你必须搞清楚科学理论是什么,本人率直的观点是：理论只是整个宇宙或其有限的一部分的一种模式,以及将该模式中的量和我们所作的观察相联系起来的一整套规则。它只存在于我们的思想感觉中,而不具有任何其他实体(不管是何种意义的)。一种理论如果能符合两个条件就是一种好理论：它必须在只有少数几个武断因素的模式基础上精确地描述各种各类的观察,并且对未来观察的结果作出明确的预言。例如：亚里士多德的理论,即一切物质都是由土、空气、火和水四个元素组成的,描述得十分简单,但是并未作出任何明确的预言。另一方面,牛顿的万有引力的理论基于更为简单的一种模式,即物体间的相互引力与其质量成正比,与其距离的平方成反比。该理论以高度的精确性预示了太阳、月亮和行星的运动。

[2] to agree with 与……相符合/to contradict 与……不一致,矛盾/to falsify 伪造,篡改/to survive 继续生存/to abandon 放弃,抛弃/to modify 修改,变更/to carry out 进行,实行

就其假设性而言,任何物理理论总是暂时性的:你永远不能论证它。实验的结果无论多少次与某种理论相符合,你决不会确信下一次实验结果将不会与该理论有矛盾。另一方面,你只要发现有一次观察与预言理论不相符,你就能否定这一理论。正像科学哲学家卡尔·波普所强调的那样,一种好的理论,其特点是该理论作出了一些预言,在原则上可以被观察所否定或证明有误。每次新的实验被观察到与预言的理论相符,则我们对该理论的信心就不断增强;但是如果发现有一次观察不相符,我们就不得不放弃或修改这一理论。虽然至少应该会发生这种情况,但是你也总会对进行观察的人的能力有所怀疑。

[3] to devise 设计,计划,想出/Mercury 水星/general theory of relativity 广义相对论/crucial 重要的,决定性的/to deal with 应付,对付,处理

在实践中,往往发生这样的情况,即一种新设计的理论实际上是先前理论的一种延伸。例如:对行星水星的精确观察显示了其运动和牛顿万有引力理论的预言有些小的差异。爱因斯坦的广义相对论所预言的运动与牛顿的理论略有不同。爱因斯坦的预言与所观察到的相一致,而牛顿的预言则不一致,这一事实正是对新理论的一个重要证实。然而,现在我们仍然将牛顿的理论运用于各种实际用途,因为在通常情况下,该预言与广义相对论的预言差别很小。(牛顿的理论还有很大的优点,即运用起来要比爱因斯坦的理论简单得多。)

[4] metaphysics 玄学,形而上学/religion 宗教,宗教信仰/omnipotent 万能的,全能的/to evolve 发展,自然而逐渐地进展/to govern 支配,治理,制约,控制

科学的最终目标是提供一种描述整个宇宙的单一理论。然而大部分科学家所实际遵循的途径是把该问题分成两个部分。首先,是一些自然法则,告诉我们宇宙是如何随着时间的变化而改变(假如我们知道宇宙在任何某一时刻是什么样子,则这些自然法则就会告诉我们今后某一时刻宇宙将会像什么样子)。其次,是宇宙起始状态的问题。一些人认为科学只是与第一部分有关,他们把宇宙的起始状况问题看做是玄学或宗教的事情。他们会说万能的上帝能随心所欲地启动宇宙。可能是这样,但是如果真是这样的话,他也能使宇宙按完全任意的方式演变,然而看起来他所选择的是使宇宙根据某些法则很有规则地自然发展。因此,我们似乎可以假设有一些法则在支配着宇宙的起始状态。

[5] all in one go 一次性,一气呵成,一步登天/to break up 分开,分成/in isolation 单独的,隔离的/to associate with 联合,联系,关联/to be independent of 独立的,不受控制的/structure 结构,构造/constitution 构成,构成的行为或方式,物的一般构造

要想一次性就设计出描述整个宇宙的理论显然是很困难的。我们只有把该问题分解,并构想成一些局部理论。每个局部理论描述并预言某种有限的观察,不去考虑其他量的作用,或者以简单的成组数字来代替它们。这种途径或许是完全错误的。假如宇宙中的一切在根本上依赖于别的一切事物,那么孤立地调查局部问题就不可能全面地解决问题。不过,这确实是我们在过去取得进步的方法。最佳的例子仍然是牛顿的万有引力理论,它告诉我们两个物体间的引力仅取决于与每个物体有关联的一个数字,即其质量,但与该物体的构成成分无关。因此,为了计算出太阳和行星的轨道,人们并不需要有关它们的结构和构成成分的理论。

[6] in terms of 就……来说,用……的话来讲/quantum mechanics 量子力学/intellectual 智力的,显示智力的/phenomena 现象,其单数形式为 phenomenon/to be inconsistent with 与……不一致/to incorporate (使)结合,(使)合并/property 特性,属性,性质

今天科学家们用两种基本的局部理论来描述宇宙——广义相对论和量子力学。它们是本世纪上半叶伟大的智力成就。广义相对论描述引力和宇宙的大规模结构,也就是说可以观察的宇宙的大小从只有几英里大到1亿亿亿英里(1之后加24个0)。另一方面,量子力学则处理极小规模的现象,如一英寸的万亿分之一。然而,不幸的是,人们知道这两种理论互相并不一致——两者不可能都正确。当代物理学的主攻方向就是寻求一种能使两者合二为一的新理论——量子引力论。目前我们还没有这样的理论,而且要有这样的理论,我们可能还有很长的路要走,但是我们已经确实知道该新理论必须具有的许多特性。

Exercises

I. Answer the following questions:

1. What is a scientific theory?
2. What is a good theory?
3. What is Aristotle's theory?
4. What is Newton's theory?
5. Why does the author say that any physical theory is always provisional?
6. What is the characteristic of a good theory according to Karl Popper?
7. Why is a new theory really an extension of the previous theory? Give an example.
8. What is the approach most scientists actually follow when describing the whole universe?
9. Why is it very difficult to devise a theory to describe the universe all in one go?
10. How do the scientists today describe the universe?

II. Translate the following words and phrases:

A. From Chinese into English.
1. 宇宙的本质
2. 科学理论
3. 一整套规则
4. 武断因素
5. 明确的预言
6. 高度的精确性
7. 广义相对论
8. 量子力学
9. 最终目标
10. 宇宙的模式
11. 万有引力理论
12. 结构和构成成分

B. From English into Chinese.
1. to be clear about
2. the simple-minded view
3. to relate…to…

4. a large class of observations _____
5. to be proportional to _____
6. in principle _____
7. to deal with _____
8. to separate…into… _____
9. the initial state of the universe _____
10. metaphysics or religion _____
11. in that case _____
12. to turn out _____
13. in a fundamental way _____
14. to calculate the orbits _____
15. to depend on _____
16. to be inconsistent with _____

III. Translate the following passage into Chinese:

Scientific knowledge is divided into mathematical sciences, natural sciences or sciences dealing with the natural world (physical and biological sciences), and sciences dealing with mankind (psychology, sociology, all the sciences of cultural achievements, every kind of historical knowledge). Apart from these sciences is philosophy. In the first place, all this is pure or theoretical knowledge, sought only for the purpose of understanding, in order to fulfill the need to understand what is intrinsic and consubstantial to man. What distinguishes man from animal is that he knows and needs to know. If man did not know that the world existed, and that the world was of a certain kind, that he was in the world and that he himself was of a certain kind, he wouldn't be man. The technical aspects or applications of knowledge are equally necessary for man and are of the greatest importance, because they also contribute to defining him as man and permit him to pursue a life increasingly more truly human.

Well-known Sayings

△ Knowledge advances by steps and not leaps.
△ Zeal without knowledge is fire without light.
△ We gain knowledge by reading, by reflection, by observation or by practice.

Lesson 40

New Findings from the Latest Scientific Research

Broadcasting Technology

[1] Sponsorship and advertising revenue from major sporting events could be dramatically enhanced by a technological leap that allows television audiences in different countries to see a variety of messages from stadium perimeter hoardings. The computer technology, specifically, the broadcasting technology, inaugurated during a special athletics meeting in May in the Olympic stadium at Atlanta, enables viewers in different countries to see the same events with contrasting advertising backdrops which match the language and markets of the country watching.

[2] The development will give companies such as car manufacturers, with brands of products unique to a particular country, the opportunity to target advertising towards the relevant market. It will also make it possible for international firms to advertise their products in different languages such as Chinese, or avoid countries that impose restrictions on items such as alcohol. Revenue could also be boosted by altering the message during the course of an event.

[3] The technology was initially developed by Orad, the Israeli defence electronics company, for military purposes. Commercially, the technology enables the computer to memorise visual pictures of the stadium. When the camera sends pictures of an event with views of a particular hoarding in the background, the computer can superimpose the correct advertising background on the hoarding, for example, an advertisement in Chinese. The recomposed pictures are then beamed to the right country.

[4] Orad and ISL, a leading sports promotion agency, have formed a Nether-lands-based joint venture, Imagine, to market the product. Sports sponsorship is presently worth around $US 11.3 billion (RMB 94 billion), while worldwide event-related advertising is over $US 145 billion (RMB 1 206 billion).

[5] The only rival is the Epsis system, developed by a Paris-based defence and multimedia group. It can only cope at present with unobstructed hoardings.

Revolutionary X-Ray Instrument

[6] A three-year collaborative effort by NASA, industry and university researchers has resulted in the development of an instrument which can generate the world's most intense source of commercial X-rays. Capable of generating beams that are more than 100 times the intensity of other conventional X-ray sources, the new instrument is expected to lead to improvements in biotechnology research and have a wide variety of applications in scientific research, medicine and industry.

[7] The revolutionary invention was developed by researchers at NASA's Marshall Space Flight Center, Huntsville, Alabama; X-Ray Optical Systems, Inc, Albany, New York; and the Center for X-Ray Optics of the State University of New York at Albany.

[8] "This new optical instrument provides something never before possible: a capability to control the direction of X-ray beams," explains Dr. Walter Gibson, Professor of Physics at the State University of New York at Albany.

[9] "At the heart of the instrument is a new type of optics for X-rays called 'Capillary Optics'. The

X-rays are controlled by reflecting them through tens of thousands of tiny curved channels or capillaries, similar to the way that light is directed through fibre optics," Gibson says. "Thus, we are able to concentrate the beams to suit the particular needs of the intended research or medical procedure."

[10] Researchers at the Marshall Flight Center are using the newly developed X-ray instrument to determine the atomic structure of important proteins which are the targets for drug design by leading pharmaceutical companies. "Our current research efforts focus on many difficult public health problems such as cancer, AIDS and heart disease," explains Dr. Daniel Carter of Marshall's Laboratory for Structural Biology.

[11] "This new capillary X-ray technology will allow us to pursue more challenging research problems in our own laboratory with a speed and effectiveness never before possible," he says. "These and future applications should have a profound impact on many areas of science and medicine. We expect this new technology to significantly accelerate the ability of researchers to gather the information necessary to design entire families of highly effective, disease-fighting drugs."

[12] The new X-ray lens system, designed by the University of New York at Albany under NASA contract, incorporates the special optics manufactured by X-Ray Optical Systems.

[13] "As a result of working with NASA and the State University of New York at Albany, we have developed X-ray optics which will provide important commercial benefits to a broad range of industries," says David Gibson, president of X-Ray Optics.

[14] "Many commercial applications of this new technology are possible, including better manufacturing control for semi-conductor circuits, better medical imaging, such as in mammography, and improved forensics." The high intensity X-ray beams will permit scientific and medical research to be performed in less time with higher accuracy. In some cases the research was not feasible in standard X-ray laboratories. Also, the instrument could permit the use of smaller, lower cost and safer X-ray sources.

Infrared Camera Has Variety of Uses

[15] A revolutionary new infrared camera developed by America's National Aeronautics and Space Administration (NASA) may present new possibilities for doctors, pilots and environmental scientists, as well as enable defence forces to identify various types of rockets by their plumes.

[16] The camera, developed at the Center for Space Microelectronics Technology at NASA's Jet Propulsion Laboratory (JPL), Pasadena, California, in partnership with Amber, part of the Raytheon group of companies, uses highly sensitive Quantum-Well Infrared Photodetectors, or QWIPS.

[17] The camera is the only one of its kind at present, according to the development team leader, Dr. Sarath Gunapala of JPL. The higher sensitivity of long-wave-length QWIPS could allow doctors to detect tumours using thermographics, or heat analysis. It could allow pilots to make better landings with improved night vision, and enable environmental scientists to monitor pollution and weather patterns. Other possible uses include law enforcement, search and rescue and industrial process control.

[18] In order for infrared light detectors to work, they must be very cold. The new camera contains a Stirling cooler, a closed-cycle refrigerator about the size of a fist. The small motor circulates cooling gas so effectively that it cools the camera from room temperature to very low temperatures—about minus 343 degrees Fahrenheit (minus 208 Celsius)—in around ten minutes.

[19] The camera can be hooked to batteries to make it more portable, while the current prototype plugs into a 110-volt wall socket for power. It is 11 centimetres wide, 26 centimetres deep and 18 centimetres high and weighs 4.5 kilograms.

Language Points and Chinese Translations

第 40 课　科学研究的最新发现

〔1〕sponsorship 发起,赞助,承办,意指赞助某项活动,赞助广播或电视节目的人或公司,为其产品做宣传、广告/revenue 收入/to enhance 增加,增进,促进/stadium perimeter hoarding 指体育场或运动场四周被用以张贴广告宣传的栅墙或招贴板/to inaugurate 为……的开始,为(展览会、运动会等)举行开幕式,相当于 to be the beginning of/contrasting 有鲜明对照的,对比,成对照/backdrop(戏台或场景后面的)背景幕,天幕

传播技术

由于技术的迅速发展,不同国家的电视观众可以从体育馆或运动场四周的广告栅墙上看到变化多样的信息,从而使重大体育比赛的承办和广告收入大幅度增加。这项计算机技术,首次使用于五月在亚特兰大奥林匹克体育场举行的特别运动会期间,使不同国家的观众收看相同的比赛节目,而与收看国的语言和市场相匹配的广告背景各不相同。

〔2〕unique 独特的,唯一的/to target 把目标对准,瞄准/to impose…on 加……于/alcohol 酒精,酒/to boost 提高,支援

该项计算机技术的发展使一些公司,例如汽车制造商,有机会将其对某一特定国家专门的品牌产品广告精准投放于相关市场。它也使一些国际公司有可能以不同的语言,如中文,为其产品作广告宣传,或者避免在那些对酒精等商品加以限制的国家做广告。在比赛期间对信息进行更改,也可以使收入增加。

〔3〕commercially 商业上,商务上/to superimpose 添加,附加,重叠,置(一物)于他物之上/to recompose 重新组成,构成/to beam sth. to 向某一特定方向播送,即 to broadcast in a particular direction

该项技术首先是由以色列奥勒德电子防御公司为了军事目的而开发的。在商业上,该项技术能使计算机储存体育场的视觉图像。当摄像机发送背景是特定招贴板的赛事画面时,计算机能够在招贴板上添加正确的广告背景,例如一则中文广告。然后这重新组成的图像定向播送至相应的国家。

〔4〕奥勒德公司和一家主要的体育运动促进机构 ISL 在荷兰成立了一家合资企业,名称为"想象",以便推销该产品。目前承办各类体育运动项目的收入约 113 亿美元(合人民币 940 亿元),而全世界与赛事有关的广告收入达 1 450 多亿美元(合人民币 12 060 亿元)。

〔5〕rival 竞争者,对手/multimedia 多媒体/to cope with 应对,对付/unobstructed 无阻隔的,无遮拦的

唯一能够与该项技术匹敌的是在巴黎的防御和多媒体小组所研制的 Epsis 系统。该系统目前仅应用于无遮蔽的广告招贴板。

〔6〕collaborative 合作的/intensity 强烈,强度/conventional 传统的,习俗的,常规的/biotechnology 生物技术

革命性的 X 光仪器

美国国家航空航天局,工业界和大学研究人员经过三年的努力合作终于研制出了一种仪器,该仪器能产生世界上最强的商用 X 光源。这种新仪器所产生的光束比传统的 X 光源强一百多倍,因此有望进一步提高生物技术的研究水平,并可广泛应用于科学研究、医学和工业等领域。

〔7〕这项具有革命性的发明创造是由美国阿拉巴马州亨茨维尔的国家航空航天局的马歇尔太空飞行中心,纽约州奥尔巴尼的 X 光学公司和奥尔巴尼的纽约州立大学的 X 光学中心共同开发完成的。

〔8〕奥尔巴尼的纽约州立大学的物理学教授 Walter Gibson 解释说:"这种新的光学仪器提供了一种前所未有的可能:控制 X 光束方向的能力。"

〔9〕optics 光学,光学镜片/capillary 毛细管/curved 弯曲的,弯形的

"该仪器的中心是一种叫'光学毛细管'的新型 X 光镜片。X 光由成千上万细小、弯曲的管道即毛细管的折射而受到控制,这与光线通过光纤维而定向的方式相类似。"Gibson 说,"所以,我们能够集中 X 光束以适应需要进行的研究或治疗进程的特定需求。"

[10] protein 蛋白质/pharmaceutical 医药的,制药的/to focus on 集中,与 concentrate 同义。

马歇尔飞行中心的研究人员们正在使用这种新研制的 X 光仪器确定一些重要蛋白质的原子结构。这些重要的蛋白质正是几家主要的制药公司进行药物配置的必需品。马歇尔结构生物实验室的 Daniel Carter 博士解释说,"当前我们进行研究的主要精力集中在许多难以解决的公共健康问题上,如癌症、艾滋病和心脏病等"。

[11] to pursue 继续进行,继续做,追求,以……为目标或目的/profound 深刻的,深远的/impact 意指 strong expression or effect 强烈的印象或影响

"这种新型的毛细管 X 光技术将使我们在自己的实验室里,以前所未有的速度和效率从事更具挑战性的研究工作。"他说,"现在和未来的应用将会对科学和医学的许多领域产生深远的影响。我们期望该项新技术将大大促进研究人员收集信息的能力,而这种信息对于设计出高效、抗病的系列药物很有必要。"

[12] lens 透镜/to incorporate 结合,使混合,合并

奥尔巴尼的纽约州立大学根据 NASA 的合同研制了新型的 X 光透镜系统。X 光光学系统公司制造的特殊镜片也融入了该系统的技术。

[13] X 光光学公司总裁 David Gibson 说,"由于和 NASA 以及奥尔巴尼的纽约州立大学共同努力的结果,我们已开发了 X 光镜片,这将给多种行业带来重要的商业利益。"

[14] to better 改善/semi-conductor circuits 半导体电路/mammgraphy 早期胸部肿瘤 X 射线测定法/forensics 法医学,相当于 forensic medicine

"这项新技术有许多可行的商业应用,包括改善半导体电路的生产控制,改善医学成像,如可以应用于早期胸部肿瘤 X 射线测定法,提高法医学技术。"这种高强度的 X 光束将使科学和医学研究更省时更准确。在某些情况下,这种研究不适宜在一般性的实验室里进行。而且,该仪器可以允许使用体积更小、费用更低以及更安全的 X 光源。

红外摄影机的多种用途

[15] infrared adj. 红外线的,n. 红外线/plume 羽毛,羽毛饰,本文中指火箭尾部喷出的羽毛状的火焰。

美国国家航空航天局(NASA)研制出的一种革命性的新型的红外摄像机为医生、飞行员和环境科学家提供了新的应用前景,也可使武装部队根据火箭尾部的尾焰辨别出各种类型的火箭。

[16] microelectronics 微电子学/propulsion 推进力/partnership 合伙,合作关系/in partnership with sb. 与某人合作,合伙/sensitive 敏感的,灵敏的/quantum 量子/photodetector 光电探测器

位于加利福尼亚州帕萨迪纳的 NASA 喷气发动机推进实验室(JPL)的太空微电子技术中心和 Raytgeon 集团公司的安珀分公司合作研制了这种红外摄像机。它使用了高灵敏度的量子阱红外光电探测器(QWIPS)。

[17] tumour 肿瘤,肿块/thermographics 热敏成像/to monitor 监视,监控/enforcement 实施,执行/to rescue 营救,援救

根据开发组组长,JPL 的 Sarath Gunapala 博士所说,该红外摄像机目前是该种类摄像机中唯一的一个。长波段 OWIPS 的更高的灵敏度可使医生利用热敏成像或热分析方法探测到肿瘤。它可使飞行员提高夜间视觉而能更好地着陆,使环境科学家能监控污染和监测各种天气变化。其他可能的用途还包括执法、搜寻和营救,以及工业过程控制等。

[18] cooler 冷却器/to circulate 使循环,使环流/Fahrenheit 华氏,华氏温度计/Celsius 摄氏的,摄氏

红外光电探测器必须处于低温状态才能工作。这种新型的摄像机安装有一个 Stirling 冷却器,即只有一个拳头大小的封闭式循环电冰箱。这小型发动机使冷气有效地循环,从而使摄像机的温度在大约十分钟的时间里从室温降至非常低的温度——华氏零下 343 度(即摄氏零下 208 度)。

[19] to hook 钩住,用钩连接/portable 轻便的,手提式的,便于携带的/prototype 原型,典型,样板/plug 插头/socket 插座,插口

该红外摄像机可安装上电池,更方便携带,而现在的原型机是把插头插入墙上 110 伏特的电源插座才能得到供电。它宽 11 厘米,长 26 厘米,高 18 厘米,重 4.5 公斤。

Exercises

I. **Answer the following questions:**

1. According to the text, what was inaugurated during a special athletics meeting in May in the Olympic stadium at Atlanta?

2. By whom and for what purposes was the technology initially developed?

3. How is the technology used commercially?

4. According to the text, how much is the sports sponsorship revenue and how much is the worldwide event-related advertising revenue at present?

5. How was the revolutionary X-Ray instrument invented?

6. In what fields does the new instrument have a wide variety of applications?

7. What capability does the new instrument provide?

8. Why does the author say that we can concentrate the beams to suit the needs of the intended research or medical procedure?

9. What can we expect the new technology to do?

10. Why does the author say that many commercial applications of the new technology are possible?

11. How was the infrared camera developed?

12. What uses does the infrared camera have?

II. **Translate the following words and phrases:**

A. From Chinese into English.
 1. 传播技术
 2. 视觉图像
 3. 广告背景
 4. 商用 X 光源
 5. 生物技术研究
 6. 原子结构
 7. 新型 X 光透镜系统
 8. 光电探测器
 9. 半导体电路

10. 医学成像 _____
11. 红外摄像机 _____
12. 环境科学家 _____
13. 微电子技术 _____
14. 量子阱红外光电探测器 _____
15. 长波段 _____
16. 热敏成像 _____

B. From English into Chinese.
1. sponsorship _____
2. major sporting events _____
3. to target advertising towards the relevant market _____
4. to market the product _____
5. to cope with _____
6. collaborative effort _____
7. to have a wide variety of applications in scientific research _____
8. to control the direction of X-ray beams _____
9. high sensitivity _____
10. heat analysis _____
11. night vision _____
12. to monitor pollution and weather patterns _____
13. industrial process control _____
14. commercial benefits _____
15. to pursue challenging research problems _____
16. prototype _____

Ⅲ. Translate the following passage into Chinese:

Right now, fiber optics is starting an unpredictable and dramatic technological revolution in both computing and communications. The National Academy of Engineering lists fiber optic communication as one of the most important scientific engineering achievements of the last 25 years. Clearly, it is every bit as revolutionary as was the transistor. A single cable can carry hundreds of thousands of times the number of channels carried by the largest copper television cable. It means that fiber optics will provide opportunities unimaginable with copper and make possible the digitization of America, including digital television, which will make HDTV as outdated as 78 rpm records. It will make it easy to shift billions of bits of data from one coast to the other in seconds. In many fundamental ways, fiber optics will change the way we view our world.

[HDTV: high definition TV 高清晰电视]

Well-known Sayings

△ *A wise man will make more opportunities than he finds.*
△ *There is scarcely a great truth but has had to fight its way to public recognition in the face of opposition.*
△ *The magnitude of a "progress" is gauged by the greatness of the sacrifice that it requires.*

Practice Exercises
Practice Exercise 1

Part I Translation

Directions: Translate the following scientific and technical terms from English into Chinese.

1. information technology _____
2. pulses of light _____
3. jet-lag _____
4. sub-sea fibre optic cable _____
5. electronic signals _____
6. video phones _____
7. space shuttle _____
8. gene _____
9. solid smoke _____
10. body clock _____
11. biorhythmic cycles _____
12. nanometer _____
13. ecosystem _____
14. natural climate variability _____
15. greenhouse effect _____
16. fossile fuel _____
17. telecommunication networks _____
18. E-mail _____
19. high energy periods _____
20. fibre optics _____

Part II Vocabulary and Structure
Section A

Directions: Complete each of the following sentences with an appropriate word derived from the underlined word on the left of the sentence.

21. <u>technique</u>   We call the age we are now living in the age of information _____.
22. <u>science</u>   At last, the experts drew a _____ conclusion from the experiments.
23. <u>contribution</u> In that area, a lot of industries _____ to the water pollution.
24. <u>economy</u>   _____, oilfields have given the Middle East countries great advantages since 1960's.
25. <u>rely</u>   Do you think that all the magazines and newspapers are _____ sources of information?
26. <u>solve</u>   Some people think that the problem of pollution is _____, but it isn't easy to find the _____.
27. <u>profession</u>   The injured soldier was reassured by the _____ treatment he received in the hospital.
28. <u>necessary</u>   The problem they raised at the meeting yesterday _____ some careful thought.
29. <u>essence</u>   It is _____ that we realize the importance of science and technology in our national economy.

30. produce   The workers' _____ increased by 10 percent when their working conditions were improved.
31. revolution   The use of computers will _____ our life and work today.
32. character   These are the _____ of the present research of the advanced technology.
33. deep   That science book shows Professor John Smith's _____ of learning.
34. chemistry   _____ is the branch of chemistry that deals with the relations between heat and chemical action.
35. care   A surgeon must help the patient to fight death and any _____ on his part will result in serious consequences.

Section B

Directions: From the four choices given, choose the ONE that best completes the sentence.

36. The new technology has many advantages, _____ are unknown to us.
    A. some of which   B. that some of which
    C. some of that   D. some which of them
37. Materials made from plastic fibres are often known by _____ special trade name as nylon.
    A. that   B. the some   C. as   D. such a
38. Dr. Albert Acheson is now _____ in a new scientific experiment.
    A. interesting   B. engaged   C. excited   D. joined
39. Colour blind people find it very difficult to _____ shades of colours.
    A. talk   B. distinguish   C. recognize   D. tell
40. The general manager requires that every employee _____ able to use a computer.
    A. is   B. is to be   C. be   D. to be
41. She _____ her success to ability more than to good luck.
    A. depends   B. belongs   C. owes   D. gives
42. With two-way radios, people can talk to each other while _____ in their cars.
    A. driving   B. to drive   C. are driving   D. driven
43. A container weighs more after air is put in, _____ proves that air has weight.
    A. it   B. that   C. which   D. what
44. They declared that they believed there was something in nature _____ gave out radiation.
    A. where   B. as   C. that   D. in which
45. How many days do you _____ the community service a month?
    A. spend for   B. devote to   C. use   D. apply to
46. Professor Black _____ in doing the experiment again though he had failed many times.
    A. insisted   B. persisted   C. consisted   D. assisted
47. Peter knows how to _____ the complicated situation.
    A. deal in   B. cope with   C. face with   D. fight against
48. Complicated _____ the problem is, the computers can solve it in a very short period of time.
    A. as   B. though   C. while   D. if
49. _____, there is no air or water on the moon.
    A. Just like knowing   B. Like is known
    C. As is knowing   D. As is known
50. It _____ the Russians that were the first to launch a man into space.
    A. has been B. is   C. were   D. was
51. The technician warns the trainees that they can't be _____ careful in doing the experiment.
    A. so   B. more   C. most   D. too

52. Hardly a man came to the exhibition _____ was deeply impressed by the functions of the robots.
    A. and   B. which   C. but   D. as
53. That is the reason _____ we are not in favour of revising the program.
    A. that   B. why   C. which   D. how
54. We understand that easy access to _____ is often the key to success in our highly developed society.
    A. information
    B. informations
    C. an information
    D. to get the information
55. The idea that the earth is flat was _____ hundreds of years ago.
    A. appointed   B. rejected   C. hesitated   D. conflicted
56. Only when they _____ the importance of the research, will they carry it on.
    A. realized
    B. will have realized
    C. have realized
    D. will realize
57. However _____, Mary failed to give a correct answer.
    A. she tried hard
    B. hard she tried
    C. she did try hard
    D. hard did she try
58. It is not the instruments that a scientist uses but how he uses them _____ make him a scientist.
    A. what   B. which   C. that   D. who
59. Her good performance in the competition proved that she was a _____ winner.
    A. worth   B. worthwhile   C. worthless   D. worthy
60. The doctor advised that Mr. Martin _____ an operation right away so as to save his life.
    A. have   B. has   C. had   D. would have

Part III Cloze

Directions: There are twenty blanks in the following passage. For each blank there are four choices marked A, B, C and D. You should choose the ONE that best fits into the passage.

A great __61__ of research work has been carried out in recent years into sleep. It is true that we already know a great deal __62__ the mechanics of sleep and that we are beginning to know about the biochemical changes __63__ in sleep. __64__, we are still a long way from finding out answers to such questions __65__ how much sleep a person really needs. __66__ the physiological bases of sleep remain very much a matter for conjecture we __67__ nevertheless have hard evidence on how much sleep people do __68__ obtain. We still need to know __69__ about the kinds of effects that sleeplessness or loss of sleep __70__. In spite of the __71__ effort which has been devoted to __72__ why men and women sleep, there is yet __73__ in the area. The fact that sleeplessness or loss of sleep causes numerous harmful effects __74__ that the body requires sleep to restore __75__ refresh itself. However, more research is needed to determine __76__ this is so or whether sleep is the result __77__ adaptation to the environment. There is also the __78__ that these two interpretations of sleep may __79__ be true although they __80__ it from different points of view.

61. A. number   B. many   C. much   D. amount
62. A. in   B. about   C. for   D. with
63. A. concerning   B. happened   C. involved   D. resolved
64. A. However   B. Thus   C. Therefore   D. So
65. A. of   B. as   C. to   D. that
66. A. While   B. Whenever   C. Why   D. With
67. A. do   B. might   C. already   D. did
68. A. for example   B. in fact   C. in conclusion D. in case
69. A. little   B. more   C. less   D. many

70.	A. results	B. causes		C. gives		D. takes	
71.	A. considerate	B. effective		C. considerable		D. exclusive	
72.	A. knowing	B. searching		C. inspecting		D. investigating	
73.	A. agreement	B. approvement		C. disappointment		D. disagreement	
74.	A. provides	B. suggests		C. rejects		D. intents	
75.	A. as	B. to		C. nor		D. or	
76.	A. why	B. whether		C. what		D. that	
77.	A. of	B. in		C. to		D. for	
78.	A. feasibility	B. capability		C. likeliness		D. possibility	
79.	A. neither	B. both		C. well		D. all	
80.	A. translate	B. interpret		C. indicate		D. predict	

Part IV Reading Comprehension

Directions: There are six passages in this part. Each passage is followed by some questions. For each question there are four suggested answers marked A, B, C and D. Read the passages carefully and choose the best answer to each question.

(1)

People who talk and sing to plants are not crazy according to Arnold Braymar, a government agriculture expert. "In fact, singing and talking to plants makes them grow better," says Braymar. The reason is quite simple—when we sing or talk to plants, we exhale carbon dioxide which plants need to survive and thrive. Plants absorb the carbon dioxide through their pores during the sun-light hours and produce oxygen which people need to survive. Singing and talking is effective, however, only during the daytime. Bedtime lullabies will not help plants to sleep better or grow faster.

81. According to this piece, singing and talking to plants _____.
    A. is helpful to the plants
    B. is necessary for the plants to grow
    C. can be harmful to people
    D. can be simple and entertaining

82. What kind of explanation does the expert give for the correctness of his claim?
    A. Superstitious.   B. Mysterious.   C. Scientific.   D. Humorous.

83. The writer of this piece seems to think that the whole matter of talking or singing to plants is _____.
    A. full of superstition   B. full of mystery
    C. crazy   D. humorous

84. Why would singing to plants only be effective during the daytime?
    A. Plants die at night.
    B. Plants only use carbon dioxide during the sunlight hours.
    C. People sleep at night.
    D. Plants do not enjoy singing at night.

85. How did the agriculture expert discover that singing and talking to plants makes them grow better?
    A. He sang and talked to his plants.
    B. He learned it in school.
    C. By using some special instruments.
    D. The answer to this question is not found in the passage above.

(2)

Have you traveled on any of the new giant airplanes? If you have not been a passenger on one of these planes, try to imagine a jet which is more than seventy meters long and more than five stories high at the tail. Such a plane costs at least twenty-five million dollars to build. It costs at least $6 000 to fill this giant with fuel.

Inside, the giant jet looks more like a great theater than a plane. It has six kitchens, and they are all needed when the plane is full of passengers. The jet holds more than 400 passengers. Imagine that number in one jet plane!

Is there any danger that the jet's engines will fail? Fortunately, the planes appear to be quite safe. On each plane there are twice as many engines as the jet needs. If two engines fail on the same side, the plane can easily use its other engines to land. There are also two mechanical pilots to take charge if the human pilots cannot fly the plane.

86. The height of the tail of the airplane is compared to _____.
    A. a building
    B. a tall pole
    C. a small plane
    D. none of the above

87. How much does it cost to build a giant airplane?
    A. $25 000
    B. $25 000 000
    C. $250 000
    D. $2 500 000

88. How many engines are there on each side of the plane?
    A. 4.
    B. 2.
    C. 6.
    D. 8.

89. Why do these planes have six kitchens?
    A. In case one or two kitchens are out of order.
    B. To be able to feed the actors in the theater.
    C. To be able to feed the number of passengers the plane can hold.
    D. None of the above.

(3)

But the success of science, both its intellectual excitement and its practical application, depends upon the self-correcting character of science. There must be a way of testing any valid idea. It must be possible to reproduce any valid experiment. The character or beliefs of scientists are irrelevant; all that matters is whether the evidence supports their contentions. Arguments from authority simply do not count; too many authorities have been mistaken too often. I would like to see these very effective scientific modes of thought communicated by the schools and the media; and it would certainly be an astonishment and delight to see them introduced into politics. Scientists have been known to change their minds completely and publicly when presented with new evidence or new arguments. I cannot recall the last time a politician displayed a similar openness and willingness to change.

90. What does the passage mainly discuss?
    A. The rewards of intellectual excitement.
    B. Practical applications of an abstract theory.
    C. An important characteristic of science.
    D. Some similarities between politics and science.

91. What did the paragraph preceding the passage most probably discuss?
    A. The scientific community.
    B. The achievements of science.
    C. Self-correction in science.
    D. Valid and invalid experiments.

92. According to the passage, if a scientist repeats an experiment several times and does not produce similar results each time, the experiment must be _____.

  A. extremely complex   B. self-corrected
  C. incorrectly recorded   D. invalid

93. According to the passage, which of the following is most essential to scientists' work?
  A. Character.   B. Beliefs.
  C. Authority.   D. Evidence.

94. The author implies that in science, arguments from authority are _____.
  A. irrelevant   B. complicated
  C. effective   D. unreliable

(4)

  Experiments with cats have been carried out at Harvard Medical School to find out what happens to individual brain cells during sleep. The cats were first made sleepy, and then a microelectrode was attached to a particular cell in their heads.

  Results show that the brain cells the scientists were looking at (those responsible for visual processing) tend to behave quite differently during sleep from in a waking state because their response to visual stimuli (something that stimulates) is much reduced. However, the scientists were surprised to discover that brain cells, even when limited to the specific type they were studying, do not all behave in the same way.

  These results are all related to "slow-wave" sleep which is not the sleep in which dreams occur. Dreams produce a quite different effect on the visual-processing brain cells, more as if dreamer were awake. The dreams of human beings have long been a source of interest to psychologists, and scientists have studied some of their physical effects on eye movements. We know that human beings have dreams and, by comparing their physical effects, scientists have shown that animals probably have them, too.

95. What are responsible for visual processing?
  A. The brain cells.   B. The microelectrode.
  C. The heads.   D. The visual stimuli.

96. What would be the best topic of this passage?
  A. Brain Cells.
  B. A Study of Brain Cells During Sleep.
  C. A Study of Visual Processing.
  D. Experiments with Cats.

97. Why do the brain cells behave differently during sleep from in a waking state?
  A. Because their response to visual stimuli is increased.
  B. Because their response to visual stimuli declines greatly.
  C. Because their response to visual stimuli is moderate.
  D. Because their response to visual stimuli slightly decreases.

98. What is "slow-wave" sleep?
  A. It is the sleep in which dreams occur.
  B. It is the dreamer who falls into sleep slowly.
  C. It is the sleep without dream.
  D. It is the sleep without producing a different effect on the visual-processing brain cells.

99. How could scientists know that animals probably have dreams?
  A. By experiments with cats.
  B. By studying "slow-wave" sleep.
  C. By studying the visual-processing brain cells.
  D. By studying physical effects on eye movements.

What we need is a nationwide network of "information superhighways", linking scientists, business people, educators and students by fiber-optic cable to process and deal with information that is available but unused.

Such a network is the single most cost-effective step America could take to become more competitive in the world economy. It is also the single most important step the United States could take to improve its proficiency in science, technology and research.

Major U. S. corporations spend millions of dollars seeking answers to questions about how to plan for the future and how to gain a competitive edge. In almost every case, all of the information they need to answer those questions is already available. But they have no idea how to find the needle in the haystack, how to distill it and how to make the judgements required to guide those corporations.

Of course, today, scientists, engineers and a few million computer hobbyists know the power of computer networking, and they take the convenience of networking for granted. But imagine that the network could transmit not just text but video and voice. It is easy to imagine uses for such a system because prototypes are already available. But the prototypes are limited because they link only a few computers. Already there's electronic mail, electronic banking, electronic shopping, electronic tax returns and electronic newspapers, but these applications are limited severely by the speed and size of our networks.

The really exciting services are yet to come. Researchers are already developing and demonstrating them. Today they are using supercomputers to organize and distill information for our productive use.

Similarly, the software being developed to allow massively parallel supercomputers to sort through these silos of data will be used to provide network users with access to a quantity of information equal to all the bits of data in the entire Library of Congress.

The interactive features made possible in a network will usher in a second information revolution.

100. What is the most appropriate title of the passage?
    A. Nationwide Multimedia Internet.
    B. Information Unused.
    C. A Most Important Communication Policy.
    D. An Improvement of Proficient Highways.

101. The purpose of building a nationwide in-line service is _____.
    A. to explore the potentialities of computerization
    B. to develop electronic circuitry
    C. to optimize the access to information through multimedia
    D. to gain a competitive edge for corporations

102. The word "cost-effective" as used in the passage can best be replaced by which of the following phrases?
    A. Yielding profit or benefit.
    B. The amount spent in producing a commodity.
    C. Producing a definite and desired result.
    D. Producing best results for the least amount of investment.

103. The example of corporations clumsily seeking solutions to their problems highlights the fact that _____.
    A. we should encourage an information revolution
    B. the U. S. could benefit greatly by efficiently processing information that is available but unused
    C. we are now being drowned by information
    D. we should automate the process of collecting information

104. What is likely to be required for the transmission of pictures or voices through a computer network?
    A. Information must be organized and distilled for productive use.
    B. An exceedingly rapid and powerful vehicle must be used to transmit enormous bits of data.
    C. The convenience of networking is taken for granted.
    D. Data bases must be sorted out to provide necessary information.

105. The following statements about prototypes of computer network are true EXCEPT _____.
    A. such prototypes are already existent.
    B. such prototypes are nonexistent as yet.
    C. such networks are limited by meagre linkage.
    D. such networks are restricted by their narrow capacities.

106. According to the passage, the key to upgrading the efficiency of the present computer networks is _____.
    A. to find the needle in the haystack
    B. to gain access to a quantity of information equal to all the bits of data in the entire Library of Congress
    C. to make the proper judgments required to guide major corporations
    D. to make the existing networks interactive

(6)

Being citizens of advanced but vulnerable economies, we must either increase the quality of our skills or see our standards of living worsen. For the future, competition between nations will be increasingly based on technological skills. Oil and natural resources will still be important, but they no longer will determine a nation's economic strength. This will now be a matter of the way people organize themselves and the nature quality of their work.

There is simply no way to rest on our past achievements. Today's competition renders out-of-data a lot of what we know and forces us to innovate. For each individual, several careers will be customary, and continuing education and retraining will be inevitable. To attain this extraordinary level of education, governments, businesses, schools and even individuals will turn to technology for the answer.

In industry, processing the information and designing the changes necessary to keep up with the market has meant the growing use of computers. The schools are now following close behind. The computer is the Proteus of machines, as it takes on a thousand forms and serves a thousand functions. But its truly revolutionary character can be seen in its interactive potential.

Today, formal education primarily consists in memorizing data—data that are now easily retrievable by computer or accessible through data banks. The challenge for educators is to restructure the curriculum to make maximum use of the new technologies so that students can learn better and prepare themselves for the information-rich world they now confront. Once we learn to use this new brain outside the brain, education will never be the same.

107. From the passage we know that a nation's economic strength used to be shown by _____.
    A. technological skills   B. oil and natural resources
    C. standards of living   D. competitions between nations

108. Today's competition forces us to innovate because _____.
    A. we have always rested on our past achievements
    B. for each person, several careers will be customary
    C. our available knowledge is no longer useful with competition
    D. we have to continue education and retraining

109. According to the passage which of the following statements is NOT true?
    A. The nature and quality of man's work has played an important part in competition between nations.
    B. Man's standards of living cannot be improved if the quality of his skills are not increased.
    C. More and more computers will be used in processing the information and designing the changes in industry to meet the needs of the market.
    D. Formal education has nothing to do with memorizing data since they are now easily derived from data banks.
110. The passage implies that _____.
    A. we must change the way in which we organize ourselves and the nature and quality of our work
    B. as computers are entering more and more fields, they bring many new problems to us
    C. if we learn to use the new brain outside the brain, we cannot avoid continuing education and retraining
    D. it is necessary to process the information and design the changes to meet the demands of the market

Part V Translation

Directions: Translate the following passages into Chinese.

(1)

If you are looking for information, library shelves are a good place to start. But if you need up-to-the-minute data or have specialized needs, you may find a computerized database more useful, less expensive, and less time consuming. A database, a file of information on one subject or family of subjects, can be stored and maintained in a computer's memory. The speed of the computer then enables you to recall any item in this file almost instantly.

The three main types of databases are statistical, bibliographic, and full text. Statistical databases store vast amounts of numerical data, such as wage and price indexes, census information, foreign exchange rates, and bond prices. Bibliographic databases store references to and summaries of articles in periodicals and newspapers. Full-text databases offer the complete texts of such materials as newspaper, magazine, and journal articles.

(2)

The "information superhighway" is more a social and commercial environment, than a static network. The "superhighway" is composed of a network, and computing resources, but more importantly, the "superhighway" defines a new environment for people, and organizations to interact and communicate with each other. It is for these reasons that the building of such a "superhighway" must be done as a cooperative task force, rather than the more traditional service provider/user model that has been used in the past. Based on these concepts the information superhighway can be defined as: "A location-independent user environment, that uses high speed networking and computing for multimedia communications."

This virtual environment allows users, for the first time, to communicate with each other in a near natural way, through the simultaneous use of voice, video and image and data. The environment is created through the merging of three rapidly evolving technologies. These are: transmission, switching, and compression.

Practice Exercise 2

Part I Translation

Directions: Translate the following scientific and technical terms from English into Chinese.

1. solar photovoltaic cells _____
2. all-purpose, one-size-fits-all PCs _____
3. massive data warehouses _____
4. economic resources _____
5. expertise _____
6. audio and visual data transmitted digitally _____
7. modem _____
8. satellite data-delivery systems _____
9. software application _____
10. multimedia _____
11. broadband service _____
12. managing platform _____
13. E-business _____
14. alternative energy technology _____
15. genetic engineering _____
16. artificial intelligences _____
17. fuel cells _____
18. download _____
19. DNA _____
20. clone _____

Part II Vocabulary and Structure

Section A

Directions: Complete each of the following sentences with an appropriate word derived from the underlined word on the left of the sentence.

21. develop   There are always a lot of new _____ in scientific research.
22. discover   The scientist's _____ may have great significance.
23. violate   The effects of watching _____ on TV are not known.
24. conceive   The _____ of sleep being controlled by serotonin is new.
25. experiment   This new kind of medicine is now being used _____.
26. achieve   The research teams should have _____ goals, or else they will be disappointed.
27. believe   Do you share the _____ that life in big cities is unbearable?
28. sense   People who have a _____ to nylon shouldn't wear nylon clothing.
29. satisfy   They are making _____ progress in the research of cloning.
30. communicate   The Russians launched a _____ satellite last month.
31. inferior   Constant negative criticism often gives one the feeling of _____.
32. mechanic   _____ in industry has put a lot of unskilled workers out of work.
33. defective   Research shows that color blindness is a visual _____ rarely found in women.
34. genetic   A _____ is a scientist who studies how _____ affect our development.

· 225 ·

35. fatality   Millions of people die of cancer every year, which is often a _____ disease.

Section B

Directions: From the four choices given, choose the ONE that best completes the sentence.

36. He is eager _____ the mastery of computer technology.
    A. at   B. for   C. to   D. of

37. The teacher told her pupils that salt water _____ at a lower temperature than fresh water.
    A. freezes   B. will be freezed
    C. was freezing   D. freezing

38. If only I _____ the books on the reading list before I attended the lecture!
    A. have been reading   B. would have read
    C. have read   D. had read

39. Scientific discoveries are often _____ to industrial production.
    A. attached   B. contrasted   C. applied   D. inclined

40. It is quite _____ that he has nicely worked out the maths problems.
    A. obvious   B. distinct   C. extraordinary D. absolute

41. Theory is based on practice and _____ serves practice.
    A. for good   B. on occasion
    C. with difficulty   D. in turn

42. The atmosphere _____ certain gases mixed together in definite proportion.
    A. consists in   B. consists of
    C. results in   D. results from

43. We have had to make a change _____ our plans about the laboratory.
    A. for   B. with   C. to   D. in

44. I had some difficulty in _____ out the plan.
    A. dropping   B. revising   C. carrying   D. drawing

45. He said that the demonstration would go on _____.
    A. as planned   B. as planning
    C. as it as planning   D. as it planned

46. Air, water and food is _____ to good health.
    A. vital   B. importance   C. convenient   D. sufficient

47. The surgeon promised to keep my brother _____ with the most effective remedies.
    A. to be treated B. on treating   C. treated   D. treating

48. You might live for two months without food; without water, you _____ die _____ less than a week.
    A. should/for   B. would/in
    C. had to/over   D. will/through

49. The desert air is so dry that it contains hardly any _____.
    A. moisture   B. atmosphere   C. vapour   D. mist

50. He has formed the most _____ relations with the German scientific circles.
    A. abstract   B. intimate   C. dramatic   D. remote

51. The information points to the fact that most wives _____ their husbands.
    A. survive   B. comfort   C. resemble   D. restrain

52. Much to the students' _____, the English exam was put off till next week.
    A. desire   B. insistence   C. relief   D. requirement

53. _____ the importance of wearing seat belts while driving.
    A. Little they realize   B. They little do realize
    C. Do they realize little   D. Little do they realize

54. The author gave an example _____ support of his argument.
    A. in   B. to   C. for   D. with

55. Because he could not find the right theme _____, his explanation was vague.
    A. to center his thoughts around   B. around which his thoughts to center
    C. in which to center his thoughts   D. on which to center his thoughts

56. Now the need _____ other people's language is becoming greater and greater.
    A. to learn   B. learning
    C. to be learned   D. being learned

57. We think the electronic computer _____ one of the most useful tools in use today.
    A. being   B. to be   C. be   D. have been

58. We prefer the country to the city _____ we have more fresh air in the country.
    A. with   B. that   C. in which   D. in that

59. Dim lights and soft music are supposed to _____ a romantic atmosphere.
    A. present   B. produce   C. preserve   D. provide

60. The fuel of the continental missile is supposed to be _____ by this device.
    A. lighted   B. fired   C. ignited   D. inspired

Part Ⅲ Cloze

Directions: There are twenty blanks in the following passage. For each blank there are four choices marked A, B, C and D. You should choose the ONE that best fits into the passage.

Scientists know that there are two basic approaches to prolonging life. One approach is the __61__ of the diseases that generally __62__ older people—diseases such as cancer, heart attack and strokes. __63__ is the delay of the process of growing old—the __64__ of the body.

In recent years scientific researchers __65__ much time in the study of the process of aging. They believe __66__, within a few years, they will develop the knowledge and the __67__ to delay the aging process for 10 to 15 years. The __68__ will be that more people will live longer, more healthful lives. __69__ scientists believe that __70__ the right diet, exercise, medical __71__ and mental attitude many people can __72__ 100 years old.

Gerontologists, people who __73__ studies of the problems of growing old, are investigating __74__ body cells slow down and __75__ die. They feel that delaying this slowing down process __76__ help postpone death. In a number of American universities, scientists are __77__ the activity of cells, the effects of diet and internal body temperature __78__ aging. If their studies are successful, the results should help __79__ the quality of life for older people in the next few years, __80__ increase the life span of the next generation.

61. A. elimination   B. deletion   C. demonstration   D. conduction
62. A. effect   B. affect   C. reflect   D. perfect
63. A. Others   B. Another   C. The other   D. One more
64. A. decaying   B. deleting   C. decreasing   D. weighing
65. A. had spent   B. had took   C. have spent   D. spent
66. A. which   B. what   C. that   D. in whom
67. A. capability   B. capacity   C. probability   D. ability
68. A. conclusion   B. result   C. summary   D. subsequent
69. A. In the present   B. In detail   C. By the way   D. At present
70. A. about   B. over   C. with   D. on

71.	A. treat	B. suggestion	C. proposal	D. advice
72.	A. begin to live	B. live to be	C. start living	D. live a life
73.	A. major in	B. engage in	C. specialize in	D. are interested in
74.	A. why	B. what	C. that	D. because
75.	A. considerably	B. suddenly	C. eventually	D. actually
76.	A. should	B. must	C. ought to	D. would
77.	A. discussing	B. concerning	C. studying	D. researching
78.	A. with	B. on	C. over	D. within
79.	A. to improve	B. improving	C. to improving	D. of improving
80.	A. as such	B. as much as	C. so far as	D. as well as

Part IV Reading Comprehension

Directions: There are six passages in this part. Each passage is followed by some questions. For each question there are four suggested answers marked A, B, C and D. Read the passages carefully and choose the best answer to each question.

(1)

Television signals cross a continent by relay towers, which pick up and amplify the straightline microwave beams. But there is no way to build towers on water, and a signal sent across the sea could not follow the curve of the earth. Its straight-line beam would soar off into space.

Scientists have solved this problem by designing a new kind of tower, a tower in the sky—a satellite. An active satellite contains amplifiers much like those in the overland microwave towers. When a microwave is beamed to it from a ground transmitter, the satellite increases the strength of the signal and reflects it to a ground receiving station beyond the curve of the globe.

Technologists know enough today to place a satellite system in medium-range altitudes, from about 5 000 to 8 000 miles in space. A system of about fifty satellites would provide many circuits, which would cover the present communication needs of the world. Telephone and telegraph messages would be carried at high speed. TV broadcasts would be shared internationally.

Plans have also been studied for high-altitude satellites as much as 22 000 miles off in space, but there are still problems with these. Some way must be found to fix such satellites in a firm position so that they will always be "on station".

81. According to the article, overland television is carried by _____.
   A. underground cables   B. relay towers
   C. sky towers   D. telegraph lines

82. Overseas television presented a problem because of difficulties in _____.
   A. building towers on water
   B. having microwaves follow the earth's curve
   C. both A and B
   D. neither A nor B

83. Whether overland or overseas, television signals need to be _____.
   A. straightened   B. curved
   C. weakened   D. amplified

84. One advance possible by this system is given as _____.
   A. internationally shared television broadcasts
   B. internationally shared weather forecasts

C. high-speed interchange on market affairs

D. rapid transmission of military information

85. Implied but not stated: _____.

    A. In Arthur C. Clarke's *The Haunted Space Suit* the problems of high-altitude satellites have been solved

    B. A system of about fifty satellites would not cover man's present needs

    C. Microwaves travel in a straight line

    D. Traveling a great distance weakens a microwave

(2)

A series of orbiting satellites and a group of sending and receiving stations located around the Earth form a communications satellite system. Since the sending and receiving stations must point their antennae directly at a satellite in order to complete a transmission, a single satellite can serve less than a third of the Earth's surface at a time. If the satellite is below the horizon, a ground station cannot use it. Therefore, a series of satellites are necessary.

Most systems use synchronous satellites that stay in one position over the Earth. Synchronous satellites are launched to an altitude of 22 300 miles. At this altitude, the satellite's revolution is synchronized with the Earth's rotation. This means that the satellite completes one orbit during the same length of time that the Earth makes one rotation on its axis. Three of these satellites, properly placed, can link stations in any two parts of the world.

86. According to the passage, all of the following are necessary for a worldwide communications satellite system except _____.

    A. ground mirrors to reflect the horizon

    B. properly placed satellites

    C. sending and receiving stations around the Earth

    D. antennae pointed toward the satellites

87. According to the passage, a series of synchronous communication satellites are necessary because a single satellite _____.

    A. reverses its antennae several times per day

    B. orbits too fast to send and receive transmissions from each ground station

    C. cannot complete transmissions with all ground stations

    D. can remain in operation only one-third of each day

88. According to the passage, when the orbit of a single satellite matches the Earth's daily rotation, the satellite will _____.

    A. transmit signals all over the world

    B. remain in a fixed position in relation to the Earth

    C. link stations in only two parts of the world

    D. complete three rotations on its axis

89. It can be inferred from the passage that synchronous satellites are called "synchronous" because _____.

    A. they can synchronize three-way transmissions to all parts of the world

    B. each one rotates on its axis simultaneously with the Earth's rotation

    C. their orbits are perfectly timed to coincide with the Earth's rotation

    D. each one's movements are synchronized to one-third of the speed of the Earth

(3)

In recent years, scientific and technological developments have drastically changed human life on our planet, as well as our views both of ourselves as individuals in society and of the universe as a whole. Maybe one of the most profound developments of the last decade is the discovery of recombinant DNA technology, which allows scientists to introduce genetic material (or genes) from one organism into another. In its simplest form, the technology requires the isolation of a piece of DNA, either directly from the DNA of the organism under study, or artificially synthesized from an RDA template, by using a viral enzyme called reverse transcriptase. This piece of DNA is then ligated to a fragment of bacterial DNA which has the capacity to replicate itself independently. The recombinant molecule thus produced can be introduced into the common intestinal bacterium Escherishchia coli, which can be grown in very large amounts in synthetic media. Under proper conditions, the foreign gene will not only replicate in the bacteria, but also express itself, through the process of transcription and translation, to give rise to large amounts of the specific protein coded by the foreign gene.

The technology has already been successfully applied to the production of several therapeutically important biomolecules, such as insulin, interferon, and growth hormones. Many other important applications are under detailed investigation in laboratories throughout the world.

90. Recombinant DNA technology consists primarily of _____.
    A. producing several therapeutically important biomolecules
    B. giving rise to large amounts of protein
    C. introducing genetic material from one organism into another
    D. using a viral enzyme called reverse transcriptase

91. Recombinant DNA technology has been used in the production of all of the following biomolecules except _____.
    A. growth hormones   B. Escherishchia coli
    C. interferon   D. insulin

92. Which of the following is not True?
    A. The foreign gene will replicate in the bacteria, but it will not express itself through transcription and translation.
    B. The bacterium Escherischia coli can be grown in large amounts in synthetic media.
    C. Research continues in an effort to find other uses for this technology.
    D. Recombinant DNA technology is a recent development.

93. Expression of a gene in Escherischia coli requires _____.
    A. the viral enzyme reverse transcriptase
    B. the processes of transcription and translation
    C. production of insulin and other biomolecules
    D. that the bacteria be grown in a synthetic media

94. The term recombinant is used because _____.
    A. by ligation, a recombinant molecule is produced, which has the capacity of replication
    B. the technique requires the combination of several types of technology
    C. by ligation, a recombinant protein is produced, part of whose amino acids come from each different organism
    D. Escherischia coli is a recombinant organism

(4)

Simply stated, computational linguistics is no more than the use of electronic digital computers in linguistic research. These machines are employed to scan texts and to produce, more rapidly and more reliably than is possible without their aid, such valuable tools for linguistic and stylistic research as word lists, frequency counts, and concordances. But more interesting and theoretically much more difficult than the compilation of lists, is the use of computers for automatic grammatical analysis and translation. A considerable amount of progress was made in the area of machine translation in the United States, Great Britain, and France between the mid-1950's and the mid-1960's, but much of the original impetus for this work has now disappeared, due in part to the realization that the problems involved are infinitely more complex than was at first envisaged. Thus, translation continues to remain as much an art as a science, if not more so.

95. According to the passage, computational linguistics involves _____.
    A. a reliance on computers
    B. a simplified computer language
    C. making electronic tools
    D. research into electronics
96. In what way have the machines referred to proven to be helpful to researchers?
    A. They can produce accurate lists of what a text contains.
    B. They can translate texts more reliably than was possible in the past.
    C. They can validate the theories of linguists and stylists.
    D. They have been used to improve grammatical analysis.
97. How does the author describe the present state of machine translation?
    A. It has been recognized as an art.
    B. It has largely been abandoned.
    C. It has received new impetus from a more artistic approach.
    D. The complex problems previously envisaged have recently been solved.
98. According to the passage, which of the following problems is the most difficult to solve?
    A. Compilation of word lists and frequency counts.
    B. Developing a theoretical approach to list compilation.
    C. Grammatical analyses and translations.
    D. Coming up with concordances which are useful for stylistic research.
99. According to the passage, when approximately was significant progress made in translations by computers?
    A. Between 1950 and 1960.   B. Before 1950.
    C. After 1965.   D. Between 1955 and 1965.
100. It can be inferred from the passage that translation _____.
    A. will never be done satisfactorily by machines
    B. is a science rather than an art
    C. is more complex than making lists
    D. is done particularly well in the United States, Great Britain, and France

(5)

Petroleum products, such as gasoline, kerosine, home heating oil, residual fuel oils, and lubricating oils, come from one source—crude oil found below the earth's surface, as well as under large bodies of water, from a few hundred feet below the surface to as deep as 25 000 feet into the earth's interior. Sometimes crude oil is secured by drilling a hole through the earth, but more dry holes are drilled than those producing oil. Pressure at the source or pumping forces crude oil to the surface.

Crude oil wells flow at varying rates, from ten to thousands of barrels per hour. Petroleum products are always measured in 42-gallon barrels.

Petroleum products vary greatly in physical appearance: thin, thick, transparent or opaque, but regardless, their chemical composition is made up of only two elements: carbon and hydrogen, which form compounds called hydrocarbons. Other chemical elements found in union with the hydrocarbons are few and are classified as impurities. Trace elements are also found, but these are of such minute quantities that they are disregarded. The combination of carbon and hydrogen forms many thousands of compounds which are possible because of the various positions and joinings of these two atoms in the hydrocarbon molecule.

The various petroleum products are refined from the crude oil by heating and condensing the vapors. These products are the so-called light oils, such as gasoline, kerosine, and distillate oil. The residue remaining after the light oils are distilled is known as heavy or residual fuel oil and is used mostly for burning under boilers. Additional complicated refining processes rearrange the chemical structure of the hydrocarbons to produce other products, some of which are used to upgrade and increase the octane rating of various types of gasolines.

101. Which of the following is NOT true?
    A. Crude oil is found below land and water.
    B. Crude oil is always found a few hundred feet below the surface.
    C. Pumping and pressure force crude oil to the surface.
    D. A variety of petroleum products are obtained from crude oil.

102. Many thousands of hydrocarbon compounds are possible because _____.
    A. the petroleum products vary greatly in physical appearance
    B. complicated refining processes rearrange the chemical structure
    C. the two atoms in the molecule assume many positions
    D. the pressure needed to force it to the surface causes molecular transformation

103. Which of the following is true?
    A. The various petroleum products are produced by filtration.
    B. Heating and condensation produce the various products.
    C. Chemical separation is used to produce the various products.
    D. Mechanical means such as the centrifuge are used to produce various products.

104. How is crude oil brought to the surface?
    A. Expansion of the hydrocarbons.
    B. Pressure and pumping.
    C. Vacuum created in the drilling pipe.
    D. Expansion and contraction of the earth's surface.

105. Which of the following is NOT listed as a light oil?
    A. Distillate oil.   B. Gasoline.
    C. Lubricating oil.   D. Kerosine.

(6)

Man is a land animal, but he is also closely tied to the sea. Throughout history the sea has served the needs of man. The sea has provided man with food and a convenient way to travel to many parts of the world. Today, experts estimate that nearly two-thirds of the world's population live within eighty kilometers of the seacoast.

In the modern technological world the sea offers many resources to help mankind survive. Resources on land are beginning to grow less. The sea, however, still offers hope to supply many of man's needs.

The riches of the sea yet to be developed by man's technology are impressive. Oil and gas exploration have existed for nearly thirty years. Valuable amounts of minerals such as manganese, iron, nickel and copper exist on the ocean floor, ready to be mined.

Fish farming promises to be a good way to produce large quantities of food. The culture of fish and shellfish is an ancient skill practised in the past mainly by Oriental peoples.

Besides oil and gas, the sea may offer new sources of energy. Experts believe that the warm temperature of the ocean can be used in a way similar to the steam in a steamship. Ocean currents and waves offer possible use as a source of energy such as hydroelectric power.

Technology is enabling man to explore even deeper under the sea. The new undersea technology is providing divers with diving suits and undersea chambers that are kept at sea-level pressure. The development of strong, new materials has made this possible.

The technology to harvest the sea continues to improve. By the year 2000, experts believe that the problems to exploit the food, minerals, and energy sources of the sea will be largely solved.

106. What is the best title for the passage?
    A. Needs of Man.　　　　　　　　　　B. Sea Harvest.
    C. Sources of Energy.　　　　　　　　D. Sea Exploring Technology.
107. It can be inferred from the passage that _____.
    A. man hasn't completely cultivated the riches of the sea
    B. technology for exploring the sea has been solved
    C. planting rice in the sea will be made possible in a short time
    D. in the near future man can live on the ocean floor
108. Why does the author mention a steamship?
    A. To illustrate that man can make use of sources of energy from the sea.
    B. To show that a steamship is better than other kinds of ship.
    C. To argue that man should use steamships more than other means of transportation.
    D. To indicate that it is warmer in the ocean than on land.
109. According to the author, technology for exploring the sea is important because _____.
    A. man cannot travel farther into space
    B. resources on land are running short
    C. it's a lot of fun diving into the sea
    D. ancient people used to explore the sea
110. The word "exploit" in the last paragraph could best be replaced by which of the following words?
    A. Evaluate.　　　B. Gather.　　　C. Develop.　　　D. Scatter.

Part V　Translation

Directions: Translate the following passages into Chinese.

(1)

Energy in nature comes in many different forms. Heat is a form of energy. A lot of heat energy comes from the sun. Heat can also come from a forest fire or, in much smaller quantities, from the warm body of a mouse. Light is another form of energy. It also comes from the sun and from the stars. Some animals and even plants produce small amounts of light energy. Radio waves and ultraviolet rays are other forms of energy. Then there is electricity, which is yet another sort of energy.

There are some things about energy that are difficult to understand. The fact that it constantly changes from one form to another makes energy rather like a disguised artist. When you think you know what energy is, suddenly it has changed into a totally different form. But one thing is certain: energy never disappears and, equally, it never appears from nowhere. People used to think that energy and matter were two completely different things. We now know that energy and matter are interchangeable. Tiny amounts of matter convert into unbelievably huge amounts of nuclear energy. The sun produces nuclear energy from hydrogen gas and, day by day, its mass gets less, as matter is converted to energy.

Cell phones, pagers, laptop computers, and personal digital assistants are here to stay, bringing increased productivity and efficiency to million of users. A survey, however, suggests that the torrent of information these portable devices unleash may be getting out of hand. From palm-top computer e-mail to cell phone voice mail, controlling these ways of receiving information is becoming a serious management problem for the people who use them.

With their advanced features and compact size, portable electronic devices offer consumers freedom, productivity, and organization. However, the ease and speed with which messages can be sent and received has increased and accelerated to such an extent that many people are receiving hundreds of electronic messages of all kinds each day. As a result, many are unable to fully maximize the features that will help them manage their information overload.

Practice Exercise 3

Part I Translation
Directions: Translate the following scientific and technical terms from English into Chinese.

1. telnet
2. three-dimensional pictures
3. CD-ROM
4. online commerce
5. WWW home pages
6. HTML (Hypertext Markup Language)
7. URLS (Uniform Resource Locators)
8. WWW browsers
9. FTP (File Transfer Protocol)
10. a proton rocket
11. olfactory technology
12. artificial sensors
13. general theory of relativity
14. quantum mechanics
15. ballistic missile technology
16. microgravity research
17. ISS (the International Space Station)
18. multimedia formats
19. a virtual shopping card
20. programming languages

Part II Vocabulary and Structure
Section A
Directions: Complete each of the following sentences with an appropriate word derived from the underlined word on the left of the sentence.

21. <u>decide</u>   Professor John William thinks that famous scientists always act very _____.
22. <u>expend</u>   The _____ of genetic counseling makes it difficult to test everyone.
23. <u>increase</u>   An _____ number of people are developing heart trouble in the U. K.
24. <u>freeze</u>   It is said that _____ food is good to health.
25. <u>rest</u>   After people take a rest, they feel energetic again. A _____ person feels energetic.
26. <u>make</u>   Orlan sweaters and plastic raincoats are man-_____ products.
27. <u>explore</u>   The astronauts have gathered informtion on the Jupiter's surface. The _____ territory will give us new knowledge about the Jupiter.
28. <u>prediction</u>   Some scientists _____ that the Arctic ice is melting, while other scientists believe that such changes are not _____.
29. <u>form</u>   Generally speaking, the first few years of a child's life are called the _____ years because he or she learns many things.
30. <u>difference</u>   The two scientists _____ a great deal in their research methods.
31. <u>precede</u>   Professor Matthew Gregory performed an experiment which was _____ in its success.

32. suspect   The research group have a _____ that the melting is caused by pollution.
33. special   They _____ in the study of environmental protection.
34. progress   The _____ melting of the Arctic ice would cause changes in weather patterns.
35. qualify   The purpose of training _____ technicians for this project is worthy of praise.

Section B

Directions: From the four choices given, choose the ONE that best completes the sentence.

36. We are interested in _____ the biologist has told us.
    A. which   B. all that   C. all what   D. that
37. My idea is that the group _____ another session to discuss the problem.
    A. may hold   B. will hold   C. should hold   D. is to hold
38. Liquids are like solids _____ they have a definite volume.
    A. in that   B. with that   C. that   D. because of
39. Large quantities of water _____ needed for cooling purposes.
    A. are   B. was   C. is   D. has
40. We _____ you came to visit our laboratory tomorrow than today.
    A. had better   B. would rather   C. rather than   D. will rather
41. A substance made up of two or more elements _____ a compound.
    A. are   B. will be   C. were   D. is
42. The scientist's achievements _____ him respect and admiration.
    A. enable   B. offer   C. supplied   D. earned
43. _____ is known to all, a body at rest will never move without the influence of an outside force.
    A. That   B. For   C. As   D. So long as
44. They had _____ it for granted that we would succeed in our experiment.
    A. made   B. taken   C. regarded   D. thought
45. To overcome the difficulties requires _____ work.
    A. many   B. plenty of
    C. many amount of   D. a great number of
46. Gasoline is processed from _____ oil.
    A. rough   B. tough   C. crude   D. raw
47. Doctors often risk making experiments _____ themselves.
    A. for   B. on   C. with   D. to
48. Mr. Smith felt powerfully _____ to the study of human nature.
    A. pursued   B. superior   C. attracted   D. similar
49. They congratulated him and also encouraged him to _____ his good work.
    A. fall to   B. approve of   C. keep up   D. participate in
50. His writing is so _____ that we cannot clarify his ideas on first reading.
    A. objective   B. obscure   C. obliging   D. obstacle
51. We have been very much pleased by your _____ of the situation.
    A. discovery   B. disposal   C. conquest   D. analysis
52. She finds it not easy to keep _____ with all the development in computer science.
    A. pace   B. time   C. touch   D. foot
53. He has not quite solved that problem yet, but he is _____ it.
    A. clearing up   B. working on
    C. making use of   D. taking action against

54. The young scientist _____ a small laboratory and devoted every spare moment to his work.
    A. furnished   B. inspected   C. marveled at   D. set up
55. But for your help, nothing _____.
    A. could do   B. could be done
    C. can be done   D. can have been done
56. _____ there is little we can do to modify the weather, we can at least know what kind of weather to expect.
    A. While   B. Since   C. Unless   D. When
57. The most important environmental influence on fish is water temperature, for fish tends to _____ the temperature of surroundings.
    A. take up   B. take to   C. take on   D. take down
58. Experts say that walking is one of the best ways for a person to _____ healthy.
    A. stay   B. preserve   C. maintain   D. reserve
59. The effects of the drug naturally wear _____ within a few hours.
    A. out   B. well   C. on   D. off
60. We are going to give you all the facts _____ so that you may judge for yourselves.
    A. at random   B. in effect   C. in essence   D. at length

Part Ⅲ Cloze

Directions: There are twenty blanks in the following passage. For each blank there are four choices marked A, B, C and D. You should choose the ONE that best fits into the passage.

Earthquakes may take place anywhere on the earth's surface. __61__, they are most __62__ to occur in certain regions. Earthquake regions are usually __63__ mountains or volcanoes. Outside these areas, earthquakes are generally __64__.

During an earthquake the pressure may __65__ at a maximum speed of 650 km/s. The duration of earthquakes __66__ an earthquake may have a duration of a second or it may __67__ intermittently for days. The __68__ of an earthquake can be measured by means of special instruments. There is also a scale of measurement __69__ the effects of earthquakes. This scale __70__ from earthquakes which are __71__ weak to be observed by man to those which are __72__ destroying everything made by man.

Some of the bad effects of earthquakes in towns can be prevented __73__ making special buildings. These have two kinds of __74__. In one kind of building the parts are made of __75__ flexible materials. The parts are __76__ together, like a basket. This structure and the properties of the materials __77__ the building to move without breaking. The other kind of building is like a box in structure. It is made of __78__, rigid materials. The lower part of the building must have a __79__ greater mass than the upper part.

There are still many problems __80__ in this field.

61. A. And   B. But   C. However   D. Therefore
62. A. certainly   B. likely   C. possibly   D. probably
63. A. near   B. beside   C. out of   D. far away from
64. A. small   B. big   C. strong   D. weak
65. A. run   B. go   C. spread   D. travel
66. A. changes   B. varies   C. differs   D. distinguishes
67. A. last   B. continue   C. keep   D. happen
68. A. force   B. strength   C. results   D. capability
69. A. basing on   B. based on   C. according to D. built on
70. A. differs   B. covers   C. changes   D. ranges

71. A. too   B. so   C. very   D. quite
72. A. able to   B. capable of C. competent for D. suitable for
73. A. by   B. if   C. with   D. in
74. A. materials   B. structure   C. composition   D. organization
75. A. light   B. heavy   C. strong   D. easy
76. A. put   B. made   C. knitted   D. woven
77. A. make   B. allow   C. enable   D. permit
78. A. light   B. flexible   C. hard   D. heavy
79. A. very   B. too   C. much   D. more
80. A. to be solved   B. solved
    C. having been solved   D. are solved

Part IV Reading Comprehension

Directions: There are six passages in this part. Each passage is followed by some questions. For each question there are four suggested answers marked A, B, C and D. Read the passages carefully and choose the best answer to each question.

(1)

It is the business of the scientist to accumulate knowledge about the universe and all that is in it, and to find, if he is able, common factors which explain the facts that he knows. He chooses, when he can, the method of the "controlled experiment". If he wants to find out the effect of light on growing plants, he takes many plants, as alike as possible. Some he stands in the sun, some in the shade, some in the dark; all the time keeping all other conditions (temperature, moisture, nourishment) the same. In this way, by keeping other conditions constant, and by varying the light only, the effect of light on the plants can be clearly seen. This method can be applied to a variety of situations.

In the course of his inquiries the scientist may find what he thinks is one common explanation for an increasing number of facts. The explanation, if it seems consistently to fit various facts, is called a hypothesis. If a hypothesis continues to stand the test of numerous experiments and remains unshaken, it becomes a law.

81. In order to investigate the effect of light on growing plants the scientist _____.
    A. has to stand in the sun
    B. can keep the same plants under different conditions of light
    C. takes as many plants as possible
    D. both B and C
82. The word "constant" in the first paragraph means _____.
    A. continual   B. faithful   C. various   D. unchanging
83. What should be kept the same in a "controlled experiment"?
    A. All the factors.
    B. The common factors.
    C. The factor under investigation.
    D. All factors except the one being investigated.
84. According to the passage, a hypothesis is _____.
    A. an explanation for a large number of facts likely to be accepted as a truth
    B. a factor which explains the facts already known to the scientist
    C. an explanation that stands the test of numerous experiments
    D. a common explanation that will definitely become a law

(2)

The great advance in rocket theory 40 years ago showed that liquid-fuel rockets were far superior in every respect to the skyrocket with its weak solid fuel, the only kind of rocket then known. However, during the last decade, large solid-fuel rockets with solid fuels about as powerful as liquid fuels have made their appearance, and it is a favorite layman's question to inquire which one is "better." The question is meaningless; one might as well ask whether a gasoline of a diesel engine is "better." It all depends on the purpose. A liquid-fuel rocket is complicated, but has the advantage that it can be controlled beautifully. The burning of the rocket engine can be stopped completely; it can be reignited when desired. In addition, the thrust can be made to vary by adjusting the speed of the fuel pumps. A solid-fuel rocket, on the other hand, is rather simple in construction, though hard to build when a really large size is desired. But once you have a solid-fuel rocket, it is ready for action at very short notice. A liquid-fuel rocket has to be fueled first and cannot be held in readiness for very long after it has been fueled. However, once a solid-fuel rocket has been ignited, it will keep burning. It cannot be stopped and reignited whenever desired (it could conceivably be stopped and reignited after a pre-calculated time of burning has elapsed) and its thrust cannot be varied. Because a solid-fuel rocket can be kept ready for a long time, most military missiles employ solid fuels, but manned spaceflight needs the fine adjustments that can only be provided by liquid fuels. It may be added that a liquid-fuel rocket is an expensive device; a large solid-rule rocket is, by comparison, cheap. But the solid fuel, pound per pound, costs about 10 times as much as the liquid fuel. So you have, on the one hand, an expensive rocket with a cheap fuel and on the other hand a comparatively cheap rocket with an expensive fuel.

85. The author feels that a comparison of liquid-and solid-fuel rockets shows that _____.
    A. neither type is very economical
    B. the liquid-fuel rocket is best
    C. each type has certain advantages
    D. the solid-fuel rocket is best

86. The most important consideration for manned space flight is that the rocket should be _____.
    A. inexpensive to construct
    B. capable of lifting heavy spacecraft into orbit
    C. easily controlled
    D. inexpensive to operate

87. Solid-fuel rockets are expensive to operate because of their _____.
    A. size   B. fuel
    C. burning time   D. complicated engines

88. Which of the following statements is not characteristic of liquid-fuel rockets?
    A. The fuel is cheap.
    B. They can be stopped and reignited.
    C. They are cheap to build.
    D. They must be used soon after fueling.

(3)

As the horizons of science have expanded, two main groups of scientists have emerged. One is the pure scientist; the other, the applied scientist.

The pure or theoretical scientist does original research in order to understand the basic laws of nature that govern our world. The applied scientist adapts this knowledge to practical problems. Neither is more important than the other, however, for the two groups are very much related.

Sometimes, however, the applied scientist finds the "problems" for the theoretical scientist to work on. Let's take a particular problem of the aircraft industry: heat-resistant metals. Many of the metals and alloys which perform satisfactorily in a car cannot be used in a jet-propelled plane. New alloys must be used, because the jet engine operates at a much higher temperature than an automobile engine. The turbine wheel in a turbojet must withstand temperatures as high as 1 600 degrees Fahrenheit, so aircraft designers had to turn to the research metallurgist for the development of metals and alloys that would do the job in jet-propelled planes.

Dividing scientists into two groups—pure and applied—is only one broad way of classifying them, however. When scientific knowledge was very limited, there was no need for men to specialize. Today, with the great body of scientific knowledge, scientists specialize in many different fields. Within each field, there is even further subdivision. And, with finer and finer subdivisions, the various sciences have become more and more interrelated until no one branch is entirely independent of the others. Many new specialties—geophysics and biochemistry, for example—have resulted from combining the knowledge of two or more sciences.

89. The applied scientist _____.
    A. does original research to understand the basic laws of nature
    B. applies the results of research to practical problems
    C. provides the basic knowledge for the pure scientist
    D. is not interested in practical problems

90. Concerning the relative importance of pure and applied scientists, the writer thinks that _____.
    A. applied scientists are more important
    B. pure scientists are more important
    C. neither are important
    D. both are equally important

91. The problem discussed in the third paragraph called for _____.
    A. selecting the best heat-resistant metal from existing metals
    B. developing a turbine wheel capable of generating heat up to 1 600 degrees Fahrenheit
    C. developing metals and alloys that would withstand terrific temperatures
    D. causing the jet engine to operate at higher temperatures

92. Finer and finer subdivision in the field of science has resulted in _____.
    A. the eradication of the need for specialists
    B. greater interdependence of all the various sciences
    C. greater independence of each science
    D. the need for only one classification of scientists

93. "The horizons of science have expanded" means that _____.
    A. scientists can see further out into space
    B. science has developed more fields of endeavor
    C. the horizon changes size from year to year
    D. scientists have made a machine for enlarging the horizon

(4)

Of all the problems facing modem astronomers, perhaps the most fascinating is: "Can intelligent life exist elsewhere?" Since the earth is an unimportant planet moving round an unimportant star, it would be a pride on our part to suppose that we are the only intelligent beings in the universe. But to obtain proof is difficult.

The main trouble is that our neighbour worlds, the bodies in the Solar System appear to be unsuitable for advanced life-forms. The Moon may be ruled out at once; it has hardly any atmosphere. Venus is little better; the surface temperature is extremely high and the atmosphere is mostly carbon dioxide. Mars with a very thin atmosphere and a severe shortage of water, may well support simple plant life but there seems no hope of finding animals, while the attractive Martians of the story-tellers have long since been given up.

Of course this has not stopped the flow of bright ideas for communicating with the supposed people on Mars. In the early nineteenth century the great mathematician Gauss suggested planting tree-patterns in Siberia, so that the Martians would see them and reply suitably. Following up this idea, the Austrian scientist Karl Littrow proposed digging very wide ditches in the Sahara, triangular in pattern, and then filling them with petrol or some such substance so that, when lit, the ditches would present Martian' observers with a "flaming triangle" which would show the existence here of intelligent minds. Even better were the plants of Charles Cros, a French writer of the eighteen-seventies, who wanted to build a large mirror to reflect the sun's rays and concentrate them on the surface of Mars, thereby making a vast burning-glass. By swinging the mirror around, Cros explained it would be practicable to write words in the Martian deserts simply by burning the sand. For many years he bombarded the French government with literature about this plan and was very disappointed when no official interest was shown.

94. The opinion of the writer is that _____.
    A. there may be other intelligent beings in the universe
    B. there are other intelligent beings in the universe
    C. people living on the earth are almost certainly the only intelligent beings in the universe
    D. people living on the earth are definitely the only intelligent beings in the universe

95. There is unlikely any life on Venus because _____.
    A. the surface temperature is too hot
    B. the weather is too cold
    C. it is severely short of water
    D. it has a very thin atmosphere

96. It seems that Mars _____.
    A. may be inhabited by attractive Martians
    B. may have some vegetable life
    C. can have no life at all
    D. may have both vegetable and animal life

97. Gauss wanted to establish contact with the Martians by _____.
    A. planting trees in triangular shape
    B. filling wide ditches with oil
    C. building a large mirror
    D. making patterns with trees

98. Charles Cros felt _____.
    A. angry when the government paid little attention to his ideas
    B. pleased when the government did take notice of his plan
    C. surprised that the officials were interested in his suggestion
    D. disappointed at the lack of interest shown in his plan

(5)

In addition to his theory of colour, Newton developed a theory of how light travels. This is known as the corpuscular theory of light, meaning that light travels as a series of tiny bits rather than in continuing waves. Newton sent his writings about light to the Royal Society, where they were given to a committee led by Hooke. Since the corpuscular theory was different from his own theory, Hooke attacked the paper. Soon others started to argue, and Hooke was supported by a scientist from Holland, Christian Huygens. At one time, Newton was so unhappy with the whole affair that he decided never again to publish any of his work.

The bitter argument continued over the years that followed. At first, Hooke and Huygens received most of the support. Later, after Newton had changed his mind and let his work on gravity be published, he became so famous, that things changed. Now people believed Newton could do nothing wrong, and for a hundred years they followed his theory.

Then, in the early part of the 19th century, the experiments of a French scientist, Augustin Fresnel, showed that light could be explained best by a wave theory. So the scientists changed sides again, saying that Newton's ideas had delayed scientific progress for a hundred years.

Strangely enough, the presently-accepted theory of light combines some of the ideas of both theories. This is known as the quantum theory and results from the work of such 20th century scientists as Albert Einstein and Max Planck. The quantum theory assumes that light is given off as separate "packages" of energy. Each "package" travels out in a fixed pattern or wave form. These "package" or light, or quanta of energy, as they are called, are given off at such a rapid rate that there is no great gap between them.

The quantum theory seems to explain the actions of light better than either of the two earlier theories. However, for many purposes, the wave theory is good enough. So it is used most often to explain light. But who is to say that new experiments and other scientists of our own time or in the future may not provide an even better theory? There is certainly still much work to be done with light and colour.

99. From this passage it seems that Newton was a scientist with _____.
   A. only one important theory
   B. two theories
   C. at least three theories
   D. very many theories

100. The corpuscular theory of light _____.
   A. was never accepted by the Royal Society
   B. was in the end accepted by Hooke and Huygens
   C. was rejected by Hooke and Huygens but immediately accepted by other scientists for the next hundred years
   D. was the most popular theory during the eighteenth century

101. The scientists who said that Newton's idea had delayed scientific progress for a hundred years were _____.
   A. right, because Fresnel's wave theory disproved Newton's corpuscular theory
   B. wrong, because Fresnel's theory has in turn been disproved
   C. right, because the quantum theory supports the wave theory
   D. wrong, because the quantum theory makes use of some of Newton's ideas

102. The quantum theory seems to be nearest in idea to that of _____.
   A. Hooke and Huygens
   B. Fresnel and Newton combined
   C. Newton
   D. Fresnel

103. The evidence of this passage suggests that _____.
   A. there would be no progress in our knowledge of light unless we questioned accepted theories
   B. the presently-accepted theory of light will very soon be replaced
   C. scientists do not know enough to be able to explain the theory of light
   D. scientists change their opinions too often

(6)

High-speed ground transportation (HSGT) technologies with vehicles speeds exceeding 150 mph can be divided into two basic categories:

(1) High-speed rail (HSR) systems, with top speeds between 150 and 200 mph, use steel wheels on steel

rails, as with traditional railroads, but can achieve higher speeds because of the design of both the rail bed and cars.

(2) High-speed magnetic levitation (MAGLEV) systems, with top speeds between 250 and 300 mph, use forces of attraction or repulsion from powerful magnets placed in either the vehicle or the guideway beneath it both to lift the vehicle above the guideway and to propel it forward. A MAGLEV vehicle can be likened to a flying train or a guided aircraft.

If linked effectively with highways and air service, HSGT technologies—particularly MAGLEV—could have a significant impact on congestion in the future.

When comparing HSR and MAGLEV technologies, MAGLEV appears to be the technology of choice. Though the new generation of HSR technology can reach commercial speeds of up to 186 mph, additional increases in speed pose great engineering problems, suggesting that rail transportation is a mature technology. MAGLEV technology, on the other hand, is in its infancy and will improve substantially with additional engineering.

In contrast to HSR, MAGLEV systems involve no physical contact between the guideway and the vehicle, which means less wear, less maintenance, less noise, and greater reliability. MAGLEV rides are as comfortable as those on airliners flying in nonturbulent air. MAGLEV trains can climb grades and bank curves without substantially reducing speed. And, as with electric HSR, there are no emissions along the guideway because MAGLEV runs on electricity, thus rendering the systems far less intrusive on existing communities than rail lines.

Though the capital costs of a MAGLEV system are somewhat higher than those of an HSR system, operating costs are about the same, and with MAGLEV's higher speeds it can attract more riders and produce more revenues.

104. What would be the most appropriate title for the passage?
    A. High-speed Ground Transportation Technologies.
    B. High-speed Rail Systems.
    C. High-speed Magnetic Levitation Systems.
    D. The way to solve a Transportation Crisis.

105. The potential top speed of innovated HSR systems can be somewhere _____.
    A. between 150 and 200 mph
    B. between 150~200 mph or higher
    C. between 200 and 250 mph
    D. between 250 and 300 mph

106. The most appropriate definition of MAGLEV could be _____.
    A. a railway system that raises the train in the air with strong magnets
    B. a railway system that makes a train float in the air with the support of magnetic tracks
    C. a railway system that makes the train rise in the air without the support of magnetic tracks
    D. a railway system that uses powerful magnets to float a swiftly moving train above its tracks

107. According to the passage, MAGLEV appears to be the technology of choice because _____.
    A. MAGLEV systems are free from the force that resists motion between two surfaces in continuous touch
    B. MAGLEV systems use forces of attraction or repulsion from powerful magnets placed in the guideway beneath the vehicle
    C. MAGLEV is in its infancy and will improve substantially without additional engineering efforts
    D. MAGLEV enjoys implicit reliability and durability

108. Compared to those of ordinary trains, MAGLEV rides are more comfortable because of _____.
    A. little maintenance   B. little noise
    C. levitation   D. greater reliability

109. According to the passage, which of the following is NOT true?
    A. HSR necessarily poses the problem of air pollution.

B. MAGLEV does not pose the problem of air pollution.

C. MAGLEV trains can climb slopes and bank curves without losing much momentum.

D. MAGLEV lines do not interfere with existing communities as much as rail lines.

110. Compared to an HSR system, a MAGLEV system is more promising in the financial aspect because _____.

   A. its initial costs are less expensive
   B. its higher speeds and reliability are a big draw
   C. its operating costs are more reasonable
   D. its capital costs are roughly the same among the business rivals

Part V Translation

Directions: Translate the following passages into Chinese.

(1)

A computer virus is a software program that attaches itself to another program in computer memory or on a disk, and spreads from one program to another. Viruses can damage data, cause computers to crash, display offending or bothersome messages, or lie dormant until such time they are set to "awaken". In today's industry, scanning is no longer considered to be an extravagance—but a necessity. Computer viruses no longer attack your computing environment only but all other computing environments which you contact. Computer viruses can attach themselves to the files being used and later propagate themselves through disks and files. Important information and hardware losses could plague your computing environment should you not take the proper precautions.

Many anti-virus products, such as KV300 and VirusScan, head up the list of proper precautions. Scheduled periodic scans of your computing environment can offer you that added assurance that you are practicing "safe computing."

(2)

Life on-line can be a much richer experience when you aren't restricted to just written words and still pictures. Even if you're new to the Net, you've probably heard about multimedia online—listening to audio, watching animations and videos, even playing in three-dimensional space. Sound and movement make information come alive.

To experience it, you'll need special pieces of software called plug-ins. The term "plug-in" refers to a small, add-on piece of software which extends the capabilities of your web browser, like Netscape Navigator or Microsoft Explorer, turning your computer into a radio or TV.

When you arrive at a web page which contains a file requiring a plug-in which you don't have, you will usually receive a message asking if you want to get it by downloading it and installing it into your computer. Most of the time, the installation will be automatic.

Practice Exercise 4

Part I Translation

Directions: Translate the following scientific and technical terms from English into Chinese.

1. long-haul fibre-optic cables   _____
2. displacement   _____
3. resonant frequencies   _____
4. electromechanical property   _____
5. spectrum   _____
6. acceleration   _____
7. harmonic content   _____
8. analog-to-digital converters   _____
9. backbone provider   _____
10. ISP (internet service provider)   _____
11. liquid Crystal display monitor   _____
12. computer chip   _____
13. audio files   _____
14. a full-screen video   _____
15. natural resources   _____
16. the ozone layer   _____
17. acid rain   _____
18. oscilloscopes   _____
19. media modality   _____
20. nature reserves   _____

Part II Vocabulary and Structure

Section A

Directions: Complete each of the following sentences with an appropriate word derived from the underlined word on the left of the sentence.

21. evidence   _____, no one has done research in this field before.
22. intelligence   An _____ person should try to use his abilities to the greatest extent.
23. absorb   The _____ of moisture by the soil is very important for the growth of plants.
24. observant   Have you ever _____ how other people's behavior differs from yours?
25. associate   Peter and John have joined an _____ which protects animals.
26. correct   That mistake isn't so bad. It's easily _____.
27. base   _____, Dr. Morgan agrees with your ideas, but he disagrees with some of the details.
28. argue   They had a rather angry _____ over the need for population control.
29. construct   All the people in our city are now working _____ to produce a better environment.
30. dense   Which has greater _____, oil or water?
31. expand   Usually, the _____ of industry will provide many new jobs.
32. authority   We believed Mr. Watson because he spoke in a very _____ manner on the subject.
33. destroy   The research indicates that a person with _____ tendencies can cause problems for everyone.

34. compete   Some people thrive on _____, but other people prefer a less _____ situation.
35. impress   You must be very careful about what you say around children because children are very _____.

Section B

Directions: From the four choices given, choose the ONE that best completes the sentence.

36. Human beings can _____ their surroundings.
    A. attend to   B. stick to   C. adapt to   D. change to
37. My approach is not to learn everything about something, but _____ something about everything.
    A. rather learning   B. to rather learn
    C. rather than   D. rather to learn
38. There has been a steady increase _____ production since the introduction of the new technology.
    A. in   B. on   C. for   D. against
39. Martin considered _____ his medical course and specializing in bacteriology.
    A. dropping   B. designing   C. denying   D. giving
40. The government decided to _____ the established policy of developing biotech.
    A. go after   B. go by   C. go ahead   D. go on
41. The doctor came to the conclusion that the patient's blindness was _____.
    A. contemporary   B. temperate   C. consistent   D. temporary
42. If the pressure is not _____ immediately, there may be an explosion.
    A. relieved   B. revealed   C. retreated   D. released
43. By the time the course ends, _____ a lot about solar energy.
    A. we'll learn   B. we are learning
    C. we'll have learnt   D. we have learnt
44. The _____ of new scientific discoveries to industrial production methods usually makes jobs easier to do.
    A. development   B. application   C. expression   D. explanation
45. Scientists had never met this problem before; it was _____.
    A. unique   B. sole   C. alone   D. common
46. Emphasis is laid on the necessity that all factors _____ into account before the project is stated.
    A. shall be taken   B. will be taken   C. be taken   D. are taken
47. Not until quite recently _____ what an air-to-air missile was like.
    A. I knew   B. did I know   C. I did know   D. knew I
48. I'd rather you _____ the international science conference since you have been working on this subject for 20 years.
    A. attend   B. have attended   C. attended   D. attends
49. _____ being used in industry, laser can be applied to operations in the hospital.
    A. Except for   B. Out of   C. In spite of   D. In addition to
50. We all _____ the achievements he has made in his experiments.
    A. admire   B. adopt   C. advise   D. adjust
51. If you don't read the newspaper, you will never know what was _____ in the world.
    A. coming out   B. going on   C. running off   D. passing by
52. _____, the design is of utmost importance.
    A. To speak practical   B. Speaking practical
    C. Practically speaking   D. In speaking practical

53. One must try his best to _____ to the new environment.
    A. adopt   B. apt   C. act   D. adapt
54. We need a lot of people who are able to deal with _____ problems.
    A. economic   B. economy   C. economics   D. economical
55. _____ such subjects, the department also taught mathematics and geography.
    A. By means of   B. In addition to
    C. With regard to   D. In consequence of
56. Many people think of deserts as _____ regions, but numerous species of plants and animals have adapted to life there.
    A. barren   B. virgin   C. void   D. useful
57. To prevent flooding in summer the water flowing from the dam is constantly _____ by a computer.
    A. conducted   B. managed   C. graded   D. monitored
58. Now the young people's attraction to stereos cannot be explained only _____ familiarity with technology.
    A. by virtue of   B. in terms of C. in quest of D. by means of
59. Can you make a clear _____ between the two scientific terms for the purpose of the discussion?
    A. separation   B. distinction C. deviation   D. devotion
60. Certain species disappeared or became _____ as new forms arose that were better adapted to the Earth's changing environment.
    A. massive   B. feeble   C. extinct   D. extinguished

Part Ⅲ Cloze

Directions: There are twenty blanks in the following passage. For each blank there are four choices marked A, B, C and D. You should choose the ONE that best fits into the passage.

Even though we have more choice of what to eat than forty years ago, the average diet of the average Britain is less healthy. 61 , according to recent research British pets, 62 specially prepared 63 food, have a healthier diet 64 most of their owners.

Health ministers were alarmed 65 recent figures which show 66 Britain has the third 67 record in Europe for heart disease. Cancer is also a growing 68 of illness and death. This has led the government to try to 69 a campaign to 70 healthier eating habits. Health ministers believe we should 71 a lesson from America, 72 death rates from heart disease have fallen. The American public is now more 73 of the link 74 diet and good health. The campaign will encourage the eating of 75 animal fat, salt and sugar than 76 at present. It will show the advantages of eating more 77 fruit and vegetables. The Health Department is going to 78 a booklet which will give guidance 79 what food to eat and what to 80 .

61. A. In fact   B. However   C. First   D. Above all
62. A. to eat   B. eating   C. eaten   D. ate
63. A. made   B. good   C. tinned   D. raw
64. A. to   B. over   C. of   D. than
65. A. at   B. with   C. by   D. through
66. A. how   B. why   C. that   D. which
67. A. bad   B. worse   C. worst   D. worsening
68. A. reason   B. cause   C. result   D. source
69. A. send   B. give   C. order   D. launch
70. A. encourage   B. develop   C. educate   D. train
71. A. have   B. find   C. take   D. make

72. A. which				B. how				C. where			D. why
73. A. afraid			B. aware			C. certain			D. frightened
74. A. among			B. within			C. behind			D. between
75. A. less				B. little			C. much				D. more
76. A. consuming		B. are consumed		C. to be consumed	D. consume
77. A. new				B. fresh			C. raw				D. recent
78. A. produce			B. sell				C. compose			D. issue
79. A. to				B. over				C. on				D. in
80. A. delete			B. avoid			C. abandon			D. discard

Part IV Reading Comprehension

Directions: There are six passages in this part. Each passage is followed by some questions. For each question there are four suggested answers marked A, B, C and D. Read the passages carefully and choose the best answer to each question.

(1)

Ever since Philo T. Farnsworth assembled the first television set in his Indiana garage in 1927, the basic technological principles for bringing electronic pictures into the home have remained the same. There have been only two major changes in the way TV sets work: the introduction of color in 1954, and the shift from tubes to transistors in the 1970s.

Now a radical change is about to take place. Digital television—which uses a different method of signal transmission—will significantly alter the way future television sets will look and perform.

The digital set, already on sale in Europe and scheduled to be introduced in the United States this fall, is a cross between a computer terminal and a TV set. Although the differences it will bring may not be dramatic, its improved quality will be increasingly appreciated, as zoom effects, stereo sound, and freeze-frame views of live shows become commonplace. Digital TV promises to give viewers a clearer, more consistent picture than has been available so far.

81. According to the passage, the first color TV was introduced _____.
    A. in the late 1920s					C. in the 1970s
    B. in the mid-1950s					D. in the mid-1980s

82. It can be inferred from the passage that Philo T. Farnsworth _____.
    A. was born in the nineteenth century
    B. invented the digital TV set
    C. lived in Indiana
    D. was a scientist

83. According to the passage, the digital TV set does which of the following?
    A. Acts as a computer.				B. Replaces stereo equipment.
    C. Provides a better picture.		D. Shifts to transistors.

84. According to the passage, which of the following statements is NOT true?
    A. There have been three major changes in television technology since 1927.
    B. Basic TV technology is the same as it was almost sixty years ago.
    C. Digital TV sets incorporate computer technology.
    D. Digital TV sets are already on sale in Europe and the United States.

85. What would be the best title for this passage?
    A. "The History of Television".
    B. "A Comparison of Television Changes".
    C. "The Qualities of the Digital Television Set".
    D. "The European Television Market".

(2)

As in business and other professions, the use of computers is a growing trend in health care. At first, computers were used only in the business office for such things as patient billing and paying for purchase. As computer technology advanced, the use of computers broadened to include patient information and communication systems.

Hospital information systems have been developed which collect, send, record, and store information. The information can be retrieved when needed. Patient records and patient care plans are on the computer in many health care facilities. Instead of recording on the patient's chart, health team members enter information into the computer. Entering information into a computer is easier, faster, and more efficient than writing on the chart. Using the computer to record observations is also more accurate and reliable.

Departments such as the x-rays department and the laboratory communicate with other units of the hospital through the computer. Instead of sending a typed report by a person for the patient's record, the information is entered into the computer. The information can be accessed at the computer in the nurses' or doctors' station. These systems provide communication links between departments in the hospital. The systems have reduced the amount of clerk's work and telephone calls between departments. Information is communicated with greater speed and accuracy.

Computers are also being used to monitor certain measurements such as blood pressures, temperatures, heart rates, and heart function. The computer is programmed to recognize normal and abnormal measurements. When the abnormal is sensed, an alarm is sounded. Monitoring by the computer has proven to be very accurate and increases early discovery of life threatening events.

86. Concerning the application of computers, we can infer from the first paragraph that _____.
    A. there is no limit for computers to be used in hospitals
    B. computers are most often used in business at present
    C. computers are more and more widely used in health care
    D. computers will replace nurses and doctors in the future
87. With the help of computers, information about patient records and care plans will be stored _____.
    A. in the health team members' files
    B. on patients' charts
    C. in doctors' personal computers
    D. in hospital information systems
88. According to the passage, when a doctor or nurse needs some information, the best way is to _____.
    A. retrieve it from his/her computer station
    B. ask a person to bring it to him or her
    C. ask for it by telephone
    D. go and get it at the department concerned
89. While monitoring the measuring of the heart rate, the computer will give a warning when it finds that _____.
    A. life threatening events are likely to happen
    B. the heart beats at the normal rate

C. the measurement is not accurate

D. the heart beats too fast or too slowly

90. The best title for this passage can be _____.

A. New Development of Computers

B. Computer Systems in Hospitals

C. Importance of Computers in Health Care

D. New Developments of Medicine

(3)

In the late 1960's many people in North America turned their attention to environmental problems, and new steel-and-glass skyscrapers were widely criticized. Ecologists pointed out that a cluster of tall buildings in a city often overburdens public transportation and parking lot capacities.

Skyscrapers are also lavish consumers, and wasters, of electric power. In one recent year, the addition of 17 million square feet of skyscraper office space in New York City raised the peak daily demand for electricity by 120 000 kilowatts—enough to supply the entire city of Albany, New York, for a day.

Glass-walled skyscrapers can be especially wasteful. The heat loss(or gain) through a wall of half-inch plate glass is more than ten times that through a typical masonry wall filled with insulation board. To lessen the strain on heating and air-conditioning equipment, builders of skyscrapers have begun to use double-glazed panels of glass, and reflective glasses coated with silver or gold mirror films that reduce glare as well as heat gain. However, mirror-walled skyscrapers raise the temperature of the surrounding air and affect neighboring buildings.

Skyscrapers put a severe strain on a city's sanitation facilities, too. If fully occupied, the two World Trade Center towers in New York City would alone generate 2.25 million gallons of raw sewage each year—as much as a city the size of Stamford, Connecticut, which has a population of more than 109 000.

Skyscrapers also interfere with television reception, block bird flyways, and obstruct air traffic. In Boston in the late 1960's, some people even feared that shadows from skyscrapers would kill the grass on Boston Common.

Still, people continue to build skyscrapers for all the reasons that they have always built them—personal ambition, civic pride, and the desire of owners to have the largest possible amount of rentable space.

91. The main purpose of the passage is to _____.

A. compare skyscrapers with other modern structures

B. describe skyscrapers and their effect on the environment

C. advocate the use of masonry in the construction of skyscrapers

D. illustrate some architectural designs of skyscrapers

92. According to the passage, what is one disadvantage of skyscrapers that have mirrored walls?

A. The exterior surrounding air is heated.

B. The windows must be cleaned daily.

C. Construction time is increased.

D. Extra air-conditioning equipment is needed.

93. According to the passage, in the late 1960's some residents of Boston were concerned with which aspect of skyscrapers?

A. The noise from their construction.

B. The removal of trees from building sites.

C. The harmful effects on the city's grass.

D. The high cost of rentable office space.

94. The author raises issues that would most concern which of the following groups?
    A. Electricians.
    B. Environmentalists.
    C. Aviators.
    D. Teachers.
95. Where in the passage does the author compare the energy consumption of skyscrapers with that of a city?
    A. In the first paragraph.
    B. In the second paragraph.
    C. In the third paragraph.
    D. In the fourth paragraph.

(4)

Because of the energy crisis, scientists in the oil consuming nations have become increasingly interested in the potential of solar energy. Some experts estimate that the present supply of fossil fuel will not last until the end of the twentieth century. The problem that solar energy researchers face is how to harness the sun's energy effectively and inexpensively. One of the most popular methods currently being tested uses rooftop solar collectors and underground storage tanks. An advantage of a properly working system of this type is that it will not create any environmental pollution. Another advantage of using solar energy is that the cost of the fuel, the sun's rays, is zero. When a solar heating system is working at maximum efficiency, it can provide up to 80 per cent of winter heating needs.

96. The main topic of this passage is _____.
    A. the shortage of fossil fuel
    B. the problems that energy researchers face
    C. an environmental pollution problem
    D. an inexpensive energy source
97. One popular solar heating system makes use of _____.
    A. roof collectors and underground storage
    B. fossil fuel conversion
    C. underground oil tanks
    D. water collection and evaporation
98. Which of the following describes an advantage of using solar energy?
    A. There is little or no environmental pollution.
    B. A large percentage of fuel costs can be saved.
    C. Fossil fuels will become more plentiful.
    D. The oil-consuming nations will not have to import oil.
99. According to some experts, the supply of fuel will not last _____.
    A. one more century
    B. an indeterminable time
    C. until the end of this century
    D. indefinitely
100. The cost of using the sun's rays for heating is _____.
    A. about the same as the cost of fossil fuels
    B. several hundred dollars per year
    C. negligible compared with other energy sources
    D. determined by the severity of the winter

(5)

All sounds come from vibrations. But not all sounds are the same. Some sounds are pleasant to hear, such as music. Other sounds are not, and these we call noise. What's the difference between the two? This is a difficult question to answer. But the sounds of musical instruments, which are usually good to hear, do have a special characteristic: musical instruments, such as the guitar and the drum, vibrate at more than one frequency. Thus, when a guitar string produces the note of A, the vibration of greatest amplitude has a frequency of 440 Hz. But there are vibrations of other frequencies present, too. They have less amplitude, and so we do not consciously hear them. But they add to the sound and form a pattern of frequencies which is pleasant to hear. It is these other frequencies(or harmonics, as they are called) which help us to identify the musical instrument we hear.

Of course, these are other characteristics of music, too. One of these is rhythm, the sequence sounds. Rhythm is not exclusive to musical sound; but it is one of the factors which help make music pleasant to hear.

101. Which statement is NOT true according to the passage?
    A. All sounds are the same.
    B. All sounds come from vibrations.
    C. Music and noise are different.
    D. Vibration is the source of sound.

102. Musical instruments vibrate _____.
    A. softly and pleasantly
    B. at the same frequency
    C. quietly and slowly
    D. at more than one frequency

103. What does the passage mainly tell us about?
    A. The difference between music and noise.
    B. The characteristics of music.
    C. Frequencies and amplitudes of sounds.
    D. Vibrations and sounds.

104. According to the passage, we can identify the musical instrument we hear _____.
    A. with the help of harmonics
    B. by touching them
    C. with the help of rhythm
    D. by looking at them

105. It can be inferred from the passage that _____.
    A. rhythm might also be with other sounds
    B. rhythm is the sequence of sound
    C. rhythm is produced by guitar and drum
    D. rhythm is characteristic of sounds

(6)

The destruction of our natural resources and contamination of our food supply continue to occur, largely because of the extreme difficulty in affixing legal responsibility on those who continue to treat our environment with reckless abandon. Attempts to prevent pollution by legislation, economic incentives and friendly persuasion have been met by lawsuits, personal and industrial denial and long delays—not only in accepting responsibility, but more importantly, in doing something about it.

It seems that only when government decides it can afford tax incentives or production sacrifices is there any initiative for change. Where is industry's and our recognition that protecting mankind's great treasure is the single most important responsibility? If ever there will be time for environmental health professionals to come to the frontlines and provide leadership to solve environmental problems, that time is now.

We are being asked, and, in fact, the public is demanding that we take positive action. It is our responsibility as professionals in environmental health to make the difference. Yes, the ecologists, the environmental activists and the conservationists serve to communicate, stimulate thinking and promote behavioral change. However, it is those of us who are paid to make the decisions to develop, improve and enforce environmental standards, I submit, who must lead the charge.

We must recognize that environmental health issues do not stop at city limits, county lines, state or even federal boundaries. We can no longer afford to be tunnel-visioned in our approach. We must visualize issues from every perspective to make the objective decisions. We must express our views clearly to prevent media distortion and public confusion.

I believe we have a three-part mission for the present. First, we must continue to press for improvements in the quality of life that people can make for themselves. Second, we must investigate and understand the link between environment and health. Third, we must be able to communicate technical information in a form that citizens can understand. If we can accomplish these three goals in this decade, maybe we can finally stop environmental degradation, and not merely hold it back. We will then be able to spend pollution dollars truly on prevention rather than on bandages.

106. We can infer from the first two paragraphs that the industrialists disregard environmental protection chiefly because _____.
   A. it is difficult for them to take effective measures
   B. time has not yet come for them to put due emphasis on it
   C. they are reluctant to sacrifice their own economic interests
   D. they are unaware of the consequences of what they are doing

107. The main task now facing ecologists, environmental activists and conservationists is _____.
   A. to arouse public awareness of the importance of environmental protection
   B. to prevent pollution by legislation, economic incentives and persuasion
   C. to improve the quality of life by enforcing environmental standards
   D. to take radical measures to control environmental pollution

108. The word "tunnel-visioned" most probably means "_____".
   A. narrow-minded   B. short-sighted
   C. able to see only one aspect   D. blind to the facts

109. Which of the following, according to the author, should play the leading role in the solution of environmental problems?
   A. The cooperation of ecologists, environmental activists and conservationists.
   B. The efforts of environmental health professionals.
   C. The industry's understanding and support.
   D. Legislation and government intervention.

110. Which of the following is true according to the last paragraph?
   A. More money should be spent in order to stop pollution.
   B. Environmental degradation will be stopped by the end of this decade.
   C. Ordinary citizens have no access to technical information on pollution.
   D. Efforts should be exerted on pollution prevention instead of on remedial measures.

Part V Translation

Directions: Translate the following passages into Chinese.

(1)

The trouble with shopping on the Internet is that you can't touch anything. Fortunately, that may be about to change with a motorised computer mouse that can give Web surfers the sensation of texture—or other physical attributes—of items pictured on the Net.

Visitors to the Web99 convention in San Francisco were able to test out the "Feel It" mouse: running the cursor over a picture of a tennis racket let a user feel the tautness of the strings. You could also feel the texture of a pair of corduroy jeans or test-drive a car, feeling how it handles the curves and accelerates on the straight. And the mouse even simulates an attempt to move through a heavy wind.

Originally developed by Stanford University and NASA, force-feedback technology was first used for flight simulation. Recently, Immersion Corporation in San Jose, California, managed to achieve the fast data exchange rates needed to provide realistic tactile sensations when someone is shopping on the Web.

(2)

The term "netiquette," a combination of "net" and "etiquette," refers to an understood agreement of social and technical guidelines for Internet behavior. Because communicating via the Internet is several steps removed from person-to-person communication, it is imperative to follow these guidelines in order to maintain good relationships with your Internet correspondents and service provider. While the codes of netiquette are not legally binding, it is important to learn them and abide by them in order to avoid misunderstandings, ostracism, and revoked Internet privileges. With the growing number of people who depend on Internet communications to conduct business and maintain personal relationships, netiquette is more important than ever.

Most rules of netiquette are based on good manners, technical understanding, and common sense. Netiquette for various Internet protocols, such as E-mail, Usenet, Newsgroups, IRC, and the World Wide Web, conforms to some general guidelines as well as to specific codes for each particular medium. The codes of netiquette usually fall under three interrelated categories: social conduct, technical courtesy, and harmful behavior.

Practice Exercise 5

Part I Translation

Directions: Translate the following scientific and technical terms from English into Chinese.

1. a Web search page _____
2. electronic banking service _____
3. attached files _____
4. text files _____
5. digital video _____
6. graphics interface _____
7. to scan an image _____
8. photodetector _____
9. high speed processors _____
10. semi-conductor circuits _____
11. infostructure _____
12. microelectronics technology _____
13. position-location devices _____
14. interactive computers _____
15. computer design automation _____
16. atomic structure _____
17. storage capacity _____
18. an E-mail phone _____
19. biochemical activity _____
20. human immune system _____

Part II Vocabulary and Structure

Section A

Directions: Complete each of the following sentences with an appropriate word derived from the underlined word on the left of the sentence.

21. prevent — Certain illness are _____ as long as you have the proper inoculations.
22. assist — Without their _____, we could never have finished the work.
23. require — Does Bill have the _____ experience to do the research job?
24. agree — They settled the problem _____ without an argument.
25. involve — The _____ of the experts with pollution problems could result in a scientific solution.
26. realize — Dr. James at last came to the _____ that the problem could not be solved by the means he had been using.
27. convenience — His schedule was very _____ arranged so he was able to work part-time while he went to school.
28. irritate — People are often _____ when they don't get enough sleep.
29. compose — It is possible for scientists to test the genetic _____ of an unborn baby.
30. disappear — _____ of the Arctic pack would enable the largest tankers to reach the newly discovered oil fields of northern Alaska.
31. behave — Sometimes a person's _____ changes greatly when he gets old.

32. variety   The weather _____ a lot in that part of the country.
33. indicate   Being tired all the time is an _____ that one may be sick.
34. recognize Her _____ of technical terms in English has increased greatly.
35. respond   They are using up the natural resources and are _____ for much of the pollution.

Section B

Directions: From the four choices given, choose the ONE that best completes the sentence.

36. Scientists _____ that there is no animal life on Mars.
    A. assume   B. detect   C. inform   D. doubt
37. Mathematics _____ the language of science.
    A. are   B. will be   C. is   D. is to be
38. Investigation shows that industry _____ only ten percent of the smog in Los Angeles.
    A. appeals to   B. accounts for   C. amounts to   D. calls on
39. Television keeps us informed about _____ events and the latest development in science and politics.
    A. new   B. past   C. fashionable   D. current
40. How long _____?
    A. do you suppose the experiment lasted
    B. did you suppose the experiment last
    C. you suppose the experiment lasted
    D. you suppose did the experiment last
41. The technician succeeded in _____ the fault in the tool machine at last.
    A. making up   B. keeping up   C. slowing down   D. tracking down
42. _____ a few minor delays, the pilot was sure that the plane would be on time.
    A. Despite   B. In spite   C. Though   D. Despite of
43. The young athlete was quite sure _____ as he entered the arena to the roar of the crowd.
    A. by himself   B. to himself   C. of himself   D. of him
44. We don't think we can take it _____, for quite a number of problems still remain.
    A. for granted   B. by chance   C. on hand   D. at will
45. If you keep on practising, you are bound _____.
    A. to succeed   B. to success   C. of success   D. of successful
46. The colour _____ from yellow through green to black.
    A. composes   B. forms   C. ranges   D. constitutes
47. The whole city _____ to welcome the astronaut.
    A. reached out   B. turned out   C. sprang off   D. brought about
48. Progress in using atomic power may make _____ to drill for oil near the North Pole or the South Pole.
    A. unnecessary   B. people unnecessary
    C. it unnecessary   D. that unnecessary
49. It is interesting to know that many new methods now in wide use have been developed from theories _____ the old methods were based.
    A. when   B. where   C. on which   D. in which
50. Be careful how you handle this instrument, as it is _____.
    A. valueless   B. priceless   C. unsaleable   D. inexpensive
51. The research indicates that a _____ person has great sensibility and he has delicate feelings and is quick to enjoy or suffer.
    A. sensory   B. sensible   C. sensitive   D. sensual

52. The boom in silver production after the nineteenth century _____ the use of innovative machinery in crafting silver flatware and vessels.
    A. duplicated   B. stimulated   C. accumulated   D. communicated
53. Today, housework has been made much easier by electrical _____.
    A. facilities   B. equipment   C. appliances   D. instruments
54. There was once an _____ idea that the earth was flat and motionless.
    A. eternal   B. offensive   C. interested   D. absurd
55. The designing of a satellite in the heavenly environment is _____ an easy job.
    A. by means of   B. by all means   C. by any means   D. by no means
56. It is often more difficult to find trained men than _____ financial support for scientific research.
    A. to get   B. getting   C. in getting   D. to getting
57. _____ the people have become masters of their own country _____ science can really serve the people.
    A. It is only then/that   B. It was that/when
    C. It was when/then   D. It is only when/that
58. To succeed in a scientific research project, _____.
    A. persistence is needed   B. one needs to be persistent
    C. one needs be a persistent person   D. persistence is what one needs
59. Research has produced many new _____ that will be used in the manufacture of a variety of goods.
    A. summaries   B. synthetics   C. emphasis   D. hypotheses
60. A conclusion was drawn _____.
    A. that identifies pressure with temperature
    B. which identifies pressure to temperature
    C. that pressure is identified to temperature
    D. that pressure is identified with temperature

Part Ⅲ Cloze

Directions: There are twenty blanks in the following passage. For each blank there are four choices marked A, B, C and D. You should choose the ONE that best fits into the passage.

Most people who travel long distances complain of jetlag. Jetlag makes business travelers less productive and more prone __61__ making mistakes. It is actually caused by __62__ of your "body clock"—a small cluster of brain cells that controls the timing of biological __63__. The body clock is designed for a __64__ rhythm of daylight and darkness, so that it is thrown out of balance when it __65__ daylight and darkness at the "wrong" times in a new time zone. The __66__ of jetlag often persist for days. __67__ the internal body clock slowly adjusts to the new time zone.

Now a new anti-jetlag system is __68__ that is based on proven __69__ pioneering scientific research. Dr. Martin Moore-Ede has __70__ a practical strategy to adjust the body clock much sooner to the new time zone __71__ controlled exposure to right light. The time zone shift is easy to accomplish and eliminates __72__ of the discomfort of jetlag.

A successful time zone shift depends on knowing the exact times to either __73__ or avoid bright light. Exposure to light at the wrong time can actually make jetlag worse. The proper schedule __74__ light exposure depends a great deal on __75__ travel plans.

Data on a specific flight itinerary and the individual's sleep __76__ are used to produce a Trip Guide with __77__ on exactly when to be exposed to bright light.

When the Trip Guide calls __78__ bright light you should spend time outdoors if possible. If it is dark outside, or the weather is bad, __79__ you are on an aeroplane, you can use a special light device to provide the necessary light __80__ for a range of activities such as reading, watching TV or working.

61. A. from   B. of   C. for   D. to
62. A. eruption   B. disruption   C. rupture   D. corruption
63. A. actions   B. functions   C. behavior   D. reflection
64. A. formal   B. continual   C. regular   D. circular
65. A. experiences   B. possesses   C. encounters   D. retains
66. A. signs   B. defects   C. diseases   D. symptoms
67. A. if   B. whereas   C. while   D. although
68. A. agreeable   B. available   C. adaptable   D. approachable
69. A. extensive   B. tentative   C. broad   D. inclusive
70. A. devised   B. scrutinized   C. visualized   D. recognized
71. A. in   B. as   C. at   D. through
72. A. more   B. little   C. most   D. least
73. A. shed   B. retrieve   C. seek   D. attain
74. A. in   B. for   C. on   D. with
75. A. specific   B. complicated   C. unique   D. peculiar
76. A. mode   B. style   C. norm   D. pattern
77. A. directories   B. commentaries   C. instructions   D. specifications
78. A. up   B. off   C. on   D. for
79. A. or   B. for   C. and   D. while
80. A. spur   B. stimulus   C. agitation   D. acceleration

Part IV Reading Comprehension

Directions: There are six passages in this part. Each passage is followed by some questions. For each question there are four suggested answers marked A, B, C and D. Read the passages carefully and choose the best answer to each question.

(1)

E-mail is a pipeline to meet friends and people with similar interests or problems. If logged on and hooked up to a national on-line information service, E-mailers can send the letters they compose at leisure on their computers by modem through the phone line to the subscribed service. E-mail addresses—either names or on-line service account numbers—automatically forward mail to the right place. A response can shoot back in no time as soon as the intended recipient checks in. And E-mailing is far cheaper than long-distance calling. But what makes E-mailing amazingly seductive is freedom from time and place. Telephone tag and different time zones are annoyances of the past once you have someone's E-mail address. Cost-effective optimum just spurs you to explore this "invisible world." Small wonder E-mailing is expanding exponentially.

An E-paper is a computerized newspaper, or "digital ink on silicon paper." The goal of electronic newspapering is ultimately to ease the consumer's data burden. E-papers are customized "news filters" that will deliver specialized information. Readers keen on anything ranging from chess tournaments to obscure medical news will be able to have respective "Daily(for)Me" information automatcally delivered to their computer screens along with the day's top news stories.

81. It can be inferred from the passage that E-mailing is accessible only to those who _____.
    A. investigate the invisible cyberspace
    B. excel in the computer operational skills

C. subscribe to a national on-line information service
D. share their thoughts and ideas generously

82. According to the passage, what most distinguishes E-mailing is its _____.
    A. chance to revive the almost lost art of letter writing
    B. freedom from pressure to respond or face-to-face confrontation
    C. global quality for one to contact people half a world away
    D. liberation from such restraints as time and locality

83. According to the passage, E-paper is _____.
    A. less versatile than the traditional model
    B. foldable paper newspaper
    C. a hollow blessing to offer vast amounts of information
    D. a digitized and individualized blend of daily information

84. According to the passage, the main object that E-newspapering strives to attain is _____.
    A. to promise readers a vast source of data supply
    B. to provide information according to personal specifications
    C. to realize the value of interactivity
    D. to advertise through an electronic medium

(2)

One of the subjects that most mystifies astronomers lies in the Large Magellanic Cloud, a neighboring galaxy to our Milky Way, and within the Tarantula Nebula, no less than 180 000 light years from earth. Designated R136a, the object gives off so much light that some scientists have speculated that it must be a star with mass some 3 000 times as great as our own. Other scientists, while agreeing as to the brightness, claim that, since R136a would then be at least 200 times as large as any other known star, what must be involved is a group of stars, each about 150 times the size of the sun, that is, comparable to the largest known to exist, all grouped so remarkably close together that, given their distance from earth, they can not be separately identified with our present technology. Whichever side is right, the known facts about R136a mean that it must create stellar winds of unimaginable speed, calculated by some who support the single-star theory at eight million miles per hour. And even if those who favor the starcluster explanation are correct, R136a would still be a thoroughly exceptional phenomenon, without parallel as far as we know in the universe.

85. How big is R136a?
    A. 180 000 light years across.
    B. 200 times the next largest star.
    C. 3 000 times as large as the earth.
    D. There is not enough evidence yet.

86. Where is R136a located?
    A. In a galaxy next to earth's galaxy.
    B. Within the Milky Way.
    C. Not far from the Tarantula Nebula.
    D. Close to the Magellanic Cloud.

87. Why is R136a a mystery to astronomers?
    A. It is in a neighboring galaxy.
    B. They are unable to determine whether it consists of one or more stars.
    C. They cannot accurately locate the Tarantula Nebula.
    D. It creates such strong stellar winds of eight million miles per hour.

88. It may be inferred from the passage that, whichever group of scientists is right, R136a is _____.
    A. a star about 3 000 times the size of our sun
    B. a group of exceptionally large stars
    C. more mystifying to astronomers than anything else in the universe
    D. different from anything else so far encountered in the universe
89. If the scientists who favor the starcluster theory turn out to be right, why would R136a still be a unique phenomenon?
    A. Because the stars would be exceptionally near each other.
    B. Because there are very few starclusters.
    C. Because it is 180 000 light years from earth.
    D. Because those who support the single-star theory would be wrong.

(3)

In these days of technological triumphs, it is well to remind ourselves from time to time that living mechanisms are often incomparably more efficient than their artificial imitations. There is no better illustration of this idea than the sonar system of bats. Ounce for ounce and watt for watt, it is billions of times more efficient and more sensitive than the radars and sonars contrived by man.

Of course, the bats have had some 50 million years of evolution to refine their sonar. Their physiological mechanisms for echo location, based on all this accumulated experience, therefore merit our thorough study and analysis.

To appreciate the precision of the bats' echo location, we must first consider the degree of their reliance upon it. Thanks to sonar, an insect-eating bat can get along perfectly well without eyesight. This was brilliantly demonstrated by an experiment performed in the late eighteenth century by the Italian naturalist Lazzaro Spallanzani. He caught some bats in a bell tower, blinded them, and released them outdoors. Four of these blind bats were recaptured after they had found their way back to the bell tower, and on examining their stomachs' contents, Spallanzani found that they had been able to capture and gorge themselves with flying insects. We know from experiments that bats easily find insects in the dark of night, even when the insects emit no sound that can be heard by human ears. A bat will catch hundreds of soft-bodied, silent-flying moths or gnats in a single hour. It will even detect and chase pebbles or cotton spitballs tossed into the air.

90. According to the author, the sonar system of bats is an example of the idea that _____.
    A. this is the age of technological triumphs
    B. modern machines are inefficient
    C. living mechanisms are often more efficient than man-made machines
    D. artificial imitations are always less efficient than living mechanisms
91. The author suggests that the sonar system of bats _____.
    A. was at the height of its perfection 50 million years ago
    B. is better than man-made sonar because it has had 50 million years to be refined
    C. should have been discovered by man many years ago
    D. is the same as it was 50 million years ago
92. Echo location in this article means the _____.
    A. location of echoes
    B. ability to determine where an echo comes from
    C. scientific term for sound waves
    D. ability to locate unseen objects by echoes

93. This article was written to illustrate _____.
    A. the deficiencies of man-made sonar
    B. the dependence of man upon animals
    C. that we are living in a machine age
    D. that the sonar system of bats is remarkable
94. The following is the main point of the article:
    A. A bat will catch hundreds of gnats in a single hour.
    B. There is a perfection in nature which sometimes cannot be matched by man's creative efforts.
    C. The phrase "blind as a bat" is valid.
    D. Sonar and radar systems of man are inefficient.

(4)

Traffic statistics paint a gloomy picture. To help solve their traffic woes, some rapidly growing U. S. cities have simply built more roads. But traffic experts say building more roads is a quick-fix solution that will not alleviate the traffic problem in the long run. Soaring land costs, increasing concern over social and environmental disruptions caused by road-building, and the likelihood that more roads can only lead to more cars and traffic are powerful factors mitigating against a 1950s-style construction program.

The goal of smart-highway technology is to make traffic systems work at optimum efficiency by treating the road and the vehicles travelling on them as an integral transportation system. Proponents of this advanced technology say electronic detection systems, closed-circuit television, radio communication, ramp metering, variable message signing, and other smart-highway technology can now be used at a reasonable cost to improve communication between drivers and the people who monitor traffic.

Pathfinder, a Santa Monica, California-based smart-highway project in which a 14-mile stretch of the Santa Monica Freeway, making up what is called a "smart corridor", is being instrumented with buried loops in the pavement. Closed-circuit television cameras survey the flow of traffic, while communications linked to properly equipped automobiles advise motorists of routes offering the best travel time.

Not all traffic experts, however, look to smart-highway technology as the ultimate solution to traffic gridlock. Some say the high-tech approach is limited and can only offer temporary solutions to a serious problem.

"Electronics on the highway redresses just one aspect of the problem: how to regulate traffic more efficiently", explains Michael Renner, senior researcher at the Worldwatch Institute. "It doesn't deal with the central problem of too many cars or roads that can't be built fast enough. It sends people the wrong message. They start thinking 'Yes, there used to be a traffic congestion problem, but that's been solved now because we have an advanced high-tech system in place.'"

Larson agrees and adds, "Smart highways is just one of the tools that we will use to deal with our traffic problems. It's not the solution itself, just part of the package. There are different strategies."

Other traffic problem-solving options being studied and experimented with include car pooling, rapid mass-transit systems, staggered or flexible work hours, and road pricing, a system whereby motorists pay a certain amount for the time they use a highway.

It seems that we need a new, major thrust to deal with the traffic problems of the next 20 years. There has to be a big change.

95. What is the appropriate title for the passage?
    A. Smart Highway Projects—The Ultimate Solution to Traffic Congestion.
    B. A Quick Fix Solution for the Traffic Problems.
    C. A Venture to Remedy Traffic Woes.
    D. Highways Get Smart—Part of the Package to Relieve Traffic Gridlock?

96. According to the traffic experts, building more roads will _____.
    A. be effective only for a short period of time
    B. mitigate the traffic problem in the long run
    C. alleviate the soaring of land costs
    D. appease the conservationists
97. According to the passage, the smart highway technology is aimed to _____.
    A. deploy sophisticated facilities on the interstate highways
    B. provide passenger vehicles with a variety of services
    C. optimize the highway capabilities
    D. improve communication between driver and the traffic monitors
98. The word "loops" as used in the sentence "the Santa Monica Freeway… is being instrumented with buried loops in the pavement" is closest in meaning to _____.
    A. close-circuit television cameras
    B. rounds of electric wires
    C. keyboard instruments
    D. ramp metering
99. According to Michael Renner, senior researcher at the Worldwatch Institute, the smart highway system focuses its attention merely on _____.
    A. the flow of traffic
    B. social and environmental disruptions
    C. efficient regulation of traffic
    D. advanced high tech approach
100. According to Larson, to redress the traffic problem, _____.
    A. car pooling must be studied
    B. rapid mass-transit systems must be introduced
    C. flexible work hours must be experimented
    D. overall strategies must be coordinated
101. Which of the following best describes the organization of the WHOLE passage?
    A. Two contrasting views of a problem are presented.
    B. A problem is examined and complementary solutions are proposed or offered.
    C. Latest developments are outlined in order of importance.
    D. An innovation is explained with its importance emphasized.

(5)

A computer is a machine designed to perform work mathematically and to store and select information that has been fed into it. It is run by either mechanical or electronic means. These machines can do a great deal of complicated work in a very short time. A large computer, for example, can add or subtract nine thousand times a second, multiply a thousand times a second, or divide five hundred times a second. Its percentage of error is about one in a billion billion digits. It has been estimated that human beings making calculations average about one mistake per two hundred digits.

The heart of an electronic computer lies in its vacuum tubes, or transistors. Its electronic circuit works a thousand times faster than the nerve cells in the human brain. A problem that might take a human being two years to solve can be solved by a computer in one minute, but in order to work properly, a computer must be given instructions—it must be programmed.

Computers can be designed for many specialized purposes—they can be used to prepare payrolls, guide airplane flights, direct traffic, even to play chess. Computers play an essential role in modern automation in many plants and factories throughout the world.

102. A computer is a machine designed to _____.
   A. perform work mathematically
   B. perform complicated calculations
   C. store and select information
   D. all of the above

103. The passage calls the vacuum tubes the electronic computer's _____.
   A. nerve cells   B. nervous system
   C. brain   D. heart

104. The speed at which an electronic computer works depends on its _____.
   A. electronic circuits   B. programmer
   C. vacuum tubes, or transistors D. instructions

105. The use of a computer for specialized purposes depends on the _____.
   A. design of the computer
   B. power used to operate the computer
   C. difficulty of the mathematical calculations involved
   D. the ability of the programmer

106. The passage implies that human beings differ from computers in that human beings _____.
   A. make fewer errors   B. work more quickly
   C. do not have to be programmed D. understand their instructions

(6)

In what now seem like the prehistoric times of computer history, the early postwar era, there was a quite widespread concern that computers would take over the world from man one day. Already, today less than forty years later, as computers are relieving us of more and more of the routine tasks in business and in our personal lives, we are faced with a less dramatic but also less foreseen problem. People tend to be overtrusting of computers and are reluctant to challenge their authority. Indeed, they behave as if they were hardly aware that wrong buttons may be pushed, or that a computer may simple malfunction.

Obviously, there would be no point in investing in a computer if you had to check all its answers, but people should also rely on their own internal computers and check the machine when they have the feeling that something has gone away. Questioning and routine double checks must continue to be as much a part of good business as they were in precomputer days. Maybe each computer should come with the following warning: for all the help this computer may provide, it should not be seen as a substitute for fundamental thinking and reasoning skills.

107. What is the main purpose of this passage?
   A. To look back to the early days of computers.
   B. To explain what technical problems may occur with computers.
   C. To discourage unnecessary investment in computers.
   D. To warn against a mentally lazy attitude towards computers.

108. According to the passage, initial concerns about computers were that they might _____.
   A. lead us into a postwar era   B. be quite widespread
   C. take control   D. take over routine tasks

109. The passage recommends those dealing with computers to _____.
   A. be reasonably doubtful about them
   B. check all their answers

C. substitute them for basic thinking
D. use them for business purposes only

110. An "internal computer" is _____.
    A. a computer used exclusively by one company for its own problems
    B. a person's store of knowledge and the ability to process it
    C. the most up-to-date-in-house computer a company can buy
    D. a computer from the post-war era which was cheap to buy

Part V Translation

Directions: Translate the following passages into Chinese.

(1)

One authority states categorically, "A computer can handle information; it can calculate, conclude, and choose; it can perform reasonable operations with information. A computer, therefore, can think." Famed mathematician Norbert Wiener foresees a computer that can learn and will "in no way be obliged to make such decisions as we should have made, or will be acceptable to us."

Probably the clearest difference between man and a computer is a quantitative one. The brain has roughly a million times as many parts as the best computer. On the other hand, the difference may lie in a spiritual factor, embraced by religion. At any rate, a computer cannot exercise free will or originate anything—not yet. Whether it ever will is still an open argument.

Computers can already do a lot of surprising things, which include predicting the weather. The computer is able to made forecasts by absorbing vast quantities of data, but this, as well as most of the other tasks now performed by the thinking machines, routine, requiring thinking of a very low order.

(2)

How would you like to do a week's worth of grocery shopping in 10 minutes? Rather than loading the kids into the minivan on shopping day, you can send them out to play and do your shopping from the comfort of your home. Thousands of busy people have traded their shopping carts for keyboards. Rather than fight the crowds in the Chicago and San Francisco areas, they log on to the Peapod, an online shopping and delivery service.

Peapod is giving us a glimpse into the future of retailing—the virtual store. Peapod is a pioneer in a rapidly expanding industry that is dedicated to enabling us to buy almost anything from PC. Peapod subscribers go shopping at the virtual grocery store by logging on to a system that lets them interactively shop for grocery items, including fresh produce, deli, bakery, meat, and frozen products. Rather than running from aisle to aisle, you simply point and click around the screen for the item you want.

The virtual supermarket is sure to change the way we shop. This interactive online approach helps take the hassle and the mystery out of grocery shopping. We can view items by category or by brand. We can even peruse the items on sale. We can request that items be arranged alphabetically, by brand, by price per unit, by package size, or, we can even request a listing by nutritional value.

In the minds of the busy people who shop online, the cost of the service is easily offset by other savings, e.g., less spent on travel.

Key to Practice Exercises

Practice Exercise 1

Part Ⅰ Translation
1. 信息技术
2. 光脉冲
3. 时差综合征,时差反应
4. 海底光纤电缆
5. 电子信号
6. 可视电话
7. 航天飞机
8. 基因
9. 固态烟雾
10. 生物钟
11. 生物节奏周期
12. 纳米
13. 生态系统
14. 自然气候多变性
15. 温室效应
16. 矿物燃料
17. 通讯网络
18. 电子邮件
19. 高能期
20. 纤维光学

Part Ⅱ Vocabulary and Structure

Section A

21. technology
22. scientific
23. contribute
24. Economically
25. reliable
26. solveable, solution
27. professional
28. necessitates
29. essential
30. productivity
31. revolutionize
32. characteristics
33. depth
34. Thermochemistry
35. carelessness

Section B

36. A 37. D 38. B 39. B 40. C 41. C 42. A 43. C 44. C 45. B
46. B 47. B 48. A 49. D 50. D 51. D 52. C 53. B 54. A 55. B
56. C 57. B 58. C 59. D 60. A

Part Ⅲ Cloze

61. D 62. B 63. C 64. A 65. B 66. A 67. A 68. B 69. B 70. B
71. C 72. D 73. D 74. B 75. D 76. B 77. A 78. D 79. B 80. B

Part Ⅳ Reading Comprehension

81. A 82. C 83. D 84. B 85. D 86. A 87. B 88. B 89. C 90. C
91. B 92. D 93. D 94. A 95. A 96. B 97. B 98. C 99. D 100. A
101. A 102. D 103. B 104. B 105. B 106. D 107. B 108. C 109. D 110. B

Part Ⅴ Translation

(1)

如果你在寻找资料,可以先去图书馆的书架上去找。但是,如果你需要最新的数据,或者你有特殊的需要,你会发现电脑里的数据库更有用,更便宜,也更省时。数据库是一个科目或一组科目的信息文件,它可被存储并保留在电脑内存中。电脑的速度能使你即刻就能调出该文件中的任何一个项目。

数据库有三种主要类型:统计、文献目录和资料全文。统计数据库储存大量的数字数据,如工资和价格指数、人口普查资料、外汇比价以及债券价格。文献目录数据库储存各类期刊和报纸文章的有关情况和内容概要。资料全文数据库提供诸如报纸、杂志以及期刊文章的全文。

(2)

"信息高速公路"与其说是一个静态的网络,不如说是一个社会和商业的环境。该"高速公路"由网络和计算机资源组成,但更重要的是,它规定了人与人之间、组织和组织之间相互作用和交流的新环境。正是这些原因,这种"高速公路"的建立需要一种共同合作的力量,而不是过去所常见的传统型服务提供商/用户模式。基于这些概念,信息高速公路可以定义为:"一种不受地理位置制约的用户环境,它使用高速网络技术和计算机技术进行多媒体通讯。"

这种环境是传输、变换和压缩三种技术的结合体,这三种技术的演变非常迅速。

Practice Exercise 2

Part Ⅰ Translation

1. 光伏电池
2. 多用途、多功能合一的个人电脑
3. 大型数据存储库
4. 经济资源
5. 专门技能(知识)
6. 声像数据数字化传送
7. 调制解调器
8. 卫星数据传送系统
9. 软件应用
10. 多媒体
11. 宽带业务
12. 管理平台
13. 电子商务
14. 替代能源技术
15. 遗传工程
16. 人工智能
17. 燃料电池
18. 下载
19. 脱氧核糖核酸
20. 克隆

Part Ⅱ Vocabulary and Structure

Section A

21. developments
22. discovery
23. violence
24. concept
25. experimentally
26. achieveable
27. belief
28. sensitivity
29. satisfactory
30. communication
31. inferiority
32. mechanization
33. defect
34. geneticist, genes
35. fatal

Section B

36. B 37. A 38. D 39. C 40. A 41. D 42. B 43. D 44. C 45. A
46. A 47. C 48. B 49. A 50. B 51. A 52. C 53. D 54. A 55. D
56. A 57. B 58. D 59. B 60. C

Part Ⅲ Cloze

61. A 62. B 63. C 64. A 65. C 66. C 67. D 68. B 69. D 70. C
71. D 72. B 73. C 74. A 75. C 76. D 77. C 78. B 79. A 80. D

Part Ⅳ Reading Comprehension

81. B 82. C 83. D 84. A 85. D 86. A 87. C 88. B 89. C 90. C
91. B 92. A 93. B 94. A 95. A 96. A 97. B 98. C 99. D 100. C
101. B 102. C 103. B 104. B 105. C 106. B 107. A 108. A 109. B 110. C

Part Ⅴ Translation

(1)

自然界的能量有许多不同的形式。热能就是一种形式。热能大多来自太阳。森林大火也可以产生热能,甚至一只老鼠温暖的身体也可以产生少许的热能。光是能量的另一种形式,也是来自太阳和星星。一些动物甚至植物也可以产生少量的光能。无线电波和紫外线也是能量形式。另外还有电能也是一种能量形式。

有关能量的一些事情很难理解。能量不断地从一种形式转变为另一种形式,就像一位化了妆的艺术家一样。当你自认为了解它的时候,它突然变成了另一种完全不同的形式。但是有一点是肯定的:能量永远不会消失,同样,它也不会无端地产生。过去,人们认为能量和物质是两种完全不同的东西。现在我们知道,能量和物质是可以相互转换的。微量的物质可以转换为令人难以置信的巨大核能。太阳利用氢气制造核能,随着物质转化为能量,其质量日复一日在减小。

(2)

手机(移动电话)、寻呼机、手提电脑和个人数码助理已成为我们的生活的一部分,它们提高了成百万用户的生产力和效率。然而,一项调查却显示这些便携设备所释放出的巨量信息有可能变得无法驾驭。从掌上电脑的电子信函到手机的语音邮件,使用者都面临着一个严重的管理问题,即如何控制这些接收信息的渠道。

由于本身小巧玲珑,又具备种种先进的特点,便携式电子设备为消费者带来了自由,提高了生产力,改进了对信息的组织。但是,信息发送与接收的便捷发展得如此之快,以至于很多人每天都会收到各种各样、成百上千的电子邮件,结果造成很多人无法充分发挥设备的特点,来帮助他们对超载信息进行管理。

Practice Exercise 3

Part Ⅰ Translation

1. 远程登录   2. 三维图像   3. 压缩光盘只读存储器
4. 网上贸易   5. 环球网主页   6. 超文本标记语言
7. 统一资源定位器   8. 环球网浏览器   9. 文件传输协议
10. 质子火箭   11. 嗅觉技术   12. 仿真传感器
13. 广义相对论   14. 量子力学   15. 弹道导弹技术
16. 微引力研究   17. 国际空间站   18. 多媒体格式
19. 虚拟购物卡   20. 程序设计语言

Part Ⅱ Vocabulary and Structure

Section A

21. decisively   22. expense   23. increasing
24. frozen   25. rested   26. made
27. explored   28. predict, predictable   29. formative
30. differ   31. unprecedented   32. suspicion
33. specialize   34. progressive   35. qualified

Section B

36. B 37. C 38. A 39. A 40. B 41. D 42. D 43. C 44. B 45. B
46. C 47. B 48. C 49. C 50. B 51. D 52. A 53. C 54. D 55. B
56. A 57. C 58. A 59. D 60. D

Part Ⅲ Cloze

61. C 62. B 63. A 64. D 65. D 66. B 67. A 68. A 69. B 70. D
71. A 72. B 73. A 74. B 75. A 76. D 77. C 78. D 79. C 80. A

Part Ⅳ Reading Comprehension

81. B 82. D 83. D 84. A 85. C 86. C 87. B 88. C 89. B 90. D
91. C 92. B 93. B 94. A 95. A 96. B 97. D 98. D 99. C 100. D
101. D 102. B 103. A 104. C 105. B 106. D 107. A 108. C 109. A 110. B

Part Ⅴ Translation

(1)

　　计算机病毒是一种附着于其他程序,藏于计算机存储器或磁盘中,并不断向别的程序扩散的一种软件程序。计算机病毒会毁坏数据,导致电脑瘫痪,显示不友好的或是骚扰信息,或者静止蛰伏,直到特定时间再"骤然发作"。在当今的产业中,病毒扫描已不再被认为是多余之举,而成为必需措施。计算机病毒不仅攻击你的计算机环境,它对你接触的所有计算机环境都不放过。计算机病毒能够附载于正在使用的文件中,然后通过磁盘和文件进行自我复制。如果你没有采取适当的防范措施,重要的信息以及硬件将会损坏,从而使你的计算机环境遭受灭顶之灾。

　　许多抗病毒产品,如 KV300 和 VirusScan,提供了一系列适当的预防措施。定期对你的计算机环境进行扫描,可以为你的"安全计算"增加一道保险。

(2)

　　当你不再仅仅限于文字和静止图片时,网上生活会丰富多彩得多。即使是个因特网新手,你也许曾听说过在线式多媒体——听音乐、看动画片和录像,甚至玩三维游戏。声音和活动画面使信息变得活灵活现。

　　要体验这些,你需要叫做"插件"的特殊软件。术语"插件"指的是一个附加的小软件,它能够扩展你的网络浏览器(比如网景的导航者或微软的探险者)的功能,把你的计算机变成一台收音机或电视机。

　　当你进入的网页含有需要使用插件程序的文件,而你却又没有这个程序时,通常你会收到一个信息,询问你是否需要下载该程序并安装到你的电脑里。多数情况下安装是自动运行的。

Practice Exercise 4

Part Ⅰ Translation

1. 远程光纤电缆 　　2. 位移 　　3. 共振频率
4. 电气机械特性 　　5. 频谱 　　6. 加速度
7. 谐波成分 　　8. 模数转换器 　　9. 主干网提供商
10. 因特网服务提供商 　　11. 液晶显示器 　　12. 电脑芯片
13. 音频文件 　　14. 全屏视频图像 　　15. 自然资源
16. 臭氧层 　　17. 酸雨 　　18. 示波器
19. 媒体方式 　　20. 自然保护区

Part Ⅱ Vocabulary and Structure

Section A

21. Evidently　　22. intelligent　　23. absorption
24. observed　　25. assoiation　　26. correctable
27. basically　　28. argument　　29. constructively
30. density　　31. expansion　　32. authoritative
33. destructive　　34. competition, competitive　　35. impressionable

Section B

36. C 37. D 38. A 39. A 40. B 41. D 42. D 43. C 44. B 45. A
46. C 47. B 48. C 49. D 50. A 51. B 52. C 53. D 54. A 55. B
56. A 57. D 58. B 59. B 60. C

Part Ⅲ Cloze

61. A 62. B 63. C 64. D 65. A 66. C 67. C 68. B 69. D 70. A
71. C 72. C 73. B 74. D 75. A 76. B 77. B 78. D 79. C 80. B

Part Ⅳ Reading Comprehension

81. B 82. C 83. C 84. D 85. C 86. C 87. D 88. A 89. D 90. B
91. B 92. A 93. C 94. B 95. A 96. D 97. A 98. A 99. C 100. C
101. A 102. D 103. B 104. A 105. A 106. C 107. A 108. C 109. B 110. D

Part Ⅴ Translation

(1)

在因特网上购物有一个问题,那便是你无法触摸任何东西。幸运的是,这种状况将要有所改变。一种机动电脑鼠标将使网上漫游者能感受到网上展示的商品的质地,或商品的其他物理特性。

在旧金山召开的网络'99大会使得参观者能够试用"触感"鼠标:将光标移向一个网球拍图片上,便能让使用者感受到球拍线的绷紧度。你还可以摸到一条牛仔裤的质地,或者试开一辆车,感受一下车的拐弯性能和开上直道后的加速功能。这种鼠标甚至能模拟在大风中逆风行车的感受。

强迫反馈技术最初由斯坦福大学和美国国家航空航天局开发,起初仅用于飞行模拟。最近,加州圣何塞市的"潜浸公司"成功地达到了数据快速交换的超高速,这种超高速能使网上购物的顾客有一种的真实触感。

(2)

"网礼"一词由网络和礼仪合成,意为国际互联网上的行为所应遵守的社会和技术准则。由于通过国际互联网交流相对于面对面交流省略了一些步骤,所以遵守这些准则尤为必要,这样会使你同互联网上的通讯对象以及网络服务提供商保持良好的关系。网礼规则不具有法律约束力,但是掌握并遵守它们很重要,只有如此才能避免误解、排斥以及被吊销互联网的使用权。随着愈来愈多的人依赖互联网通讯进行商务活动和维持个人联络,网礼比过去任何时候都更加重要。

大多数网礼规则建立在良好举止、技术理解和常识的基础之上。不同的互联网协议,如电子信箱、使用网、新闻组、IRC以及万维网,其网礼均符合一些总的准则和为每一媒介设定的特殊规则。这些网礼规则通常分成相关的三类:社会行为、技术礼貌和有害行为。

Practice Exercise 5

Part Ⅰ Translation

1. 网络搜索页   2. 电子银行业务   3. 附加文件
4. 文本档案   5. 数字视频   6. 图形界面
7. 扫描图像   8. 光电探测器   9. 高速处理器
10. 半导体电路 11. 信息基础设施 12. 微电子研究
13. 定位装置   14. 交互式计算机 15. 计算机设计自动化
16. 原子结构   17. 存储容量   18. 电子邮件电话
19. 生化活度   20. 人类免疫系统

Part Ⅱ Vocabulary and Structure

Section A

21. preventable   22. assistance   23. required
24. agreeably   25. involvement   26. realization
27. conveniently 28. irritable   29. composition
30. Disappearance 31. behavior   32. varies
33. indication   34. recognition   35. responsible

Section B

36. A 37. C 38. B 39. D 40. A 41. D 42. A 43. C 44. A 45. A
46. C 47. B 48. C 49. C 50. B 51. C 52. B 53. C 54. D 55. D

56. A　　57. D　　58. B　　59. B　　60. D

Part Ⅲ　Cloze

61. D　　62. B　　63. B　　64. C　　65. A　　66. D　　67. C　　68. B　　69. A　　70. A
71. D　　72. C　　73. C　　74. B　　75. A　　76. D　　77. C　　78. D　　79. A　　80. B

Part Ⅳ　Reading Comprehension

81. C　　82. D　　83. D　　84. B　　85. D　　86. A　　87. B　　88. B　　89. A　　90. C
91. B　　92. D　　93. D　　94. B　　95. B　　96. A　　97. C　　98. B　　99. C　　100. D
101. B　　102. D　　103. D　　104. A　　105. A　　106. C　　107. D　　108. C　　109. A　　110. B

Part Ⅴ　Translation

(1)

一位权威人士断言,"计算机能够处理信息,能够计算、推理和选择,能够利用信息资料进行合理操作。因此,计算机能够思考"。著名数学家诺伯特·威纳预见到一种计算机,它能够学习,而且"绝不会被迫做出我们会做出的或是我们可接受的那种决定"。

也许人脑与计算机的最明显的区别在于数量的不同。人脑的部件大概是最先进的计算机的100万倍。另一方面,差异可能有时在于精神因素,即人脑受到宗教的影响。不管怎样,计算机不能按自己的意愿自行其是或创造任何事物,至少目前是如此。至于将来是否具有这个能力,一直存有不同看法。

计算机现在已经能够做许多令人惊讶的事情,包括预报天气。计算机能够引用输入大量数据进行天气预报。但这项工作及大多数现在能由会思维的机器完成的工作都是些常规工作,只需要很简单的思考。

(2)

你想不想在10分钟之内完成一周的食品采购？你不必每一个采购日用小车带上孩子们了,而是可将他们放出去嬉戏,你在家中舒舒服服地进行采购。现在成千上万的人已经把购物小推车换成了键盘。他们在芝加哥和旧金山地区已经不再拥挤购物,而只是登录到 Peapod 网站上。Peapod 是一个网上采购与送货服务系统。

Peapod 为我们展现出未来零售业的一个画面——虚拟商店。在一个迅猛扩大的、确保人们能从个人电脑上购买几乎是任何物品的产业中,Peapod 可谓是一个先驱者。Peapod 的用户通过登录到一个计算机系统完成在虚拟商店中的购物。该系统允许人们进行交互式采购,物品包括新鲜瓜果蔬菜、熟食、面包点心、肉类以及冷冻商品。你不必一条通道接一条通道地实地采购,你只需简单地在屏幕上点击一下你所想要的物品。

虚拟超级市场确实会改变我们的购物方式。这种交互式在线购物方式有助于避免在食品店购物时的烦恼和神秘化。我们既可以按照产品分类,也可以按照品牌察看货物。我们甚至可以详细读到出售的各种商品的目录。我们可以要求按照字母顺序、品牌、单价、包装尺寸、甚至营养成分的高低给商品排序。

在网上购物的忙碌的人们的心目中,服务费很容易被省下的其他费用所弥补,比如减少了路上的开支。